D0960109

LOSING THE LONG GAME

Also by Philip H. Gordon

Winning the Right War

Allies at War (with Jeremy Shapiro)

Winning Turkey (with Omer Taspinar)

The French Challenge (with Sophie Meunier)

Cold War Statesmen Confront the Bomb (co-edited with John Lewis Gaddis, Ernest R. May, and Jonathan Rosenberg)

France, Germany, and the Western Alliance

A Certain Idea of France

LOSING THE LONG GAME

The False Promise of Regime Change in the Middle East

Philip H. Gordon

St. Martin's Press
New York
A Council on Foreign Relations Book

The Council on Foreign Relations (CFR) is an independent, nonpartisan membership organization, think tank, and publisher dedicated to being a resource for its members, government officials, business executives, journalists, educators and students, civic and religious leaders, and other interested citizens in order to help them better understand the world and the foreign policy choices facing the United States and other countries. Founded in 1921, CFR carries out its mission by maintaining a diverse membership, including special programs to promote interest and develop expertise in the next generation of foreign policy leaders; convening meetings at its headquarters in New York and in Washington, D.C., and other cities where senior government officials, members of Congress, global leaders, and prominent thinkers come together with CFR members to discuss and debate major international issues; supporting a Studies Program that fosters independent research, enabling CFR scholars to produce articles, reports, and books and hold roundtables that analyze foreign policy issues and make concrete policy recommendations; publishing *Foreign Affairs*, the preeminent journal of international affairs and U.S. foreign policy; sponsoring Independent Task Forces that produce reports with both findings and policy prescriptions on the most important foreign policy topics; and providing up-to-date information and analysis about world events and American foreign policy on its website, www.cfr.org.

The Council on Foreign Relations takes no institutional positions on policy issues and has no affiliation with the U.S. government. All views expressed in its publications and on its website are the sole responsibility of the author or authors.

First published in the United States by St. Martin's Press, an imprint of St. Martin's Publishing Group

www.stmartins.com

Library of Congress Cataloging-in-Publication Data

Names: Gordon, Philip H., 1962- author.
Title: Losing the long game : the false promise of regime change in the Middle East / Philip H. Gordon.
Description: First edition. | New York : St. Martin's Press, 2020. | Includes bibliographical references and index.
Identifiers: LCCN 2020024211 | ISBN 9781250217035 (hardcover) | ISBN 9781250217042 (ebook)
Subjects: LCSH: United States—Foreign relations—Middle East. | Middle East—Foreign relations—United States. | Regime change—Middle East. | Middle East—Politics and government—1945-1979. | Middle East—Politics and government—1979-
Classification: LCC DS63.2.U5 G594 2020 | DDC 327.56073—dc23
LC record available at https://lccn.loc.gov/2020024211

Our books may be purchased in bulk for promotional, educational, or business use. Please contact your local bookseller or the Macmillan Corporate and Premium Sales Department at 1-800-221-7945, extension 5442, or by email at MacmillanSpecialMarkets@macmillan.com.

First Edition: 2020

10 9 8 7 6 5 4 3 2 1

I never knew a man who had better motives for all the trouble he caused.

—journalist Thomas Fowler on CIA agent Alden Pyle in Graham Greene's *The Quiet American*

. . . a man hears what he wants to hear and disregards the rest.

—Simon and Garfunkel, "The Boxer"

How can we lose when we are so sincere?

—Charlie Brown, in Charles Schulz's *Peanuts*

Contents

LOSING THE LONG GAME

INTRODUCTION

The Regime Change Temptation

Since the end of World War II, the United States has set out to oust governments in the Middle East on an average of once per decade. It has done so in places as diverse as Iran, Afghanistan (twice), Iraq, Egypt, Libya, and Syria, to count only the instances where regime change—the removal of a country's leaders and transformation of its political system—was the goal of U.S. policy and where an administration made sustained efforts to bring it about. The motives for U.S. interventions in all of these countries have been equally varied, including countering communism, competing with geopolitical rivals, preventing the development of weapons of mass destruction (WMD), combating terrorism, saving civilian lives, and trying to promote democracy. And the methods by which the United States has pursued regime change have also been extraordinarily diverse: sponsoring a military coup, providing covert or overt military assistance to opposition groups, invading and occupying, invading and not occupying, providing airpower to opposition forces, and relying on diplomacy, rhetoric, and sanctions alone. What is common to all these efforts, however, is that they invariably failed to achieve their ultimate goals, produced a range of unintended—and often catastrophic—consequences, carried extraordinary financial and human costs, and in many cases left both the target country and the United States worse off than they were before.

This book is the story of how regime change in the Middle East has proven so tempting to American policy makers for decades and of why it always seems to go wrong. I've called the book *Losing the Long Game* because regime change often seems to work out in the short term—leading to premature declarations of victory by its proponents—but then ends up failing badly as costs mount, unintended consequences arise, and instability spreads in the wake of the apparent initial success. In fact, the long-term results of regime change in the region are so consistently disappointing—regardless of the reasons why it was tried or the manner in which plans were executed—that it is surprising so many policy makers and analysts keep coming back to it as a viable policy option, hoping that somehow it will work out better next time. The track record also shows that the reason for the recurring failure is not just a matter of poor implementation or lack of sustained follow-up—the most common excuses of regime change proponents. Instead, it shows that there are inherently high costs, unexpected consequences, and insurmountable obstacles that make it exceedingly difficult for the United States to replace objectionable Middle Eastern regimes and leaders without creating new, different, and often bigger problems.

With few exceptions, the history of U.S. regime change efforts in the region reveals remarkably familiar patterns. Once U.S. policy makers become determined to remove a given regime, they overstate the threat, underestimate the costs and risks, overpromise what they can accomplish, and prematurely claim success if and when the targeted regime falls. Invariably, however, stability quickly proves elusive, a security vacuum develops, insecure and suspicious neighbors interfere, allied contributions fall short, and long-standing ethnic, sectarian, geopolitical, and personal rivalries emerge that the United States is unable to control. As unexpected challenges emerge and costs mount, those who conceived of and oversold the policy blame the results on implementation, and an "if only" phase begins—"if only" we had sent more troops, or fewer troops, or different troops, or more money, or better diplomats, or "if only" we had followed up on any one of a number of other policy options that were not pursued. Books and articles are written by key protagonists, explaining that victory could have been achieved if only U.S. leaders had been wiser, more determined, and willing to commit adequate resources to the task. Over time, the American public sours on the results of the intervention and tires of the costs of trying to make it a success, and the policy is shelved, usually after a new president enters office and blames the problem on the ill-conceived or poorly implemented strategy of his predecessor. This rejection of the policy then lasts until the next time leaders consider trying it again—sometimes in the very same country where it failed the first time.

Not every case of Middle East regime change conforms exactly to this pattern, of course. In some cases, certain U.S. goals are met initially before problems emerge later; in others, some objectives are achieved while new, different, and unexpected problems are created; in many cases, the United States derives strategic benefits from its intervention while the citizens of the target countries pay the price; and in some cases the result is a disaster for almost all concerned. In other words, to paraphrase Tolstoy, every unsuccessful attempt at regime change is unsuccessful in its own way. But the patterns and outcomes are consistent enough—across a wide range of countries, circumstances, and administrations—that future U.S. leaders would be wise to take them into careful account before concluding, yet again, that U.S. efforts to oust existing regimes will prove worth the high costs and risks.

Debates about the pros and cons of regime change in the Middle East and elsewhere have gone on for many decades, and as both an analyst and a policy maker I've been involved in them for nearly thirty years. The issue took on renewed practical relevance in 2018, however, when President Donald Trump withdrew the United States from the 2015 nuclear deal with Iran—apparently pinning his hopes on a strategy of regime change there. To be sure, the Trump administration didn't officially embrace that goal and insisted it just wanted to change Iranian behavior. But it was hard to avoid the conclusion that regime change was the actual policy. Trump alleged in 2017 that the nuclear deal had come "just before what would have been the total collapse of the Iranian regime" and that it had impeded the Iranian people's ability "to reclaim their country's proud history, its culture, [and] civilization."[1] While the administration said it only wanted to negotiate a "better deal," Secretary of State Mike Pompeo used his first speech in May 2018 to spell out demands on Iran—including completely and indefinitely ending all uranium enrichment, abandoning ballistic missile development, providing international nuclear inspectors unqualified access anywhere and everywhere, and abandoning all its regional allies—that seemed designed to be rejected.[2] Trump surrounded himself with prominent proponents of regime change (including Pompeo, National Security Adviser John Bolton, and Trump's personal attorney Rudolph Giuliani), lent strong rhetorical support to Iranian protesters ("TIME FOR CHANGE!" he tweeted in January 2018), and set up the special Iran Action Group at the State Department to coordinate a "maximum pressure" campaign.[3] Encouraged by outside supporters in think tanks and Congress—many of whom had been strong proponents of regime change in Iraq fifteen years previously and in Syria more recently—the administration seemed to see the solution to the Iran problem as a sanctions campaign that would cripple the regime and lead to a popular uprising to overthrow it. As the scholar and former Bush administration official Eliot Cohen observed, Trump's "real theory of victory" in Iran was not that the Iranian regime would negotiate a new and better deal but "that American sanctions, rather, will bring down a regime whose economy is already collapsing."[4]

Facing skepticism that the administration sought only to influence Iranian policy, Pompeo acknowledged to an interviewer in May 2019 that he didn't actually expect Tehran's behavior to change, but "what can change is the people can change the government. What we're trying to do is create space for the Iranian people."[5] In Trump's more simplistic formulation, a fight with the United States would mean the "official end of Iran." "Never threaten the United States again!" he warned in a May 2019 tweet.[6] As Trump's Iran policy unfolded—demonizing the Iranian regime, exaggerating intelligence about weapons of mass destruction and Iranian links to al-Qaeda, associating with unsavory opposition groups, and overselling the likely benefits of confrontation—it was hard to avoid having flashbacks to 2002 and the run-up to the Iraq War.[7]

A U.S. policy of promoting regime change in Iran would certainly be in America's interest if it led to a new government that treated its people better, abandoned its nuclear program, stopped supporting terrorism and meddling in its neighbors' affairs, and was ready to cooperate politically, militarily, and diplomatically with the United States. Far less clear was whether that goal could be achieved by the United States through the imposition of economic sanctions, diplomatic isolation, covert action, or military force; whether the results would be the intended ones if it somehow were accomplished; and what the costs and side effects—for Americans, Iranians, and the region—would be of trying and failing to do so.

Trying to think through those questions led me to think even more about the track record of previous U.S. regime change efforts, which turns out to be replete with cautionary tales of hubris, overreach, and magical thinking. A look back at previous efforts since World War II—ironically, the first of which was a 1953 intervention in Iran that contributed to some of the very problems later generations of Americans would seek to solve with regime change again—shows no case of clear success, some catastrophic failures, and universally high costs and unintended consequences. In every case it has proven far more costly and difficult than expected, and in no case has it led to anything even close to stable democracy, despite the promises of some of its proponents. If the U.S. experience in the region over the past seventy years is any guide, the prospect that external pressure—whether through economic isolation or covert or overt military intervention—can bring about the replacement of adversarial regimes in the region with more stable, friendly, and democratic ones is poor. If past is prologue, any administration that pursues such an approach should do so with its eyes wide open, and the American public should be very skeptical about its claims and promises.

More broadly and on a more personal level, my interest in this issue arose from my own direct experience with regime change in the Middle East as a member of the Obama administration from 2009 to 2015. First as assistant secretary of state for European and Eurasian affairs and then as the White House coordinator for the Middle East at the National Security

Council, I was closely involved in efforts to try to stabilize two countries where the previous administration had ousted regimes—Iraq and Afghanistan—and also in Obama's own, ultimately unsuccessful efforts to promote political transitions in Egypt, Libya, and Syria. Obama's experience with Middle East regime change would prove to be another cautionary tale, full of painful lessons about the limits of America's ability to foster positive change in the region and about the risks of pursuing regime change without the will or means to bring it about.

By the time Obama took office in January 2009, the United States had already invested nearly $2 trillion and had suffered thousands of casualties in post-intervention Iraq and Afghanistan yet was still struggling to stabilize both. The 2003 Iraq invasion—originally sold as a way not just to prevent the development of weapons of mass destruction but also to put Iraq on a path to democracy and transform the Middle East—had instead led to widespread violence and instability, empowered Iran and its proxies in Baghdad, fanned the flames of Kurdish separatism, exacerbated Islamist extremism globally, and instigated seething resentment and a violent rebellion among Sunni Arabs not just in Iraq but across the region, in Europe, and beyond. Afghanistan was not in much better shape, with the Taliban still controlling significant parts of the country and the government in Kabul—like that in Baghdad—weak, corrupt, and often uncooperative. Whereas in Iraq Obama had tried to manage the situation by withdrawing most U.S. forces and turning over security responsibilities to the Iraqis (to reduce U.S. burdens and because the Iraqis demanded it), in Afghanistan he instead deployed tens of thousands of additional U.S. troops to help the government provide security and combat terrorism. That military surge brought the total number of American and allied forces to more than 100,000, but they were still unable to turn the tide. By the time Obama left office, almost fourteen years after the United States had ousted the regimes of those two countries—and notwithstanding extraordinary investments of money, political capital, and lives—the prospects for security, stability, and democracy in both countries remained dim. To be sure, in both cases hostile dictatorships had been eliminated, but the goal of making America safer by eliminating the sources of extremism and promoting political stability was a long way from being achieved.

Even more telling were Obama's own—unanticipated—attempts to implement regime change in the region. Obama had come to office as a foreign policy "realist" with a professed admiration of President George H. W. Bush and his national security adviser, Brent Scowcroft, both of whom were well-known regime change skeptics. Obama had strongly opposed President George W. Bush's invasion of Iraq and considered his "freedom agenda" for the Middle East unrealistic and unwise. Yet in another great irony of history, whereas the younger Bush had for all practical purposes abandoned that agenda by the end of his presidency, Obama—driven by unexpected public uprisings in the region—would soon find himself trying to implement it. Despite his instinctive opposition to U.S. intervention in the Middle East and skepticism about what the United States could accomplish there, Obama ended up throwing U.S. support behind opposition forces in Egypt, Libya, and Syria that were trying to replace those regimes—and even falling prey to some of the same wishful thinking as his predecessors. In Egypt, he sided with revolutionary protesters and used U.S. diplomatic leverage to help drive its longtime president, Hosni Mubarak, from power. In Libya, he declared that the dictator Muammar Qadhafi had to go and then launched a NATO-led bombing campaign that was ostensibly limited to protecting civilians but that in reality targeted—and eventually brought about—the violent ouster of Qadhafi's regime. And in Syria, far from "doing nothing," as many of his critics allege, Obama in 2011 called on President Bashar al-Assad to step aside and eventually invested heavily in a political, military, and diplomatic campaign designed to oust him. All these cases were of course very different from one another: the United States used no military force against its ally in Egypt, it led an allied military intervention against the regime in Libya, and it relied on proxies and partners to promote regime change in Syria. But the results in all these cases were similar: a failure to engineer a successful political transition to pro-Western democracy—or even to more effective, tolerant, or cooperative autocracy for that matter—and a legacy of protracted violence, sectarianism, instability, and geopolitical competition.

As the coordinator for Middle East policy at the White House, I was closely involved with all these efforts and did all I could to help them succeed. But I also saw how whatever we did inevitably came up against some harsh realities that thwarted success, and I observed firsthand that despite enormous differences in the way successive U.S. administrations approached these issues going back to Iraq and even further, the results were similarly disastrous. A few months after I left government in 2015, I wrote an article in *Politico* called "The Middle East Is Falling Apart" in which I made the following observation:

> When implying the United States can "fix" Middle Eastern problems if only it "gets it right" it is worth considering this: In Iraq, the U.S. intervened and occupied, and the result was a costly disaster. In Libya, the U.S. intervened and did not occupy, and the result was a costly disaster. In Syria, the U.S. neither intervened nor occupied, and the result is a costly disaster.[8]

As obvious as the point seemed to me, the argument got a lot of attention. The *New Yorker* editor, David Remnick, wrote that it neatly summarized the "dispiriting reality of American foreign policy in the twenty-first century," while Jeffrey Goldberg, the editor of *The Atlantic,* even labeled it the "Gordon dictum."[9] The argument also caused some controversy, and plenty of criticism, from those—including many friends and colleagues—who thought I was being too negative about America's ability to shape world events or, worse, who blamed me and my colleagues for "allowing" the Middle East to spin out of control. On Twitter, for every commentator who thought the quotation concisely summarized the challenges of U.S. foreign policy in the Middle East, there were others who thought I was just looking for an excuse for what they saw as Obama's inaction. The point I was trying to make, however, is that the issue was not so much that we didn't "get it right" as that there isn't always a "right" way of getting it. It wasn't just rotten luck that two successive and very different administrations—Bush's and Obama's—happened to apply the wrong tactics to the wrong situations; it was that there were powerful reasons why using American power to install stable and friendly democracies in place of Middle Eastern dictatorships was simply beyond our reach, and why trying to do so had consequences that we did not foresee and did not like.

To be sure, these were all hard cases in which the status quo, prior to the American intervention, was hardly appealing. In foreign policy, inaction has costs and consequences that must be weighed against the costs of action, and particularly in the Middle East the "road not taken" is also fraught with danger and risk. In most of the cases discussed in this book, it must be acknowledged that the costs of inaction would likely have included enduring or even increased repression, human rights abuses, violence against civilians, and continued risks of regional conflict or even terrorist attacks against Americans or others. But when the menu includes only bad options, such outcomes must be weighed against the results of a choice to seek to remove—usually violently—an existing regime and to accept all the costs of pursuing that goal and the unpredictable consequences that follow. And when the United States sacrifices thousands of American and local lives, spends billions or trillions of dollars, alienates potential partners, exhausts the U.S. military, violates international laws and norms, fans the flames of nationalistic resentment, and undermines public support for international engagement, even a "wash"—exchanging one set of problems for another—is simply not good enough.

Nor can it be said, after such a wealth of experience, that regime change is a sound concept, with success proving elusive only because successive administrations failed to follow up effectively. As we'll see in the chapters ahead, administrations of very different orientations tried very different approaches to the challenges of filling the political and security vacuum created by the overthrow of an existing regime, yet doing so always proved beyond their reach. That evidence suggests not that the problem results from incompetent officials from both major parties somehow failing to find the magic formula for making it a success but that there's something inherently difficult and inevitably costly about removing Middle Eastern governments and institutions and replacing them with something better.

My focus in this book is on the broader Middle East, because that is where U.S. regime change policy has been most active in recent decades and where it is most relevant today as policy makers and pundits continue to debate whether to pursue it in places such as Iran, Syria, Yemen, the Palestinian territories, and even in traditionally U.S.-aligned countries such as Saudi Arabia, Qatar, and Egypt.[10] But it is important to note that the track record in other parts of the world has not been much better. Scholarly studies looking at dozens of cases of regime change from all over the world have concluded that most attempts fail and that even when the United States manages to replace unwanted systems or governments, the result is rarely democracy or better relations with the United States.[11] Indeed, most U.S. attempts to change regimes in other parts of the world over the decades—whether overt or covert—show familiar patterns of exaggerated threats, wishful thinking, costly or failed military interventions, premature declarations of victory, and often disastrous long-term results. And of course the poor historical track record of regime change in the greater Middle East is hardly limited to the United States. The Franco-British invasion of Suez in 1956, Egypt's effort to overthrow the regime in Yemen in the early 1960s, the Soviet-backed coup in Afghanistan in 1978, the Israeli attempt to destroy the Palestine Liberation Organization leadership in Beirut in 1982, and the Saudi-led coalition's 2015 intervention to oust the Houthi regime in Yemen are all examples of Middle Eastern regime change attempts that ultimately backfired badly.

U.S. proponents of regime change, of course, like to point to Japan and Germany after World War II—and more recently to interventions in Latin America and the Caribbean—as examples of how the policy can succeed. In their 2003 book advocating an invasion of Iraq, for instance, Lawrence Kaplan and William Kristol cited Japan, Germany, Austria, Italy, Grenada, the Dominican Republic, and Panama as "*only a few of the nations* whose democratic systems were at first 'imposed' by American arms."[12] (They never identify the other, allegedly more numerous examples of U.S.-imposed democracy.) Kristol and Robert Kagan have also argued that those who "caution against the difficulties of occupying and reforming [countries such as Iraq and Serbia] . . . may wish to reflect on the American experience in Germany and Japan—or even the Dominican Republic and Panama."[13] The writer Joshua Muravchik even claims that "a significant part of the democratic world is democratic as a result of direct American coercion" and points to "Japan, West Germany, Austria, Italy, Grenada, the Dominican Republic, and Panama" as places that "have democratic systems imposed by American arms."[14] Danielle Pletka, another prominent advocate of both the 2003 Iraq War and U.S. intervention in Syria more recently, asserted in *The New York Times* in 2016 that "regime change has often succeeded," citing the cases of Germany, Italy, South Korea, and Taiwan.[15]

It is certainly true that the results of regime change in Japan and Germany (and Italy and Austria) were spectacularly positive—all became prosperous democracies and allies of the United States—and that regime change was at the time the only way to deal with the threats those countries posed. That said, the differences between these cases and the current ones we face in the Middle East are such that those precedents would not be particularly relevant even if Americans were somehow prepared to devote the four years of total war and nearly two million U.S. troops and occupation forces that were necessary—but not sufficient—to achieve American goals in those cases.[16]

Prior to the war, Japan, Germany, Italy, and Austria were all relatively advanced industrial states with functioning, and in some cases democratic, institutions. They were relatively homogeneous culturally, linguistically, and ethnically, not artificial entities fractured along the sectarian, religious, and national lines that make it so hard to develop and maintain democratic institutions and internal peace. By the time the war ended, the leaders of these regimes were also all so thoroughly discredited by more than a decade of failed, reckless aggression and the domestic repression and misery that went along with it that U.S. forces were—unlike in later cases in the Middle East—broadly seen by the public as liberators, not as outside invaders seeking to occupy their lands.

Moreover, because of the long-term strategic importance of Europe and Japan, the sacrifices that had been made to win the war, and great confidence in U.S. relative power in the late 1940s and early 1950s, the U.S. public was ready and willing to commit the massive resources and take the risks of rebuilding and nation building in Asia and Europe. The Soviet threat and emerging Cold War reinforced this willingness, persuading Americans to support the Marshall Plan (which cost nearly $150 billion in today's dollars over just four years) and deploy hundreds of thousands of troops to Europe and Japan. Germany benefited from being bordered on one side by friendly, supportive, and prosperous partners that (unlike after World War I) understood their interest in Germany's success, while Japan sought security in alliance with the United States to ensure its survival. None of these conditions are remotely analogous to the situations of the states in the Middle East today, and none are likely to be in the near future. In short, if the best argument proponents of regime change can come up with for trying it today in the Middle East is that "it worked in Germany and Japan," they don't have useful guidance for, say, how to approach Iran, Syria, Libya, or Saudi Arabia today.

Some other post–World War II precedents from Latin America and Asia are also worth keeping in mind. In Guatemala in 1954, inspired in part by the low-cost "success" of the coup in Tehran a year before, the Eisenhower administration decided to get rid of the left-leaning, democratically elected Guatemalan government of Jacobo Arbenz Guzmán. Afraid that Arbenz would align Guatemala with the Soviet Union and threaten U.S. economic interests, Eisenhower authorized CIA support for a military coup and found a suitable, exiled opposition leader—Carlos Castillo Armas—to lead it. With support from mercenaries from the United States and Central America, Castillo Armas forced Arbenz from power on June 18, 1954, and soon thereafter "legitimized" his presidency in a rigged plebiscite. The coup, however, led to a long series of corrupt military dictators and decades of civil war that left 200,000 Guatemalans dead, more than 90 percent of whom were killed by the government.[17] And one of its many unintended consequences was that it forced out of the country large numbers of leftists who ended up working to undermine some of the right-wing, pro-American regimes in the region. Ironically, one of them was Che Guevara, who fled to Mexico, where he would meet and join forces with Fidel Castro to help topple the U.S.-supported regime in Cuba.[18]

A few years later, with Castro having taken power in Havana, Eisenhower tasked the CIA with bringing about "the replacement of the Castro regime with one more devoted to the true interests of the Cuban people and more acceptable to the U.S."[19] However, when Eisenhower's successor, John F. Kennedy, launched the operation—an amphibious assault by some fourteen hundred Cuban paramilitaries at the Bay of Pigs on April 17, 1961—it backfired spectacularly. Instead of producing a popular uprising against Castro, the failed operation bolstered Castro's standing, increased suspicions of Washington across all of Latin America and beyond, demonstrated that even the powerful United States could be defeated, pushed Cuba further into Moscow's arms, and led directly to the Soviet decision the following year to deploy nuclear missiles to Cuba, producing the most dangerous confrontation of the Cold War. In the years and decades that followed, the United States persisted with efforts to oust the Castro regime—including assassination attempts, diplomatic isolation, and crippling economic sanctions—but never succeeded. Even successfully overthrowing a rival regime on a small, nearby island turned out to be more complicated than the advocates of that policy thought.

Less synonymous with failure than the Bay of Pigs, but ultimately even more disastrous, was the U.S. attempt to engineer a change in the leadership of the South Vietnamese government in 1963. Frustrated at seeing South Vietnam failing in its struggle against the communist North and its local supporters, the Kennedy administration authorized a coup against the corrupt and ineffective South Vietnamese president, Ngo Dinh Diem, who was overthrown and executed by other military officers with a bullet to the back of the head (complicating the plotters' plans to claim his death was by suicide). Far from solving the problem of South Vietnamese government legitimacy, however, the coup only exacerbated it and drew the United States deeper into the conflict. Diem's eventual successor, Nguyen Van Thieu, turned out to be even weaker, more corrupt, and less effective than his predecessor, and the United States would spend the next decade—at the cost of some fifty-eight thousand American lives—trying and failing to support him. Foreshadowing later efforts by U.S. political and military leaders in Afghanistan and Iraq, Presidents Lyndon Johnson and Richard Nixon and their top generals would spend much of that decade claiming, falsely, that the military campaign was making great progress and that success was just around the corner.

In Chile in 1970, the United States turned to intervention once again to try to prevent a leftist leader from threatening U.S. economic and geopolitical interests. The Nixon administration saw Salvador Allende, a Marxist who had formed a government after winning a plurality of votes in a three-way presidential election in September 1970, as a threat that had to be stopped at all costs. With Allende nationalizing critical industrial sectors (including big American firms) and threatening—or so Washington believed—to take Chile into the Soviet orbit, Secretary of State Henry Kissinger authorized the CIA to support a military coup to oust him on September 11, 1973. Allende died, probably by suicide, in the attack on the presidential palace. As in the previous cases, the Chile coup had some positive benefits for the United States, because the new leader, General Augusto Pinochet, reached agreements with the nationalized American firms and kept Chile staunchly in the Western camp. He also began a process of capitalist economic reform that would lay some of the groundwork for future economic growth. At the same time, Pinochet launched a campaign of horrible repression, including widespread torture, summary executions, and "disappearances" of regime opponents; he even authorized the murder of Allende's former ambassador to the United States and his American assistant, sending intelligence agents to blow up their car at a Washington, D.C., traffic circle in 1976.

About a decade after the Chile coup, the Reagan administration authorized the CIA to provide billions of dollars in covert assistance to the "contra" rebels in Nicaragua, who were fighting the Marxist Sandinista government. The Sandinistas had overthrown the right-wing dictatorship of Anastasio Somoza in 1979 and went on to win broadly free and fair elections in 1984, but they were also clients of the Soviet Union, so Reagan wanted them gone. After Congress banned U.S. assistance to the rebels in the wake of widespread human rights abuses, the administration responded by imposing a total U.S. trade embargo on Nicaragua and by maintaining support for the contras through secret and illegal arms sales to Iran.[20] The Sandinistas were eventually ousted (in 1990) in a democratic election, but the price of that outcome was high—more than thirty thousand killed and massive human rights abuses including murder, kidnapping, rape, and terrorist attacks on civilians—and the outcome fragile. Ironically, since 2018 Nicaragua has experienced the largest and deadliest protests since the Sandinista era—protests targeting President Daniel Ortega, the very leader the United States spent a decade trying to overthrow!

Finally there are the cases of Grenada and Panama, where the United States used military power to oust hostile governments at modest costs. The United States invaded the small Caribbean island of Grenada in October 1983 to overturn a coup by an extreme left-wing faction that it feared would turn the island into a Soviet outpost. The invasion—undertaken at the invitation of neighboring islands (and under the guise of saving a small group of U.S. medical students)—was tactically successful, U.S. forces suffered fewer than twenty fatalities, and a degree of democratic governance was restored. And in Panama in December 1989, the George H. W. Bush administration sent in a force of some thirty-five thousand troops to oust the government of General Manuel Noriega, whom it accused of threatening U.S. citizens, human rights abuses, and drug trafficking. U.S. casualties were again limited (twenty-three fatalities and 235 wounded, with Panamanian deaths in the hundreds), and the invasion largely achieved its goal of restoring moderate government and democracy. There is a decent case to be made that in Panama and Grenada the United States achieved its objectives at reasonable cost, but if they are indeed exceptions, those exceptions only underscore the rule. The U.S. ability to alter the political futures of one or two small, nearby states hardly means it can do the same thing in Iran, Syria, or Iraq. Just by way of comparison, deploying as many troops on a per capita basis to Afghanistan today as were sent to Panama in 1989 would require a force of at least half a million soldiers.

Some proponents of regime change also bring up Bosnia and Kosovo as cases where U.S.-led military intervention can work if only the political will is there and sufficient military force is used. It's true that in 1995 U.S. airpower and willingness to deploy twenty thousand U.S. troops (as part of a NATO force of sixty thousand) to Bosnia succeeded in stopping the war, and in 1999 sustained NATO bombing and the credible threat of a ground invasion led the Serbian strongman Slobodan Milosevic to withdraw his security forces from the disputed province of Kosovo, from which they had previously expelled nearly one million Muslims. But it is notable that in both cases the intervening powers explicitly *eschewed* regime change and in fact went so far as to work with the very leaders who were responsible for the conflict—Milosevic in Belgrade, President Franjo Tudjman in Zagreb, and even the Bosnian Serb leadership in the self-declared Republika Srpska, which was granted significant autonomy as part of the peace settlement. Working with these leaders—whose ethnic nationalism was responsible for the war in the first place—was certainly distasteful, but it was the recipe for ending a war that had led to hundreds of thousands of deaths and refugees. The same was true four years later in Kosovo, where it took three months of NATO bombing and the threat of a ground invasion just to get Serbian forces out of the rebellious province. Insisting on regime change as part of that operation not only would likely have fractured the international coalition that was implementing it but would have required a longer and costlier war, with highly uncertain outcomes. Ultimately, defeat and humiliation in Kosovo, along with subsequent U.S. efforts to strengthen democratic forces in Serbia, might even have led Milosevic to fall more quickly than if regime change had been an explicit policy goal: he held and lost elections eighteen months later. The fact that it took a sustained bombing campaign by the strongest military alliance in history, the threat of invasion, and a willingness to deploy thousands of peacekeeping forces indefinitely to achieve even limited political objectives on Europe's borders should give pause to those who argue that modest amounts of military force can bring about maximalist political objectives—regime change—anywhere in the Middle East.[21]

Whatever the track record in other parts of the world, the Middle East today is particularly unpropitious for successful regime change. It is made up mostly of artificial and often economically underdeveloped states plagued by deep ethnic and religious divisions with little history of democracy and the rule of law. Its main opposition parties are not primarily liberals, who form a distinct minority in all its countries, but Islamists, nationalists, or minorities of one form or another who are no more committed to democracy or freedom or good relations with the United States than most of the current leaders. The strong history of resentment of the United States makes it particularly hard for Americans to fill the vacuum once a regime is toppled, and geopolitical rivalries among the main actors in the region—to say nothing of outside players such as Russia and China, who posture as the defenders of the principle of national sovereignty—mean that some of them will always have a stake in American failure as well as the means to bring it about. Under these circumstances, it may not be a coincidence that the only country that has emerged from the "Arab Spring" more stable, inclusive, and democratic than it was before the revolutions broke out has been Tunisia, where the geopolitical stakes are limited and where the United States played hardly any role.

The case against regime change in the Middle East in this book is a practical, not a moral, one. It goes virtually without saying—or at least it should—that the United States and most people in the Middle East would be better off if there were different leaders, governments, institutions, and systems in many of the countries of the region today. But the question is not whether we should wish for such changes to take place. The question is whether active, coercive measures by American policy makers to undermine or overthrow those regimes make positive changes more or less likely, and whether the very fact of taking such actions is likely to advance U.S. interests or undermine them. The benefits of getting rid of hostile regimes need to be balanced with the costs, risks, and consequences of doing so, and in most cases the latter have exceeded the former, despite lots of wishful thinking that it would be the other way around.

Nor is the problem with regime change some form of American malevolence, as many critics at home and around the world seem to assume. Many of those critics have in common a principled opposition to the use of military force and often accuse the United States of exercising power for its own sake or acting exclusively on behalf of powerful corporations seeking profits or oil. They see the United States as an imperialist, mercantilist power that undermines world order and international law by seeking material gain at the expense of weaker states, often contending that "the search for markets, and for access to natural resources, is as central to American history as it has been to the history of every great power in every age."[22] There is no doubt that economic interests and a desire to wield and demonstrate power influenced American decisions to pursue regime change in Middle Eastern countries, and those factors played a role in some—though hardly all—of the interventions discussed here. But my argument is not that the United States always seeks regime change for impure motives—often the motives are honorable ones—but that doing so rarely serves, and often undermines, U.S. long-term interests, regardless of intentions. Donald Trump, of course, has floated the view that after invading Iraq, we should have "taken the oil" and even claims to have done so himself in Syria.[23] But that sort of thinking has fortunately been more the exception than the rule in American history, and even Trump—for all his falsehoods and bluster—has not actually implemented such illegal, immoral, and impractical ideas.[24]

There is something appealing about the can-do American spirit that lures its leaders and top officials to believe, often sincerely (and like generations of financial pundits before them), that "this time is different" and that with enough commitment, willpower, and resources friendly democracies can be established in the Middle East.[25] But there is something dangerous about it as well. Whereas in other fields of human endeavor—medicine, for example—we seem to accept that there are certain problems and challenges that we did not create and cannot entirely resolve (and that trying to do so sometimes makes things worse), the U.S. policy debate about the Middle East suffers from the fallacy that there is an external American solution to every problem, even when decades of painful experience suggest that this is not the case. The next time U.S. leaders or analysts argue that the solution to a Middle Eastern problem is to use coercive efforts to get rid of an adversarial regime, Americans should take it as axiomatic that the benefits of doing so will be less than promised and the costs will be higher than expected.

The alternative to regime change is not—as a growing number of Americans would apparently have it—simply withdrawal or resignation. I do not share the view, often expressed both by Trump himself and by some of his critics on the left, that the United States has little at stake in the Middle East and that relative energy independence means Americans can now ignore what happens there. On the contrary, the United States has enduring interests in the Middle East that include preventing the proliferation of weapons of mass destruction, containing terrorism, ensuring the free flow of oil, preventing mass refugee flows, and saving human lives. I support efforts, sometimes including the threat or use of military force, to protect those interests. And I believe there are often practical things the United States can and should do to reduce conflict, alleviate suffering, promote prosperity, deter atrocities, and advance political reform. In most cases, however, a mix of containment, deterrence, diplomatic engagement, support for partners, selective military actions, arms control, economic investment, and the restoration of the United States as a respected, prosperous, and democratic alternative will produce better results than the pursuit of costly, quixotic, and unrealistic campaigns to overthrow regimes.

While there are no easy fixes to the massive challenges the United States faces in the region, the global track record of engagement, diplomacy, and containment is simply better than the track record of regime change, whether in places where regime change was achieved such as Iraq, Afghanistan, and Libya or in places where dictators held on to power such as Syria, Cuba, and North Korea. As I argue in this book's conclusion, even the fall of the Soviet Union, the model for many current proponents of regime change, actually came about not primarily through military confrontation and economic sanctions but through long-term containment, internal corrosion, generational change, détente, and a realization by its leadership that the course it was on could no longer be sustained, just as the diplomat George F. Kennan predicted when he spelled out the original containment policy in 1945. If Americans fail to draw the right lessons from nearly seventy years of failed attempts at regime change in the Middle East, they are bound to repeat them—with enormous costs for all involved.

The next seven chapters are the stories of how and why the United States pursued its perceived national interests by intervening—through a wide range of different means—to change governments and institutions in the Middle East over the past seventy years, and how those interventions turned out. Every case started with high hopes and often the best of intentions. But all came with exceedingly high costs, and none turned out well.

CHAPTER 1

Original Sin

Iran, 1953

"What they had in mind was nothing less than the overthrow of Mosaddeq."[1]

That was the pithy summary of British thinking provided by the CIA's chief of Middle East operations, Kermit "Kim" Roosevelt, to top American officials following a brief visit to London in November 1952. Only a few days before Roosevelt arrived in Washington, the Republican Dwight D. Eisenhower had soundly defeated the Democrat Adlai Stevenson in the U.S. presidential elections, a result that would bring to power a U.S. administration much more sympathetic to what the British "had in mind" in Iran. The thirty-six-year-old Roosevelt, a grandson of former president Theodore Roosevelt, who had a similar appetite for action, adventure, and intrigue, would end up playing a central role in the momentous events that would follow. He and those who sponsored his mission did so out of a genuine sense that U.S. interests would be well served by getting rid of an insolent, hostile, and potentially unstable Iranian regime. But in pursuing that worthy goal, they had no idea what forces they would ultimately unleash. The coup that Eisenhower would agree to sponsor might (or might not) have prevented Iran from tipping into the Soviet camp, but it also aborted Iran's democratic development, empowered a cruel (and not always cooperative) dictator, fueled visceral anti-Americanism, and ultimately led to a revolution founded on enduring hostility toward and direct confrontation with the United States.

That Eisenhower would end up embracing British plans for a coup in Tehran to prevent Iran from falling into communist hands may seem puzzling because Mohammad Mosaddeq was hardly a communist. An upper-class lawyer who had been involved in Iranian politics since he was elected to Iran's new parliament, the Majlis, at age twenty-four, Mosaddeq was by the early 1950s a towering figure not just in Iran but around the world. A descendant of the Qajar dynasty that had ruled Iran from 1796 to 1925, he was a powerful speaker but also a strange and emotional man, prone to fits of tears and laughter, who was frequently ill and often held meetings while still in bed wearing pajamas. A fierce nationalist who hated Iran's corrupt monarchs as much as he did the British who had dominated his country ever since they discovered oil there in 1908, Mosaddeq regularly deployed his eloquence to rail against both dictatorship and colonialism. Although no friend of the shah, Iran's head of state, Mosaddeq was named prime minister in April 1951 after the Majlis overwhelmingly insisted on his appointment to stand up to the British and fight for their oil rights.[2] Recognizing the global significance of that fight, *Time* magazine named Mosaddeq "Man of the Year" for 1951, ahead of Winston Churchill, Harry Truman, Dean Acheson, and Douglas MacArthur. Calling Mosaddeq "Iran's George Washington," *Time* wrote that his "acid tears dissolved one of the remaining pillars of a once great empire" and that "in his plaintive, singsong voice he gabbled a defiant challenge that sprang out of a hatred and envy almost incomprehensible to the West."[3]

The primary target of Mosaddeq's ire was the hated Anglo-Iranian Oil Company (AIOC), and the feelings were mutual.[4] Taking advantage of its monopoly on Iran's oil production, the British-dominated company treated its Iranian workers miserably and paid them little, while Iran—according to contracts signed in 1933 with the shah's father and predecessor, Reza Shah—was allowed to keep only 16 percent of the company's massive profits. Thanks to creative accounting and a total lack of transparency—as well as an unwillingness to allow any Iranian role in company management—the Iranian share was almost certainly much less than even that. AIOC had no Iranian directors and paid taxes in Britain but not in Iran (in fact, AIOC paid more in taxes to Britain than the total amount of revenues received by Iran).[5] When Mosaddeq sought to negotiate a better deal—perhaps something close to the fifty-fifty split American oil companies had agreed to with other oil-producing states, including Saudi Arabia—he was met with categorical British rejection. The revenues from AIOC were too critical to a postwar British economy already under enormous strain, and London refused to even consider revising the 1933 agreement. In retrospect, cutting a more reasonable deal with Mosaddeq in 1951 might have salvaged Britain's special role in Iran, allowed London to continue to reap vast profits, and helped nurture Iran's incipient democratic development while maintaining good ties with the West. But British leaders at the time refused to compromise. They failed to seize that opportunity, thinking instead they could avoid the inevitable by interfering in the politics of Iran. Not unlike the Trump administration in its approach to Iran some seventy years later, the British were trying to have almost everything. But they would end up with nothing.

With no hope for an equitable deal with London, on April 30, 1951, the Majlis voted unanimously to nationalize AIOC.

Mosaddeq, whom the shah had just reluctantly named prime minister, astutely linked his confirmation by parliament to the decision to nationalize, knowing the measure had overwhelming public support. Even though Iran offered to compensate the British for their previous investments in infrastructure—notwithstanding all the profits they had taken and even as Britain's own Labour government was nationalizing industries back home—the reaction in London was furious and uncompromising. Launching its own version of a "maximum pressure" campaign against Iran (to use the language the Trump administration would adopt some sixty-five years later), the British government sought to bring the Mosaddeq government to its knees by declaring a boycott of Iranian oil (and pressing international oil companies to join them), stopping ships, sabotaging oil installations, and blockading Iranian ports. Britain sued Iran at the United Nations Security Council and International Court of Justice—moves that backfired when Mosaddeq used those platforms to denounce unjust treatment by the British. The hard-line British foreign secretary, Herbert Morrison, developed plans for the U.K. to seize the massive Abadan refinery and to invade and occupy Iran with seventy thousand troops.[6] Only opposition from Prime Minister Clement Attlee—and from the Truman administration—prevented an all-out invasion.

Determined to maintain its control over Iran's oil, London looked to Washington for support, but it got little from the Truman administration. With the Cold War at the top of the U.S. foreign policy agenda (especially following the Soviet-backed North Korean invasion of South Korea in June 1950), Truman and his top advisers saw Mosaddeq as a bulwark against the influence of the communist Tudeh Party and urged London to accommodate Iranian demands. Truman even sought to empower and build a relationship with Mosaddeq by hosting him for a very positive visit to Washington in October 1951.[7] Presciently, some U.S. officials saw the Iranian more as the nationalist that he was than as a potential Soviet proxy. Assistant Secretary of State for Near Eastern Affairs George McGhee considered him a "conservative and patriotic Iranian nationalist with no reason to be attracted to socialism or communism," while the U.S. ambassador to Iran, Henry Grady, privately reported that Mosaddeq "has the backing of 95 to 98 percent of the people of the country."[8] In June 1951, Grady publicly argued that "since nationalization is accomplished fact, it would be wise for Britain to adopt a conciliatory attitude." He told *The Wall Street Journal* that "Mosaddeq's National Front party is the closest thing to a moderate and stable political element in the national parliament."[9] Truman's secretary of state, Dean Acheson—hardly known for any reluctance to take tough stands against foreign leaders—also advised the British to make further concessions and decried AIOC's "inflexibility."[10] Compared with what would happen next, it seems clear more flexibility would indeed have been wise, but the British had other ideas.

Eisenhower's election in November 1952 was the game changer. The new president was, like Truman, broadly sympathetic to the anticolonialist movements then spreading across Asia and Africa, and, also like Truman, he feared that a failure to accommodate them could drive those countries into communist hands. But the Eisenhower administration was also obsessed with the growing communist threat and more open to taking direct U.S. measures to stop it. With the United States bogged down in a costly conventional military campaign in Korea, Eisenhower, along with Secretary of State John Foster Dulles and the CIA director, Allen Dulles, was looking for lower-cost ways to fight the Cold War. So when the British began pitching the idea of a coup, for which their own internal planning had already begun, they found a newly receptive American audience.[11]

The overwhelming priority for the British was to protect their own oil and geopolitical interests, but they also knew what buttons to push in Washington to help them do so. In the spirit of what the British prime minister Harold Macmillan would later that decade call Britain "playing Greece to America's Rome," U.K. officials were tasked with the mission of persuading the powerful Americans to use their might to advance British interests. Ever since 1951, Foreign Office internal guidance was "to stress to the Americans that the danger of communism increases the longer Mosaddeq remains in power."[12] And when a senior agent in the Secret Intelligence Service, Christopher Montague Woodhouse, arrived in Washington to sell the British idea only a few days after pitching it to Roosevelt in London, he did just that.[13] As Woodhouse later admitted, "Not wishing to be accused of trying to use the Americans to pull British chestnuts out of the fire, I decided to emphasize the Communist threat to Iran rather than the need to recover control of the oil industry."[14]

The message was music to the Dulles brothers' ears, and once Eisenhower and his team took office in January 1953, U.S. decision making on Iran advanced rapidly. At a meeting of the National Security Council on March 4, John Foster Dulles warned that in the case of a communist takeover in Iran "not only would the free world be deprived of the enormous assets represented by Iranian oil production and reserves, but . . . in short order the other areas of the Middle East, with some sixty percent of the world's oil reserves, would fall into Communist control."[15] One month later, Allen Dulles approved $1 million in secret funding for use "in any way that would bring about the fall of Mosaddeq."[16] The objective "was to bring to power a government which would reach an equitable oil settlement and which would vigorously prosecute the dangerously strong Communist Party."[17]

As would be the case in later approaches to regime change, it wasn't long before U.S. analyses started to bolster the case for intervention and officials began to see what they wanted to see. Whereas Truman administration officials viewed Mosaddeq as a genuinely popular nationalist who could help stave off the communists, the Eisenhower team was increasingly convinced—or convinced itself—of the opposite. Cables from the U.S. embassy in Tehran described Mosaddeq as "lacking in stability," "clearly dominated by emotions and prejudices," and "not quite sane." The National Front, the embassy now reported, was composed of "the street rabble, the extreme left . . . extreme Iranian nationalists, some but not all of the more fanatical religious leaders, [and] intellectual leftists, including many who had been educated abroad and did not realize that Iran was not ready for democracy."[18] The U.S. and British ambassadors sent their respective capitals a rare joint analysis arguing that the longer Mosaddeq remained in power, the likelier it was that Iran would fall to communism. Not all U.S. officials saw the risk of Iran turning communist if Mosaddeq stayed in power; the CIA station chief in Tehran, Roger Goiran, and Assistant Secretary of State for Near Eastern Affairs Henry Byroade, were notable exceptions, and even the U.S. ambassador to Iran, Loy Henderson, was ambivalent. But the political leaders in Washington would ignore their analysis in favor of those that fit better with their worldview.[19]

Influenced by their most optimistic hopes, top American officials even began to convince themselves that a U.S. intervention to overthrow Mosaddeq would be politically popular in Iran. On March 2, 1953, Secretary of State Dulles noted—summarizing the embassy's recent reporting—that "there appears to be [a] substantial and relatively courageous opposition group both within and outside Majlis. We gather Army Chiefs and many civilians [are] still loyal to [the] Shah and would act if he gave them positive leadership, or even if he merely acquiesced in move to install [a] new government."[20] Ambassador Henderson asserted that "during last six months there has been sharp shift in basis [of] Mosaddeq support among political leaders" and that most elements of the original National Front were now "in open or tacit opposition."[21] Just two months beforehand, Henderson was reporting that Mosaddeq "had near-total support from the Iranian population and was not likely to fall," an analysis that suggested a policy of engagement. Now he was suddenly asserting that "most Iranian politicians friendly to the West would welcome secret American intervention which would assist them in attaining their individual or group political ambitions."[22] And it was just what Washington wanted to hear.

The assessment that Mosaddeq faced growing opposition and might resort to communist support to stay in power was no doubt based in part on real trends in Iran, where a clear power struggle between Mosaddeq, the shah, and others was under way. But it also represented a serious overstatement of the threat and wishful thinking in Washington about the desire of Iranians to see the shah empowered at the government's expense—let alone at the hands of the Americans and the British. Mosaddeq was indeed obstinate, mercurial, emotional, and inflexible, but he was also broadly popular, strongly anticommunist, and probably the only hope to avoid dictatorship or chaos in Iran. A National Intelligence Estimate (NIE) updated as recently as January 1953 assessed that Mosaddeq would likely remain in power throughout the year and that he "almost certainly desires to keep US support as a counterweight to the USSR."[23] More recent research also suggests that the Tudeh Party had "neither the intention nor the capability of seizing power in the near term."[24] But once Washington had decided to act, it could not resist the temptation to inflate the threat, which led to a self-fulfilling prophecy: the more the United States and Britain pressured Mosaddeq—with crippling sanctions, harsh public criticism, denial of financial assistance, and eventually propaganda and covert action—the more the subsequent instability created space for the communist threat to actually grow. In that sense U.S. policy had become as much the cause of political instability as its remedy.

By the spring of 1953, however, the administration's mind was largely made up. In May, the CIA consultant Donald Wilber spent several weeks in Cyprus with Norman Darbyshire of the U.K.'s Secret Intelligence Service to flesh out more detailed arrangements for what would come to be called Operation Ajax. The British had already been developing a network of anti-Mosaddeq figures centered on General Fazlollah Zahedi, a senior military officer under Reza Shah in the 1920s and 1930s, and three brothers from the Rashidian family, who would help to organize the opposition.[25] The plan would consist in bribing journalists, editors, Islamic preachers, and opinion leaders to undermine the government and fan the flames of distrust. Stories would be planted "to show Mosaddeq as a Communist collaborator and as a fanatic," and thugs would be hired to organize protests and create chaos and instability on the streets.[26] The shah would fire Mosaddeq, who was bound to resist, creating a pretext for his arrest, his ouster, and the restoration of the shah's unquestioned rule.[27]

On July 19, Roosevelt arrived in Iran and began to implement the plan, paying agents to spread chaos on the streets of Tehran and bribing members of parliament to abandon the government. The cautious, young shah—aware of Mosaddeq's popularity—was reluctant to approve the action, but he was eventually brought on board, mostly due to threats from Roosevelt but also in part by his sister Ashraf, who was enlisted by the CIA to help persuade him.[28] Still dealing with the British-led global oil boycott, Mosaddeq begged for assistance from the United States, but Eisenhower declined to help, by then convinced that the only hope was to squeeze Iran financially to prepare the ground for the coup.[29] As instability mounted—including after the resignation en masse of all National Front deputies and a fraudulent referendum Mosaddeq used in an effort to shut down parliament and hold new elections—on August 14 the shah signed royal decrees dismissing Mosaddeq and naming General Zahedi prime minister. Mosaddeq was tipped off about the move, however, and when the commander of the Imperial Guard, Nematollah Nassiri, tried to deliver the decrees, loyalist soldiers were standing by to repel them and arrest Nassiri. Concluding the coup had failed, Zahedi went into hiding, and the shah fled to Baghdad, thinking he might never return. Policy makers in Washington also gave up, and on August 18 the CIA sent Roosevelt a cable that said, "Operation has been tried and failed and we should not participate in any operation against Mosaddeq which could be traced back to US. Operations against Mosaddeq should be discontinued."[30]

But Roosevelt did not give up. Working with anti-Mosaddeq forces and some of his paid agents, Roosevelt encouraged continued protests and rioting in Tehran, while Mosaddeq—who abhorred violence—made the fatal mistake of telling his own supporters to stand down. On August 19, military units recruited by Roosevelt took over the police station, the Foreign Ministry, and army headquarters. General Zahedi left the CIA safe house where he was hiding and promptly declared himself "the lawful prime minister by the Shah's orders," while the CIA and U.S. embassy disseminated news of the shah's decree dismissing Mosaddeq to make him appear to be acting beyond the law.[31] Zahedi's forces surrounded the ousted prime minister's residence and—after a bloody battle in which as many as three hundred loyalists were killed—arrested him. The shah returned from Baghdad, reclaimed the throne, and concluded—quite wrongly, it would turn out—that the Iranian people loved him after all. The CIA promptly sent in a further $5 million, followed by another $68 million in emergency aid from the U.S. government, to consolidate what it considered a remarkable success.[32]

In the wake of Mosaddeq's fall, coup proponents felt vindicated, and important U.S. policy goals were undeniably achieved. Without expending significant resources, the United States had helped get rid of a disruptive nationalist and sent a signal to the entire region about its determination to counter potential communist influence there. The operation kept Iran out of the Soviet camp and installed a strong partner in Tehran who, initially at least, implemented some progressive reforms and would go on to buy massive volumes of U.S. weapons and establish extensive military and intelligence cooperation with the United States. The coup also benefited U.S. oil companies, which received a 40 percent stake in a market from which they had previously been excluded.[33] For the Eisenhower administration, the low-budget, high-payoff move to oust Mosaddeq was so seemingly successful it would serve as a model to be emulated elsewhere, including in Guatemala City the following year and in the later plans to overthrow Castro in Cuba. It is thus fair to argue that viewed through the geopolitical perspective in which U.S. leaders saw the issue, the overthrow of Mosaddeq and the empowerment of the U.S.-friendly shah were at least initially a success.

While these achievements were real, however, they also

tended to obscure a wide range of more negative, unintended—and eventually disastrous—consequences, for the people of Iran, the stability of the region, and ultimately the interests of the United States. The most immediate casualty of the coup—beyond the Iranians who were killed on the day—was the prospect for the democratic development of Iran. Since the 1906 Qajar promise of a constitutional government, followed in 1909 by a constitutional revolution, Iran had been on a path, however bumpy and uncertain, to more representative government. After the autocratic Reza Shah was forced to abdicate and to give way to his young son Mohammad Reza during World War II, the restored Majlis was given real powers, and a balance of power had emerged among the shah, the prime minister, and the parliamentary parties.[34] Iran's relatively free elections and assertive parliament were exceptional in the region, and Mosaddeq, as much as he hated the British, admired and hoped to emulate their constitutional monarchy and democratic institutions.

Such hopes were destroyed with the coup, and the reinstalled shah immediately set out to crush all dissent. Fearing that Mosaddeq's execution would create a backlash, the shah instead had him tried for treason, sentenced to three years in prison, and then held under house arrest until his death in 1967. Mosaddeq's foreign minister, Hossein Fatemi, on the other hand, was arrested, tortured, and executed by firing squad, as were some of the student leaders close to Mosaddeq. The shah also cracked down on Tudeh, arresting some two thousand suspected communists by the end of 1953 and another thousand by the end of 1954.[35] He blatantly rigged elections in 1954 and the following year fired Zahedi, replacing him with a series of weak prime ministers who posed no political threat. From then on, the once-powerful Majlis was reduced to the role of a rubber stamp, and prime ministers became little more than what the scholar Barry Rubin later called "executive assistants" to the shah.[36]

In 1957 the shah—with extensive help from the CIA, a fact not lost on a subsequent generation of Iranians—created an intelligence service that would come to be known around the world for its brutality.[37] The National Intelligence and Security Organization (known by its Persian acronym, SAVAK) would go on to arrest tens of thousands of regime opponents and use torture, rape, and executions to perpetuate the shah's rule. In 1967, Mohammad Reza Shah named himself "king of kings," and over the course of the following decade spent tens of billions of dollars on private palaces and weapons.

Perhaps even more tragically, the shah's brutal elimination of both the nationalist and the communist opposition led to a political vacuum that was filled by Islamic clerics, some of whom Washington had paid in 1953 as part of its campaign to oust Mosaddeq.[38] It was not that the shah was afraid of repressing religious figures when necessary—he reportedly killed, arrested, tortured, or exiled at least six hundred clerics during the 1970s alone—but because mosques were sacred, they became the one place in Iran where dissent could be expressed and opposition could develop.[39] With no other outlets for dissent, the Islamic movement became the leading voice for Iranian resentment of the shah and of his close ties to the United States, providing fuel to what would eventually become the 1978–79 revolution.[40]

There is obviously no guarantee that Iran's democratic development would have continued had Mosaddeq not been overthrown. What is certain, however, is that the coup and the policies that followed it destroyed any chance that it might do so. While it might have staved off the hypothetical prospects of political instability or a communist takeover, the coup delegitimized the monarchy, emasculated the parliament, and empowered autocratic Islamists all at the same time.

Defenders of U.S. policy in 1953 tend to argue that the coup itself was a great success and the only problem was that the United States failed to curb the shah's excesses in the years that followed. "If only" U.S. policy makers had managed to persuade the shah to govern better, the logic runs, the coup would have paid off even in the long run. It is an easy argument to make in retrospect, but in reality (and as always) U.S. leverage over the dictator it had helped install was limited, and the shah knew it. Presidents Kennedy and Johnson restricted weapons sales and pushed for domestic reforms in Iran, consistent with their support for economic development and social change across the third world, but they were ignored in Tehran.[41] Nixon and Kissinger—concerned about driving Iran into the Soviet camp (and in particular about losing access to the TACKSMAN listening post that was critical for monitoring Soviet missile tests)—set aside any attempt to curb domestic repression and agreed to provide whatever advanced weapons the shah claimed he needed.[42] Nixon and Kissinger knew U.S. support for those policies fostered growing resentment within Iran, but the confident shah scoffed at the notion that Washington had alternative strategic partners. "Who else in the area," he asked rhetorically, "can supply a credible military deterrent in the Gulf? Pakistan, Saudi Arabia, the small, weak Gulf States? Of course not."[43] Even President Jimmy Carter, who had made the promotion of human rights a core element of his foreign policy, had only limited influence on the shah, who called Carter's bluff at a press conference with American reporters in 1976: "What will you do if one day Iran will be in danger of collapsing? Do you have any choice?" The only alternatives to supporting him, the shah claimed, were "an all-out nuclear holocaust or other Vietnams."[44] These were arguments that American officials would hear time and again from other allies and proxies in the region—from Hosni Mubarak and

Hamid Karzai to Saudi kings—and the officials never had a good response. What was Washington going to do, pull the plug on a proxy it had helped put in power in the first place?

Many years later, Christopher Montague Woodhouse, one of the original British planners of the coup, acknowledged, "It is easy to see [the 1953 coup] as the first step towards the Iranian catastrophe of 1979. What we did not foresee was that the Shah would gather new strength and use it so tyrannically, nor that the U.S. government and the Foreign Office would fail so abjectly to keep him on a reasonable course."[45] But in fact they should have known that keeping the shah "on a reasonable course" would prove easier said than done. And the hope that the shah, after coming to power in a coup, would not use his new strength "so tyrannically" was simply naive.

Eisenhower himself was not immune to the same sort of wishful thinking. In an October 8, 1953, entry in his diary, the president recorded his hopes at the time that "if the British will be conciliatory and display some wisdom; if the Shah and his new premier, General Zahedi, will be only a little bit flexible, and the United States will stand by to help both financially and with wise counsel, we may really give a serious defeat to Russian intentions and plans in that area."[46] He should also have known, however, that British "conciliation" and Iranian "flexibility" were never in the cards and that America's "wise counsel" was unlikely to be followed.

Perversely, in fact, the shah's weakness actually allowed him to resist pressure to follow Washington's lead on foreign policy, as would so often be the case with leaders who owed their positions to the United States. To be sure, Iran sided with Washington on most regional disputes, opposed Arab radicals, and in 1955 even joined the Baghdad Pact, a U.S.-led regional defense agreement. But Iran's perceived and real national and regional interests did not suddenly change when Mosaddeq was overthrown. Far from the shah's Iran being America's "unconditional ally," as former secretary of state Henry Kissinger once asserted, in many ways it was the other way around.[47] Examples of Tehran going its own way under the shah include helping to create the Organization of Petroleum Exporting Countries in 1960 and leading the effort to boost oil prices (when Washington was desperate to lower them); refusing the U.S. request to deploy nuclear missiles in Iran in 1962, just before the Cuban missile crisis; siding with the royalist opposition in Yemen against the republican forces backed by the United States; providing U.S. spare parts to Pakistan after the United States had imposed an embargo during the 1971 war with India; providing weapons to Turkey in its 1974 war with Greece; taking over the Persian Gulf islands of Abu Musa and Greater and Lesser Tunbs that were also claimed by the United Arab Emirates (UAE); and developing a domestic nuclear program with the potential to violate nuclear nonproliferation norms.[48] Most important, in 1971 the shah took over the international consortium that had run Iranian oil production since 1953—essentially completing the nationalization of that sector that was one of the main reasons why Mosaddeq was overthrown—and supported the 1973 Arab oil boycott that quadrupled oil prices and sent the U.S. and world economies into a deep recession. Americans were unable to prevent any of these developments, notwithstanding the billions of dollars in assistance and weapons sales they provided to Iran.[49]

Finally and most significant, U.S. complicity in empowering and then supporting the brutally repressive shah provided fuel for deep-seated Iranian hostility toward the United States, powerfully contributing to the 1978–79 revolution and the confrontational policies of the regime that followed it. As Barry Rubin observed, the coup "formed the essential backdrop to

[the] 1978–79 revolution" and was the "main rationale used to justify [the] seizure of the American embassy in November 1979."[50] After decades of domination and mistreatment by the British, Iranians were of course already deeply resentful of foreign influence; that was in many ways the source of Mosaddeq's popularity in the first place. But by assisting in the overthrow of a popular Iranian government and the empowerment of the repressive and illegitimate shah, Washington virtually guaranteed that such resentment would grow exponentially and that it would be directed in particular at the United States. Iran's Islamic movement, led by the Ayatollah Ruhollah Khomeini, picked up that mantle enthusiastically and would never let it go. In the long run, the historian Malcolm Byrne concluded, the CIA's support for the shah's return "would breed Iranian anti-Americanism and play a central role in shaping the attitudes of the post-Shah regime."[51] Those attitudes consisted of profound, unrelenting anti-Americanism that ultimately led not only to the seizure of the American embassy but to decades of terrorist attacks against U.S. targets and an all-out geopolitical effort to reduce American influence in the region that continues to this day.

That U.S. support for the coup would create a domestic backlash was no surprise to its original proponents, most of whom worked hard to keep it secret—even from large parts of the U.S. government. Ambassador Loy Henderson told the shah on August 16, just after he fled to Iraq, that "for his prestige in Iran he never indicate that any foreigner had had a part in recent events," advice the shah readily accepted.[52] And as Eisenhower noted in his diary, "If knowledge of [U.S. support for the coup] became public, we would not only be embarrassed in that region, but our chances to do anything of like nature in the future would almost totally disappear."[53] But of course it could not be kept secret—as early as 1954 some anonymous sources leaked word of the U.S. role to *The Saturday Evening Post*—and the result was a powerful myth in Iran, cynically manipulated by the leadership of the Islamic Republic, that the United States bore responsibility for all the troubles that followed.[54]

In recent years, a number of revisionist scholars have sought to downplay the role of the United States in the coup, suggesting that subsequent criticism of the U.S. intervention has been overstated. Authors such as Darioush Bayandor, Abbas Milani, and Ray Takeyh have challenged the caricature of outsiders simply changing the course of Iranian politics by throwing a few dollars around and emphasized the important role played by Iranian actors themselves.[55] Takeyh, a colleague of mine at the Council on Foreign Relations, even goes so far as to suggest the notion that the United States toppled Mosaddeq is a "myth" and that U.S. actions were "ultimately insignificant" because the regime was "bound to fall and the shah was bound to retain his throne and expand his power."[56] While acknowledging that the United States and Britain had a policy of seeking to oust Mosaddeq, these authors argue that their attempt to do so on August 15–18, 1953, failed and that Iranians themselves were solely responsible for the successful revolution that took place on August 19.

Top Trump administration officials and other leading critics of the Islamic Republic today have embraced this narrative, apparently as a way to downplay American responsibility and instead to shift the blame for what has happened since to the Iranian religious establishment itself. Asked in May 2019 whether the memory of the 1953 coup might be a factor in Iranian resistance to American efforts to influence Iran today, Brian Hook, the U.S. special representative for Iran, asserted that "Mosaddeq was overthrown by the religious establishment, the military, and the political leaders"—not the CIA. Like the revisionists, Hook claimed that the administration had "declassified a range of materials that speak to this," and pointed to the Iranian clerics' desire to downplay their own support for the coup as a reason why most Iranians and others continue to blame the United States.[57]

The argument that the United States and Britain did not play a leading role in organizing and executing the coup, however, does not hold up to scrutiny. Iranians obviously played a central role in the events in Tehran in 1953—the coup took place in Iran, after all—but the hypothesis that Mosaddeq's overthrow would have happened anyway is highly dubious and overlooks the importance of even the perception that the United States was responsible for imposing the shah, a perception that would fuel Iranian anti-Americanism for decades to come. The idea that Washington bears little responsibility for the coup because its relative role on the single day of August 19 cannot be precisely determined also ignores the importance of the propaganda campaign, economic sanctions, and support to the Iranian opposition that purposefully set the stage for what took place on that day. In fact, the United States would bear significant responsibility for the coup even if its agents did nothing on the day itself, which was of course not the case. According to the historian Mark Gasiorowski, who examined the primary source documents and interviewed many of the coup plotters themselves, "While it is impossible to say what would have happened if the CIA had not instigated the coup, there is no reason to think that [any] Iranians . . . would have overthrown Mosaddeq any time soon."[58]

Takeyh and others challenge this conclusion by pointing to official documents released in 2013 and 2017, but those documents, in fact, only underscore the central importance of the

U.S. role. They include the release of the CIA's own previously secret internal history, which concluded that the coup "was carried out *under CIA direction as an act of U.S. foreign policy*, conceived and approved at the highest levels of government."[59] The CIA authors concluded that "when it became apparent that many elements in Iran did not approve of Mosaddeq's continuing gamble or the direction in which he was pushing their country, the execution of a U.S.-assisted coup d'état seemed a more desirable risk than letting matters run their predictable course."[60] Indeed, according to the historian Malcolm Byrne, "all 21 of the CIA items . . . reinforce the conclusion that the United States, and the CIA in particular, devoted extensive resources and high-level policy attention toward bringing about Mosaddeq's overthrow, and smoothing over the aftermath."[61] Further papers released in 2017 add British documentation to what was previously known and confirm that senior Iranian clerics received "large sums of money" from U.S. officials in the days leading up to the coup.[62] They also include the publication of declassified excerpts from Eisenhower's secret diary, which show that he certainly thought the United States was responsible for contributing to the "restoration of the Shah to power . . . and the elimination of Mosaddeq," including as part of the August 19 events.[63] Whereas Takeyh claims that Eisenhower was skeptical of Roosevelt's description of his role in the coup (pointing to Eisenhower's comment that it read like a "dime store novel"), the documents show Eisenhower was impressed with his agent's accomplishments, noting again in the diary, "We can understand exactly how courageous our agent was in staying right on the job and continuing to work until he reversed the entire situation."[64] Far from downplaying Roosevelt's role, Eisenhower secretly awarded him the National Security Medal in a ceremony in the Oval Office in 1954.[65]

It is certainly fair for analysts today to push back against

Iranian attempts to instrumentalize the 1953 coup and blame the United States for the many problems—and the brutal, Islamic regime—that followed it. Mosaddeq was no saint, and his ouster spared the United States from having to work with a confrontational, nationalistic leader and replaced him with an ostensible ally, which brought the United States concrete strategic benefits for a considerable amount of time. But it is also impossible to deny the reality that the United States played a major—and by now long-admitted—role in overthrowing the Iranian government in 1953, and that the intervention had disastrous longer-term consequences not just for the Iranian people but ultimately for the United States itself. The U.S. intervention in 1953 might have prevented a hypothetical Iranian pivot into the Soviet camp, but it also halted—for the foreseeable future—Iran's democratic development. It made the United States complicit in the establishment of a brutal, corrupt, and tyrannical regime on which American influence proved limited, and it created the conditions for a violent revolution that produced another brutal, corrupt, and repressive regime—this time founded on hostility toward Washington.

There is no guarantee that maintaining the Truman administration's policy of engagement with Mosaddeq and attempting to negotiate a more equitable oil deal—the main alternative to helping topple the Mosaddeq government in 1953—would have led Iran to evolve in a freer, more democratic, less extremist, and less anti-American direction. What is fairly certain, however—after forty years of the Islamic Republic's deeply repressive government, efforts to spread sectarian revolution around the region, state-supported terrorism, development of an expansive nuclear program, and conflict with the United States—is that in the long run U.S.-sponsored regime change in Iran could not have turned out much worse.

CHAPTER 2

"We Won"

Afghanistan, 1979–92

Christmas 1979 was already unlikely to be a very peaceful one for Jimmy Carter. Radical Iranian students were still holding the fifty-two Americans they had taken hostage seven weeks before, unemployment and inflation were soaring, and Carter's prospects for reelection were sinking as quickly as the lines at gasoline stations, driven by the energy crisis that resulted from the Iranian revolution, were growing. Little did Carter know it as he spent the day at Camp David with his family—rising at 5:30 a.m. at the request of his young daughter to exchange gifts and presumably enjoy a brief respite from world politics—but later that night his life was going to get even more complicated. Confirming warnings Carter had received earlier that week from the U.S. intelligence community, the Fortieth Red Army was spending Christmas Day moving two motorized rifle divisions into Kabul to prop up its communist government against a growing Islamist insurgency.[1] Within days, some fifty thousand Soviet troops would be deployed throughout the country, giving Moscow a strategic foothold in Southwest Asia and the wider Middle East. It was a nightmare top U.S. policy makers had long feared. Now it was happening on their watch.

As the scale of the invasion became clear, Carter would have to cut his vacation short. By December 28, he was back in Washington, sending "the sharpest message I have ever sent [Soviet leader Leonid] Brezhnev" and chairing National Security Council meetings to put in place policies that would have momentous consequences for Afghanistan, the United States, the Soviet Union, and the entire world.[2] Those policies would begin with a limited, covert operation to increase the costs of Soviet occupation by arming and training Afghan rebels, expand considerably under Ronald Reagan into an ambitious plan to force the Soviet army to withdraw, and end up under George H. W. Bush—not so much deliberately as by default—becoming a policy of U.S.-backed regime change in Kabul that would culminate in the violent overthrow of the Afghan government in 1992. The consequences of those measures would eventually include one of the most savage civil wars of modern times, the death and displacement of millions of Afghans, the arming and inspiration of thousands of extremist fighters, the creation of a security vacuum in Afghanistan, the rise of the Taliban, *another* U.S. regime change operation to oust the Taliban after the 9/11 terrorist attacks, and nineteen years and counting of a war that has cost more than $1 trillion and thousands of lives. But all that would be for Carter's successors to handle; he had a Soviet invasion to worry about.

The story of regime change in Afghanistan—the first one, at least—actually begins more than six months before that invasion, with Carter's decision in the summer of 1979 to provide military support to the anticommunist rebels there. In a series of high-level meetings earlier that spring, senior administration officials began looking at options to "reverse the current Soviet trend and presence in Afghanistan." They wanted "to demonstrate to the Pakistanis, Saudis, and others our resolve to stop the extension of Soviet influence in the Third

World," as Undersecretary of State David Newsom summed it up on March 30.[3] Participants in that meeting also examined whether U.S. policy should include assisting the insurgency—"sucking the Soviets into a Vietnamese quagmire," as the Pentagon official Walter Slocombe put it—but they worried that doing so might lead to Soviet escalation. Cold War hawks such as National Security Adviser Zbigniew Brzezinski favored tougher measures to increase the costs on Moscow for backing the communist government, while others in the administration, including Secretary of State Cyrus Vance, wanted to avoid steps that could imperil other goals, including pending arms control agreements that were already fragile.

After months of internal debate, on July 3, 1979, Carter issued a presidential "finding" that authorized—under the code name Operation Cyclone—direct covert aid for the insurgents, including propaganda, psychological operations, and radio equipment, as well as some $500,000 in cash and nonmilitary supplies.[4] To avoid escalation, no weapons were provided, a restriction that would only last, however, until the Soviet invasion. Carter would respond to that invasion by authorizing the provision of covert lethal aid, including small arms, to the Afghan rebels, along with a U.S. grain embargo, a boycott of the 1980 Moscow Olympics, and the suspension of efforts to ratify the new Strategic Arms Limitation Treaty (all announced publicly). The first arms, mostly .303 Enfield and Kalashnikov AK-47 rifles, were dispatched with alacrity, and by July 1980, according to then CIA official Robert Gates, "the covert program had been dramatically expanded to include all manner of weapons and military support for the Mujahedin."[5] By then Carter had already requested from Congress a more than 5 percent increase in the U.S. defense budget and announced what would become known as the Carter Doctrine, a pledge in his January 1980 State of the Union address that the United

States would use whatever means necessary, including military force, to prevent a foreign power (the Soviet Union) from threatening U.S. vital interests in the Persian Gulf.

The goal of these measures was to raise the costs of the intervention on Moscow and deter further aggression, not the ouster of the Kabul regime or even the withdrawal of Soviet troops from Afghanistan, both of which were deemed unrealistic. Even Brzezinski, who saw the invasion as an opportunity "to finally sow shit in [the Soviets'] backyard," warned against being "too sanguine about Afghanistan becoming a Soviet Vietnam." He pointed out in a December 26 memo to Carter that "the guerrillas are badly organized and poorly led. They have no sanctuary, no organized army, and no central government—all of which North Vietnam had. They have limited foreign support, in contrast to the enormous amount of arms that flowed to the Vietnamese from both the Soviet Union and China. The Soviets are likely to act decisively, unlike the U.S. which pursued in Vietnam a policy of 'inoculating' the enemy."[6] A week later, he wrote that "our ultimate goal is the withdrawal of Soviet troops from Afghanistan. Even if this is not attainable, we should make Soviet involvement as costly as possible."[7] Brzezinski even contended—arguably quite presciently, given how things turned out—that a "massive insurgency" would not be in America's best interest. It would be better, he wrote, to support the more modest goal of a "low-level . . . insurgency" that would make it possible "to keep the Islamic states mobilized against the Soviets in Afghanistan."[8]

Most of the U.S. intelligence community agreed that attempting to defeat the Soviet army in Afghanistan was futile and that too much covert aid for the rebels "might provoke a Soviet retaliation against Pakistan."[9] Indeed, according to the former head of the CIA's Near East Division, Frank Anderson, until about 1985 the agency's Afghanistan team believed that the Soviet occupation of Afghanistan was an "irreversible fact"; there was "no hope" that the rebels could expel the Soviets.[10] Carter's CIA director, Stansfield Turner, also acknowledged that some intelligence professionals believed that by providing support to the rebels, the United States would be putting money into a "hopeless cause."[11]

Carter was defeated in the November 1980 presidential election, but by then the basic structure of U.S. policy on Afghanistan was already firmly in place: the United States was providing the rebels with covert assistance, including arms, through Pakistan and with significant financial assistance from Saudi Arabia. But also in place were clear limits on that assistance and a narrow focus on raising the costs of Soviet occupation, not expelling the Red Army, let alone ousting the government in Kabul or trying to bring down the Soviet Union. As one Carter administration official put it, "The question here was whether it was morally acceptable that, in order to keep the Soviets off balance, which was the reason for the operation, it was permissible to use other lives for our geopolitical interests."[12] The Carter administration's answer to that question was yes, it was acceptable, but only within those well-defined parameters.

The president who took office in January 1981 would have a different answer. Ronald Reagan had criticized Carter's response to the Soviet invasion as weak, quipping about the grain embargo that it wasn't Soviet "pigs, cows and chickens that invaded Afghanistan" but the Red Army, and therefore that it should be punished, not American farmers.[13] For the incoming foreign policy team, especially Reagan's close friend William Casey, the CIA director, confronting Soviet expansionism was an overwhelming priority that justified almost any cost or risk. Their nightmare was that Moscow would build on a successful invasion of Afghanistan to drive farther southward, potentially acquiring a warm-water port on the Indian Ocean and threatening the oil supplies from the Middle East.

Of all the cold warriors in Reagan's cabinet, Casey, a deeply religious Catholic who, like Reagan, saw the Cold War in Manichaean terms of good and evil, was perhaps the most determined and ideological. It was he who would end up leading the expansion of covert support to the Afghan rebels. In this sense, Casey was a reincarnation of John Foster and Allen Dulles, who had played central roles in the development of plans for the anticommunist interventions in Iran, Guatemala, and Cuba. And just like the Dulles brothers, Casey spent little time thinking about the longer-term consequences of such initiatives, which were subordinated to the overwhelming priority of confronting the communists.

Once in office, Reagan would escalate the U.S. covert support program, though at first only gradually. U.S. funding for the rebels—matched more or less dollar for dollar by the Saudis according to a deal the Carter administration had struck with their intelligence chief, Prince Turki al-Faisal—went from around $30 million in 1981 to $60 million in 1983 and was still only $200 million by fiscal year 1984.[14] Reagan also gradually increased the quality and quantity of arms provided, which eventually included bazookas, mortars, grenade launchers, mines, recoilless rifles, and 20-millimeter anti-aircraft guns. All the weapons provided to the guerrillas were designed and manufactured by China, Egypt, or Eastern Europeans—to maintain the covert nature of the program and the pretense that they had been captured on the battlefield from Afghan or Soviet troops.[15] The additional weapons helped the mujahideen, but decades-old anti-aircraft weapons were no match for Soviet airpower, which was ruthlessly used to attack opposition fighters, supply lines, and civilian targets.

The Reagan administration enthusiastically led the effort to expand support to the Afghan fighters, but the funding for operations came from an equally enthusiastic Congress, driven initially to a large degree by one member, the Democratic representative from Texas Charlie Wilson. A former naval officer, Wilson was a larger-than-life character—as active on the Dallas social scene as he was in the House of Representatives—who made it his personal mission to turn Afghanistan into a Soviet quagmire. As dramatized by Tom Hanks in the 2007 film *Charlie Wilson's War,* Wilson traveled frequently to the country, met with rebel leaders, socialized with top Reagan administration officials, drank heavily, unapologetically chased women, and used his perch on the House Appropriations Committee to ensure that increasing amounts of covert money and arms would flow. Starting in the fall of 1983, Wilson began to make amendments to annual defense appropriations bills, adding tens of millions of dollars to Department of Defense budgets to pay for the CIA's Afghanistan programs. Like Casey, Wilson was genuinely committed to the Afghan rebels' cause. But also like Casey, his primary goal was to punish the Soviet Union, in part as "payback" for having supported the communists who fought U.S. forces in Vietnam. "There were 58,000 dead in Vietnam and we owe the Russians one and you can quote me on that," Wilson told *The Washington Post* in January 1985.[16]

Congressional support, in fact, was hardly limited to Wilson but included staunch anticommunists from both major parties. An October 1984 congressional resolution, which passed 97–0 in the Senate, stated that "it would be indefensible to supply the freedom fighters with only enough aid to fight and die, but not enough to advance their cause of freedom."[17] A few months later, Congress set up the Task Force on Afghanistan to examine the needs of the opposition and to press the administration for more action. That effort was led by the liberal

Massachusetts Democrat Paul Tsongas and the conservative Wyoming Republican Malcolm Wallop, who claimed "the only opposition to the resolution has come essentially from the CIA and the Department of State."[18] Ironically, the strong congressional support for U.S. escalation in Afghanistan took place at the very time that congressional Democrats were simultaneously cutting support for Nicaraguan rebels because of their human rights violations. But Democratic sympathies for the Sandinistas, who had been elected, were far greater than for the communist dictatorship in Kabul, so the egregious human rights violations by the Afghan rebels were overlooked. As one senior administration official put it, "Over the last two years as the Nicaraguan operation became the bad war, the one in Afghanistan became the good war."[19]

Even by the standards of the familiar U.S. tendency to overstate common values with proxies, Reagan would stand out for his readiness to portray U.S. support for the opposition in moral terms. Carter had already started referring to the rebels as "freedom fighters," but Reagan took the hyperbole to an extreme. In 1982, the administration issued a proclamation establishing Afghanistan Day, an annual celebration of Afghans who were "defending principles of independence and freedom that form the basis of global security and stability," including "the right to practice religion according to the dictates of conscience."[20] The following day, Reagan dedicated a flight of the *Columbia* space shuttle to the mujahideen and proclaimed that "just as the Columbia . . . represents man's finest aspirations in the field of science and technology, so too does the struggle of the Afghan people represent man's highest aspirations for freedom."[21] In 1983, Reagan met with a group of mujahideen leaders in the Oval Office and underscored how "very honored" he was to be meeting with "Afghanistan's freedom fighters," whose story he wanted to be known to "everyone in the free world."[22]

And in his 1986 State of the Union address, Reagan assured the "freedom fighters" that the United States would "support with moral and material assistance your right not just to fight and die for freedom, but to fight and win freedom."[23] Reagan never went so far as to claim the Afghan rebels were the "moral equivalent of the Founding Fathers," which he said in 1985 about the Nicaraguan contras, but the implication of his rhetoric was the same.[24]

The mujahideen were many things, including courageous, determined, and resilient, but democrats and lovers of American-style freedom they were not. Their leaders included Gulbuddin Hekmatyar, the corrupt and extremely violent Pashtun leader known for methods that included narcotics profiteering, executions, and torture; Ahmad Shah Massoud, the media-savvy Panjshiri guerrilla who would be murdered by al-Qaeda on the eve of 9/11; Abdul Rasoul Sayyaf, a fundamentalist militia commander close to Saudi Arabia; Abdul Rashid Dostum, the Uzbek chieftain and former communist general who would shift loyalties multiple times over the years; Burhanuddin Rabbani, a fundamentalist Tajik viewed suspiciously by the Pashtun majority; Ismail Khan, a commander based in western Afghanistan who had close ties to Iran; and Jalaluddin Haqqani, founder of the extremist Haqqani network who would benefit from the financial support of Osama bin Laden.[25] Even though only some factions were labeled "Islamist" (as opposed to the "traditionalist" camp that was open to the return of the former king), they were all deeply religious and wanted to see Afghanistan ruled under sharia law. Even the more "moderate" of them, such as Massoud, were fighting to bring Islamic revolution to Afghanistan. They opposed not only the communist regime's links to Moscow but also its policies of secular education, schooling for girls from the age of eleven, and raising the marriage age to prevent child exploitation. From the start, to imagine that these warlords would ever work together peacefully, or that a postcommunist government under any of them would support religious or any other kind of freedom, was to live in a fantasy world. But it was what Reagan and many members of Congress deemed necessary to justify supporting them.

In March 1985, the Reagan administration clarified its policy in Afghanistan in National Security Decision Directive (NSDD) 166, which made clear that the "ultimate goal" of that policy was "the removal of Soviet troops from Afghanistan and the restoration of its independent status."[26] According to Robert Gates, the "new objective" was "to win."[27] They might not yet have called it regime change, but it would soon become clear that Reagan's definition of winning did not mean leaving in place Afghanistan's existing political leadership and institutions, which they assumed would collapse when the Soviets left. In a still classified annex, the directive reportedly tasked the CIA to achieve its objectives "by all means necessary" and spelled out detailed methods, including training in explosives and the direct targeting of Soviet officers.[28] The administration also continued to increase covert assistance, which was increased to $250 million per year, almost 80 percent of all covert assistance globally. Combined with economic aid, the total U.S. support package to the opposition now approached some $500 million annually, helping to sustain some 200,000–300,000 full- or part-time insurgents.[29]

Even more consequential was Reagan's decision in March the following year to start providing a new weapon to the rebels—the infrared, shoulder-fired Stinger missile.[30] Prior to that point, the Pakistani president, Muhammad Zia-ul-Haq—who controlled the quantity, quality, and timing of all arms deliveries to the rebels—had opposed Stinger deliveries lest they reveal the extent of the still secret American and Pakistani roles in the war.

But 1985 was a difficult year for the rebels—the bloodiest to date—as the Soviets counter-escalated against the growing U.S. aid, relying increasingly on Special Forces and taking advantage of weak rebel air defenses to attack mujahideen forces and supply lines. With the rebels facing growing shortages of food, ammunition, and medical supplies, Zia authorized the United States to begin deploying the Stingers, initially via Pakistani trainers and later directly to the rebels themselves. On their very first day in the field in September 1986, Stinger-wielding mujahideen shouted, "*Allahu akbar!*"—God is great!—as they turned three Soviet Mi-24 helicopters into fireballs. The loss of air superiority forced Soviet helicopter pilots to fly at higher altitudes, which resulted in higher civilian casualties but also better protected opposition troop formations and supply lines. It also led to mounting Soviet casualties, not just of draftees, but of elite and better politically connected pilots, who increasingly went back home in body bags. From 1986 to 1987 the United States provided nearly a thousand Stingers to the rebels, leading to the downing of 269 Soviet planes and helicopters.[31] The changing military balance—and enemy deaths—improved morale among the resistance, which for the first time started to believe it could actually win the war.[32]

And by 1987 the Soviet leadership now believed it as well. Back in 1979, in Russia's own version of wishful thinking about military intervention in Kabul, Brezhnev had assured the Soviet ambassador in Washington, Anatoly Dobrynin, that the operation to stabilize the new Afghan government would be "over in three to four weeks," a view shared by leaders of the Soviet General Staff.[33] Instead, the project had become a costly quagmire, and the casualties and costs were becoming a political problem back home. After Brezhnev's death in 1982 and a succession of ineffective, geriatric leaders, the desperate Politburo had turned in March 1985 to the fifty-four-year-old Mikhail Gorbachev to try to revive a stagnant Soviet economy and Moscow's declining geopolitical position. Faced with falling oil revenues, the challenge of a rapidly growing U.S. defense budget, Reagan's antiballistic-missile Strategic Defense Initiative, and the costs of subsidizing allies in places as diverse as Nicaragua, Angola, and Cuba, Gorbachev knew from the start that the occupation of Afghanistan was an unsustainable burden. He told the Afghan leader, Babrak Karmal, as early as October 1985 that Soviet forces would ultimately have to be withdrawn and immediately began exploring negotiations and options for achieving that goal.[34] That process would take several years, but with Soviet casualties mounting and morale plummeting, by 1987 its completion had become imperative, and on April 14, 1988, Moscow agreed to begin withdrawing from Afghanistan in May.[35] On February 15, 1989, the last Soviet soldier, Colonel General Boris Gromov, symbolically walked across the Soviet-Afghan "Bridge of Friendship" to Russia, and the Soviet occupation—after almost a decade of war—was over.

Back in Washington, the sense of delight at the Soviet withdrawal was palpable. In a *Washington Post* article titled "How the Good Guys Won in Afghanistan," the former Reagan White House official Zalmay Khalilzad—who would become Trump's envoy to Afghanistan almost thirty years later—declared his "great satisfaction" at "an unprecedented, magnificent victory."[36] At CIA headquarters in Langley, Virginia, the agency's director, William Webster, and his colleagues "had a little party" and toasted the event with champagne.[37] From Islamabad, the CIA officer in charge of running the covert Afghan operation, Milton Bearden, sent back perhaps the shortest cable in U.S. diplomatic history—"WE WON"—devoting a full page to each letter lest anybody fail to see the significance of the event.[38] It was perhaps not as detailed or sophisticated as Kennan's famous 1946 more than five-thousand-word "Long Telegram" from Moscow spelling out the Cold War doctrine of containment, but it neatly summed up the entire government's sense of satisfaction and accomplishment.

In one sense, Bearden and his colleagues were right to be proud and could even be forgiven for gloating, given what they had accomplished—with no U.S. casualties and at relatively low financial cost—against overwhelming odds. In many other ways, however, the declaration of victory would prove wildly premature. The all-encompassing focus on "bleeding" and then driving out the Soviets—important geopolitical objectives to be sure—obscured some of the inevitable consequences of doing so, including the collapse of Afghanistan's political system; the arming, empowerment, and inspiration of a global jihadist movement; and U.S. dependence on Pakistan. Proponents of U.S. support to the mujahideen would attribute Afghanistan's later troubles to U.S. failures to manage these consequences, but doing so, as always, would prove far easier said than done.

The first problem was Washington's inability to fill—in any remotely satisfactory way—the security vacuum that inevitably resulted from the Soviet withdrawal. At the time, nearly all experts assessed that it wouldn't be long before the communist regime of Mohammed Najibullah fell and the rebels could move in and set up a new government. In his *Post* article, Khalilzad confidently asserted that Najibullah "won't survive" without the Soviet military presence and that he did not "take seriously analyses that postulate a protracted conflict between the resistance forces and the Najibullah government."[39] The U.S. intelligence community shared that assessment, predicting in a special estimate in March 1988 that the "Najibullah regime will not long survive the completion of Soviet withdrawal" and that it might even fall before the withdrawal was complete.[40] The CIA assessed that Najibullah would be replaced by a regime that "will be Islamic—possibly strongly fundamentalist, but not as extreme as Iran. . . . We cannot be confident of the new government's orientation toward the West; at best it will be ambivalent, and at worst it may be actively hostile, especially toward the United States."[41] President Zia of Pakistan assessed in July 1988 it would be "a matter of weeks, or at the most a few months," before the Kabul regime fell, while Pakistani intelligence officials assured Prime Minister Benazir Bhutto the mujahideen would sweep to victory as soon as the last Soviet soldier left.[42] But these judgments would all turn out to be faulty. Indeed, the possibility that Najibullah would last more than three more *years*, or that he might be replaced not by a new government but by no government at all, did not seem to be seriously considered in Washington. Nor, for that matter, did the option of cutting off assistance to the mujahideen, even though the stated U.S. policy goal—the withdrawal of Soviet forces—had been accomplished and the United States had no realistic plan for how to stabilize Afghanistan after a jihadist victory. Already in 1987, Reagan had ruled out an aid cut-off even if the Soviets left because "you can't suddenly disarm [the rebels] and leave them prey to the other government," and the incoming George H. W. Bush administration concurred—in large part based on the assumption that the Kabul regime would soon fall anyway.[43] The Bush foreign policy team, of course, was led by "realists" such as National Security Adviser Brent Scowcroft, Secretary of State James Baker, and Chairman of the Joint Chiefs of Staff Colin Powell, who were not exactly fans of regime change and would specifically and controversially forgo that option in Baghdad after forcing Iraq out of Kuwait only two years later in the Gulf War. When it came to Afghanistan, however, preoccupied with Iraq and the momentous events surrounding the end of the Cold War, assuming the regime would fall anyway, and with no good alternative options, they embraced regime change in Kabul—not as deliberate policy so much as by default. "We don't have a plan B," conceded a senior U.S. official in 1989.[44] According to Bruce Riedel, the NSC official responsible for the region at the time, there was "not a single DC [Deputies Committee] or PC [Principals Committee] meeting about Afghanistan" from 1991 to 1993.[45]

To the extent they focused on it at all, U.S. officials sought to empower local commanders they believed to be relatively moderate, such as Massoud, Khan, and the Pashtun leader Abdul Haq.[46] As soon as the Soviets left, however, extremists such as Hekmatyar started moving to wipe out their erstwhile allies in a violent battle for control; civil wars are not good conditions in which to foster moderates, and picking winners among warlords proved beyond Washington's grasp. In March 1990, Hekmatyar even joined forces with the hard-line communist defense minister, Shahnawaz Tanai, to attempt a coup, underscoring the reality that power, and not ideology, would be what mattered in post-Soviet Afghanistan.[47] From 1989 to 1992, Hekmatyar's forces would focus their attacks as much on other Afghan factions as on the communist government, killing thousands of fighters and civilians alike in a brutal quest for power.[48]

The deck was further stacked against the "moderates" because Pakistan, which retained near-total control over the flow of arms to the opposition, was determined to see its proxies in power, regardless of American concerns. For their own reasons, throughout the war the Pakistanis had disproportionately funneled most weapons to the most Islamist and anti-Western forces, a tendency that continued and even accelerated after the Soviets left.[49] While the Red Army was still in Afghanistan, the Pakistani intelligence chief, Hamid Gul, disingenuously insisted to the Americans that his job was "to get the Russians out" and that he was "not concerned about anything else."[50] In fact, he had plenty of other concerns, including satisfying the strong desire of President Zia and the Inter-Services Intelligence agency (ISI) to turn Afghanistan into a Pashtun-dominated Pakistani satellite state. "We have earned the right to have [in Kabul] a power which is very friendly toward us," Zia asserted in a July 1988 interview. "We have taken risks as a front-line state, and we will not permit a return to the prewar situation, marked by a large Indian and Soviet influence and Afghan claims on our own territory. The new power will be really Islamic, a part of the Islamic renaissance which, you will see, will someday extend itself to the Soviet Muslims."[51] In other words, a U.S. policy focused on containing the Soviets had now been hijacked by Pakistan and turned into a plan to install an Islamist government in Kabul, contain India, and spread Islam throughout the region. And there was little Washington could do about it.

In fact, in another unintended consequence of pursuing regime change in Kabul, U.S. dependence on Pakistan for success in the Afghan theater became so complete that Reagan administration officials not only allowed Islamabad to call the shots in Afghanistan but looked the other way as Pakistan developed nuclear weapons.[52] In support of U.S. nonproliferation policies, in 1979 President Carter had canceled a sale of 110 fighter-bombers to Pakistan and persuaded France not to sell Islamabad a nuclear reprocessing plant. Once the Afghan campaign started, however, South Asia nonproliferation goals took a backseat to working with the Afghan resistance, which Secretary of State George Shultz admitted to Reagan in 1982 would be "effectively dead" without Pakistani support.[53] Notwithstanding congressional legislation—the 1985 Solarz amendment to the Foreign Assistance Act—that required the United States to cut off funding for any international partner that illegally tried to procure nuclear weapons material, the Reagan administration continued to increase assistance and arms sales to Pakistan even after it conducted a secret nuclear weapons "cold test" (a test without fissionable material) in March 1983. The arms sales included nuclear-capable F-16s, previously available only to NATO allies and Japan, as well as $3.2 billion in military assistance that could be put toward their purchase. In a July 1987 classified briefing to Congress, State Department talking points specifically referenced concern "about weakening the President's hand in discussions with the Soviets on Afghanistan, which is at a critical stage," and for that reason later that year Reagan ignored a memo from the head of the U.S. Arms Control and Disarmament Agency asserting that the "facts certainly support" an aid cutoff because Pakistan was violating U.S. nonproliferation law.[54] There is no guarantee, of course, that even a cutoff of all assistance to Pakistan would have curbed or prevented its acquisition of nuclear weapons, or its later proliferation of nuclear capabilities to North Korea and Iran. But what is certain is that this major U.S. national security interest was directly undercut by the decision to prioritize regime change in Afghanistan.

With Bush administration officials largely preoccupied elsewhere, American support to the Afghan opposition remained on autopilot, and arms continued to flow, with Pakistan steering many of them to the extremists. Along with the Pakistanis, the Saudis were playing a double game of giving lip service to American goals while buying off extremists within the kingdom, some of whom were in turn funding the extremists in Afghanistan. Hekmatyar, in particular, benefited from as much as $25 million a month flowing in via Pakistan from private Saudi and Arab funding, including from Osama bin Laden.[55]

Meanwhile, fighters from across the Muslim world—largely from Saudi Arabia, Yemen, and Algeria—continued to flock to Afghanistan, drawn by the opportunity to wage a jihad that would expel the infidels from Muslim lands. According to the journalist and terrorism expert Peter Bergen, the Saudi national airline even gave a 75 percent discount to Saudis who traveled to join the jihad.[56] No one will ever know for sure, but the CIA estimated that a cumulative total of around twenty thousand foreign fighters ultimately took part in the war, while the Pakistanis put the number around thirty-five thousand.[57] They didn't make much of an impact on the battlefield—the Afghans did all the heavy fighting—but, as we would learn later, the battlefield had an effect on them.[58]

Contrary to later myths and unfounded conspiracy theories, the CIA never supported or worked with bin Laden, al-Qaeda, or any of these fighters directly, and it did not recruit them; they came on their own to fight the Soviets. But U.S. assistance did help ensure the victory of their cause and bolstered the intoxicating myth that their violent movement was able to destroy a superpower, an outcome that would embolden them for future struggles, including against the United States. "Mr. President, I am afraid we have created a Frankenstein's monster that could come back to haunt us in the future," Prime Minister Bhutto of Pakistan presciently told President George H. W. Bush on a June 1989 visit to Washington.[59] Numerous Afghans, especially secular ones and the exiled tribal leadership, had also warned about this risk, but those warnings went unheeded given the more immediate priority of winning the war. "For God's sake, you're financing your own assassins," one told the journalist Steve Coll. But the Americans, Coll writes, "had been convinced by Pakistani intelligence . . . that only the most radical Islamists could fight with determination."[60] As early as 1981, other Afghans told "government officials . . . members of Congress . . . and anyone who would listen" that Pakistan's favorite client, Hekmatyar, was corrupt, extremist, and anti-American, but their warnings went unheeded.[61]

The CIA director Gates would later acknowledge, with more than a little understatement, that "a lot of [the mujahideen] weren't people you'd invite home for dinner" but insisted the reality was "that you had to make do with the strategic situation you found in Afghanistan."[62] Similarly, Bearden admitted that "you wouldn't want any of these guys marrying your daughter" but plaintively explained that even the "darkly troubled" Hekmatyar "had a number of commanders who were reasonably effective."[63] Like the rest of official Washington, both underestimated—or chose not to think about—the trouble these unsavory partners would later cause.

Remarkably, most U.S. officials didn't really start focusing on what might happen in the aftermath of a Soviet withdrawal until that goal was accomplished. A year after the regime fell, the U.S. ambassador to Pakistan during the war, Robert Oakley, admitted, "*There was no recognition until very recently* that these people might come back to the United States or raise hell in other Muslim countries." Charles Hill, an aide to Secretary of State George Shultz at the time, said that there was "no naivete about who these guys were, they weren't sweethearts," but that "*it never crossed anybody's mind*" that their campaign against infidels would continue against targets including the United States once the war was over. Another senior U.S. official noted that "tremendous battles" about "whether we were creating a monster" *took place only after* the Soviet pullout. "Before the Soviet pullout, it was open season, just kill as many Russians as possible." "Anyone here who suggested we should be concerned about the politics of the groups we were aiding," added Barnett Rubin, a scholar who advised the U.S. government on Afghan affairs, "*was considered terminally naive*. The objective was to kill Russians."[64]

Ironically, the Russians themselves had shown more concern about the spread of Islamic fundamentalism that could result from U.S. support for the rebels than the United States did. In September 1987, when the Soviet foreign minister, Eduard Shevardnadze, informed Secretary of State Shultz that Moscow had decided to withdraw, he expressed great concern about the risk of Islamic fundamentalism and asked for American cooperation to deal with it after the withdrawal. The KGB director, Vladimir Kryuchkov, made the same point in a meeting with then CIA deputy director Gates on December 4, 1987, reminding him that the United States already had its hands full with another difficult Islamic republic—Iran. Focused on the shorter-term goal of defeating the Soviets, however, the Americans dismissed the concern. According to Gates himself, hard-liners at the CIA and elsewhere in the U.S. government saw the Soviet warnings as nothing more than an attempt to "deflect attention from Soviet failings."[65] As the military historian Andrew Bacevich later cuttingly observed, "That instigating large-scale war in Afghanistan might entail long-term hazards for the United States exceeded the imaginative capacity of U.S. policymakers."[66]

Such hazards, in fact, were not merely long term, because veterans of the Afghan campaign—where they had honed their skills as recruiters, trainers, fighters, or bomb makers—almost immediately turned their attention to waging global jihad and attacking Americans. After several of those former fighters took part in the first World Trade Center bombing, in 1993, Thomas Lippman reported in *The Washington Post* that "many current and former government officials, independent analysts and Arab diplomats are now saying Washington 'created a monster' by encouraging a rebellion based on religious zealotry without stopping to analyze what would happen if the zealots triumphed."[67] One such former official was Robert Gates, who admitted in his memoirs a few years later that the CIA failed to recognize the importance of Arab volunteers in Afghanistan until around 1986. "We expected post-Soviet Afghanistan to be ugly," Gates wrote, "but never considered that it would become a haven for terrorists operating worldwide."[68]

Zbigniew Brzezinski, who was as responsible as anyone for launching the covert program in the first place (even if initially only to punish and contain the Soviets), would long defend the operation, maintaining that it was an "excellent idea" whose geopolitical benefits vastly exceeded its costs. In a 1998 interview, Brzezinski asked, "What is more important in world history? The Taliban or the collapse of the Soviet empire? Some stirred-up Moslems or the liberation of Central Europe and the end of the Cold War?"[69] Before 9/11, two more decades of war in Afghanistan, scores of global terrorist attacks, and Russia's reemergence as a geopolitical adversary, the answer might have seemed obvious. But the problem of what he dismissed as "stirred-up Moslems" would in the longer run turn out to be far greater than Brzezinski and others seem to have imagined at the time.

The war also took a terrible humanitarian toll on Afghanistan. Out of a population of around 15 million, 1–1.5 million Afghans were killed—a stunning 10 percent of the population—with around the same number injured, and more than 5 million fled to refugee camps in Pakistan and Iran, while some 3 million were internally displaced.[70] The economy and infrastructure were left in ruins, Kabul's population was reduced from 2 million to 500,000, and thousands of Afghans were executed by either the communist government or its opponents. In the terms of Milton Bearden's famous 1989 cable, "we" might have "won" in 1989, but the fighting in the country continued for three more years after the Red Army left until the communist regime was ousted and then for four more years after that, when Kabul fell to a group of ultrareligious extremist "students" known as the Taliban. When the Taliban completed their violent takeover in 1996, they instituted a dystopian form of governance in which education for girls was banned, men were forced to wear beards, music was illegal, art was destroyed, and thousands more were beheaded or had limbs amputated in public to reinforce the provisions of their interpretation of seventh-century Islamic law. Proponents of arming the mujahideen might argue these were problems only for Afghans while U.S. interests were secured. But viewing the problem that way overlooks the fact that the Taliban also gave refuge to bin Laden and al-Qaeda, allowing them to use the country as a safe haven in which they could train, recruit, and plan global terrorist attacks, including the August 1998 Africa embassy bombings, the October 2000 attack on the USS *Cole* in the Gulf of Aden, and of course 9/11. This was not exactly the outcome optimistic Americans had sought—or promised—when they set out to bleed the Soviets in 1979.

Could the United States have helped topple the communist regime but also found a way to prevent the mess that Afghanistan became after its demise? Would the "victory" of regime change have proven less Pyrrhic "if only" subsequent U.S. policy had been different? Many would argue it could have been, and indeed the conventional wisdom in the years since then is that the Bush and Clinton administrations are responsible for failing to stabilize Afghanistan in the 1990s. Already in the early 1990s, Peter Tomsen, special envoy to Afghanistan from 1989 to 1992, argued from inside the government that U.S. "perseverance" could have "at little cost" contributed to a "favorable moderate outcome" that would include sidelining the extremists, building good relations with Afghanistan, curbing terrorism, and providing more stability in the region.[71] After the Taliban took over in 1996, Khalilzad argued that the United States had "stopped paying attention" and failed in its "moral obligation" to help the Afghans achieve peace. He recommended deepened diplomatic engagement with Afghanistan and its neighbors "to promote an end to Taliban military offensives" and "the establishment of a broad-based national government."[72] Bruce Riedel was also critical of U.S. disengagement, later writing, "In retrospect it was easy to see that the U.S. neglect of Afghanistan was a major mistake. Because Afghanistan was left to the warlords and the ISI, not only did the Afghan people suffer tremendously but a very toxic environment was created that would give rise to the Taliban and al Qaeda."[73] Even President George W. Bush would implicitly blame his father's administration for neglecting Afghanistan after the Kabul regime was overthrown and vow not to "repeat [the] mistake" of failing to consolidate initial military success.[74] And many years later, Robert Gates, a senior official at the time, told the Afghan people that walking away from Afghanistan in the wake of the Soviet withdrawal had been a "tragic miscalculation."[75] We not only failed to invest in postwar Afghanistan, Peter Bergen notes, but "the United States willfully turned its back on the country, closing the U.S. embassy there in 1989 and providing zero aid at all. This made us blind to what the hell was going on there—the rise of the Taliban and al Qaeda."[76]

It is certainly true that the first Bush administration and the Clinton administration largely ignored Afghanistan as it descended into further hell during the 1990s. Bush, as noted, was preoccupied with other major challenges, like coping with German unification, the end of the Cold War, and the Iraqi invasion of Kuwait, while Clinton came to office on a platform of focusing "like a laser beam" on the economy and cutting U.S. budget deficits and was soon consumed by conflicts in the

Balkans—not exactly a great time to propose nation building in Afghanistan. In that sense neither administration ever really made a major effort to follow up on the "success" of ousting the Russians or the Afghan communist regime. Thus we will never know if more diplomatic engagement, financial assistance, or even a massive peacekeeping force could have spared Afghans—and the rest of the world—from their tragic fate, or at least prevented the rise of al-Qaeda.

That said, the argument that a more attentive United States could have brought stability to Afghanistan if only it invested more was the sort of hindsight that has been applied to all failed interventions, and there are reasons to doubt it. It raises the difficult questions of just what would have been necessary to install a functioning government after a decade of civil war, how to "sideline the extremists" who had been armed to the teeth, how to rebuild institutions that had barely existed in the first place, how to curb Pakistani influence given Islamabad's core national interest and proximity to the conflict, and how to persuade Americans to bear the costs of huge and indefinite investments in Afghanistan with so many competing challenges on their plate. As the next chapter will show, even devoting enormous resources to nation building in Afghanistan over a long period of time would be far from a clear recipe for success.

All the alternatives to regime change in Afghanistan after the 1979 Soviet invasion, of course, would have had their own set of costs and consequences. Failing to back the insurgents in the first place would have been a missed opportunity to accelerate the decline of the Soviet Union, at the time Washington's top geopolitical concern. And cutting off support to the mujahideen after Soviet forces had left—while consistent with the more limited initial aim of "bleeding" the Soviets—might not have prevented them from maintaining their insurgency anyway with help from others and might have allowed a repressive communist dictator to remain in place. These would have been far from ideal outcomes, but in such a situation there were no ideal options available. And while high, the costs of pursuing these alternative approaches would have paled in comparison with those of an indefinite postwar military deployment to Afghanistan—as the past two decades have made clear—or with those of continuing to fuel the violent insurgency, which is essentially what was done, with horrific consequences, in 1989. Imposing pain on Moscow in Afghanistan certainly contributed to the Soviet Union's collapse, but that process was already under way before the United States escalated in Afghanistan; the Politburo, after all, had turned to Gorbachev in desperation even before the first of the U.S. Stingers were deployed. And whereas ending U.S. support for the jihadists after the Soviet withdrawal might have seemed like snatching defeat from the jaws of victory and a betrayal of American allies, in retrospect it might have helped avoid some of the tragedies that befell Afghans and the entire world in the thirty years that would follow.

CHAPTER 3

"We Have Turned a Corner"

Afghanistan, 2001

With the ashes of the World Trade Center still smoldering, just nine days after the worst terrorist attacks in American history, President George W. Bush stood before a joint session of Congress and told the world how the United States was going to respond. He identified the 9/11 perpetrators as members of the al-Qaeda organization based in Afghanistan and declared the Taliban government that was harboring them to be complicit in murder. Bush gave an ultimatum directly to the Taliban: deliver to the United States all the leaders of al-Qaeda, release unjustly imprisoned foreign nationals, close every terrorist training camp in Afghanistan and hand over every terrorist and those supporting them, or be removed from power. These demands, he said, were "not open to negotiation or discussion. The Taliban must act and act immediately. They will hand over the terrorists, or they will share in their fate."[1]

In the days and weeks that followed, top administration officials debated whether to focus initially only on al-Qaeda or whether to also go after the Taliban up front. At Camp David on September 15 and 16, Deputy Secretary of Defense Paul Wolfowitz made a case for a broader campaign, even including Iraq, but Bush deferred that question for the time being. Instead, the

United States would go after al-Qaeda initially while trying to persuade the Taliban to expel the terrorists or change its own leadership—a sort of conditional regime change. Congressional support for the approach was overwhelming. On September 18, the Authorization for Use of Military Force "against those nations, organizations, or persons . . . who planned, authorized, committed, or aided" the September 11 attacks—or against those who "harbored such organizations or persons"—passed in the Senate 98–0 and in the House 420–1.[2] The only member of Congress who voted against the bill was the California Democrat Barbara Lee, who warned—all alone but presciently—that it could lead to an "open-ended war with neither an exit strategy nor a focused target."[3]

Administration officials approached the idea of pursuing regime change again in Afghanistan with caution. On September 23, National Security Adviser Condoleezza Rice remarked on television that the Taliban was "a very repressive and terrible regime" and that the "Afghan people would be better off without it" but left open the question of whether the United States would pursue that goal. "We will see what means are at our disposal to do that," she said.[4] Vice President Dick Cheney also made clear that in "the long term—we need the Taliban to be gone," but the focus for now was going to be destroying al-Qaeda and trying to get the Taliban to replace its leader, Mullah Omar, "with someone more amenable to what we need done with respect to al Qaeda."[5] Secretary of State Colin Powell explained that the nature of Afghanistan's regime was "not uppermost in our minds right now."[6] "We want Afghanistan to be terrorist-free," he explained. "If the Taliban can do that, fine. If not, we will work with someone else as long as they make it terrorist-free."[7]

Any possible window for the Taliban leadership to save itself closed quickly, however, and once it did, the regime's fate was sealed. This time, in contrast to the 1980s, the United States would not just provide covert assistance to the Afghan opposition through third parties but also participate directly and openly in a relentless and sustained military assault. As early as September 26, a CIA paramilitary team landed in northeast Afghanistan and began to deliver arms, equipment, and military advice to the "Northern Alliance," a Panjshir valley–based group of mostly Tajik and Uzbek fighters still resisting the Taliban.[8] Two weeks later, on October 7, a U.S. bombing campaign began with precision air strikes from sea-launched cruise missiles, carrier-launched aircraft, long-range bombers, and strike aircraft from quickly assembled bases in Uzbekistan. The narrow mission of the operation was to destroy al-Qaeda and its infrastructure, but it became rapidly clear this war was only going to end with the Taliban's demise. Indeed, by mid-October, an Afghanistan strategy memo drafted by the Pentagon made clear that one of its goals was to "terminate the rule of the Taliban and their leadership."[9] As of October 11, Bush was still telling the Taliban, "if you cough . . . up [bin Laden] and his people, we'll reconsider what we're doing to your country," but the Taliban refused.[10] On November 10, the day the Northern Alliance took control of the northwestern town of Mazar-e-Sharif, Bush told the United Nations that the Taliban's days were "drawing to a close" and when they were gone the world would say "good riddance."[11] Three days later, Kabul—the capital city run by the Taliban for the past five years—fell without a fight. Kunduz was overrun on November 26, and by December 6 Kandahar, the Taliban's birthplace and last remaining stronghold, was in Northern Alliance hands. Bin Laden and other al-Qaeda fighters would remain in the mountainous eastern border region of Tora Bora for a few more weeks, but the war was essentially over, and the Taliban regime was gone.

The methods, duration, and costs of Operation Enduring Freedom in 2001 were very different from Operation Cyclone in the 1980s. After the Soviets had invaded Kabul in 1979, it took the United States more than a decade to adopt a policy of regime change and a total of some thirteen years to achieve that goal, whereas after the 9/11 attacks the whole process took less than three months. But there would be eerie and troubling similarities as well, including the temptation to declare victory before it was achieved and to vastly underestimate the degree of effort and resources that would be required to maintain stability and build functioning institutions after the previous regime was removed. Perhaps even worse, the illusion of a quick and easy victory in Afghanistan would lead, two years later, to the misplaced confidence that regime change might also succeed in Iraq. Few at the time could have imagined that nearly twenty years later—after thousands of U.S. and Afghan fatalities and a cost of almost a trillion dollars—the war would still be going on, the Afghan government would still be fragile, and the Taliban would remain a major force.

The war's eventual costs and consequences were not immediately obvious, however, and the temptation to declare victory prematurely was, as always, irresistible. Already on December 17, Powell announced that we had "destroyed al Qaeda in Afghanistan and ended the role of Afghanistan as a haven for terrorist activity," while a month later Bush declared in his State of the Union address that U.S. troops had "rid the world of thousands of terrorists, destroyed Afghanistan's terrorist training camps, saved a people from starvation, and freed a country from brutal oppression."[12] In April 2002, Rice said that the results of the Afghanistan operation "speak for themselves: al Qaeda has been deprived of its home base; its leadership is on the run; many of its operatives have been captured or killed; the Taliban regime has been routed; Afghanistan has been transformed from a terrorist-sponsored state into a country led by people who are trying to create a better future."[13] The commander of CENTCOM, Tommy Franks, who led the ground invasion, would soon boast about how with just a few thousand troops the United States had "destroyed an army the Soviets had failed to dislodge with more than a half million men" and that U.S. forces had "liberated twenty-five million people and unified the country."[14] In fact, the Soviets never had more than around 100,000 troops in Afghanistan at any given time, and the country, even after the Taliban's fall, was a long way from being "unified."

To be fair, some officials, particularly Secretary of Defense Donald Rumsfeld and Deputy Secretary of Defense Paul Wolfowitz, readily admitted that al-Qaeda was not fully defeated, with Wolfowitz rightly observing as the Taliban were about to fall that "the hardest job begins now."[15] Ironically, however, these were the officials least in favor of devoting resources to the aftermath of regime change and most ready to advocate it elsewhere, largely based on the notion that Operation Enduring Freedom demonstrated the almost unlimited potential of American military power. Rumsfeld claimed the war was "a demonstration of the kind of defense transformation that the President envisioned," while Wolfowitz and Franks called the campaign "revolutionary."[16] As Andrew Bacevich observed, for these and other "like-minded officials in the national security establishment (and for hawks generally), Enduring Freedom had demolished any need for the United States to constrain its use of force. The risks appeared manageable, the costs modest, the prospective payoff great."[17]

Some outside commentators drew even more breathless conclusions. The *Washington Post* columnist Charles Krauthammer proclaimed in January 2002 that "Afghanistan demonstrated that America has both the power and the will to fight, and that when it does, it prevails. The demonstration effect of the Afghan war has already deeply changed the Near East."[18] And Max Boot, another neoconservative writer, was so impressed by the apparent ease of victory in Afghanistan that he used it as an argument for a new "American empire" in the region. "Afghanistan and other troubled lands today," Boot argued in *The Weekly Standard*, "cry out for the sort of enlightened foreign administration once provided by self-confident Englishmen in jodhpurs and pith helmets."[19]

Unfortunately, however, bringing peace and stability to Afghanistan—or even extricating U.S. forces from the country—would prove no easier after a quick and direct U.S. military campaign than after a long and indirect one. As impressive and unprecedented as it was, using a combination of cruise missiles, precision-guided munitions, and men on horseback to overthrow a government halfway around the world would indeed turn out to be "the easy part" compared with figuring out what to do next. In fact, Boot's analogy with the British Empire proved close to the mark, but not in the way that he meant: the British had fought three bloody wars in Afghanistan from 1839 to 1919, before the Afghans finally drove them out, only to see the Russians replace them.[20]

The first big problem—just as in 1993—was how to fill the inevitable political and security vacuum created by the destruction of a regime that had brought a degree of order to the country for the first time in more than two decades—at the price, of course, of imposing its grotesque practices and backward beliefs. The U.S.-led military operation had proceeded so quickly, and in tactical terms so successfully, that little serious thought was given to what would come next, and little advance planning could be done. In his mid-October Afghanistan strategy memo, Rumsfeld argued it was "not in U.S. power to assure a specific outcome [and] U.S. preference for a specific outcome ought not paralyze U.S. efforts to oust Al-Qaida and the Taliban." He insisted that the administration "not agonize over post-Taliban arrangements to the point that it delays success over Al-Qaida and the Taliban," and ignored warnings that a tactical partnership with the Northern Alliance could result—as Milton Bearden presciently put it—in "the coalescing of Afghanistan's majority Pashtun tribes around their Taliban leaders and the rekindling of a brutal general civil war that would continue until the United States simply gave up."[21] The overwhelming, short-term priority of defeating the terrorists and their protectors was understandable, but the result was that Washington had no idea what to do after that initial goal was achieved. When he heard Bush's speech to Congress, the Afghanistan expert Barnett Rubin said to himself he hoped the reason why Bush didn't mention postwar plans was that he could not discuss them in public. Instead, "it turned out there wasn't any postwar plan."[22]

Some administration officials, in fact, did argue from the start that a major U.S. troop presence would be necessary once the Taliban were defeated. Indeed, according to Bob Woodward, at a meeting of the NSC on October 3, "everyone in the room knew they were entering a phase of peacekeeping and nation building. The overriding lesson from the 1990s in Afghanistan was: Don't leave a vacuum. The abandonment of Afghanistan after the Soviets were ousted in 1989 had created the conditions for the rise of the Taliban and the virtual takeover of the country by bin Laden and al Qaeda."[23] With this in mind, Powell would urge Bush to consider deploying a substantial U.S. peacekeeping force, including outside Kabul. Powell later said in an interview that his model was the 1989 invasion of Panama, where U.S. forces spread quickly around the country after the dictator Manuel Noriega was overthrown. "The strategy has to be to take charge of the whole country by military force, police or other means," Powell argued.[24] Based on informal conversations with European allies, Powell's director of policy planning, Richard Haass, thought that a force of twenty to forty thousand peacekeepers could be created, half of whom could be Americans.[25] James Dobbins, a veteran diplomat who had worked on peacekeeping operations in Bosnia, Somalia, and Haiti and who would become the administration's envoy to the Afghan government, argued it would be "naïve and irresponsible" to leave Afghanistan without first establishing order.[26]

But if the "lesson" of the 1990s was that the United States should not leave a vacuum in Afghanistan, it was ultimately a lesson that would go unheeded, or at least it was a lesson that had implications the administration was not prepared to accept. Recalling Bush's strong opposition to using the U.S. military for peacekeeping and with one eye already on Iraq, Rumsfeld and other colleagues at the Pentagon argued strongly against devoting the sorts of resources to Afghanistan that a genuine attempt at nation building would require. Misreading the lessons of the Soviet experience, where the problem was not so much an oversized force as the fact that Moscow was trying to impose an alien, centralized, secular, and communist regime on unwilling Afghans, Rumsfeld, Wolfowitz, and Douglas Feith argued that U.S. military deployments should remain small and limited to Kabul.[27] That position had the merit of avoiding a long and costly troop deployment and allowing the United States to continue to transform its military away from large forces, but it was inconsistent with the administration's other stated goals of setting up a national government in Kabul, protecting Afghan civilians, permanently eliminating al-Qaeda and the Taliban, and limiting Pakistan's influence. During the presidential campaign, Condoleezza Rice had scoffed at the notion of the "82nd Airborne escorting kids to kindergarten," but it turned out that maximalist objectives could not be achieved with limited resources and commitment.[28]

Pentagon officials also underestimated the monumental difficulties of establishing functioning institutions after decades of civil war and state collapse in a country that had never been governed from the center. After the Taliban fell, Tommy Franks suggested to the White House that a total of ten thousand U.S. troops "seemed about right" for the postwar mission, an optimistic calculus for a country of more than twenty million people with no government to speak of, meddlesome neighbors, ungoverned territory across the border in western Pakistan, a devastated economy, and more personal weapons than India and Pakistan combined.[29] By way of comparison, NATO sent *twenty times* that many troops per capita to Bosnia in 1995, despite the far more challenging conditions of Afghanistan.[30] But big military deployments were dangerous, unpopular, and expensive, and other potential theaters of war awaited. Even with his popularity soaring, Bush was reluctant to ask the American people to bear the burden of long and costly deployments halfway around the world in a country whose name had almost become synonymous with quagmire.

The administration also might have missed an opportunity to minimize resistance to the new Afghan government when it categorically ruled out amnesty, or a future role in politics, for the defeated Taliban—possibilities that Karzai wanted to explore. In December 2001, senior Taliban leaders tried to negotiate a peace deal with Karzai that might have included a cease-fire and recognition of Karzai as the country's legitimate leader.[31] But Rumsfeld made clear that any plan to allow the Taliban leader, Mullah Omar, to "live in dignity," as part of a negotiated settlement, was not on the table, and the Bush administration ruled out engagement with Taliban leaders.[32] As

Steve Coll put it, "The Bush administration's policy was: The Taliban have been defeated, they remained illegitimate, and stragglers should be hunted down, imprisoned, and interrogated about Al Qaeda. . . . The Taliban could expect no future in Afghan politics unless they fought for it."[33] The problem was that fighting for a role in Afghan politics is exactly what the Taliban would do, for the indefinite future.

The extent of the security challenges created by that fight would become painfully clear as early as March 2002, when U.S. and coalition forces set out to clear a group of al-Qaeda and other terrorist remnants from the Shah-i-Kot valley and mountains around Kunduz, in Operation Anaconda.[34] From March 2 to 16, the U.S. Tenth Mountain Division and 101st Airborne's Third Brigade, backed by Black Hawk helicopters, B-52s, and AC-130 gunships, fought a fierce battle against al-Qaeda and associated militia, who resisted using mortars, artillery, sniper rifles, rocket-propelled grenades (RPGs), and man-portable air defense systems. Spread out and hiding in mountain passes they knew better than their attackers, the terrorists kept the fight going for two full weeks, downing two Chinook helicopters with RPGs, killing eight Americans, and wounding approximately eighty others. The surprising intensity and duration of the battle revealed what U.S. forces would be up against and highlighted the wishful thinking that had gone into earlier assessments of what amount of military force would be needed.[35] Franks would go on to claim that Operation Anaconda was an "unqualified and complete success," but to paraphrase Sheriff Martin Brody in *Jaws*, it also demonstrated that the U.S. military was going to need the equivalent of a bigger boat.[36]

Yet for all the reasons that led it to limit the American military presence in the first place, the Bush administration would go in the opposite direction. In May 2003—not coincidentally two months after the invasion of Iraq—Rumsfeld announced the end of "major combat operations" and a shift to stabilization and rebuilding in Afghanistan. The top Afghanistan commander, Lieutenant General Dan K. McNeill, claimed that the U.S. force presence could likely be reduced by the following summer because "the Afghans can take over most of the controls." There would still be some combat operations and some areas would be "a little bit messy" for some time to come, "but in most of the country you'll find more security than has existed here in decades."[37]

In fact, Afghanistan in subsequent years turned out to be more than "a little bit messy." By 2004, a low-level insurgency was taking place in the south and east of the country, where rebel fighters were now mimicking tactics that were proving so effective in Iraq. That July, relief organizations such as Médecins sans Frontières were forced to shut down operations given the lack of security, and in September President Hamid Karzai was nearly assassinated in a rocket attack on his helicopter in Gardez.[38] By 2006, after a "deal" between the Pakistani president, Pervez Musharraf, and tribes in the border area essentially gave them free rein, a "spring offensive" created further chaos, with Taliban attacks surging by some 200 percent since the previous December.[39] Suicide attacks, virtually unheard of in Afghanistan previously, rose from near zero in 2002–4 to 27 in 2005 and 139 in 2006, while the use of remotely detonated roadside bombs doubled during the same period from 783 to 1,677, and direct arms attacks rose from around 1,500 to over 4,500.[40] The security situation was clearly deteriorating, but by this time, as David Rohde and David Sanger later observed, "the American sense of victory had been so robust that the top CIA specialists and elite Special Forces units who had helped liberate Afghanistan had long since moved on to the next war, in Iraq."[41]

I saw the declining security situation for myself on a visit to the country in December 2005 as part of a delegation that NATO had sponsored with the hope of convincing pundits and analysts like me that the security situation was under control. Our delegation included the terrorism expert Peter Bergen, who had been one of the first Western journalists ever to interview Osama bin Laden; Reuel Marc Gerecht, a former CIA case officer and neoconservative writer; Steven Simon, a former State Department and National Security Council official who was working on terrorism in the White House on 9/11; Gerard Baker, then a columnist for the *Financial Times*; and Walter Slocombe, the former Pentagon official who had first raised the possibility of "sucking the Soviets into a Vietnamese quagmire" way back in 1979. Now, four years after what had seemed to be a successful invasion, it looked as if the quagmire might be our own.

Traveling from Kabul to Kandahar to Herat, we saw some positive signs as the country prepared for the inauguration of its first parliament in more than thirty years, one that would include sixty-eight women. NATO had increased its troop deployment to fifteen thousand and now included troops from thirty-seven different countries. We were mostly greeted by friendly waves from people milling about towns and on streets and were impressed by the Italian-led Provincial Reconstruction Team base in Herat, which to our pleasant surprise included a first-rate restaurant with gnocchi and an espresso machine.

But the security problems were also plainly apparent. Violence was still on the rise, with more suicide attacks against NATO forces in the six months prior to our visit than in the entire period since 2001. The day after we left Kabul, on a helicopter flight to Kandahar, the capital was hit by a car bomb. We then got stranded in Herat when the main transport plane of NATO's International Security and Assistance Force (ISAF), a Danish C-130, broke down. ISAF's other transport plane (there were only two, itself a bad sign) was prevented by national "caveats"—the restrictions certain NATO members put on their armed forces—from flying at night to pick us up. The country's lack of infrastructure and inability to provide security on the roads made it impossible to get back to Kabul any other way. (When we inquired as to how long it would take us to drive back to Kabul, a U.S. colonel said without apparent irony that if we set off by Christmas, we could "probably get to Kabul by March.") When we finally did make it back to the capital for our departure the next day, our Italian security detail was attacked by an al-Qaeda suicide bomber after dropping us off at the airport, injuring three soldiers and killing three passersby.[42]

The lack of security that was apparent to us was not so apparent to—or at least not readily acknowledged by—many of those charged with running the war, however. In 2007, troubled by reports of problems in the field, Secretary of State Rice asked the State Department counselor Eliot Cohen, a military historian, to conduct an independent assessment of the war. What Cohen found during several trips to the country was a familiar "pattern of briefings at military headquarters, whether at Kabul or in the regions. The commanders starting a rotation would say, 'This is going to be difficult.' Six months later, they'd say, 'We might be turning a corner.' At the end of their rotation, they would say, 'We have achieved irreversible momentum.' Then the next command group coming in would pronounce, 'This is going to be difficult . . .'" Rice and Bush, Cohen concluded, were getting "an awful lot of happy talk from people who should know better."[43] And as if to demonstrate the point, in September 2007, Dan McNeill, the general who in 2003 had said the Afghans could soon take over "most of the controls," was again optimistically claiming "great progress and significant gains in the Afghan National Army," even as the security situation continued to erode.[44]

In reality, by this time it was clear that the United States and NATO had insufficient resources to cope with the growing challenges, but it was now also clear that new resources would not be immediately forthcoming. The escalating war in Iraq, considered by the administration the "central front in the war on terror," would starve Afghanistan not just of CIA specialists and Special Forces but of combat troops, diplomats, air force spotters, scarce Predator drones, and money. From 2002 to 2008, military spending and economic assistance for Iraq was more than $600 billion compared with around $170 billion for Afghanistan.[45] Never an administration spending priority, Afghanistan was continuing to take a backseat to Iraq, and it showed.[46]

There is no guarantee, of course, that regime change would have succeeded in Afghanistan had it not been simultaneously tried in Iraq. Afghanistan had always been deeply divided along tribal and ethnic lines, and it was just emerging from more than two decades of brutal civil war, with national and even local institutions destroyed, millions of internally displaced citizens, and millions more refugees abroad. With a sanctuary for an Afghan resistance next door in ungoverned parts of Pakistan—which was determined at all costs to preserve a subordinate Afghanistan as "strategic depth" for its far greater priority of geopolitical competition with India—it may be that U.S. ambitions for the country were simply unrealistic and no amount of focus or resources could have succeeded in building a functional and legitimate new government in Kabul. What is certain, however, is that it was impossible to achieve that goal while devoting the bulk of available resources—the most advanced specialists and equipment, more than three times as many troops, and almost four times as much money—to regime change in Iraq at the same time. By the end of Bush's term, top administration officials admitted that what they were doing in Afghanistan was, as Secretary of State Rice put it, "not working."[47] "The United States is not losing in Afghanistan," concluded the administration's final strategy review, "but we are not winning either, and that is not good enough."[48]

Barack Obama took office in January 2009 determined to reverse these trends. Although strongly opposed to the Iraq War, he had favored doing more in Afghanistan, now widely seen as the "good war." He wanted to show Americans and the world the difference between a war of necessity and a war of choice, and between a truly multilateral effort and a mostly unilateral one. As an Obama foreign policy adviser during this period, I believed the same thing. In a 2007 book, *Winning the Right War,* I argued that more U.S. and allied troops and greater pressure on Pakistan could have a positive impact on security and help make Afghanistan a success. "Especially if the United States withdraws more than 100,000 troops from Iraq," I wrote, "coming up with fewer than 10,000 more for Afghanistan should not be difficult and would help send a message to the Taliban and Afghan people in general that NATO is not going to withdraw."[49] But this would itself turn out to be wishful thinking.

In his first several years in office, Obama made a genuine effort to test the proposition that more resources could help turn the tide. In February 2009, he ordered the additional deployment of 17,000 troops to Afghanistan, and in May he fired the failing commander there and replaced him with the hard-charging general Stanley McChrystal, who had made his name hunting down al-Qaeda terrorists in Iraq. After the conclusion of a military policy review led by McChrystal (and the deployment of 4,000 more troops in November), Obama announced on December 1 that the United States would send a further 30,000 troops to Afghanistan while also rallying NATO partners to send more as well. At the time responsible for Europe at the State Department, I worked closely with Secretary of State Hillary Clinton on an intense, and ultimately successful, effort to get NATO allies and other partners to devote an additional 8,000 troops and some $4 billion to try to make the Afghan surge work. There were 58,000 international forces in Afghanistan when Obama took office; by the end of his first year there were more than 100,000, and by the end of 2011 there were over 150,000.[50]

Unfortunately, however, greater inputs did not translate into better results, because a weak and corrupt government in Kabul struggled to extend its control over areas that remained stubbornly sympathetic to the resurgent and defiant Taliban. One of the first tests of McChrystal's new and better-resourced approach to counterinsurgency came in a February 2010 operation in the city of Marja, a Taliban stronghold in Helmand province. It was the largest joint operation of the war to that point, involving some fifteen thousand international troops. Marja was meant to be an "opening salvo" in a campaign to reverse the Taliban's momentum, and initially it worked, with U.S. forces taking over the city of some eighty thousand residents, with limited casualties (eight American and three British soldiers were killed in the operation). Despite more aggressive patrolling, however, it was not long before the Taliban came back, and by the end of the year U.S. forces were facing a "full-blown insurgency," with "firefights all over, every day," as one marine observed.[51] Just as Operation Anaconda had demonstrated eight years before, permanently suppressing Afghanistan's violent resistance was going to take more troops, for a longer time, than American military planners or their bosses were prepared to accept. Al-Qaeda fighters had been driven out of Helmand province in November 2001 but almost a decade later—notwithstanding a surge in U.S. forces—they were back as if they had never left.

Security would continue to deteriorate throughout 2010–11, with the CIA depicting "an eroding stalemate with the Taliban" and assessments of Taliban numbers increasing.[52] By the end of 2010, as Steve Coll later wrote, "it did not require an expeditionary battalion of anthropologists and political scientists to discover much of what was at issue. Daily reading of *The New York Times, The Washington Post,* and *The Wall Street Journal* alone would provide any Obama cabinet member a directionally reliable sense of rising Afghan anger over civilian casualties and intrusive night raids, at least in Pashtun areas of the country; popular disgust at the predatory Afghan government and police; and declining faith that American-led troops could defeat the Taliban."[53] And even by the end of 2011, with international troop deployments at their peak, the National Intelligence Council was still predicting a grim future: the next group of political leaders after Karzai would likely be "corrupt and unlikely to improve governance"; the goal of establishing capable Afghan National Security Forces at the scale America had planned "might not be viable"; and Afghan security forces would likely not be as effective against the Taliban as ISAF commanders predicted, even if they would not collapse outright.[54]

Yet the tendency of military commanders—and often their political bosses—to claim success even in the face of these assessments persisted, just as Eliot Cohen had observed during the previous administration. In December 2009, McChrystal said he thought we were at "an inflection point" with "a new clarity in our mission," and later that year he told ABC News he believed "we had turned the tide." Then, in February 2010, he said that in Helmand province Afghan forces had "clearly turned the corner."[55] On December 16, 2010, Obama personally showed up in the White House briefing room, where he admitted to ongoing challenges but also insisted—like so many before him—that we had made "significant progress" and "considerable gains toward our military objectives."[56] On March 15, 2011, General David Petraeus testified that the Taliban's momentum had been "halted" and its "gains reversed," and on June 4, 2011, Secretary of Defense Gates pointed to "significant military gains" that included "ejecting the Taliban from population centers and their traditional strongholds in the south and east."[57] Later that same month Obama said that progress meant "we have turned a corner where we can begin to bring back some of our troops."[58] A month after that, Petraeus also claimed we had "turned the corner," insisting that "we're seeing progress for the first time in many years. We have halted the momentum of the Taliban in much of the country."[59] And in September 2012, the new defense secretary, Leon Panetta, rejected claims that U.S. strategy was failing and insisted—yet again—that we had "turned the corner."[60]

Emphasizing progress and boosting military and public morale were understandable tendencies of military and government officials, but all the hopeful assessments in the world would not change the reality that the Taliban were holding firm or even gaining ground—even in the face of more determined U.S. efforts. After a decade in Afghanistan, we had turned so many corners that we seemed to be back in the same place we started—trying to bolster a weak, ineffective government against a violent resistance receiving support from outside.

In December 2019, after an intensive investigation and long legal battle, *The Washington Post* obtained a trove of documents that demonstrated that government military and political officials consistently overstated progress in Afghanistan in an attempt to maintain public support for the war.[61] The dogged investigative journalism was enormously impressive—revealing, for example, that the Pentagon was putting out glowing official reports of progress even as Rumsfeld was getting deeply pessimistic assessments from the field.[62] But the revelations did not come as a shock to anyone who had been following the issue—and the gap between spin and reality—all along.

Later, many would argue that the problem was that Obama undermined the effectiveness of his otherwise worthwhile troop surge by setting an artificial deadline for the troops to start coming home eighteen months later. It seems unlikely, however, that pledging to stay indefinitely or even sending more forces would have made a fundamental, long-term difference. As U.S. leaders learned in Vietnam in the 1960s and 1970s—and as the French had discovered in both Vietnam and Algeria before that—politicians' solemn pledges to maintain military operations in the face of determined resistance go only so far; the only way really to convince some insurgents you'll stay and fight forever is to actually do so. In April 2002, after all, Bush lamented America's withdrawal from Afghanistan in the 1990s and swore that "we're not going to make that mistake again." Bush insisted in a speech at the Virginia Military Institute, "We're tough, we're determined, and we're relentless. We'll stay until the mission is done."[63] Apparently, the Taliban didn't take him at his word, and they probably wouldn't have believed Obama either.

As for sending even more troops and leaving them in Afghanistan for longer, it would almost certainly have made at least a tactical and temporary difference, but after more than a decade during which force size correlated poorly with improved security conditions, it was becoming clear that more troops alone could not overcome the consequences of a corrupt and ineffective government, profound national divisions, residual sympathy for the Taliban, and ongoing interference from Pakistan. Counterinsurgency strategy—the approach based on the notion that security can best be achieved by protecting the public with a large and locally integrated troop presence—made sense in theory but in practice was difficult to implement. A counterinsurgency strategy resourced according to accepted military best practices—around 20 soldiers per 1,000 locals—would mean some 600,000 troops for Afghanistan, in other words around more than four times the number of forces the United States and its partners were able to muster even when Obama made it a diplomatic and budgetary priority.[64] As the British special representative to Afghanistan, Sherard Cowper-Coles, presciently argued to visiting Obama administration officials in July 2009, the international coalition's "hold-build-transfer" approach to taking territory from the Taliban was "based on wishful thinking," Afghan capacity was "an illusion," and NATO countries simply didn't have enough troops to execute it.[65] Another British official, Rory Stewart—who had also served in Iraq and lived and worked in Kabul—testified to Congress a few months later that such a strategy was "particularly implausible in Afghanistan." The "fundamental problem" of U.S. strategy in Afghanistan, he warned, was that it was "trying to do the impossible. It is highly unlikely that the US will be able either to build an effective, legitimate state or to defeat a Taliban insurgency."[66] The Taliban had the great advantage, the White House Afghanistan coordinator Douglas Lute pointed out, that "we spend $60 billion a year. They need $60 million a year."[67]

Even as it was, Obama's limited military surge would cost the United States more than an additional $50 billion per year, was increasingly controversial domestically, and was leading to a spike in U.S. casualties—around 385 killed and 3,900 wounded per year in contrast to around 115 killed and 560 wounded per year during George W. Bush's second term.[68] The reality was that all too many Afghans did not support the U.S.-backed government and they had a powerful ally next door that helped many of them undermine it. Karl Eikenberry—U.S. ambassador to Afghanistan from 2009 to 2011 and a former commander of U.S. forces there—was also prescient when he reportedly made the case to Washington in November 2009 that more troops would not end the insurgency as long as Pakistan provided sanctuary to insurgents and sought to keep its Afghan neighbor weak.[69] More U.S. troops, deployed indefinitely, would certainly have made a difference. But they would not have made the Taliban go away.

The security problems were compounded by the fact that U.S. relations were also deteriorating with Karzai, the leader in whom so much hope had been invested when he was first named to run the government in December 2001. In the uncertain, early days after the Taliban fell, U.S. officials felt lucky to find Karzai, a former deputy foreign minister in the first postcommunist government who had been living in Pakistan and had been helpful in organizing Pashtuns in his hometown of Kandahar. With his striking appearance, flowing colorful robes, and fluent English, Karzai seemed to be just the sort of decent, cooperative ally the United States and its partners would need as they tried to establish a new, "broad-based, gender sensitive, multi-ethnic and fully representative government" in Kabul.[70]

But it would not be long before Karzai, once seen as the solution, would be seen as part of the problem. As Andrew Bacevich has observed, Karzai in Afghanistan was not unlike President Diem in South Vietnam in the late 1950s and early 1960s: "His credentials as a nationalist untainted by corruption but with a Western orientation made him in Washington's eyes a seemingly ideal partner." But just as the Eisenhower administration found out with Diem, the Bush administration would learn that "Karzai had a mind of his own."[71] The same thing might have been said about Diem's eventual successor, Nguyen Van Thieu, about Iran's Mohammad Reza Shah, or any of a number of subsequent leaders helped to power by the United States. In the case of Karzai as in the other cases, an initial honeymoon would become a tension-filled marriage that would ultimately end in a bitter divorce.

By the time Obama took office, Karzai's relations with the United States had already seriously eroded, with bitter disputes about drug policy, corruption, and the civilian casualties that resulted from American military action. Karzai famously gave voice to his frustrations at a February 2008 dinner in Kabul with a group of visiting U.S. senators, complaining that the United States "hasn't done anything" to help Afghanistan, infuriating then senator (and soon to be vice president) Joe Biden.[72] It was downhill from there, and the frustrations were mutual: Eikenberry reportedly considered Karzai an inadequate strategic partner who refused to accept responsibility for defense, governance, or development.[73] Even direct cash payments reportedly from the CIA to Karzai—ostensibly to support government functions—were not enough to keep him on board, because his domestic priorities far outweighed any desire to keep the Americans happy.[74] By 2013, Karzai was publicly vilifying his American allies, ordering U.S. Special Operations forces out of a Taliban-dominated province, railing against alleged CIA plots, rejecting U.S. terms for handing over detainees, and even equating the United States with the Taliban as forces that were working to undermine his government.[75] In another familiar pattern, it was not long before the United States would end up actively working to get rid of the very leader it had helped, with such hope, to empower in the first place.[76]

In his final year in office in 2014, Karzai refused to sign a long-term security agreement with the United States and claimed in farewell remarks to Afghan officials, "We don't have peace because Americans didn't want peace."[77] His message back to Washington, conveyed via two *Washington Post* journalists, was this: "To the American people, give them my best wishes and my gratitude. To the U.S. government, give them my anger, my extreme anger."[78] Obama had devoted an enormous amount of effort and resources to Afghanistan but ended up with little to show for it.[79]

After leaving office, the American president looked back wistfully. "As I write," he reflected two years later, "the war in Afghanistan continues. The Taliban remain active, and the Afghan government is struggling to gain full control of its country. From the beginning, I knew it would take time to help the Afghan people build a functioning democracy consistent with its culture and traditions. The task turned out to be even more daunting than I anticipated. Our government was not prepared for nation building. Over time, we adapted our strategy and our capabilities. Still the poverty in Afghanistan is so deep, and the infrastructure is so lacking, that it will take many years to complete the work." The president who wrote those words was George W. Bush, in 2010, but it could just as well have been Obama in 2019.[80]

As Obama's troop surge peaked in 2011, an American businessman and reality TV star tweeted his deep disapproval: "When will we stop wasting our money on rebuilding Afghanistan? We must rebuild our country first." "It is time to get out of Afghanistan," the same man tweeted on February 27, 2012.

"We are building roads and schools for people that hate us." And the next year as well he called on the United States to "get out" and stop "wasting our blood and treasure."[81]

Donald Trump had long opposed spending American money on foreign military interventions, so when against all odds he took office in 2017, it was assumed that withdrawing troops from Afghanistan would be among his top priorities. According to Bob Woodward, during his first year in office Trump considered Afghanistan a "disaster," railed against the costs of the ongoing U.S. military presence, and repeatedly asked his national security adviser H. R. McMaster, "What the fuck are we doing there?" "We ought to just exit completely," Trump insisted.[82]

Yet it turned out that leaving Afghanistan would not be so easy, even for Trump. In his final years in office, Obama had mostly completed the promised drawdown of U.S. forces and passing of control to the Afghans, but the difficult security situation prevented the completion of that process, so there were still around eleven thousand U.S. soldiers (including some two thousand previously undeclared Special Operations forces on a counterterrorism mission) in country when Trump took office.[83] After heated internal debates, in which McMaster and Secretary of Defense James Mattis—both of whom had served in Afghanistan as senior military officials—strongly opposed withdrawing those troops, in August 2017 Trump backed off. In a rare expression of candor, he admitted that "decisions are much different when you sit behind the desk in the Oval Office," and he would therefore act against his instincts and increase the U.S. military presence in Afghanistan by nearly four thousand troops, to nearly fifteen thousand. In his statement announcing the decision, Trump also blasted Pakistan for providing "safe havens for terrorist organizations" and insisted the United States would no longer pay Pakistan "billions and billions of dollars at the same time they are housing the very terrorists we are fighting." Trump added that the United States would seek to integrate "all instruments of American power" and that "conditions on the ground, not arbitrary timetables, will guide our strategy from now on" and—echoing almost exactly Bush's words from 2002, almost fifteen years previously—insisted that "we will be here until the mission is done."[84] Secretary of State Rex Tillerson described the new approach as a "dramatic shift in terms of the military strategy" and insisted it was "sending a message to the Taliban that we are not going anywhere. We're going to be here. We're going to continue to fight for the Afghan government, support the Afghan security forces."[85]

Trump and his top advisers called the strategy "an entirely new approach from what has happened in the past" (the words of UN ambassador Nikki Haley), but what was striking was how much it sounded just like all the old ones.[86] Additional troops, more diplomacy, and more pressure on Pakistan were its core components just as they were for the two administrations that preceded him, when they faced similar challenges and dilemmas. "Soldier Excited to Take over Father's Old Afghanistan Patrol Route" was the headline in *The Onion* that underscored just how long the U.S. military had been doing mostly the same thing and hoping for better results.[87]

Also remarkably familiar was the pattern of "happy talk" that had accompanied previous "new approaches." In November 2017, the commander of U.S. forces in Afghanistan, General John Nicholson, called Trump's plan a "game changer" that put Afghan forces on a "path to win." Momentum was now "with Afghan security forces," Nicholson asserted, and the United States and its Afghan partners had again "turned the corner."[88] Echoing this optimism, a State Department spokesperson asserted that "Taliban attacks against Afghan population centers have failed to take and hold urban areas and instead resulted in heavy casualties for the attacking Taliban fighters." In the face of reports about Taliban gains, the spokesperson highlighted "an ever increasing capability of the Afghan National Defense and Security Forces," which "remain in control of all provincial capitals."[89] It was an assessment that was virtually identical to so many others that had been made by similar officials over the previous seventeen years.

And it was just as disconnected from reality. Since 2001, the United States had spent close to $1 trillion on war costs for Afghanistan, or an average of more than $50 billion per year.[90] Nearly twenty-five hundred U.S. military service members had died, along with more than one thousand coalition forces, from the U.K., Canada, France, Germany, Italy, Poland, and dozens of other countries. More than twenty thousand Americans had been wounded in action, and tens or hundreds of thousands of others were afflicted by a range of mental and physical disabilities. And yet the Taliban were still gaining ground, the Afghan government was losing domestic support, suicide attacks were up, civilian casualties were rising, poppy cultivation was growing, and the Afghan public was losing faith—with majorities now saying the country was headed in the wrong direction.[91] Americans were also losing faith; whereas almost no one had questioned the initial intervention in 2001, now a clear majority of Americans thought the United States had "mostly failed" in Afghanistan, and only 45 percent still thought intervening was the "right decision."[92] The war was still costing U.S. taxpayers some $45 billion per year, but genuine progress seemed as elusive as ever.[93]

In December 2018—only two months after CENTCOM's chief, General Joseph Votel, insisted "the Taliban's strategy for waiting us out is an untenable one"—Trump directed the Pentagon to reduce by half the number of U.S. troops in

Afghanistan and accelerated peace talks with the Taliban.[94] The lead U.S. negotiator, Zalmay Khalilzad, who had played a key role in U.S. Afghanistan policy going all the way back to the initial efforts to oust the Soviet-backed regime in the early 1980s, excluded the Afghan government from the talks and pursued a deal that would pave the way for U.S. troop withdrawals in exchange for Taliban commitments to negotiate long-term peace with the Afghan government and refrain from allowing terrorists to act against the United States from Afghan soil. Many experts assessed that such an arrangement could lead to a return of the Taliban to power, taking the country back more or less to where it was when the United States intervened in 2001.[95] But with Americans tired of "endless wars," and little prospect of defeating the Taliban, the administration pressed ahead. On February 29, 2020, the United States and the Taliban announced an agreement that, if implemented, would lead to a complete departure of U.S. troops from Afghanistan within fourteen months, just under two decades after they first arrived.[96] Afghanistan's future remained highly uncertain, but what was certain was that this was not the outcome U.S. officials—or most Americans—had in mind when the Taliban were removed from power in 2001.[97]

After the 9/11 attacks, the United States had no realistic alternative to striking back militarily at al-Qaeda, trying to capture or kill bin Laden, and ousting the Taliban regime when it refused to cooperate with Washington to achieve those goals. But the United States did have a choice to make about what to do afterward, and that was where regime change in Afghanistan went wrong. If Washington was not prepared to devote far more troops, money, time, and political capital to Afghanistan for an indefinite period—a commitment apparently beyond what most Americans were comfortable with and certainly incompatible with the decision made less than two years later to pursue regime change in Iraq—it would have been better off forgoing nation building and pursuing more limited political and counterterrorism goals. Such an approach could have included the destruction of al-Qaeda's infrastructure and deployment of limited military forces to defend Kabul, train Afghan security forces, and undertake selected counterterrorism missions. But it would have accepted the reality of conservative Pashtun or even Taliban rule in large parts of the country—not unlike the situation that continued to exist on the Pakistani side of the border, where the majority of Pashtuns live, or what would eventually emerge in much of Afghanistan anyway. The United States could also have supported the Karzai government's early desire to explore a potential peace deal with the Taliban from a position of strength—rather than waiting nearly twenty years before U.S. intervention fatigue and Trump's determination to withdraw U.S. troops would lead it to do so from a position of far greater weakness. Focusing on an alleged lack of U.S. resolve or mistakes made since 2001 overlooks the reality that powerful local factors—including the nature of Afghan society and the leverage of determined neighbors such as Pakistan—were always going to dictate Afghanistan's future more even than American military power and financial resources. Ousting the regime that harbored those who attacked the United States in 2001 was necessary; spending the next two decades trying to turn Afghanistan into something it had never been before was a costly mistake.

CHAPTER 4

"Mission Accomplished"

Iraq, 2003

On April 9, 2003, Corporal Edward Chin of the Third Battalion, Fourth Marines Regiment placed a heavy iron chain around the neck of a forty-foot-tall statue of Saddam Hussein on Baghdad's Firdus Square. The statue had been erected a year before to honor the Iraqi president's sixty-fifth birthday, but its own first birthday would also be its last. As a crowd of Iraqis cheered wildly—their earlier attempts to topple the massive structure with sledgehammers had failed—Chin and his fellow marines used an M88 armored recovery vehicle to pull it down, symbolizing the end of Saddam's twenty-four-year reign of terror. The cast-iron likeness of the dictator's head was dragged through the streets as local Iraqis hit it repeatedly with shoes, celebrating their newfound freedom.

The incident—televised live on CNN and seen to mark the fall of Baghdad—was cause for some cheering back home as well. While more than 130 American troops had been killed and some oil wells were burning in the desert, the U.S.-led Iraq War had gone faster and better than many had predicted, and the sense of relief and vindication in Washington was palpable. Vice President Dick Cheney, one of the war's most avid proponents, threw a dinner party that evening at his official

Massachusetts Avenue residence, where he was feted with victory toasts by friends including the former Reagan administration official Ken Adelman, who had famously predicted that the march to Baghdad would be a "cakewalk." The next day in *The Washington Post*, Adelman soberly insisted now was "not an occasion for gloating" but then went on to do exactly that, proclaiming that "administration critics should feel shock over their bellyaching" and expressing huge pride in his old friend Secretary of Defense Donald Rumsfeld. "Now we know," Adelman concluded, "at least now we know."[1]

It was not exactly clear what Adelman thought we knew, but presumably it was that the American military was now so powerful that overthrowing regimes in the Middle East was just not that difficult and that ousting Saddam, as he had written before the war, would prove to be the "greatest victory in America's war on terrorism."[2] This was certainly the conclusion reached by other prominent supporters of the war, many of whom could hardly contain their glee over what seemed to be an easy, inexpensive, and portentous victory. Even before Saddam's statue was toppled, David Brooks of *The Weekly Standard* had already concluded that U.S. military dominance was "now so overwhelming that the rules of conflict are being rewritten," confirming that "Vietnam comparisons" and "rampant quagmire forebodings" had been "ludicrous."[3] Now that "the war in Iraq is over," as Brooks saw it at the end of April, the average American citizen could see that the United States was an "incredibly effective colossus that can drop bombs onto pinpoints [and] destroy enemies that aren't even aware they are under attack." It had "a ruling establishment that can conduct wars with incredible competence and skill [and] a federal government that can perform its primary task—protecting the American people—magnificently."[4]

Bill Kristol, the editor of *The Weekly Standard* and another leading proponent of regime change in Iraq, seemed equally certain that "the battles of Afghanistan and Iraq have been won decisively and honorably" and that the era of "American fecklessness" in the Middle East was over.[5] At an April 22, 2003, panel discussion at the American Enterprise Institute (AEI), the former Speaker of the House Newt Gingrich, AEI's vice president Danielle Pletka, and the columnist Charles Krauthammer all agreed. Krauthammer concluded that the war "has had a deep impression in the region and around the world," pointing to signs of diplomatic progress in North Korea and Iran and expressing confidence that other tyrannies were now taking note of U.S. power. The Iraq War marked "a revolution in military doctrine, a revolution in national security doctrine, and also a revolution in the region and in the world in understanding what the power of the United States is and what it is capable of doing." The Bush administration had "redefined the world, reoriented American foreign policy and put in place a profound new approach." It would "stand in history as one of the more remarkable achievements, both intellectually, militarily and diplomatically," of "the most successful and the most impressive [national security team] since the Truman-Acheson-Marshall team and the others of the late 1940s."[6]

The administration itself was more restrained in drawing such definitive, far-reaching conclusions so soon, but only slightly. On May 1, President Bush—riding a 77 percent public approval rating—flew a U.S. Navy S-3B Viking jet out to declare victory on the aircraft carrier USS *Abraham Lincoln,* across which was draped a huge red, white, and blue banner stating, "Mission Accomplished." It was true that Bush himself was not responsible for having the banner placed there, but his message was perfectly consistent with its words. While noting the United States still had "difficult work to do," the president declared the "end of major combat operations" and announced that "we have seen the turning of the tide." "In the battle of Iraq," Bush proudly proclaimed, "the United States and its allies have prevailed."[7]

Of course, the United States had not really prevailed, and the mission—not just ousting Saddam, but fighting terrorism, deterring Iran, and establishing a peaceful and stable democracy in Iraq—was far from accomplished. On the contrary, over the coming weeks and months, widespread rioting and looting would morph into a civil and sectarian war, a struggle for political power, and a violent jihadist insurgency that the United States had not expected and for which it was ill-prepared. No weapons of mass destruction or evidence of Iraqi involvement in 9/11 would be found, and stable, inclusive democracy would not develop in Iraq, let alone spread across the region. The war would cost the lives of some fifty-five hundred Americans and hundreds of thousands of Iraqis, leave thousands more mentally and physically wounded, shatter American credibility and popularity, allow Iran to dominate the Iraqi political system, reinforce al-Qaeda's narrative, and inspire a new generation of Islamist extremists. And it would cost American taxpayers an average of more than $300 million per day for the next ten years.[8]

The decision by George W. Bush to oust Saddam Hussein in 2003 resulted, indirectly, from the decision his father made not to do so in 1991. Having successfully driven the Iraqi army out of Kuwait in January of that year, President George H. W. Bush decided not to expand that mission beyond what the international coalition had agreed. As Bush and his national security adviser, Brent Scowcroft, later wrote, by marching to Baghdad, the United States "would be committing ourselves—alone—to removing one regime and installing another and if the Iraqis themselves didn't take matters into their own hands, we would be facing . . . some dubious 'nation-building.'"[9] Their decision was supported at the time by all of Bush's top advisers, who would continue to defend it for years to come. Secretary of Defense Dick Cheney insisted that taking Baghdad would have carried a "real danger of being bogged down" and that the United States had to avoid going "willy-nilly" into Arab capitals; he doubted, in any case, that a successor government would be "notably friendlier to the United States."[10] Secretary of State James Baker argued that regime change in Iraq would have empowered Iran and presciently observed that even if Saddam's regime were toppled, "U.S. forces would still have been confronted with the specter of a military occupation of indefinite duration."[11] Chairman of the Joint Chiefs of Staff Colin Powell believed toppling Saddam could have led to Iraq being "fragmented into separate Sunni, Shia, and Kurd political entities," and General Norman Schwarzkopf, who had commanded coalition forces in the war, said that overthrowing Hussein would have left the United States like "the dinosaur in the tar pit . . . left there bearing the costs of that occupation."[12] Even the former Pentagon official Paul Wolfowitz, who would later conclude that failing to topple Saddam had been a mistake, was still suggesting as late as 1994 that expanding the coalition's mandate would have been analogous to "MacArthur's disastrous experience in Korea after the stunning victory at Inchon." He warned against the notion that "the occupation of Iraq would be as easy as the liberation of Kuwait" and wrote that "even if easy initially, it is unclear how or when it would have ended."[13]

At the time, Bush and his advisers had hoped that Saddam's humiliating defeat itself would lead the Iraqi people—or perhaps another Iraqi general—to get rid of the dictator. In February 1991, Bush called on the Iraqi military and the Iraqi people to "take matters into their own hands and force Saddam Hussein, the dictator, to step aside," but then stood by as Saddam's forces slaughtered the Iraqi Shia who rose up against him in response to Bush's appeal.[14] Dissatisfaction with U.S. policy rose throughout the 1990s as Saddam consolidated his rule, and by decade's end a small group of intellectuals—including Wolfowitz—had begun to make the case for a do-over in Iraq. With the Cold War over and the Soviet Union gone, these American strategists were coming to believe the United States could and should use its power to change the world for the better, and Saddam Hussein's Iraq was seen as a good place to start. Even the famously cautious George H. W. Bush thought victory in the Gulf War meant we had "kicked the Vietnam syndrome once and for all" and with the U.S. economy surging in the late 1990s and on the heels of military successes in places like Bosnia and Kosovo, the case for using American power as a force for good was gathering steam.[15]

No proponents of that worldview were more passionate or articulate than the leaders and members of the Project for the New American Century (PNAC). Launched in June 1997 and modeled on the Cold War–era Committee on the Present Danger, PNAC was created by two long-standing proponents of a more assertive and ideals-based American foreign policy, Robert Kagan and William Kristol. Signatories of PNAC's original statement of principles included a number of future top officials of the Bush administration, including Dick Cheney, Eliot Cohen, Zalmay Khalilzad, Peter Rodman, Donald Rumsfeld, and Paul Wolfowitz. They would make regime change in Iraq a focus of their work, and within six years some of them would find themselves implementing it.

On January 26, 1998, PNAC's founders and others wrote a letter to President Bill Clinton making the case for regime change in Iraq. Because containment was eroding, they argued, "the only acceptable strategy is one that eliminates the possibility that Iraq will be able to use or threaten to use weapons of mass destruction. In the near term, this means a willingness to undertake military action as diplomacy is clearly failing. In the long term, it means removing Saddam Hussein and his regime from power."[16] When Clinton failed to heed their urgent warning, the same group wrote another letter, this time to Speaker of the House Newt Gingrich and the Senate majority leader, Trent Lott, insisting that it was now "imperative that Congress take what steps it can to correct U.S. policy toward Iraq." "U.S. policy," they wrote, "should have as its explicit goal removing Saddam Hussein's regime from power and establishing a peaceful and democratic Iraq in its place."[17] Sympathy for their position among not just congressional Republicans but also many Democrats would result in the 1998 Iraq Liberation Act, which stated it "should be the policy of the United States to support efforts to remove the regime headed by Saddam Hussein from power" and appropriated $97 million in assistance to the Iraqi opposition.[18] Clinton, politically wounded by the scandal caused by his affair with White House intern Monica Lewinsky, signed the legislation, although he had no intention of doing what would have been necessary to implement it. Instead, he focused on reinforcing containment, including by launching a four-day bombing campaign against Iraqi military and security targets in December 1998. Mocked by critics at the time as a "pinprick" attack designed to distract from White House scandals, Desert Fox actually significantly degraded Iraq's military capabilities and likely deterred attempts to restart its WMD programs.[19]

In the fall of 2000, Kagan and Kristol published an edited book of essays called *Present Dangers,* making the case for a far more assertive U.S. foreign policy that would prioritize spreading democracy around the world, including in the Middle East. In the chapter on Iraq, the former Reagan administration Defense Department official Richard Perle denounced the Clinton administration for being "content to leave Saddam in power"—as if that were a mere policy preference—and warned, wrongly it would turn out, of the "increasing strength of Saddam's position and the accelerating decline of our own." Perle did not call for immediate or direct U.S. military intervention—an outright invasion of Iraq was still a radical position in the pre-9/11 world—but argued that "as a last resort . . . we should build up our own ground forces in the region so that we have the capacity to protect and assist the anti-Saddam forces in the northern and southern parts of Iraq."[20] Implicit in the recommendation was the alluring idea that regime change would not have to be costly for the United States, because the Iraqi opposition could overthrow Saddam with U.S. "assistance" alone.

In retrospect, the most interesting essay in the book was by Wolfowitz, who as Bush's deputy secretary of defense would end up being one of the most passionate proponents of American military action. In this essay, however, Wolfowitz cautioned against the hubris of thinking that Washington in particular could impose democracy everywhere. "We cannot ignore the uncomfortable fact that economic and social circumstances may better prepare some countries for democracy than others," he wrote. "Oddly, we seem to have forgotten what Vietnam should have taught us about the limitations of the military as an instrument of 'nation-building.' Promoting democracy requires attention to specific circumstances and to the limitations of U.S. leverage. Both because of what the United States is, and because of what is possible, we cannot engage either in promoting democracy or in nation-building as an exercise of will." Wolfowitz also rejected the facile World War II comparisons favored by some proponents of regime change. "We must proceed by interaction and indirection, not imposition. In this respect, post–World War II experiences with Germany and Japan offer misleading guides to what is possible now, even in a period of American primacy."[21] The advice was excellent but would be ignored by Wolfowitz himself, and the administration he served, just a few years later.

Whatever the momentum for regime change in Congress and intellectual circles, George W. Bush did not take office with the intention of invading Iraq. On the contrary, he had famously campaigned for the office by promising a more "humble" foreign policy and warned against the notion that "our military is the answer to every difficult foreign policy situation."[22] Like practically all Republicans, before running for president, Bush had supported the Iraq Liberation Act—at the time it was a convenient way to attack Clinton for weakness—but there was no sign he intended to do more than boost support for the Iraqi opposition once he was elected. His top foreign policy advisers agreed. In an article in *Foreign Affairs* in January 2000, Condoleezza Rice—a Scowcroft protégée who would go on to serve as Bush's first national security adviser—had written that regimes such as those in Iraq and North Korea were "living on borrowed time, so there need be no sense of panic about them." She called for the first line of defense to be "a clear and classical statement of deterrence—if they do acquire WMD, their weapons will be unusable because any attempt to use them will bring national obliteration."[23] Vice President Cheney told NBC's *Meet the Press* during the campaign that the administration wanted to "maintain our current posture" on Iraq, and Powell noted in his January 2001 confirmation hearings that U.S. policy would be to "keep [the Iraqis] in the rather broken condition they are in now."[24] After his first trip to the Middle East in February 2001, Powell underscored that there was no need for panic about Saddam Hussein, because "we have kept him contained, kept him in his box," while Rumsfeld said that "Iraq is probably not a nuclear threat at the present time."[25] In the late summer of 2001, some in the Pentagon were still pushing for an "invigorated policy of regime change" in Iraq, but even this meant primarily more support for the opposition and expanded safe zones, not a full-scale invasion.[26] And as the summer ended, as Ivo Daalder and James Lindsay have written, the idea of regime change in Iraq had "gained little traction," and there was no reason to believe it would be on the agenda anytime soon.[27]

And then 9/11 happened. The death of nearly three thousand Americans in a single terrorist attack changed everything, including the regime change debate. Bush now suddenly considered containment of Saddam much "less feasible" and drew the lesson that "if we waited for a danger to fully materialize, we would have waited too long," while Cheney, once a cautious realist, "became consumed with the possibility that Iraq or other countries could distribute biological or chemical weapons to terrorists."[28] According to the journalist Ron Suskind, Cheney would even conclude that if there were a "one percent chance" that al-Qaeda could obtain a nuclear weapon, "we would have to treat it as a certainty in terms of our response," and the administration began to operate on that principle.[29] The objective facts about Iraq—the state of its possible WMD programs, the risk of its potential support for terrorism, Saddam Hussein's susceptibility to containment and deterrence, and the costs and risks of an invasion—did not change at all with 9/11. But U.S. assessments of all those things changed dramatically.

In the days following the attacks, Bush did not heed calls

by Rumsfeld and Wolfowitz to consider going after Iraq immediately, but he came back to it quickly. On September 20 he told Prime Minister Tony Blair of the U.K. that the "first job" was al-Qaeda and the Taliban and "Iraq we keep for another day."[30] By late November—even before the Afghanistan campaign was finished—he was warning publicly that Saddam Hussein would "find out" what would happen if he refused to cooperate with UN weapons inspectors.[31] Bush soon began pressing the Pentagon for specific Iraq war plans and asking speechwriters to start drafting language for his upcoming State of the Union address to justify a war in Iraq.[32] In December, Vice President Cheney warned that while nothing was "inevitable," Saddam Hussein should "be thinking very carefully about the future and . . . looking carefully to see what happened to the Taliban in Afghanistan."[33]

In January 2002, Bush warned in his State of the Union address that Iraq represented a "growing, grave danger" and insisted that "time is not on our side," while in February top officials including Powell started making the case that "the people of the region and the people of the world and the people of Iraq will be better off with a new regime."[34] Speaking somewhat more colloquially, in March Bush dropped by a meeting Rice was having with Senators John McCain, Joe Lieberman, and Lindsey Graham and said, "Fuck Saddam, we're taking him out," after learning they were talking about Iraq.[35] The Pentagon continued to shift assets from Afghanistan to the Gulf, and that summer, when the State Department official Richard Haass visited Rice in the White House in early July to urge caution about an Iraq invasion, he was brushed aside, with Rice explaining to her old friend that the president had "made up his mind."[36] At an August 5 dinner at the White House with Bush, Secretary of State Powell raised his own private concerns, telling Bush that by invading Iraq, he would "be the proud owner of 25 million Iraqis," but learned that the president had, indeed, made up his mind.[37]

Looking back, there does not appear to have been a single day on which the decision to invade Iraq was made—there was never a decisive meeting of the National Security Council or a formal decision memo signed by the president—but it is clear that the decision in principle was made more than a year before the invasion was launched and that it was a direct product of the 9/11 attacks. Nor does there appear to have been a single *reason* why the United States went to war. Instead, like most decisions—in politics as in life in general—the decision to invade Iraq resulted from a combination of factors, in this case including genuine concerns about weapons of mass destruction, the belief that only freedom and democracy could undercut the sources of Middle East terrorism, and the desire to reestablish the perception of American power that took such a blow on 9/11.[38] As Wolfowitz later candidly admitted, "For reasons that have a lot to do with the U.S. government bureaucracy, we settled on the one issue that everyone could agree on which was weapons of mass destruction," but the other factors were at least as important.[39]

For those already convinced of the need to get rid of Saddam Hussein, the 9/11 attacks provided decisive closing arguments. Kagan and Kristol wrote in *The Weekly Standard* that the risks of catastrophe were now "no longer abstract" and dismissed concerns that an Iraq war would distract from Afghanistan or al-Qaeda as "nonsense." "Can it really be that this great American superpower, much more powerful than in 1941, cannot fight on two fronts at the same time against dangerous but second-rate enemies?"[40] Danielle Pletka, who already before 9/11 argued for "promoting armed resistance" as we had done "well in places like Afghanistan and Nicaragua in the 1980s," now complained that "there are always a million excuses not to do something like this," while Richard Perle argued that there could be no victory in the war on terrorism without a "Phase 2," and "at the top of the list for Phase 2 is Iraq."[41] Even some former skeptics were now persuaded. The former CIA Iraq analyst and Clinton administration official Kenneth Pollack, who in 1998 had called "rollback" in Iraq a "fantasy," now bluntly concluded that "the United States should invade Iraq [and] eliminate the present regime."[42] His 2002 book *The Threatening Storm: The Case for Invading Iraq* helped persuade many—including congressional Democrats—that regime change in Iraq was not just a project for the political right.[43]

For David Brooks, the 9/11 attacks not only bolstered the case for war but discredited all those who had failed to overthrow Saddam before and anyone who questioned the need to do so now. He mocked "the same prognosticators of doom" who "repeat their false predictions, and the bright and the beautiful nod at their sage counsel." "And the idea that we should pay attention to the people who took the last invasion of Iraq and turned that military triumph into a stunning political defeat, is simply mind-boggling. But the veterans of Bush I—who should *live in ignominy* for letting Saddam think the United States doesn't have the guts to take him out, who should *hide in disgrace* for the way they abandoned the Kurds to their slaughter—instead ride high. It is an amazing example of the establishment's ability to protect their most incompetent members."[44] Regime change in Iraq was an obvious choice, and anyone who thought otherwise deserved neither attention nor respect.

Once the decision was made, the regime change playbook was opened and familiar patterns kicked in. The urgency and magnitude of the threat were exaggerated, the costs and risks of intervention were downplayed, best-case scenarios were used for action while worst-case scenarios were used for failing to act. Everything was seen through the prism of what benefits would accrue from the successful implantation of democracy in Iraq, while less thought was given to whether that goal could be accomplished and what might result if it was not.

First came the overstatement of the threat, which was used to win support for urgent action. There were, of course, good reasons to consider Iraq highly dangerous and to suspect it had weapons of mass destruction programs. Saddam Hussein was a reckless, brutal dictator who had invaded Iraq's neighbors, killed thousands of his own people with poison gas, and undeniably pursued nuclear, chemical, and biological weapons programs before the 1991 Gulf War. The U.S. intelligence community believed he was trying to rebuild such capabilities, and Iraq's refusal to cooperate with UN weapons inspectors was good reason for additional suspicion. But whereas before 9/11 the U.S. government admitted to uncertainty about the state of Iraq's WMD programs and believed Saddam could be contained, suddenly that uncertainty was gone, deterrence was deemed impossible, and urgent action was said to be required. Information that confirmed the worst U.S. suspicions—some of which was provided by Iraqi defectors with a strong interest in getting the United States to overthrow Saddam—was welcomed, while other information that raised questions about WMD was dismissed. As the head of the British Secret Intelligence Service, Richard Dearlove, observed in July 2002, once regime change was decided, "the intelligence and the facts were being fixed around the policy" to justify it.[45] It was neither the first nor the last time that U.S. officials would begin to see what they wanted to see once they had decided to pursue regime change in the Middle East.

In a series of speeches during 2002, Bush made the case for action to prevent any possible development of WMD and promised to "take the battle to the enemy, disrupt his plans, and confront the worst threats before they emerge."[46] "While there are many dangers in the world," he maintained, "the threat from Iraq stands alone—because it gathers the most serious dangers of our age in one place."[47] Rice argued over and over again that the United States had to act even in the face of uncertainty because "we don't want the smoking gun to be a mushroom cloud," because "history is littered with cases of inaction that led to very grave consequences for the world."[48]

Cheney turned up the temperature—and stretched the intelligence—in an August 26, 2002, speech to the Veterans of Foreign Wars. He asserted that "many of us are convinced that Saddam will acquire nuclear weapons fairly soon" and warned that if Saddam Hussein got such weapons, he "could then be expected to seek domination of the entire Middle East, take control of a great portion of the world's energy supplies, directly threaten America's friends throughout the region, and subject the United States or any other nation to nuclear blackmail. *Simply stated, there is no doubt that Saddam Hussein now has weapons of mass destruction.* There is no doubt he is amassing them to use against our friends, against our allies, and against us."[49] A month later, Rumsfeld compared a journalist's question about the possibility that the United States would not find WMD in Iraq to "looking down the road for every conceivable pothole you can find and then driving into it." Rumsfeld impatiently explained that he did not "get up in the morning and ask myself that [question]" because "we know they have weapons of mass destruction! We know they have active programs! There isn't any debate about it!"[50] Cheney added on September 8, again on *Meet the Press* (but again erroneously), that we knew "with absolute certainty" that Saddam was using his procurement system to acquire the equipment he needs in order to enrich uranium to build a nuclear weapon."[51]

Cheney and others also overstated potential links between Saddam Hussein and al-Qaeda. On *Meet the Press* on December 9, 2001, the vice president said, "It's been pretty well confirmed that [the 9/11 plotter Mohamed Atta] did go to Prague and he did meet with a senior official of the Iraqi intelligence service . . . last April."[52] That meeting and other alleged links between Iraq and al-Qaeda were in fact not confirmed at all, and turned out not to have existed, yet administration officials such as Rumsfeld would continue to call them "accurate and not debatable."[53] Such assertions helped persuade some 70 percent of Americans to conclude, wrongly, that Saddam Hussein was involved in the 9/11 attacks.[54]

The case that Iraq was pursuing weapons of mass destruction was broadly backed by the U.S. intelligence community, which in October 2002 put out a National Intelligence Estimate that asserted that Iraq was "reconstituting its nuclear program" and "has established a large-scale, redundant and concealed BW [biological weapons] agent production capability."[55] A rushed product that did not get the scrutiny it should have, the NIE misled policy makers by presenting certain "judgments"—such as the case that Baghdad possessed chemical and biological weapons—as established facts. But administration officials eager to make the case for war ignored the uncertain level of confidence behind other judgments as well as the various caveats that accompanied them—such as the dissent of the State Department's Bureau of Intelligence and Research.[56] Skeptical of the intelligence community's caution—as usual, intelligence officials were less enthusiastic about regime change than their policy counterparts—Cheney and Rumsfeld in effect both established their own, separate intelligence shops in the Office of the Vice President and the

Office of the Secretary of Defense, respectively. Both were led by strong proponents of regime change in Iraq—the former by the vice president's national security adviser, I. Lewis "Scooter" Libby, and the latter by Undersecretary of Defense Douglas Feith—and were staffed with strong, like-minded officials determined to find links between Iraq and al-Qaeda and proof of Iraqi WMD.[57] Cheney and his top advisers even made repeated trips to CIA headquarters in Langley, a highly unusual practice that some CIA officials believed was designed to pressure the analysts to tell them what they wanted to hear.[58] Other CIA officials, including the then director, George Tenet, reject that charge, but even Tenet later observed that Libby and Wolfowitz "never seemed satisfied with our answers regarding allegations of Iraqi complicity with al-Qa'ida."[59] Another senior intelligence official, Michael Morell, also gave the visiting policy makers the benefit of the doubt but still found the degree of intelligence analysis they were doing "unprecedented"; Morell would later write that Libby's efforts to get the CIA to accept his own conclusions about Iraqi ties to al-Qaeda were "the most blatant attempt to politicize intelligence that I saw in thirty-three years in the business."[60]

When Cheney was pressed to explain why he reached conclusions about Iraq that others—like European allies or the International Atomic Energy Agency—did not share, he would often assert that "they haven't seen the intel we have," a frightening and un-rebuttable point that helped mislead the public into support for the war.[61] In his 2003 State of the Union address, Bush would assert, misleadingly, that the British government had "learned that Saddam Hussein recently sought significant quantities of uranium from Africa," that Saddam "tried to purchase high-strength aluminum tubes suitable for nuclear weapons production," and that Iraq had "mobile biological weapons labs."[62] All these assertions helped build the case for war in Iraq, but all of them were also misleading, unsubstantiated, or simply wrong.[63]

The culmination of the administration's efforts to make a compelling case for war, of course, was Secretary of State Powell's presentation to the UN Security Council on February 5, 2003. With the aid of secret recordings, graphics, and props such as a mock-up of a vial of anthrax, Powell spoke solemnly to the world for more than an hour about the U.S. government's certainty that Saddam Hussein had chemical and biological weapons, an active nuclear weapons program, and operational links with al-Qaeda terrorists.[64] Powell's known reservations about the war and his credibility derived from a lifetime of service made him the perfect vehicle to testify to the world that the United States had all the proof it needed, that everything he said was "evidence, not conjecture," and that it was "facts and conclusions based on solid intelligence."[65] But despite Powell's great efforts to weed out all the unsubstantiated accusations some of the war's strongest proponents sought to include in his remarks, he would still end up making assertions that were simply not true. In his zeal to make the case for regime change, even the administration's most credible spokesman overstated it, leaving what he called an indelible "blot" on his record and an even bigger one on that of the United States.[66]

If the misjudgments about weapons of mass destruction were understandable, overlooking the risk of instability, resistance, and civil strife was not. Yet whether out of naïveté, wishful thinking, or deliberate manipulation as a marketing tool, proponents of regime change in Iraq vastly undersold those risks and overpromised the benefits regime change would bring.

In their 2003 book, *The War over Iraq,* Lawrence Kaplan and William Kristol asserted that "installing a decent and democratic government in Baghdad should be a manageable task for the United States" and even claimed Iraq was "ripe for democracy" based on the progress the Kurds had made in their U.S.-protected enclave in the north.[67] The authors wrote that "predictions of ethnic turmoil in Iraq are even more questionable than they were in the case of Afghanistan. Unlike the Taliban, Saddam has little support among any ethnic group, Sunnis included, and the Iraqi opposition is itself a multiethnic force." They approvingly cited the Iraqi exile Rend Rahim Francke—a prominent Washington, D.C.–based proponent of regime change—who asserted that civil war was somehow "contrary to Iraqi history" and that even the Kurds were enthusiastic supporters of a united Iraq (an assertion that could have been rebutted simply by asking them).[68]

Top U.S. officials both bought and sold these rosy perspectives, often sounding like the Kevin Costner character Ray in the movie *Field of Dreams,* relying on faith that "if you build it, he will come." In a speech at AEI in February 2003, Bush insisted that "there was a time when many said that the cultures of Japan and Germany were incapable of sustaining democratic values. Well, they were wrong. Some say the same of Iraq today. They are mistaken."[69] Condoleezza Rice frequently made the same point, arguing that only "dogmatic cynics and cultural determinists" doubted that "democracy will succeed in this region."[70] These were proclamations based more on faith than logic or history. On a trip to Manila in October 2003, Bush even evoked the U.S. "liberation" of the Philippines in 1898 as an example of how military intervention could lead to democracy, overlooking the fourteen years of occupation, an insurgency that cost four thousand American lives, and decades of corrupt dictatorship that followed.[71]

The most famously erroneous prediction was that of Vice President Cheney, who asserted on March 16, 2003, on *Meet the Press* that U.S. troops would be "greeted as liberators." The host, Tim Russert, pressed him: "If your analysis is not correct and we're not treated as liberators, but as conquerors, and the Iraqis begin to resist, particularly in Baghdad, do you think the American people are prepared for a long, costly, and bloody battle with significant American casualties?" "Well, I don't think it's likely to unfold that way, Tim," responded Cheney reassuringly. "Because I really do believe that we will be greeted as liberators. *I've talked with a lot of Iraqis in the last several months myself,* had them to the White House. The president and I have met with them, various groups and individuals, people who have devoted their lives from the outside to trying to change things inside Iraq. And like Kanan Makiya, who's a professor at Brandeis but an Iraqi, he's written great books about the subject, knows the country intimately, and is part of the democratic opposition and resistance. *The read we get on the people of Iraq* is there is no question but [that] they want to get rid of Saddam Hussein and they will welcome as liberators the United States when we come to do that."[72]

Wolfowitz also based his highly optimistic analysis on selected meetings with groups and individuals with an interest in seeing the United States invade Iraq. Meeting a group of Iraqi American exiles in Dearborn, Michigan, he reveled when the crowd chanted, "Yes! Yes! Yes!" to his question about whether Iraq was capable of democracy, and later that day told a Detroit newspaper that "ethnic differences in Iraq are exaggerated."[73] In congressional testimony a few days later, he drew on what he heard in Dearborn to tell members of the House Armed Services Committee that the Iraqis were "23 million of the most educated people in the Arab world who are going to welcome us as liberators. . . . The notion that we're going to earn more enemies by going in and getting rid of what every Arab knows is one of the worst tyrants . . . is just nonsense." Wolfowitz dismissed comparisons with the Balkans and noted that Iraq had no record of "ethnic militias fighting one another," so large postwar peacekeeping forces would not be required.[74] He was also confident free Iraqis would reject Islamic extremism or theocratic rule, again basing his arguments in part on his personal contacts. "Look, fifty percent of the Arab world are women," he told an audience in August 2003. "Most of those women do not want to live in a theocratic state. The other fifty percent are men. *I know a lot of them.* I don't think they want to live in a theocratic state."[75]

Whereas many Iraq and regional experts, including within the U.S. government, warned that regime change in Iraq would lead not to inclusive democracy but to control by theocratic Iran, proponents of the war also dismissed that concern. Richard Perle argued that "the evidence suggests that the Shi'ites of Iraq are far more independent than the State Department supposes" and that "concern with Iran's possible influence in Iraq is not sufficient to justify accepting a unified Iraq ruled by Saddam Hussein. On the contrary, if an Iraq without Saddam Hussein would best serve our interests, efforts to remove him should not be affected by fear of Iran's influence."[76]

One of the most influential voices in convincing all these officials and analysts that U.S. troops would be welcomed in Iraq was Ahmed Chalabi, the head of the Iraqi National Congress (INC), the group of exiles some U.S. officials hoped to put in power in Iraq. The INC's American supporters placed great faith in Chalabi's confidence that the "Iraqi people will welcome U.S. troops in Iraq . . . as liberators," even though he hadn't lived in Iraq for decades and had a dubious record that included being convicted of fraud in Jordan in 1992.[77] For proponents of regime change such as the *Washington Post* columnist Jim Hoagland, however, Chalabi was a "dedicated advocate of democracy" who had "sacrifice[d] most of his fortune so he can risk his life to fight Saddam," while for Richard Perle he was "far and away the most effective individual that we could have hoped would emerge in Iraq."[78] Far from the first or last exiled aspiring leader who convinced Americans of his democratic bona fides, Chalabi would end up leading the aggressive de-Baathification efforts that helped fuel insurgency in Iraq before the United States gave up on him, ultimately raiding his house in May 2004 on suspicions that he was spying for Iran.[79]

As they downplayed the risk of instability, the administration and its supporters also dismissed the notion that large numbers of U.S. troops or heavy financial expenditures would be necessary for regime change in Iraq. Such assessments derived not only from genuine overconfidence and the desire by Rumsfeld and others to cut the size of U.S. military forces but also—and perhaps primarily—from the need to sell the war domestically. Warning that a war could cost billions of dollars and require the indefinite deployment of large numbers of U.S. troops was no way to win domestic or international support for the war, so the administration took every opportunity to lowball projected requirements.[80] As a Defense Department official told the journalist George Packer, "The senior leadership at the Pentagon was very worried about the realities of the post-conflict phase being known . . . because if you are Feith or if you are Wolfowitz, your primary concern is to achieve the war."[81]

It was not as if no one were warning of potentially high costs or the risk that regime change could require large forces and a lengthy occupation. Former military officers such as the retired CENTCOM commander Anthony Zinni and the retired Marine Corps general Joseph P. Hoar did so in congressional testimony, with Zinni calling plans to overthrow Saddam on the cheap "pie in the sky," a "fairy tale," and a potential "Bay of Goats."[82] Much of the Republican foreign policy establishment, including the former secretaries of state Henry Kissinger, James Baker, and Lawrence Eagleburger, and the former national security adviser Brent Scowcroft, were also highly skeptical, as was the Republican senator and Vietnam veteran Chuck Hagel.[83] Scowcroft even wrote a *Wall Street Journal* article titled "Don't Attack Saddam" that was read by many as reflecting the views of his former boss George H. W. Bush.[84] Groups of regional and defense specialists assembled by organizations such as the National Defense University, the Army War College, and the Council on Foreign Relations warned that an intervention could cause massive instability, which large numbers of troops would be required to police.[85] Journalists such as James Fallows presciently compared taking over Iraq to the United States' taking on a "fifty-first state," while a group of scholars of international security affairs placed a large ad in *The New York Times* arguing that if the United States invaded Iraq, it "would have to occupy and police [the country] for many years to create a viable state."[86] Two of those scholars, John Mearsheimer and Stephen Walt, accurately predicted in the same newspaper in February 2003 that because "the United States would have to occupy Iraq for years, the actual cost of this war would likely be larger" than the administration expected and that "because most of the world thinks war is a mistake, we would likely get little help from other countries."[87] In October 2002, an unknown Illinois state senator, Barack Obama, warned that "even a successful war against Iraq will require a U.S. occupation of undetermined length, at undetermined cost, with undetermined consequences" and that an invasion "without a clear rationale and without strong international support will only fan the flames of the Middle East, and encourage the worst, rather than best, impulses of the Arab world, and strengthen the recruitment arm of al-Qaida."[88]

Within the government, top State Department officials including Powell, Richard Armitage, Haass, and Assistant Secretary of State for Near Eastern Affairs William Burns, backed by analysts at the National Intelligence Council, also tried to underscore the immensity of the task.[89] In the spring of 2001, Director of Policy Planning Haass wrote Powell a memo arguing that "the only sure way to oust the regime and put something better in its place is through prolonged military occupation and nation-building. This would be costly by any and every measure and impossible to sustain politically either at home or in the region in the absence of a clear cause, such as Iraqi use of WMD or a new invasion of Kuwait."[90] The following summer, Burns led the drafting of another memo to Powell that included a long list of things that could go wrong during or after an invasion of Iraq as well as the warning that the effort could require planning "to stay five years, maybe four if we're lucky, ten if we're not."[91] A large State Department effort called the Future of Iraq Project accurately foresaw many of the challenges the occupying Americans would ultimately face there, while a comprehensive study by the State Department's Policy Planning Staff of past U.S. nation-building efforts warned that "without order and security at the local level, all else is jeopardized." It concluded that "the larger the gap between ambition and situation, the larger must be our commitment in time and resources."[92]

The "gap between ambition and situation" in Iraq was certainly large, but proponents of the war were not convinced heavy U.S. commitments would be required. Max Boot insisted that invading Iraq "will hardly require half a million men, since Hussein's army is much diminished since the Gulf War, and the U.S. will probably have plenty of help from Iraqis, once they trust that it intends to finish the job this time."[93] Lawrence Kaplan and William Kristol assessed that "initially as many as 75,000 U.S. troops may be required to police the war's aftermath, at a cost of $16 billion a year," but were confident that "as other countries' forces arrive and as Iraq rebuilds its economy and political system, that force could probably be drawn down to several thousand soldiers after a year or two."[94] Even analysts like Kenneth Pollack who acknowledged a big invasion force would be necessary to oust Saddam Hussein optimistically suggested that the United States could then "try to turn the question of future Iraqi political arrangements over to the UN, or possibly the Arab League," or that it might "bring in those countries most directly affected by the outcome—the Saudis, Kuwaitis, Jordanians, and Turks."[95]

My own view at the time—as I wrote in a series of newspaper articles and debated with Pollack, whose office was down the corridor from mine at the Brookings Institution—was that while Saddam clearly posed a threat, he could be contained. As I put it in the *Financial Times* in November 2001, "advocates of a change of regime [in Iraq] systematically understate the costs and risks" and "for now, the costs and risks of containment appear lower than those of attempting to overthrow Mr. Saddam."[96] I also supported using the threat of military force to try to compel Saddam Hussein to accept verifiable disarmament, while warning that we should be prepared to take yes for an answer even if that meant leaving Saddam in power, because invading and occupying Iraq would be a far more costly and onerous task than many of its proponents seemed to assume.[97] I became a footnote in the Iraq debate when one of my articles, co-authored with the Brookings military affairs analyst Michael O'Hanlon, prompted Ken Adelman to make his famous "cakewalk" prediction. In December 2001, O'Hanlon and I argued in *The Washington Post* that regime change in Iraq would be a much bigger challenge than in Afghanistan and that the risks of an invasion included Iraqi use of WMD and significant U.S. military casualties. We concluded that "even after the victory was won . . . large numbers of occupation forces, many of them surely American, would probably be needed for years—unless the United States were willing to run the risk that Iraq would descend into a protracted state of civil war."[98]

Six weeks later, Adelman dismissed our "fearmongering" and predicted instead that invading Iraq would be a "cakewalk," because "it was a cakewalk last time . . . they've become much weaker . . . we've become much stronger . . . and now we're playing for keeps."[99] To be fair, Adelman was focused on the initial invasion and did not address what might happen in the longer run, though that itself was a telling omission, typical of regime change proponents. Other analysts did consider the post-invasion phase, however, and their optimism would prove even more unfounded. Patrick Clawson of the Washington Institute for Near East Policy dismissed our analogy to the Balkans as "entirely irrelevant," because "the problem in Iraq is not warring ethnic groups [but] a brutal dictator from whose rule the people want to be liberated." "*Security will be a subsidiary issue,*" Clawson concluded. "The United States will not have to provide many if any forces; if Iraqis need the assistance of foreign military forces, they are more likely to turn to moderate Arab states such as Jordan, Egypt or Morocco. And Iraqis will be able to pay for what aid they need, thanks to having the world's second-largest oil reserves."[100] The notion that neighbors will be willing and able to play a constructive role in peacekeeping after a government is overthrown is one of the more persistent myths in the history of regime change.

The administration itself tried to avoid speculation about

how many postwar troops would be required; again, any discussion of a large peacekeeping effort risked undermining public support. But in February 2003, Chief of Staff of the Army Eric Shinseki testified to the Senate Armed Services Committee that based on his experience in the Balkans, postwar Iraq could require "something on the order of several hundred thousand soldiers."[101] Wolfowitz was furious at such off-message remarks and was quick to rebut them, telling the House Budget Committee a few days later that Shinseki's estimate was "wildly off the mark." There were many reasons, Wolfowitz argued, to "suggest that peacekeeping requirements in Iraq might be much lower than our historical experience in the Balkans," including likely contributions by other countries and plans to train "free Iraqi forces" once "purged of their Baathist leadership." "It's hard to conceive that it would take more forces to provide stability in post-Saddam Iraq than it would take to conduct the war itself and to secure the surrender of Saddam's security forces and his army. Hard to imagine."[102] Actually, it was easy to imagine, but Wolfowitz and others refused to do so.

Because they vastly underestimated the long-term need for U.S. troops, administration officials and their supporters also vastly underestimated the long-term costs of the war. When the White House economic adviser Larry Lindsey suggested that the "upper bound" for those costs could be on the order of some $100–$200 billion—a figure that would prove to be only a fraction of the eventual costs—he was rebuked by senior administration officials and soon found himself out of a job.[103] Rumsfeld hesitated to provide his own official figures given all the uncertainties but privately suggested total war costs would be "something under $50 billion."[104] Wolfowitz dismissed predictions by outside economists such as Yale's William Nordhaus that a war could ultimately cost taxpayers as much as

$1.6 trillion not only because a long occupation would not be needed—as some were "foolishly suggesting"—but because the costs of war could easily be covered by Iraqi oil sales.[105] "There is a lot of money to pay for this that doesn't have to be U.S. taxpayer money," he told the House Appropriations Committee in March 2003. "We are dealing with a country that can really finance its own reconstruction and relatively soon."[106] Richard Perle also had "no doubt" that "the Iraqis can finance, largely finance, the reconstruction of their own country," while Kenneth Pollack wrote reassuringly that it was "unimaginable that the United States would have to contribute hundreds of billions of dollars and highly unlikely that we would have to contribute even tens of billions of dollars."[107] In April 2003, the administration's Office of Management and Budget budgeted a total of $2.5 billion for postwar reconstruction, a figure that would turn out to be closer to the *weekly* cost of the war for the next ten years.[108]

At a congressional hearing on Iraq in November 2002, a prominent expert witness offered up yet another reason why regime change in Iraq would allegedly be in the interest of the United States and its allies in the region. "If you take out Saddam, Saddam's regime," argued the then Israeli opposition leader, Benjamin Netanyahu, "I guarantee you that it will have enormous positive reverberations on the region. And I think that people sitting right next door in Iran, young people, and many others, will say the time of such regimes, of such despots is gone."[109] The notion that democracy in Iraq would spread throughout the Middle East, undermine the regime in Iran, and eliminate the sources of terrorism that led to 9/11 was a powerful factor in the decision to go to war, and it would also turn out to be a huge miscalculation.

Kaplan and Kristol explained the theory this way: "Iraq's experience of liberal democratic rule in turn could increase the pressure already being felt by Teheran's mullahs to open that society. Iraq's model will be eyed warily by Saudi Arabia's theocrats to the south, where male unemployment stands at 30 percent, population growth is rapid, and the populace is restive for change. Meanwhile, Iraq could even replace Saudi Arabia as the key American ally and source of oil in the region. A democratic Iraq would also encourage the region's already liberalizing regimes—such as those in Qatar, Morocco and Jordan—to continue on their paths toward democracy."[110]

This appealing vision was widely shared. Richard Perle wrote that "Saddam's replacement by a decent Iraqi regime would [likely] open the way to a far more stable and peaceful region. A democratic Iraq would be a powerful refutation of the patronizing view that Arabs are incapable of democracy."[111] Max Boot saw a "historic war aim" as being the chance "to establish the first Arab democracy" and to "turn Iraq into a beacon of hope for the oppressed peoples of the Middle East."[112] Robert Kagan and William Kristol argued that "a devastating knockout blow against Saddam Hussein, followed by an American-sponsored effort to rebuild Iraq and put it on a path toward democratic governance, would have a seismic impact on the Arab world—for the better."[113] For the former CIA director James Woolsey, "this could be a golden opportunity to begin to change the face of the Arab world . . . just as what we did in Germany changed the face of Central and Eastern Europe."[114] And Donald Rumsfeld asked rhetorically, "Wouldn't it be a wonderful thing if Iraq were similar to Afghanistan—if a bad regime was thrown out, people were liberated, food could come in, borders could be opened, repression could stop, [and] prisons could be opened? I mean, it would be *fabulous*."[115]

For Bush himself, "the establishment of a free Iraq at the

heart of the Middle East will be a watershed event in the global democratic revolution," and a new regime in Iraq would serve as a dramatic and inspiring example of freedom for other nations in the region. "Success in Iraq," he argued, could "also begin a new stage for Middle East peace, and set in motion progress toward a truly democratic Palestinian state."[116]

The problem with all these arguments was not the theory. A successful liberal democracy in Iraq likely *would* have had a positive effect on the region, and there can be little doubt that "liberal democratic rule" throughout the Middle East would have indeed been "fabulous." The problem was that the prerequisite of all those positive reverberations was establishing that liberal democracy in Iraq in the first place, and that turned out to be a pipe dream.

Maintaining security after the fall of Baghdad was always going to be a monumental task, but decisions by the administration made that task even greater. One, of course, was the failure to send adequate troops to prevent looting and protect the population. Once desperate Iraqis concluded the United States could not or would not protect them, they took matters into their own hands, turning against rival sects, tribes, religions, and their occupiers all at once. Avoiding the deployment of large numbers of U.S. troops to police Iraqi cities was understandable given the costs that would have been necessary and fears of creating a backlash against occupation, but their absence led to a degree of anarchy that made a successful transition impossible. Another catastrophe was the decision in May 2003 by the head of the Coalition Provisional Authority, Paul "Jerry" Bremer, a self-confident former diplomat with no experience in the Middle East, to disband the Iraqi army and fire all of the top echelons of the Baathist regime. Doing so immediately put hundreds of thousands of resentful—and well-armed—Sunnis out of work and led them to fear for their place in the new, Shia-dominated Iraq.[117] Bremer would later claim that these decisions were widely supported at senior levels of the U.S. government and that in any case the Iraqi army had simply disintegrated on its own.[118] Other officials dispute that claim, however, and even Bush would later acknowledge the decisions had an unforeseen "psychological impact" and should have at least been debated further within the government.[119] Bremer had a point that keeping too many high-level Baathists in place and maintaining a Sunni-dominant army would have created its own set of problems—there were no good options for filling the security vacuum in Iraq—but whether approved by others or not, Bremer's decisions almost certainly contributed to a violent insurgency that the United States could not control. Post-invasion Iraq demonstrated an eternal and inescapable regime change dilemma: large numbers of U.S. forces were expensive and ran the risk of provoking an insurgency among those who lost power, while a light footprint left a vacuum that would be filled by the best-armed and most violent groups. In a country with meddlesome neighbors and so deeply divided along ethnic, religious, and political lines, the "sweet spot" didn't exist.

Even as security deteriorated, the administration and many of its supporters remained in a state of denial—reflecting the same sort of wishful thinking that led to the war in the first place. Rumsfeld initially dismissed the looting, noting that "stuff happens and it's untidy, and freedom's untidy, and free people are free to make mistakes and commit crimes and do bad things."[120] He called the insurgents "dead-enders" and professed to be shocked at the negative press coverage of the violence, and just as in Afghanistan top military officials kept seeing "turning points" and claiming that the insurgency was "waning."[121] Neither the deaths of Saddam's sons, Uday and Qusay, on July 22 nor Saddam's own capture on December 13—after which Bremer triumphantly proclaimed "Ladies and Gentlemen, We got him!"—would have the positive effect officials had hoped for.[122] The accelerated transfer of sovereignty to the Iraqi government in June 2004 was also supposed to calm things down; instead, empowering a Shia-dominated government in Baghdad only increased the fears of Iraq's minority populations and fueled the growing insurgency.

Outside supporters of the war also kept seeing progress. Max Boot returned from an August 2003 visit "more optimistic than he went," because he saw an occupation that was making "tremendous strides among the Shiites," shops "overflowing with goods," and "little animosity . . . directed toward the Americans, who are generally seen as liberators."[123] A month later, Danielle Pletka was also confident that security in Iraq was improving—based on declining numbers of military "engagements" and more Iraqis "stepping forward with information" since the deaths of Uday and Qusay. Pletka concluded that additional troops would be not only unnecessary but even counterproductive.[124] Even more wildly optimistic was Fred Barnes of *The Weekly Standard,* who after a spring 2004 trip saw "impressive momentum that was about to turn into an economic boom." He witnessed "solid economic growth, sure to be followed by torrid growth," because Iraq's economy was "among the freest in the world." If Barnes saw any problems, it was with the "attitude of many Iraqis" who were constantly "whining" and "squabbling" and apparently unable to "forgive America for having liberated them." They were "sullen and suspicious" and in desperate need of an "attitude adjustment." Notwithstanding growing allegations about torture and abuses in U.S.-run prisons, Barnes was also somehow confident based on his short reporting trip that the "tales of mistreatment" were "largely mythical" and certainly didn't justify the Iraqi journalists' "hysterical" reactions. Despite the "impressive momentum" he witnessed in Iraq, Barnes did admit without irony to having quickly learned there that "the transformation of the country into a peaceful, free market democracy is a bigger, more demanding, and far more difficult project than *you* ever dreamed."[125]

By the end of 2005, more than two thousand Americans had been killed, extremists had taken over major cities such as Ramadi and Fallujah, and increasingly sophisticated roadside bombings and other attacks were proliferating, but Vice President Cheney still insisted the insurgency was in its "last throes" and Condoleezza Rice was claiming "unprecedented progress."[126] If the United States had followed the advice of the naysayers, she argued, it would have missed "a Lebanon that is free of foreign occupation and advancing democratic reform. A Palestinian Authority run by an elected leader who openly calls for peace with Israel. An Egypt that has amended its constitution to hold multiparty elections. A Kuwait where women are now full citizens." And while she admitted Iraq was facing "a horrific insurgency," she was proud that it had "held historic elections, drafted and ratified a new national charter, and will go to the polls again in coming days to elect a new constitutional government."[127] Echoing U.S. military leaders in Afghanistan, well into 2006 Cheney was still claiming that Iraq had "turned a corner" and was predicting people would look back at 2005 as the year "when we began to get a handle on the long-term future of Iraq."[128] But of course no corner had been turned. By the end of 2006, the war was costing more than $7 billion per month, over three thousand Americans had died, more than twenty thousand had been wounded, and the conflict had morphed into a full-fledged insurgency and civil war at the same time.[129] The reality of the administration's attempts to spin what they knew was a horrific situation was captured in a memorably cynical quotation from the Coalition Provisional Authority spokesman Dan Senor: "Off the record: Paris is burning. On the record: Security and stability are returning to Iraq."[130]

In January 2007, with his popularity collapsing and only 31 percent of Americans still supporting the war, Bush announced the bold decision to double down on his Iraq gamble, sending in an additional twenty thousand U.S. troops, including an extra five brigades for Baghdad.[131] Under new commanders, including Generals David Petraeus, Ray Odierno, and H. R. McMaster, U.S. forces would also change tactics, emphasizing the protection of the local population and working with those Iraqis—especially in Sunni-majority parts of the country—where populations were turning on al-Qaeda elements among them. The surge—as it became known—would eventually help bring down the violence, but it would also come at an exceedingly high cost.[132] The summer of 2007 was the deadliest one yet for U.S. forces—more than nine hundred U.S. troops would be killed—and the annual cost of the war increased to a staggering $130 billion. The surge showed that with enough force and the right tactics the United States could help keep violence in Iraq from spinning out of control, but only with a fabulously expensive and potentially indefinite military deployment that was increasingly unpopular both at home and in Iraq.[133] As the Bush administration came to an end, the Iraqi government was demanding that it agree to a deadline by which all U.S. forces would leave the country, and the American people had elected a new president who had strongly opposed the war and campaigned on a promise to quickly bring those troops home.

Bush's surge was tactically successful, in the sense that it helped local Iraqis resist the extremists who had essentially taken over the majority-Sunni provinces. At the same time, it failed in its strategic objective, which was to provide space for political reconciliation and for democratic government to take hold. Indeed, far from taking advantage of the relative calm to reach out and bring Sunnis into the government or to reconcile with the Kurds in the north, the government of Prime Minister Nouri al-Maliki—now backed by tens of thousands of additional American troops—became increasingly authoritarian, corrupt, and sectarian. Under heavy pressure from the United States, Maliki tolerated the formation of "Concerned Local Citizens" militias in Sunni-majority provinces to fight al-Qaeda—so long as the United States paid for them—but he never delivered on his pledges to incorporate those fighters into Iraqi security forces (ISF), which he instead used as a tool to expand his own power. Nor was Maliki willing or able to take legislative steps to help heal Iraq's divisions, such as modifying the harsh de-Baathification laws, empowering Iraq's provinces, giving Sunnis a major voice in government, or implementing energy-sharing arrangements with the Kurds.[134] These unmet promises left many of Iraq's Sunnis unemployed and resentful, thus fueling the very insurgency that the U.S. troops and their local partners were trying to stamp out.[135]

In this sense, as was the case with Mohammad Reza Shah, Carlos Castillo Armas, Nguyen Van Thieu, Augusto Pinochet, Hamid Karzai, and a number of other U.S.-backed leaders before and since, Maliki's story was a cautionary one. Handpicked out of obscurity by U.S. officials in December 2005, despite his violent past and close ties to Iran, Maliki was identified as "the right guy for Iraq," as Bush would put it late the following year, claiming to have "watched a leader emerge."[136] But it would quickly become clear that he was not the "right guy" at all, and the very fact of strong and visible U.S. support seemed to make him all the more determined to prove his nationalist bona fides and defy American wishes. Highly suspicious, and knowing how badly the Americans needed him and how poor other U.S. options were, Maliki turned the Iraqi police and security services into his own personal militia, replaced competent military professionals with unqualified political cronies, and alienated Iraq's Sunnis, Kurds, and other minorities. While he confronted Shia militias that opposed him—such as Muqtada al-Sadr's Mahdi Army—he turned a blind eye to others, including Iran-backed terrorist groups such as Asa'ib Ahl al-Haq and Kata'ib Hezbollah, that continued to attack U.S. forces.[137] At times Maliki gave U.S. forces permission to target those groups, but he cut deals with the militias when doing so served his own political interests. By 2008, top U.S. officials were already wondering if they had made a mistake, but it was too late: Maliki had been their choice among a range of poor options, and Washington would stick with him for better or worse. Years later, even strong proponents of the war would acknowledge that it ended up empowering these Iran-backed militias and that there was little Iraq's own leaders, even with U.S. support, could do about it.[138]

By the time Bush left office, violence in Iraq had been reduced considerably, and bilateral agreements were in place to provide a legal framework for U.S. troops in Iraq and to guide the future strategic relationship. The conditions seemed ripe enough to allow the outgoing president to claim to have salvaged a degree of success from the invasion of Iraq and for the new president to implement his commitment to bring U.S. troops home. But a still-broken Iraq's ability to govern itself without large numbers of U.S. troops—even after six years of massive deployments—would prove to be an illusion.

Opposed to the Iraq War from the start, Obama had pledged

during his presidential campaign to withdraw all U.S. combat forces from the country within sixteen months of taking office. After consulting his new national security team and the commanders on the ground—most of whom were concerned that too rapid a drawdown could sacrifice the hard-fought gains from the surge—Obama settled on an eighteen-month withdrawal timetable for the combat forces with a plan to leave in place a "transitional force" of up to fifty thousand troops until the end of August 2010, when they would also return home.[139] Just as Bush had redirected U.S. military resources from Afghanistan to Iraq in 2003, now Obama wanted to shift them back while also prioritizing the deep financial crisis at home.

In addition to enabling Obama to deliver on his campaign pledge to quickly end the U.S. combat role in Iraq, the timetable had the merit of keeping enough U.S. forces in place to help provide security for the parliamentary elections scheduled for early 2010, because a successful outcome—potentially the first democratic, peaceful political transition in the country's history—would facilitate the U.S. withdrawal. But while the voting on March 7 took place relatively smoothly and free from violence, the results were frustratingly ambiguous. Maliki's predominantly Shia State of Law coalition, expected to win a majority and land him a second term as prime minister, ended up with two fewer seats (eighty-nine to ninety-one) in the parliament than Ayad Allawi's Sunni-dominant Iraqiya party, leaving neither group in a position to form a government. (Allawi himself was a secular politician of Shia origin, but the vast majority of Iraqiya members were Sunni.) Far from bringing Iraqis together, the political stalemate divided the country further as the political leaders jostled for power, with Maliki maneuvering to ban dozens of Iraqiya candidates for alleged Baathist links and to deny Allawi the chance to form a government, even though his party had the largest bloc of seats in parliament. Some Obama officials argued that an Allawi-led government—by including Sunnis and demonstrating a peaceful transfer of power—would be best for Iraq. But others were convinced that only a strong, Islamist Shia leader—that is, Maliki—would have the legitimacy to govern and that any alternative would lead to Shia resistance or even violence.[140] After ten months of deadlock, during which Allawi was never able to expand his support enough to form a government, Washington finally threw its full weight behind Maliki for prime minister and managed to broker a deal that left Iraq's presidency in Kurdish hands, appointed a Sunni speaker of the parliament, and put Allawi in charge of a newly created—and mostly symbolic—security council. The concept was "power sharing," but it would quickly become clear—starting when Maliki appointed himself defense, interior, and national security minister—that sharing power was not in Maliki's plans.

Still, Obama forged ahead with his commitment to withdraw U.S. forces, hoping, as he had long argued, that it would lead Iraqis to take on more responsibilities for themselves. With enduring concerns among the commanders on the ground and outside experts that Iraqi politics were still fragile and Iraqi forces were not yet ready to provide security, Obama throughout 2011 considered options for leaving in place a residual U.S. force. Rejecting proposals to maintain as many as twenty thousand troops in Iraq as inconsistent with ending the U.S. combat role (and his desire to cut the military budget), in August 2011 Obama settled on a proposal for around five thousand troops, with a mission of training Iraqis, counterterrorism support, and deploying U.S. F-16s to help protect Iraqi airspace. The American public's war weariness and Obama's desire to reduce commitments in Iraq were not the only obstacles to the deployment, however. Maliki faced his own domestic opposition to maintaining a U.S. military presence in

Iraq, and a powerful faction in the Iraqi parliament—to say nothing of the Shia militias who were still firing on American troops—wanted the Americans completely out. On top of all that, the American insistence that the Iraqi parliament ratify legal protections for remaining U.S. forces—as it had done in 2008—was more than the Iraqi political traffic would bear. With neither the Americans nor the Iraqis overly enthusiastic about reaching an agreement on a residual force—and neither side willing to run the political risk of compromise on the legal immunities issue (only the Kurdish members of the Iraqi parliament were willing to approve the American conditions)—the talks broke down, and in October 2011 Obama decided that all U.S. troops would leave Iraq on schedule.[141]

Obama's announcement—and the logic that complete U.S. withdrawal would lead Iraqis to come together and handle their own affairs—showed that wishful thinking was not a monopoly of Iraq War proponents. "After nearly nine years," Obama declared, the remaining U.S. troops in Iraq would come home, and "America's war in Iraq will be over."[142] Iraq, he added after a December meeting with Maliki in Washington, was now "sovereign, self-reliant and democratic." "A war is ending. A new day is upon us."[143] With top Obama advisers insisting Iraq was "secure, stable, and self-reliant," and now "less violent, more democratic, and more prosperous than at any time in recent history," the Iraq War debate had in a way come full circle.[144] Obama and other long-standing opponents of the war were now claiming Iraq as a democratic success story, while proponents of that invasion, who had promised a quick transition to Iraqis, were now insisting Iraq could only survive with continued deployments of large numbers of U.S. troops.

It would not take long to see just how fragile Iraq in fact remained. Indeed, literally within days of U.S. forces leaving in 2011, Maliki showed his authoritarian and sectarian hand, announcing arrest warrants against Sunni rivals including the Iraqi vice president, Tariq al-Hashimi (sentenced to death for treason), and finance minister, Rafi al-Issawi. Once feared to be too weak and in need of U.S. protection and empowerment, Maliki was now becoming too strong and using the very security forces the Americans had trained to pursue his own sectarian agenda.[145] Maliki's tactics, as the reporter Ned Parker has written, ominously echoed "the pattern laid down by his predecessors, from Iraq's post-Ottoman monarchs to its prime minister, Abdul Karim Kassem, to Saddam himself: put yourself first, and guard power with a ruthless security apparatus."[146]

As his critics had warned, and especially in the absence of U.S. forces, Maliki's repressive sectarianism fueled Sunni resentment, which exploded in the spring of 2014 with a sudden Islamic State of Iraq and Syria (ISIS) assault on Iraqi territory and institutions. With very little warning, ISIS forces bolstered by fighters from Syria and elsewhere marched across Iraq, capturing vast swaths of territory, including Iraq's second-largest city, Mosul, in June. By the end of the year, ISIS controlled nearly sixty thousand square kilometers (or 13 percent) of Iraqi territory and an estimated 6.3 million people (19 percent of the population). It held Iraq's biggest oil refinery (Baiji) and largest dam (Mosul) and had Baghdad itself in its sights.[147] In the Situation Room that summer, President Obama was briefed that while Baghdad was unlikely to fall, if ISIS blew up the Mosul Dam—or even failed to maintain its complex grouting system properly—Iraq's capital (including the U.S. embassy) could be flooded with fifteen feet of water, potentially killing hundreds of thousands.[148] Eleven years after the initial U.S. invasion, Iraq not only was not a free, stable, and functioning democracy but was being attacked from within by an extremist movement that was even more violent, repressive, and hostile to the United States than Saddam.

Proponents of regime change in Iraq would later argue that Iraq was by this time on a path to success, when Obama snatched defeat from the jaws of victory by withdrawing too soon.[149] But while developments would clearly demonstrate that Iraq was not able to stand on its own, it is far from clear that a residual U.S. military presence—had a way been found to maintain one—would have prevented the ISIS resurgence in the absence of significant political change. When a Sunni insurgency flared up in 2003–6, after all, even 130,000 U.S. troops were not enough to contain it, and only two years of hard fighting by additional "surge" forces from 2007 to 2009 managed to tamp it down. Mosul alone was a city of nearly two million people, and it was telling that by 2014 at least part of its Sunni population was so frustrated with Baghdad's sectarian repression—and the lack of progress on issues such as modifications to de-Baathification and the widespread mistreatment of Sunnis—that it appeared willing to take its chances with ISIS rather than continue to live under the corrupt Iraqi Security Forces. Many of the ISF were so poorly trained and unmotivated that they simply dropped their weapons and took off their uniforms when faced with determined ISIS forces. As James Jeffrey, the U.S. ambassador to Iraq at the time, later wrote, "With troops we would have had better intelligence on al Qaeda in Iraq and later ISIS, a more attentive Washington, and no doubt a better-trained Iraqi army. But the common argument that U.S. troops could have produced different Iraqi political outcomes is hogwash. The Iraqi sectarian divides, which ISIS exploited, run deep and were not susceptible to permanent remedy by our troops at their height, let alone by 5,000 trainers under Iraqi restraints."[150]

The argument that a stable Iraqi democracy would have

emerged if only Obama hadn't pulled out U.S. forces also overlooks the fact that the firm commitment to withdraw all U.S. forces had already been agreed to by Bush, because the Iraqis had insisted on it. With so much invested in Iraq's success, Bush had been dead set against any unconditional withdrawal deadlines, but by 2008 he was left with no choice, and the Status of Forces Agreement he negotiated included the commitment that U.S. troops would be out of Iraqi cities by 2009 and would "withdraw from all Iraqi territory no later than December 31, 2011." If Bush—so committed to success in Iraq regardless of political consequences—was unable to resist Iraqi demands that the United States commit to withdrawing all its troops from Iraq, it's hard to see how Obama could have maintained a large number of U.S. troops there.

With enough political determination, and a willingness to compromise on the issue of immunities for U.S. troops (which would have had its own risks and complications and created a political firestorm), Obama probably could have persuaded the Iraqis to agree to a small residual force.[151] But the real point is that more than a decade after the United States had intervened in Iraq—with so much blood and treasure having been invested—the country was still not on a stable, self-sustaining path. On the contrary, a repressive, sectarian leader—empowered and supported by the United States because the alternatives all seemed worse—was ruling with an iron fist reminiscent of previous Iraqi dictators and alienating much of the population. Sunnis were rising up violently, and Kurds were doing oil deals with neighboring Turkey and plotting a path to the independence they had long desired.

When ISIS surged across Iraq in 2014—ironically fueled in large part by the consequences of U.S. efforts to change the regime in neighboring Syria—the United States had little choice but to intervene militarily again, ultimately conducting tens of thousands of air strikes, reintroducing more than five thousand ground troops, and putting together an international coalition of some sixty-four countries to defeat the group now known as the Islamic State (IS). That campaign, launched by the Obama administration in 2014 and continued by Trump starting in 2017, ultimately managed to destroy the so-called IS caliphate and help the Iraqi government take back control of most of its territory, but not before IS terrorists had killed, raped, or enslaved thousands of Iraqis, and thousands of civilians and combatants were killed during what was essentially the third U.S.-led war in Iraq of the past thirty years. The war also left some two million Iraqi Sunnis, Kurds, and Yazidis displaced from their homes and living in camps or overcrowded shelters, and emboldened up to 150,000 Shia militia fighters, some of whom were controlled by Iran.[152] These groups' refusal to take direction from the government in Baghdad undermined Iraqi sovereignty, while their actions to prevent displaced minorities from returning to their homes planted the seeds for a potential IS revival.[153] In September 2017, 93 percent of Kurds voted for full independence from Iraq, leading Baghdad to seize Kurdish-held territory (including the oil-rich city of Kirkuk), further fueling tensions between the two communities and undermining prospects for a unified Iraq.[154]

In May 2018, Iraq again held parliamentary elections. The two largest blocs of seats went to coalitions led by the radical Shia cleric Muqtada al-Sadr, who had led the insurgency against the U.S. occupation and continued to call for the departure of all U.S. troops, in alliance with the communists, and Hadi al-Ameri, the Iran-backed Shia militia leader whose forces had killed hundreds of Americans and conducted terrorist attacks against Sunnis for many years. Applauding the fact that the elections took place without significant violence, *The Washington Post* called the result a "positive sign" for Iraq and potentially "the most significant event of the year" in the region.[155] It was a sign of how low the bar for success had fallen in the two decades since the first significant calls for regime change in Iraq. A competitive and relatively free and fair vote was indeed a step in the right direction, and the subsequent appointments of the moderate politicians Barham Salih and Adil Abdul Mahdi as president and prime minister kept those posts out of the hands of the extremists. Even their well-intentioned efforts, however, were not enough to overcome Iraq's deep divisions, and throughout 2019 and 2020, Iraq faced massive public protests and a widespread revolt against the entire system the United States had tried to set up after the war—leading to a violent government crackdown and reopening questions about the country's ultimate political fate. The Iraqi political system seemed so dysfunctional, and U.S. policy since 2003 such a failure, that some original proponents of regime change in Iraq began to conclude that it was time to try it again.[156] After all the promises made about how regime change in Iraq would lead to democracy, undermine terrorism, prevent weapons of mass destruction, and reverberate positively around the region, Americans could be forgiven for having expected something more.

It is tempting to blame the disaster that emerged in Iraq on "implementation," and certainly the Bush administration made enormous mistakes by underestimating the eminently foreseeable security and political challenges Iraq would face in the aftermath of regime change. The wishful thinking and happy talk U.S. officials thought necessary to sell the controversial war proved catastrophic, leading the administration to underprepare for the chaos and mislead the American public about what it was getting into. At the same time, given the depth of the country's divisions and aims and the influence of some of its neighbors, it's far from clear that any amount of military force or advance preparation could have prevented most of the problems that plagued the country, the region, and U.S. forces after the U.S. invasion. As the 2006–8 military surge demonstrated, even the deployment of over 150,000 U.S. troops, at an enormous cost in terms of money and casualties, was not sufficient to prevent a surge in sectarianism, provide lasting stability, or win the support of the Iraqi or U.S. public. The real lesson of the past twenty years in Iraq is that the only way to have avoided the calamitous repercussions of regime change would have been to not invade the country in the first place.

No one should pretend, of course, that continuing to contain Saddam Hussein's Iraq in the early years of the twenty-first century would have been easy or without its own high costs. Such costs would have included maintaining targeted economic sanctions that inevitably hurt the Iraqi public, allowing Saddam to continue his corrupt, brutal, and repressive regime, maintaining indefinite no-fly and no-drive zones over parts of the country, conducting periodic military strikes to destroy potential WMD infrastructure, and maintaining military support for Iraq's neighbors to deter potential Iraqi attacks. No one knows where such a policy would have led over time, and the best that could have been hoped for might have been an eventual internal military coup, followed by a willingness to cooperate with weapons inspectors in exchange for the lifting of international sanctions (not an unimaginable Iraqi concession, however, given that the alleged WMD programs didn't actually exist). The costs of that alternative approach can never be known for sure, though it is worth remembering that prior to 9/11 they were deemed bearable, even by most of those who would later argue they were not. What we do know is that the costs of shifting the policy from containment to regime change included thousands of American deaths, hundreds of thousands of Iraqi deaths, tens of thousands of physically or mentally wounded on both sides, and more than a trillion dollars, while leading to the expansion of jihadist extremism around the world, a tarnished U.S. reputation, Iranian domination of Iraq, and still today, almost twenty years later, an enduring risk of anarchy, terrorism, and civil war. Compared with that, containment does not look so bad.

CHAPTER 5

"The Transition Must Begin Now"

Egypt, 2011

Beer and vodka were not typically consumed in large quantities in the Eisenhower Executive Office Building, but the night of February 11, 2011, was an exception. Earlier that evening, the Egyptian dictator Hosni Mubarak, who had ruled Egypt for the previous thirty years, finally resigned, and not just Egypt but the whole of North Africa seemed on the verge of freedom. Only ten days previously, some of Barack Obama's younger aides—the National Security Council staffers Ben Rhodes, Samantha Power, Denis McDonough, and Michael McFaul—had overcome the objections of their more conservative, senior colleagues—Vice President Joe Biden, Secretary of State Hillary Clinton, Secretary of Defense Robert Gates, and National Security Adviser Tom Donilon—and persuaded the president to call on Mubarak to step down. When Mubarak did so, an apparent miracle in a region where dictators rarely left peacefully, the younger advisers' feelings of hope and vindication were overwhelming. Several of them celebrated in the office of McFaul, who as an academic at Stanford was a longtime advocate of democracy promotion. All of them knew that huge challenges lay ahead and took nothing for granted, but they could not help feeling that they had played a major role in pushing Obama onto the "right side of history." It was why some of them had joined the government in the first place. "It was a great day," McFaul told me later. "We knew how rare it was for these things to actually happen."[1]

The feelings of joy and relief were all the more warranted because persuading Obama to support measures, however modest, to intervene in the domestic politics of a Middle Eastern country was no minor task. Indeed, Obama came to office as a foreign policy "realist" who had expressed admiration for the foreign policies of the first president Bush—a champion of regional stability and order—while harshly criticizing those of the second, who after 9/11 put democracy promotion front and center.[2] Whereas George W. Bush at least rhetorically made it U.S. policy to "seek and support the growth of democratic movements and institutions with the goal of ending tyranny in our world," Obama often underscored the need to deal with "the world as it is" and the priority of nation building at home.[3] In practice, of course, Bush largely backed away from that agenda after the Iraq invasion went awry and Hamas won Palestinian elections in 2006, but the lessons of both those events only reinforced Obama's tendency to believe that spreading democracy in the region was an overly ambitious goal. As Obama's first NSC senior director for the Middle East and North Africa, Daniel Shapiro, put it, the new president was "modest about U.S. influence on internal matters, realistic about what could be achieved, and cognizant of the importance of working in partnership with strategic allies to achieve other regional goals."[4] A few weeks before announcing his candidacy for the presidency in 2006, Obama called for "a strategy no longer driven by ideology and politics but one that is based on a realistic assessment of the sobering facts on the ground and our interests in the region."[5]

To be sure, Obama had his own idealistic streak, frequently

citing Martin Luther King's belief that in the long run the "arc of the moral universe . . . bends toward justice." In his landmark "New Beginnings" speech about U.S. relations with the Muslim world in Cairo in June 2009, Obama insisted that freedom of speech, rule of law, and honest government were "not just American ideas" but "human rights" and that "we will support them everywhere." But Obama also emphasized—articulating a core pillar of what might be seen as an Obama doctrine—that "no system of government can or should be imposed upon one nation by any other." He devoted most of the speech to other priorities, including combating extremism, the Israeli-Palestinian issue, Iraq, Afghanistan, Iran, women's rights, and economic development.[6] The Obama administration, Vice President Biden explained to an international audience early in the administration's first term, would "advance democracy not through the imposition of force from the outside, but by working with moderates in government and civil society to build those institutions that will protect that freedom."[7]

Trying to square this realist approach with the potential for internal unrest in the region, some of Obama's National Security Council officials tried to get ahead of the curve and in early summer 2010 launched a process to consider how to confront the growing challenge of repression and frustration. Obama's top advisers for the Middle East, democracy, and human rights—Dennis Ross, Samantha Power, and Gayle Smith—convened a series of meetings to consider how the United States might promote gradual political change while stopping short of what they saw as the Bush administration's ambitious, disruptive, and ultimately unsuccessful attempts at democracy promotion. The effort led to a presidential directive, which in August 2010 tasked the NSC to undertake a review of the lessons of political transitions. The classified document presciently noted that the Middle East and North Africa were entering a period of potential instability because of rising public discontent with the authoritarian regimes that had ruled them for decades. The study considered precedents from places like Indonesia, the Philippines, and Serbia and set up working groups to examine the best ways to promote gradual reform, but while its goals were idealistic, its proposed actions were modest. They included potentially immediate steps—such as freeing political prisoners—to demonstrate visible change, engagement with the full spectrum of opposition groups, and an emphasis on sequencing presidential elections ahead of parliamentary votes and the drafting of a new constitution.[8] The administration would seek to manage the risk of instability by promoting more openness, gradual political reform, and more effective governance.[9] As Samantha Power later summed it up, "The United States needed to act while we still had time to support political *evolution* in the Middle East. Otherwise, we would find ourselves figuring out how to respond to *revolution*."[10]

Neither Obama nor Clinton talked much about democracy promotion in their first months in office; one journalist said the word seemed to be "banished" from the administration's vocabulary.[11] The administration cut funding for democracy assistance by nearly 30 percent, and Clinton focused her efforts at the State Department on three *d*'s—defense, diplomacy, and development—but democracy did not make the cut.[12] Where Egypt was concerned, Obama declined to label Mubarak an "autocrat," instead calling him a "stalwart ally" and "force for stability and good."[13] Many would later point to Clinton's prescient warning in a January 2011 speech in Doha, Qatar, that "in too many places, in too many ways, the region's foundations are sinking into the sand" as an example of at least her own early support for democratic change.[14] But while conscious of the region's fragility, Clinton, like Obama, sought to work with the region's leaders, not to replace them.

Watching the growth of protests in Cairo, Clinton saw not so much opportunity as risk, warning Obama, "It all may work out fine in twenty-five years, but I think the period between now and then will be quite rocky for the Egyptian people, for the region, and for us."[15]

"Quite rocky" would prove an understatement. Within weeks of that warning, the president, who was hoping to manage gradual, orderly change, would find himself demanding that Egypt's longtime president leave power immediately and then working to support a far-reaching political and institutional transition that would quickly go off the rails. As the limits on the U.S. ability to influence Egypt's evolution became painfully clear, Mubarak's departure would be followed not by freedom and stability but by a transitional military regime; an autocratic, divisive, and religiously conservative president from the Muslim Brotherhood; massive public protests; a military coup that involved mass killings and widespread arrests; and the restoration of a regime that would turn out to be far more repressive than Mubarak's. U.S. support for revolution in Egypt would also produce its own share of unintended consequences, not least by inadvertently encouraging others in the region—from Libya, Yemen, and Syria—to rise up against their own dictators, equally noble causes but with even more catastrophic results. The United States, of course, did not instigate or implement regime change in Egypt; the Egyptians did that. But the Obama administration ended up embracing and promoting it, with high expectations but results that would fall far short of what those celebrating in McFaul's office—or even the president they had persuaded to support it—had in mind.

Egypt's revolution started not in Cairo but in Tunis, on December 17, 2010, when a fruit vendor named Mohammad Bouazizi triggered massive protests when he set himself on fire after being humiliated by officials from the corrupt and autocratic government of Zine el-Abidine Ben Ali. The sight of their fellow North Africans winning their freedom by chasing Ben Ali from power—the dictator fled to Saudi Arabia in January 2011—inspired Egyptians to rise up against their own entrenched military regime. Egyptians were fed up with the military regime's poor economic performance, stifling political environment, security sector abuses, and rampant corruption, all now exacerbated by Mubarak's apparent plans to turn over power to his businessman-son Gamal. Even the army, the bastion of Mubarak's authority (and beneficiary of a central role in the Egyptian economy), resented the notion that power would be handed to someone from outside their ranks. In late January, tens of thousands of Egyptians of all sects and social classes began to gather regularly at Cairo's Tahrir Square to demand changes, including that Mubarak step down.[16] The eighty-two-year-old leader was caught off guard and troubled when the police forces (which effectively disbanded after failing to control the rallies) and military proved reluctant to crack down on the protesters.

The U.S. government was also caught off guard—the working groups created by the presidential directive had not yet finished their work—and Obama remained inclined toward caution. There was little reason to believe that Mubarak would fall quickly as had Ben Ali, and plenty of reason to worry about the consequences if he did. If Mubarak did suddenly resign, the Egyptian constitution required a presidential election to be held within sixty days, which could well lead to instability or Islamist rule, because the long-banned Muslim Brotherhood was by far the best organized political opposition. The religiously conservative Brotherhood was internally autocratic, generally anti-American, and ideologically illiberal; its most recent draft party platform required that Egypt's president be a male Muslim, not something Hillary Clinton was likely to be enthusiastic about. So even after large crowds gathered at Tahrir Square on January 25 for a "Day of Rage," the administration's instinct was to help defuse the protests. Later that day, Clinton insisted publicly that "the Egyptian government is stable and is looking for ways to respond to the legitimate needs and interests of the Egyptian people."[17] In his State of the Union address that same evening, Obama talked about the "democratic aspirations of all people" in the context of Tunisia, but he did not mention Egypt.[18]

After even bigger protests on January 28 were followed by a defiant speech by Mubarak, Obama's patience began to wear out. He phoned Mubarak that night to urge him to hand over effective control of the government to his intelligence chief, Omar Suleiman, hoping that a visible change at the top—to avoid triggering elections, Mubarak could maintain a ceremonial role as president while Suleiman began a process of reform—might satisfy the protesters. But while "the dynamic was established that day that the president wanted to get rid of Mubarak," as Ben Rhodes saw it, U.S. demands remained limited, and Obama remained cautious in public.[19] In a statement later that evening, Obama noted Mubarak's commitment to "a better democracy and greater economic opportunity" and said he told Egypt's leader he had "a responsibility to give meaning to those words."[20]

Still focused on working with Mubarak, the next day Obama accepted Undersecretary of State Bill Burns's suggestion that he send former ambassador to Egypt Frank Wisner to Cairo. Obama instructed Wisner—who knew the Egyptian president well from his time there—to warn Mubarak not to use force against the protesters and to respond to their demand that neither he nor his son run in the upcoming elections. "The White

House demanded neither an immediate exit by Mubarak nor fundamental immediate change to the Egyptian regime," *The New York Times*'s David Kirkpatrick reported. "Its goal was to let Suleiman manage a succession, possibly to himself."[21] Wisner conveyed that message to Mubarak at his palace in Cairo on Monday, January 31.

With pressure mounting from all sides—the Egyptian military leadership had made clear it would not use force against the protesters—Mubarak addressed the nation in a televised speech after midnight on February 2. In a long and rambling speech, he announced he would not run for reelection in September and that Gamal would not be a candidate either—the main concessions Washington was demanding. At the same time, however, Mubarak's exact intentions were confused; he said he remained "absolutely determined to finish my work," and his tone was defiant. "This is my country," he declared. "This is where I lived, fought, and defended its land, sovereignty and interests. I will die on its soil."[22] Somehow Mubarak managed to announce that he was accepting some of the protesters' core demands while sounding as if he were rejecting them. "He buried the lede," thought NSC Middle East adviser Dennis Ross, who watched the speech from the White House Situation Room.[23]

Obama also watched the speech from the Situation Room, where his advisers had already assembled to discuss the U.S. response and where the extraordinary generational divide among them would occur. The most senior officials around the table (who included Biden, Clinton, Gates, Donilon, and Chairman of the Joint Chiefs of Staff Michael Mullen) remained cautious, reluctant to push Mubarak out the door. Some of them knew the Egyptian leader personally, remembered when Egypt was still a disruptive force in the region, and recognized all Mubarak had done over the decades to cooperate with the United States on security and counterterrorism, maintain Egypt's peace treaty with Israel, and provide military overflights and access to the Suez Canal. They were also old enough to remember what happened in Iran following the fall of the shah, hardly a precedent anyone wanted to follow. They all believed that Mubarak should be given time to manage his own departure and treated with respect; if the United States humiliated him, Gates said, "it would send a message to every other ruler to shoot first and talk later."[24] Asked to consider two possible presidential statements, one calling for Mubarak's immediate departure and the other calling for an orderly transition, Obama's most senior officials all supported the latter.

When Obama asked for the assessments of the room's "backbenchers," however, he got very different advice. Breaking with Clinton, Bill Burns—who had previously run the State Department's Near East bureau and had served as ambassador to Jordan—said he thought Mubarak was finished and that continued U.S. support would be counterproductive. White House counterterrorism adviser John Brennan, a former CIA station chief in the Middle East, acknowledged that Mubarak had been a valuable security partner for the United States, but he was now "toast"; failing to take a clear stand would only diminish the United States in the eyes of the protesters. And then one by one, a series of other backbenchers—including Rhodes, Power, Shapiro, the vice president's national security adviser, Antony Blinken, and other younger advisers—all made the case that Obama should get on what some called "the right side of history," which meant embracing the protesters and calling for Mubarak to go now.[25] Another young NSC staffer, Kelly Magsamen, said it felt as if generational change in U.S. foreign policy were taking place, for the better.[26] "This was a once-in-a-generation chance to achieve meaningful reform in the Arab world," Rhodes thought, and Obama—who had been widely criticized for failing to support public protests after a flawed election in Iran in 2009—agreed.[27] To refuse to embrace change in Egypt would be a betrayal of Obama's vision of political change as outlined in his original Cairo speech, and doing nothing would make the United States no different from Russia or China.[28] The cabinet officials at the table were taken aback, Gates wondering how anyone could know which side of history was the "right" one and the White House chief of staff, Bill Daley, wondering what some of the younger advisers knew about Egypt.[29] But as Clinton later recalled it, she and her front-bench colleagues lost the debate because "other members of the team appealed . . . to the president's idealism and argued that events on the ground were moving too quickly for us to wait."[30] Clinton and Gates both felt that Mubarak had actually agreed to do what Wisner had asked of him, but it was "too little, too late"—for the protesters in Cairo and the president and some of his advisers.[31]

To say Obama's call to Mubarak later that night was not well received would be an understatement. Mubarak thought Obama was naive about Egypt and warned—as he had all along—that the Muslim Brotherhood would take over if he stepped aside without a transition plan in place. "You don't know Egypt," he told Obama. "I know my people."[32] Mubarak told Obama it would be unnecessary to speak again the following day because the protests would be over soon, but Obama was no longer prepared to wait. In a public statement after the call, he called the Egyptian protesters an "inspiration to people around the world" and made clear the United States was on their side. "To the people of Egypt, particularly the young people of Egypt, I want to be clear," Obama said. "We hear your voices." "What is clear, and what I indicated tonight to President Mubarak, is my belief that an orderly transition must be meaningful, it must be peaceful, and it must begin now."[33]

Obama wondered aloud after the call if he would have handled the situation the same way had he, like some of his advisers, known Mubarak personally—in the way he knew King Abdullah of Jordan, for example—but the decision had been made.[34] The next day, lest Mubarak or anyone else not understand the urgency of Obama's demand, the White House press secretary, Robert Gibbs, explained, "Now means yesterday. . . . Not September, now means now."[35]

U.S. policy was now set, but the enduring divisions would emerge only a few days later when Frank Wisner, speaking as a "private individual" because his official mission to Cairo was over, made a public case for continuing to work with Mubarak. Speaking by video link to the high-profile Munich Security Conference on Saturday, February 5—where Clinton had in person already reiterated the U.S. view that Mubarak should step aside—Wisner opined that Mubarak "must stay in office" in order to steer through the changes that Egypt needed. Far from being an obstacle, Wisner insisted, Mubarak remained "utterly critical in the days ahead," and outsiders should refrain from creating a "negative force" inside Egypt.[36] The White House was furious about the lack of message discipline and demanded that Clinton get her former envoy in line.[37] But while distinctly off message, Wisner was only saying out loud what some of Obama's top advisers—including Clinton herself—were saying just a few days before and what some of them continued to think. Wisner himself would in fact never come around, arguing years later, "We ought to have been calling for an orderly transition, not telling Mubarak 'get out of town, get out of government,' with no strategy for what happens next. We needed a responsible path to stability and evolution, not revolution."[38] The irony is that this was precisely the strategy Obama and his team had originally endorsed, before it was overtaken by events.

Whatever goodwill Mubarak might have won from the protesters with his belated concessions was undermined by his defiant language and squandered as his police forces arrested activists and his supporters beat up protesters in Tahrir Square and elsewhere. So the protests continued and so did U.S. pressure on Mubarak. On February 6, Clinton again stressed that an "orderly transition" meant not just Mubarak not running again but "dialogue and constitutional reform, creating a new approach to political parties, [and] setting up an election."[39] On February 8, Gibbs called Suleiman's refusal to lift the emergency law and comments about Egypt not being ready for democracy "particularly unhelpful," and two days later Obama reiterated that the United States would "do everything that we can to support an orderly and genuine transition to democracy in Egypt."[40] With the protests continuing and the Egyptian military unwilling to act against them, the writing was on the wall. On February 11, Suleiman announced in a terse statement that Egypt's president was stepping down, and thousands of Egyptians poured into the streets, chanting "Egypt is free" and "God is great."[41] A regime that had lasted for almost sixty years—since Egypt's army first seized power—appeared to be on its way out.

As Mubarak's departure was announced, Obama expressed understandable satisfaction. He acknowledged "difficult days ahead" but spoke of the "privilege to witness history taking place" and expressed confidence that Egyptians could find the way forward "peacefully, constructively, and in the spirit of unity that has defined these last few weeks." Egyptians had made it clear that "nothing less than genuine democracy" would carry the day, and Obama noted with satisfaction that "it was the moral force of nonviolence—not terrorism, not mindless killing . . . that bent the arc of history toward justice once more."[42] "It seemed," Ben Rhodes agreed, that "history might at last be breaking in a positive direction in the Middle East."[43]

But even as Obama and his team steeled themselves for "difficult days," they probably could not have imagined just how difficult those days would be. Developments in Egypt would demonstrate once again, even after what looked like a peaceful transition of power with a modest American role, that getting rid of a country's leader was easier than successfully putting a new regime in place. They would also demonstrate that the U.S. ability to steer events in a positive direction was not what U.S. officials thought or hoped.

The first problem was that while Mubarak had left the scene, power remained in the hands of his generals, which in turn remained unacceptable to the Egyptian people. On February 12, the Supreme Council of the Armed Forces (SCAF), under the leadership of Field Marshal Hussein Tantawi, dissolved parliament and announced that it would "manage the affairs of the country" for a temporary period of up to six months, during which time it would organize parliamentary and presidential elections.[44] The seventy-five-year-old Tantawi, who had served in the Egyptian army for nearly six decades, would prove to be as stubborn and inflexible as Mubarak, governing under draconian emergency laws—not exactly the democratic breakthrough the United States or the Egyptian protesters had in mind. When the SCAF tried to extend its rule further, Egyptians again took to the streets to "reclaim the revolution," and Tantawi agreed to hold the elections that would lead to his—and the entire Egyptian regime's—undoing.[45] In January 2012, the Muslim Brotherhood won a remarkable 47 percent of the votes, with another 25 percent going to the even more religiously extreme Salafists, giving Egypt a parliament dominated by Islamists for the first time in its history.[46] Even more consequentially, in presidential elections held six months later, the Brotherhood candidate Mohammad Morsi—a former hard-line spokesman of the organization's Guidance Bureau—narrowly defeated the establishment candidate, the retired air force general Ahmed Shafik.[47] Clinton could not help but recall later that "those of us who favored the stodgy-sounding 'orderly transition' position were concerned that the only organized forces after Mubarak were the Muslim Brotherhood and the military."[48] The election results had proved her point as the military gave way to the uncertainty of Brotherhood rule.

When the votes were first tallied showing 52 percent for Morsi and 48 percent for Shafik, reports arrived in Washington suggesting that the SCAF was going to declare Shafik the winner anyway. But the Obama administration warned strongly against doing so, with Clinton publicly declaring that it was "imperative" for the generals to "turn over power to the legitimate winner."[49] "To this day," then ambassador Anne Patterson later told me, "I don't know how we in the U.S. government would have handled it if the military had declared Shafik the winner."[50] Satisfied at having kept the democratic process on track, the United States officially accepted the election results, and Obama called to congratulate Morsi on what his spokesman called a "milestone in [Egypt's] transition to democracy."[51]

Contrary to accusations of some critics then and since, the administration was not sympathetic to the Brotherhood, and Obama frequently pointed out that he—and certainly Clinton—did not exactly have much in common with a party with such regressive views on women's rights and other social issues. But Obama's strongly held view was that a freely and fairly elected Egyptian leader should be given a chance to govern according to democratic rules. Some of Obama's top advisers, including Tom Donilon and Dennis Ross, were deeply skeptical—as were U.S. allies in Israel and the Gulf, who were shocked that the United States would lend support to a group some of them viewed as a serious national security threat.[52] But Obama had seen moderate Islamic government function in Indonesia and had also invested heavily in Turkey's leader Recep Tayyip Erdogan, who seemed to be conducting a similar experiment in Turkey. From Obama's point of view, demonstrating that democracy and moderate Islamism could succeed in Egypt—and letting voters decide if they wanted to go in a different direction in a subsequent election—would be a major step forward for the entire Muslim world.

Morsi's initial moves suggested it just might work. After the election, he pledged to be the president of all Egyptians, promised cabinet posts for women and Copts, and resigned from the Brotherhood to symbolize his new role.[53] He announced that he would continue to support the U.S.-Egypt defense relationship and abide by the 1979 peace treaty with Israel, and he refrained from implementing some of the Brotherhood's previous rigid ideological positions, such as rescinding a law that allowed wives to divorce their husbands. In July, Obama issued an invitation for Morsi to visit him in the White House and pushed ahead with an accelerated $1 billion debt relief package to encourage this relatively constructive approach.[54] Pentagon officials sought to maintain the defense relationship with Egypt, and even use the transition as an opportunity to wean it away from expensive and anachronistic heavy weapons systems such as fighter jets and tanks and instead focus on more relevant priorities like border security, maritime security, and counterterrorism.[55]

But it was not long before both the limits to Morsi's flexibility and the deep opposition to his rule within Egypt would become apparent. For every step that showed Morsi understood the need to respect the views of all Egyptians, there were others that suggested he really did believe in the Brotherhood's slogan "Islam is the solution" and that he was determined to govern Egypt according to his campaign chant "The Quran is our constitution, and Sharia is our guide!"[56] To execute a genuine transfer of power after decades of dictatorship, Egypt would need a Nelson Mandela, and Morsi was no Mandela.

A major turning point came on August 12, when after less than two months in office Morsi took advantage of military embarrassment over an attack in the Sinai that killed sixteen Egyptian soldiers to dismiss all its top leadership, including Tantawi, Chief of Staff Sami Anan, and the heads of the Egyptian army, navy, and air force. He would replace them with his "own people," including, ironically, the then relatively junior head of military intelligence, Abdel Fattah al-Sisi, whose religious piety and professions of support for democracy Morsi thought—quite wrongly, it would turn out—would ensure loyalty to the Islamist regime. Around the same time, a new, Brotherhood-affiliated minister of information, Salah Abdul Maqsud, began a press crackdown that would include efforts to replace fifty leading establishment editors and journalists.[57]

On November 22, 2012, Morsi went further, passing a decree making him immune from court intervention and putting his decisions beyond legal challenge.[58] "The President is authorized to take any measures he sees fit in order to face any threats posed to the January revolution," a spokesperson announced. "His decisions cannot be appealed or canceled."[59] The decree unsurprisingly created an uproar, with demonstrations calling for Morsi's ouster, members of the Constituent Assembly threatening to walk out, and the opposition leader Mohammad el-Baradei tweeting that Morsi had "usurped all state powers and appointed himself pharaoh."[60] As the pressure mounted, Morsi would soften the new directive by limiting the types of decisions that would be free from judicial appeal, but the episode demonstrated his profound distrust of the Egyptian judiciary, part of a "deep state" he believed to be determined to prevent him from governing.[61] It would later turn out that Morsi took the dramatic action when he got word that Egypt's Supreme Constitutional Court—which had already disbanded the Brotherhood-led parliament—was preparing to dissolve the committee drafting a new constitution and that it might even move to annul his election and put the generals back in charge.[62] In postrevolutionary Egypt, even paranoids had enemies.

Those in Egypt who were in fact working toward Morsi's failure had plenty of help from outside. The leaders of Saudi Arabia and the United Arab Emirates had been shocked by developments of the Arab Spring and by what they saw as a U.S. betrayal of long-standing allies: If the United States was willing to abandon an ally of thirty years in the face of protests, what would it mean if they ever got in trouble? Seeing Morsi—and what they believed to be his vision of empowered, Islamist masses across the region—as a direct threat to their interests, Riyadh and Abu Dhabi responded with a major campaign to undermine Egypt's new leader through public pressure and criticism, direct support for Egypt's opposition, and offers to compensate Egypt for any lost U.S. aid if the military were to remove Morsi from power.[63] Ultimately, these countries would end up directly supporting the military intervention that would overthrow Morsi and contributing billions of dollars to the Sisi regime afterward.[64] Like Pakistan in postwar Afghanistan, and Iran in postwar Iraq, it would be yet another example in the region of well-intentioned American plans being thwarted by neighbors with a bigger stake and deeper commitment than the United States.

I saw for myself how hard it was going to be to consolidate

Egypt's democratic transition during the spring of 2013, not long after taking over the Middle East portfolio at the White House. In March, I joined Secretary of State John Kerry on a trip to Europe and the Middle East that included a stop in Cairo. Invoking his own political engagement as a young man following the Vietnam War, Kerry made a powerful case to Egyptians from across the spectrum to settle their disputes peacefully and within democratic norms. But he made little headway either with non-Islamist Egyptians who felt that Morsi was an extremist who was going to impose his ideology on them or with Islamists who felt it was "their turn" to run Egypt according to their own beliefs. In bilateral meetings, Morsi politely heard Kerry out but failed to convince him he was genuinely committed to inclusivity, while Sisi professed to support civilian rule but also warned Kerry he would not "let the country go down the drain."[65] In retrospect, Sisi was cryptically signaling his undemocratic intentions.

Two months later, I returned to Cairo on my own, naively thinking I could pick up our diplomatic effort where Kerry had left off, but the gaps among Egyptians were by then even greater, and my ability to close them far smaller. With pressure building on the government and rumors of a military intervention circulating more than ever, I looked for common ground among the parties, but found none. When I pressed Morsi's top foreign policy adviser, Essam el-Heddad, to do more to bring members of the opposition into the government, I was lectured about how they had tried to do so but faced unmitigated hostility from a "deep state" that only sought their demise. When I raised human rights with a top official in Morsi's Freedom and Justice Party, he asked me where the United States was when he was in Mubarak's jails. On the other side of the political divide, representatives of the former regime insisted Morsi was the one who refused to share power and that his support for Islamic law threatened their freedom. It was clear they saw Morsi not just as a neophyte from a different class and culture but, worse, as a determined Islamist who would erase thousands of years of Egyptian history by folding Egypt into an amorphous "caliphate." In a private meeting, one high-ranking former Egyptian diplomat told me bluntly what others only implied: the way to save Egypt from this menace was for the military to intervene, and the United States should not stand in the way. Six weeks later—in the wake of massive public demonstrations and backed by a broad coalition of Christians and Muslims, political leaders, and even hard-line religious Salafis—Sisi would depose Morsi and take over the government, effectively restoring the former, military-backed regime.[66]

The Obama administration would later be criticized for failing to prevent the coup and for failing to curb the excesses that followed it, but the story of its attempts to steer Egypt in a better direction actually demonstrates both the limits of U.S. influence in Egypt and the unintended consequences of even the "soft" version of regime change that took place in 2011. Even though Sisi had clearly overthrown an elected Egyptian government, Obama at a meeting of the National Security Council on July 4, 2013, decided not to formally declare the intervention to have been a "coup," which according to U.S. law would have required a cutoff in all U.S. financial assistance.[67] I and some other advisers, including Power and Rhodes, thought the administration should make such a declaration, but Obama and his more senior advisers feared the consequences of a full aid cutoff (which could last indefinitely if democracy was not restored) and worried about further alienating an Egyptian government that might be around for some time. Certain that a coup determination would not lead

Sisi to relinquish power anyway, Obama decided to make no determination at all. An NSC spokesperson explained that "the law does not require us to make a formal determination as to whether a coup took place, and it is not in our national interest to make such a determination." We would instead work with Congress to try to use our aid to push Egypt toward "a stable, democratic, inclusive, civilian-led government that addresses the needs and respects the rights and freedoms of all its people."[68] A few weeks later, the State Department spokesperson, Jen Psaki, was even pithier: "We have determined we're not going to make a determination."[69]

The attempt to steer a middle course between disapproving of the coup and continuing to provide military aid to Egypt became unsustainable six weeks later, when on August 14 Sisi's security forces killed nearly a thousand supporters of the Morsi regime who were protesting the military takeover on Cairo's Rabaa Square.[70] In response, Obama immediately announced the suspension of large military exercises and, after extensive further internal debate, two months later suspended the delivery of military equipment, including F-16 fighter jets, Apache attack helicopters, Abrams tank kits, Harpoon anti-ship missiles, and $260 million in cash transfers.[71] There could be no "business as usual," Obama said, and the aid would not be restored until there was "credible progress toward an inclusive, democratically elected civilian government through free and fair elections."[72]

But even this tougher approach had little impact. The new Egyptian leaders wanted their military equipment, but they were never going to refrain from confronting what they considered an existential threat—from the Muslim Brotherhood—just to get it back, especially when they had Gulf allies giving them many times that amount in unrestricted aid. The Egyptians also knew that while the official U.S. government position was that assistance would not be restored until those far-reaching conditions were met, at least some senior U.S. officials wanted to lower the bar and protect the strategic relationship. Kerry, for example, repeatedly signaled his sympathy for Sisi's position, claiming in August 2013 that by intervening, the generals had "restored democracy" to Egypt, as desired by millions of Egyptians.[73] He publicly said he took Sisi's commitment to human rights at face value, advocated for the restoration of a suspended "strategic dialogue," and expressed confidence that "the full amount" of U.S. aid would be restored.[74] Secretary of Defense Chuck Hagel held a similar view, spending hours on the phone with Sisi ostensibly to urge him to put Egypt back on the path to democracy, but often conveying the impression that his real interest was restoring the defense partnership and building a relationship with someone he suspected would be running Egypt for a long time to come.[75]

As time went by, a pattern emerged whereby NSC-drafted talking points about the imperative of taking credible steps toward democracy would often get diluted by those—at State and Defense—delivering the message. But even Obama would signal that there were limits to how much leverage on Egypt the United States was going to try to exert. Speaking at the UN General Assembly in September 2013, he acknowledged that while democratically elected, Morsi had "proved unwilling or unable to govern in a way that was fully inclusive," that the government that replaced him "responded to the desires of millions of Egyptians who believed the revolution had taken a wrong turn," and that "the United States will at times work with governments that do not meet, at least in our view, the highest international expectations, but who work with us on our core interests."[76]

The internal debate about restoring defense assistance—and normalizing relations with Egypt more generally—went on for more than a year, during which time the U.S. demands gradually diminished. Obama continued to deny Sisi the honor of a visit to the Oval Office, but in September 2014 he agreed to meet the Egyptian leader in New York during the UN General Assembly and pressed for lesser steps such as the release of detained journalists and secular activists, the repeal of a repressive 2013 protest law, and access to the Sinai for the U.S. military to monitor how U.S. military equipment was being used.[77] A confident Sisi, delighted with the imprimatur of a presidential meeting even if not in Washington, resisted even these modest measures, claiming that Egypt was facing existential threats and only a firm hand could keep it safe.

When the issue came to a head at a March 31, 2015, NSC meeting, Obama's advisers were again divided, this time along both generational and bureaucratic lines. Younger, NSC-based officials such as Rhodes, some of the NSC Egypt experts, and Power (who by then had replaced Susan Rice as the U.S. ambassador to the UN) argued for continuing to restrict the assistance until at least some of the U.S. conditions were met, whereas more senior officials at the State and Defense Departments, including Kerry, Hagel's successor, Ash Carter, and Chairman of the Joint Chiefs of Staff Martin Dempsey, made the case for restoring it. Obama's heart was with the former group—he had told me privately the day before the meeting that his inclination was to reject the recommendation of most members of the NSC's Principals Committee that the assistance be fully restored—but he would ultimately go in the other direction. Speaking to the group assembled in the Situation Room from a video screen in Cairo, the U.S. ambassador to Egypt, Stephen Beecroft, made the case that the assistance cutoff was doing more harm than good and that for all Sisi's ostensible power his ability to take some of the measures the United States demanded was limited by forceful resistance in the Egyptian bureaucracy. Those who made the case for restricting assistance believed U.S. credibility was at stake and that proponents of restoring it overstated the costs and consequences of possible cuts or changes to the program: Egypt needed the United States more than the United States needed Egypt. But when no one could credibly argue—when pressed by the president—that doing so would lead to fundamental change or bring democracy to Egypt, a fatalistic Obama agreed to resume delivery of the aid.[78]

Obama would leave office deeply frustrated by his inability to affect Egypt's course and resigned to the reality that democracy in Egypt, for now at least, was not in the cards. In 2011, he had set aside his instinctive caution and realism and supported revolution, only to see that approach lead to instability and the effective restoration of the old regime.

In the years after Sisi's takeover, repression in Egypt grew significantly, with the jailing, torture, or deaths of thousands of Egyptian Islamists, liberals, journalists, and others, the effective banning of democracy and human rights organizations, and a heavy crackdown on press freedom.[79] The repression only intensified after Obama gave way to Trump, who maintained the yearly $1.3 billion military package and ended any pretense of seeking to steer Egypt back on course to democracy. Trump welcomed Sisi to the Oval Office in April 2017, calling him a "fantastic guy" and complimenting his shoes, and then hosted him again in April 2019, even as Sisi was pushing through constitutional amendments that would allow him to remain in office until 2034. Asked if he had any problems with that effort, Trump said, "I can just tell you he's doing a great job.

Great president."[80] Meeting Sisi at the G7 summit in Biarritz, France, in September 2019, Trump would lightheartedly refer to the Egyptian leader as his "favorite dictator."[81]

The United States in Egypt had thus come full circle. With the best of intentions, it had helped push out Mubarak in an attempt to lead Egypt to a better and more democratic regime. It ended up—after years of political chaos, an Islamist experiment, a military coup, and thousands of casualties—embracing a more repressive version of the old one.

It's important to put the U.S. role in these events in perspective. Contrary to the arguments of some of Obama's critics—at home, in Israel, and in the Gulf—Obama did not "throw Mubarak under the bus." If that analogy is to be used, it would be more accurate to say Obama warned Mubarak that a bus was heading his way and urged him—if firmly—to get out of the way. As the then director of the State Department's Policy Planning Staff, Jake Sullivan, later told me, for many administration officials "getting on the right side of history" meant embracing what *was going to happen* as much as it meant trying to determine *what should happen*.[82] In that sense, it goes too far to argue that pushing Mubarak out was "one of the biggest mistakes of Obama's presidency," as one prominent foreign policy observer put it, because his real options were highly limited at the time.[83] But it's also necessary to admit that U.S. efforts to use diplomatic leverage to promote a democratic transition in Egypt failed and that those efforts had major costs and unintended consequences. We'll never know if an "orderly transition" under Mubarak—perhaps with a clear schedule for his departure, the exclusion of his family from the line of succession, and delayed parliamentary elections until institutions were strengthened and political parties other than the Muslim Brotherhood's Freedom and Justice Party had time to organize—would have been possible. But there can be little doubt that would have been a better outcome than what happened when the United States tried to engineer a quick democratic transition that proved tragically out of reach.

CHAPTER 6

"We Came, We Saw, He Died"

Libya, 2011

You could never accuse President Nicolas Sarkozy of France of lacking a flair for the dramatic. But informing Secretary of State Hillary Clinton that French fighter jets were already in the air and about to launch air strikes in Libya was extraordinary even by his standards. In Paris to attend Sarkozy's emergency summit on Libya at the Élysée Palace on March 19, 2011, Clinton had received reports earlier that day that the French were planning to launch the early strikes, so she was not entirely caught off guard. And although exasperated by Sarkozy's showmanship, she had no intention of taking responsibility for blocking an action that might prevent a massacre of Libyan civilians. So Clinton did not demand that Sarkozy recall the planes, and soon thereafter four Rafale jets struck several Libyan armored vehicles that were advancing on the rebel stronghold in Benghazi.[1]

In the hours and days that followed, the United States itself would launch hundreds of air strikes and more than a hundred Tomahawk cruise missiles from submarines and destroyers positioned off the Libyan coast, pummeling the country's dilapidated air defenses, giving NATO complete control of the Libyan skies, and leaving Muammar Qadhafi's forces vulnerable to an opposition counteroffensive. Seven months later, after some thirty thousand NATO sorties and ten thousand air strikes, the Libyan armed forces were finally defeated by the Western-supported rebels, and Qadhafi was pulled from a pipe near his hometown of Sirte, beaten, and killed, as recorded by a cell-phone camera for all to see. Upon hearing the news, Libyans danced and celebrated, much as Iraqis had after the fall of Saddam Hussein. As in Iraq, however, the celebrations—and the expectations that Libya was on a path to democracy and stability—would turn out to be tragically premature.

The path to regime change in Libya—not exactly a project on Barack Obama's original to-do list as president—had begun seven months earlier, on February 15, 2011, with Qadhafi's brutal reaction to the protests that began largely in the eastern Libyan city of Benghazi. Determined to avoid a similar fate as his counterparts in Egypt and Tunisia, both of whom had just been chased from power, Qadhafi took quick preemptive action to try to deter the protests, including by arresting the prominent human rights lawyer Fathi Terbel. That move backfired, however, only bringing more Benghazians into the streets. Within a week, rebels calling for Qadhafi's ouster would seize control not just of Benghazi but of the eastern Libyan city of Tobruk and some cities in the west, including Misrata, a commercial hub. In late February, the Libyan interior and justice ministers resigned, as did the Libyan ambassadors to the United States, United Nations, and elsewhere, some of whom also defected and denounced Qadhafi.[2] It appeared the regime was finished and that another North African domino was going to fall.

In desperation, Qadhafi sought to turn the tide, and save himself, by threatening harsh consequences for the rebels, threats that would ironically contribute more than anything else to the ultimate efforts to remove him. On February 21, Qadhafi's son Saif—seen by some as a potential reformer who had spent years courting Western pundits to try to polish Libya's image—made a partly conciliatory speech in which he offered a range of potential concessions including a new flag, national anthem, and confederal structure for Libya.[3] Saif admitted that Libya's security services had made "mistakes" after initial protests, implying that the regime wanted to avoid a crackdown, but also blamed Islamists and exiled Libyans for the protests and warned of consequences if the opposition refused to stand down. "Libya is made up of tribes and clans and loyalties," he emphasized. And if the unrest continues, "forget about democracy, forget about reform. . . . It will be a fierce civil war."[4]

The next day, Muammar Qadhafi himself upped the ante, in his own, rambling seventy-five-minute televised speech. He, too, offered vague potential concessions to the rebels, including amnesty to those who disarmed and safe passage to Egypt for rebels who wanted to defect.[5] But Qadhafi also warned that if the rebels didn't accept those offers, he would "chase them house to house." In defiant words reminiscent of Mubarak's less than two weeks before, Qadhafi insisted, "I am not going to leave this land. I will die here as a martyr, I shall remain here defiant." Antigovernment protesters were "rats and mercenaries" who deserved the death penalty, and his supporters would "cleanse Libya house by house" unless the protesters surrendered. "All of you who love Muammar Gaddafi, go out on the streets, secure the streets, don't be afraid of them. . . . Chase them, arrest them, hand them over," Qadhafi said.[6]

Qadhafi's hyperbolic threats—designed to intimidate his adversaries into backing down so he could avoid the fates of Mubarak and Ben Ali—instead proved to be his undoing. In fact, despite years of human rights abuses (including an infamous massacre at Tripoli's Abu Salim prison in 1996), Qadhafi had tended to avoid large-scale killing of civilians—

traditionally opting to buy off and cut deals with Libyan tribes instead.[7] He might well have massacred civilians had the West not intervened, but it's also possible, as British Libya scholar George Joffé and others have argued, that such fears were "vastly overstated" because Qadhafi understood he could not control all of Libya through violence alone.[8] In that sense, Qadhafi's downfall might have resulted from the same sort of desperate and counterproductive attempt to deter his adversaries with bravado that led to the demise of Saddam Hussein. Just as Saddam's refusal to allow inspectors to search his country for weapons of mass destruction that he did not have contributed to a U.S. decision to overthrow him, Qadhafi's efforts to stay in power by threatening more violence than he intended to carry out led to a Western military intervention against him.

Whatever the reality, the United States and its partners did not feel they had the luxury of waiting to find out if Qadhafi's threats were real or not, and they moved quickly to embrace the goal of his departure. Having seen Ben Ali and Mubarak quickly fall, Washington assumed that Qadhafi would also not last long, and so without much internal debate, on February 25, 2011, Obama called on the Libyan dictator to step down. "When a leader's only means of staying in power is to use mass violence against his own people," Obama said in a White House statement after a phone call with the German chancellor, Angela Merkel, "he has lost the legitimacy to rule and needs to do what is right for his country by leaving now."[9] Clinton added in a statement later the same day, "We have always said that the Qadhafi government's future is a matter for the Libyan people to decide, and they have made themselves clear. . . . Qadhafi has lost the confidence of his people and he should go without further bloodshed and violence."[10] In the days and weeks that followed, Obama and other top U.S.

officials—sometimes together with European counterparts such as Sarkozy and Prime Minister David Cameron of the U.K.—would repeat their conviction that the Libyan dictator should "step down from power and leave" immediately.[11] France recognized the opposition Transitional National Council (TNC) as Libya's legitimate government during a meeting with its leader, Mahmoud Jibril, on March 10, and the European Union as a whole called for Qadhafi "to relinquish power immediately" on March 11.[12]

Calling for Qadhafi to go was one thing. Figuring out how to achieve that result was another, and it soon led to a major U.S. policy debate about whether to intervene militarily, and if so, how. Already, as so often in the past, there was growing clamor for military action from leading members of Congress and prominent pundits. On March 3, the then chairman of the Senate Foreign Relations Committee, John Kerry, called for a no-fly zone and floated the idea of bombing Libyan air force runways, asserting that "the global community cannot be on the sidelines while airplanes are allowed to bomb and strafe."[13] The following day, two other committee members, Senators Joe Lieberman and John McCain, also called on the administration to implement a no-fly zone "immediately."[14] In the press, former head of the State Department's Policy Planning Staff Anne-Marie Slaughter and columnists such as Nicholas Kristof of *The New York Times* and James Traub of *Foreign Policy* were among those calling for prompt U.S. military action.[15] On March 15, a group of foreign policy specialists including Max Boot, Elizabeth Cheney, Robert Kagan, Reuel Marc Gerecht, William Kristol, and other prominent advocates of the 2003 invasion of Iraq wrote a letter to President Obama imploring him to "urgently institute a no-fly zone over key Libyan cities and towns . . . [and] to explore the option of targeted strikes against regime assets."[16] As a State Department official familiar with Obama's anti-interventionist instincts, I initially detected little appetite among top administration officials for military action in Libya. But I also recall going down to the State Department gym for a late evening workout that second week of March, seeing a parade of politicians and pundits on CNN calling for U.S. military action, and realizing that the pressure to act militarily was only going to grow.

The momentum was fueled by familiar assertions that such military operations would be relatively easy. On March 7, for example, former Speaker of the House Newt Gingrich said on Fox News, "The United States doesn't need anybody's permission. We don't need to have NATO, who frankly, won't bring much to the fight. We don't need to have the United Nations. All we have to say is that we think that slaughtering your own citizens is unacceptable and that we're intervening. And we don't have to send troops. All we have to do is suppress his air force, which we could do in minutes."[17] Former Bush administration Middle East official Elliott Abrams agreed that only a "small amount of effort [is] needed from the United States to ensure that Qaddafi is defeated."[18] Nicholas Kristof favorably cited the retired air force general Merrill McPeak's conclusion that "I can't imagine an easier military problem" than setting up a no-fly zone in Libya.[19] A Libyan opposition spokesman promised, "We are capable of controlling all of Libya, but only after the no-fly zone is imposed," while the French activist Bernard-Henri Lévy suggested that with early military action "bombing three airports would have been sufficient" to stop Qadhafi.[20] Anne-Marie Slaughter was hopeful that "if the international community lines up against him and is willing to crater his runways and take out his anti-aircraft weapons, he might well renew his offer of a negotiated departure."[21]

Even Donald Trump, before anyone had any idea his views

might one day matter, joined the bandwagon of those claiming military intervention would be easy. "I can't believe what our country is doing," Trump complained in a video recording posted on YouTube in February. "Qadhafi . . . is killing thousands of people, nobody knows how bad it is, and we're sitting around, we have soldiers all over the Middle East, and we're not bringing them in, to stop this horrible carnage." Trump promised it would be "very easy and very quick" to "stop this guy" and that afterward Americans would be very popular among Libyans who would reimburse us for our efforts out of their oil sales.[22] Trump would later call the Libya intervention a "disaster" and deny ever having called for it; in fact he argued passionately in favor of it—and insisted it would be quick and easy—at the time.[23]

The administration itself was divided, in many ways along similar lines to the generational gaps that emerged on Egypt—with younger, more idealistic advisers arguing for assertive U.S. action while some more senior officials remained cautious. Proponents of military action also included veterans of the Clinton administration—such as Deputy Secretary of State Jim Steinberg and Ambassador to the United Nations Susan Rice—who recalled the consequences of U.S. inaction in the face of massacres in Rwanda and Bosnia. As Steinberg later explained, "The thing about Rwanda that's important is it showed the cost of inaction. But I think the reason Bosnia and Kosovo figured so importantly is they demonstrated there were ways of being effective and there were lessons of what worked and didn't work."[24] As on Egypt, other, younger officials, including Rice, Power, and Rhodes, felt strongly that the United States should act more assertively, and they advocated efforts to protect Libyans from a violent dictator, prevent likely atrocities, and deter other dictators from repressing their own people with violence. With the French planning to table an imminent UN Security Council resolution calling for a no-fly zone, Rhodes later recalled, U.S. opposition to action would mean joining the Russians and *standing in the way* of protecting civilians, not exactly a position any of them were comfortable with.[25]

On the other side of the argument were senior cabinet officials like Vice President Joe Biden and Secretary of Defense Robert Gates who seemed to be thinking more about the costly precedents of Iraq and Afghanistan than about Bosnia or Rwanda. Biden argued that military action would create a political vacuum that would be difficult to fill, worried not just about the "day after" but the "decade after." He reminded colleagues of former secretary of state Colin Powell's line about Iraq that "if you break it you own it" and made clear he did not want to own Libya.[26] Gates was even more skeptical of military action, asserting in a speech at West Point on February 25 that any future defense secretary proposing "to again send a big American land army into Asia or into the Middle East or Africa" needed to "have his head examined."[27] He would later recall asking colleagues, "Can I finish the two wars I'm already in before you guys go looking for a third one?"[28] Qadhafi, Gates believed, was "not a threat to us anywhere. He was a threat to his own people, and that was about it."[29]

Gates and other Defense Department officials were particularly skeptical about setting up a no-fly zone, the favored remedy of most of those calling for military action but wanting to avoid sending troops. "Let's just call a spade a spade," Gates said. "A no-fly zone begins with an attack on Libya to destroy the air defenses. That's the way you do a no-fly zone. And then you can fly planes around the country and not worry about our guys being shot down. But that's the way it starts."[30] At a Pentagon press conference on March 1, Admiral Mike Mullen, chairman of the Joint Chiefs of Staff, said that a no-fly zone would be "an extraordinarily complex operation to set up."[31]

And the White House chief of staff, Bill Daley—reflecting the caution still felt by his boss—said on *Meet the Press,* "Lots of people throw around the phrase of 'no-fly zone,' and they talk about it as though it's just a game, a video game or something, and some people who throw that line out have no idea what they're talking about."[32]

Somewhere in the middle of the two camps was Clinton, who was initially more skeptical of intervention than many later press portrayals of her as an instinctive hawk. She regularly pulsed her staff for their views and brainstormed with them about options. As she later reflected, "We had learned the hard way in Iraq and elsewhere that it's one thing to remove a dictator and another altogether to help a competent and credible government take his place."[33] Having seen up close the costs of inaction in Rwanda, the benefits of intervention in Bosnia, and the disaster of the Iraq War, she understood the costs and risks of both action and inaction in Libya.

A critical factor in Clinton's thinking—perhaps not surprising for the country's top diplomat—was the degree to which a potential intervention in Libya would have international and regional support. On March 10, Clinton testified to Congress that she believed the United States needed "international authorization to act in Libya," adding, "I know that's how our military feels."[34] That same day, she and Gates participated in a Principals Committee meeting on Libya, and both at that point opposed military intervention, at least in the absence of clear international support.

I saw the importance Clinton placed on international perspectives myself when I accompanied her to a Group of Eight (G8) foreign ministers meeting in Paris on March 14, 2011. Just prior to the G8, she met with the United Arab Emirates foreign minister, Abdullah bin Zayed, who pledged Emirati support for a no-fly zone and potential military campaign.

Only two days before, the Arab League, which had already suspended Libya's membership, had called on the UN Security Council to "impose immediately a no-fly zone" over Libya and to recognize the National Transitional Council as the country's new government.[35] These steps—exceptional for the typically cautious and divided organization—underscored that the United States would have strong Arab support if it acted in Libya, a critical factor in winning support in Washington.[36]

The Europeans also played a pivotal role, in particular at the G8 foreign ministers meeting hosted by the French. Normally at such gatherings, the United States speaks first as the *primus inter pares*, but in this case Clinton asked me to arrange for her to speak last, because she had no clear guidance on Libya from the divided and still deliberating administration in Washington. So the Europeans—the Italian foreign minister, Franco Frattini, the British foreign secretary, William Hague, and the French foreign minister, Alain Juppé—all presented their views, and one by one they made passionate appeals for U.S. leadership and military action. Frattini, in particular, warned that Qadhafi's massacres would send thousands of migrants across the Mediterranean that Italy could not absorb, while Juppé, under pressure from his impatient president, stressed that time for action was running short. Less than a decade after the Iraq War, it was unusual to say the least to watch Europeans—led by the French and the Italians—lecture a U.S. secretary of state about the costs of inaction and the compelling need to use military force in the Middle East.

Another important factor in leading Clinton and others to support action was the belief—admittedly based on little evidence—that Libyan opposition leaders were genuinely representative or committed to democracy, rule of law, human rights, and good relations with the United States. Back at her Paris hotel at 10:30 p.m. after the G8 meeting, Clinton met with the TNC leader, Mahmoud Jibril, an English-speaking political scientist who had received his doctorate at the University of Pittsburgh. Jibril was accompanied by Bernard-Henri Lévy, who had played a prominent role in introducing Libyan opposition leaders to the French government while pressing Paris to intervene in Libya. Clinton found Jibril, who said all the right things about how a future Libya would be governed, "impressive and reasonable" and was "won over," an important factor in her ultimate decision to support military intervention.[37] Clinton wasn't the only one persuaded by the TNC's well-coached efforts to present themselves as pro-American liberals. John McCain was similarly enthusiastic about the fact that Jibril and other opposition leaders had studied in U.S. universities and that the TNC was made up of "lawyers, doctors, women activists," while Clinton's British counterpart, William Hague, made the case that "these people at the top of this organization are genuine believers in democracy and the rule of law. It is quite inspiring."[38] The U.K. chief of the Defence Staff, David Richards, recalled a "quorum of respectable Libyans" assuring the Foreign Office that militant Islamist militias would not benefit from the rebellion as being a key factor pushing Britain toward war, concluding later that "with the benefit of hindsight, that was wishful thinking at best."[39] The State Department's lead Libya analyst, Andrew Miller, later concluded that "we were the victims of our own efforts to market the Libyan opposition as a credible, democratic, and competent alternative to Qadhafi. . . . We bought into our own propaganda."[40] It was not the first or the last time that articulate and well-meaning exiles would play a major role in persuading U.S. and U.K. officials to support intervention in the Middle East.

The U.S. debate on the use of force would come to a head at a meeting of the National Security Council on the afternoon of March 15, with Clinton participating by secure phone from Cairo, where she had traveled from Paris to help support the transition under way there. With Qadhafi's forces still encircling Benghazi and his threats continuing, top U.S. officials considered their options, focusing in particular on whether to support the French and British proposals to impose a no-fly zone on Libya. Biden, Gates, Mullen, Donilon, Daley, Brennan, and Deputy National Security Adviser Denis McDonough all opposed U.S. military intervention, while Clinton, Rice, Power, Blinken, and Rhodes emphasized a U.S. moral responsibility to act.[41] Clinton also argued, based on her recent consultations, that the Libyan opposition was credible and that most Arab and European leaders favored and would support military intervention, while Rhodes, in charge of communications, wondered how the administration could explain a decision not to join others in acting to save Libyan lives.[42]

Obama was sympathetic to the need to act, but—after a briefing by Mullen—was unpersuaded that a no-fly zone alone would make a real difference, because Libyan air forces were not being heavily used and ground forces posed the real threat to civilians. A frustrated Obama insisted his team come back later that same evening—after he attended a long-scheduled dinner with military commanders—with options that would make a real difference on the ground.[43] When the NSC reconvened, participants considered a wider objective of trying to protect Libyan civilians by attacking Libyan forces on the ground, a potentially more effective mission but one that would entail more costs and risks. After further debate, Obama admitted he was "as worried as anyone about getting sucked into another war," but determined the United States could not just stand by and permit a humanitarian disaster in Benghazi. "We can't underestimate the impact on our leadership," he concluded. "Let's make a difference."[44] He approved a military plan according to which the United States would provide certain unique capabilities—such as cruise missiles to destroy Libyan air defenses, advanced intelligence and reconnaissance, and in-air refueling—while relying on others to carry out the bulk of military operations. And he made clear that he expected the U.S. role to be limited to an initial phase, after which others would be expected to bear the bulk of the military burden. Gates would later report that Obama told him it was a 51–49 decision.[45]

The NSC meeting ended with Obama authorizing Rice to try to win support at the UN Security Council for the wider mission so that if the United States did intervene, it would be at least doing so with a legal mandate and multilateral support. To almost everyone's collective surprise, two days later that effort resulted in UN Security Council Resolution 1973, which authorized not only a no-fly zone over Libya but enforcement of the previously agreed arms embargo, the freezing of Libyan regime assets, and most consequentially "all necessary measures" to protect civilians and civilian populated areas.[46] The resolution got ten votes in favor but even more surprisingly was not vetoed by Russia or China, which both abstained while reiterating their preference for a negotiated solution. Two days later, Clinton found herself back in Paris, with Sarkozy telling her that the French planes were already in the air.

In many ways, the NATO operation went exactly as planned. After destroying Libyan air defenses in the opening days of the conflict with Tomahawk cruise missiles, A-10 Warthogs, and electronic jammers, the United States would continue to provide 75 percent of intelligence, surveillance, and reconnaissance data to enforce an arms embargo as well as 75 percent of refueling planes used—an essential contribution to reduce loitering time of allies' strike aircraft. But beyond that, NATO allies and other partners made major military contributions to a NATO mission whose formal tasks included policing the arms embargo, patrolling the no-fly zone, and protecting civilians. France and the United Kingdom flew more than 40 percent of sorties, destroying more than one-third of overall targets; Italy and Greece provided access to critical air bases; Belgium, Canada, Denmark, Norway, and the UAE deployed fighters for combat operations; and Jordan, the Netherlands, Spain, Sweden, Turkey, and Qatar helped enforce the no-fly zone. It was an impressive display of collective action and a demonstration—in contrast to the 2003 Iraq War and other past conflicts—that NATO and others could act without the United States having to carry an excessive military burden.[47]

The air operations prevented Qadhafi from using airpower and stopped his forces from retaking all of Libyan territory. It quickly became clear, however, that this was not going to be a quick or easy military mission—certainly not one in which the U.S. military role would last only "days, not weeks," as Obama had suggested.[48] Indeed, any hope that Qadhafi would see the writing on the wall and voluntarily give up power also proved to be wishful thinking, notwithstanding extensive efforts to offer the Libyan dictator a way out while threatening consequences if he refused. In July 2011, the NSC's Derek Chollet, Assistant Secretary of State Jeffrey Feltman, and the U.S. ambassador to Libya, Gene Cretz, traveled to Tunis to try to negotiate Qadhafi's departure with his chief of staff and interpreter, but they got nowhere.[49] Just as Mubarak had done in Egypt, Qadhafi's officials insisted that the Americans "did not know our country" and that if Qadhafi fell, the result would be a takeover by terrorists.[50] The Libyan officials "expressed genuine disappointment, believing that since the reopening of ties in 2003, the United States would 'protect them.'"[51] Notwithstanding periodic rumors about interest from various Qadhafi advisers,

Cretz ultimately concluded that "there was never a serious offer from Qaddafi to step down from power" and that "none of those characters around him ever had the gumption to raise the issue with him personally."[52] Just like Mosaddeq, Najibullah, Mullah Omar, and Saddam Hussein before him (and Bashar al-Assad later), Libya's dictator saw relinquishing power—even with Western promises of safe harbor—as an effective death sentence. If the United States and others wanted Qadhafi to leave power, they would have to take it from him.

Qadhafi's refusal to depart voluntarily also exposed a tension—if not to say an outright contradiction—in the U.S. mission in Libya. Ostensibly, it was not regime change but, as authorized by UNSCR 1973, simply "protecting civilians." Keen to reassure the public and Congress that there would be no "mission creep," when announcing the operation on March 18, Obama stressed, "We are not going to use force to go beyond a well-defined goal, specifically the protection of civilians in Libya."[53] White House spokesman Jay Carney also assured reporters that it was a "time-limited, scope-limited military action . . . with the objective of protecting civilian life in Libya from Muammar Qaddafi and his forces," while Hillary Clinton insisted "there is nothing in there [the UN Security Council resolution] about getting rid of anybody."[54] In a speech to the National Defense University on March 28, Obama reiterated the goal of Qadhafi's departure but stressed that "broadening our military mission to include regime change would be a mistake" and reminded his audience of the costs of making that mistake in Iraq.[55] In London with Clinton for the Friends of Libya conference two days later, I dutifully went on the BBC to insist that "the military mission of the United States is designed to implement the Security Council resolution, no more and no less . . . protecting civilians against attacks from Qadhafi's forces and delivering humanitarian aid," while on March

31 Deputy Secretary of State Jim Steinberg assured a Senate hearing that "our military operation has a narrowly defined mission that does not include regime change."[56]

In fact, however, while it was technically true that the mission was "protecting civilians," the assumption within the administration that Libyan civilians could never be safe so long as Qadhafi was in power meant regime change was the actual mission after all. This led to a convenient syllogism: *the mission is protecting civilians; Qadhafi threatens civilians; ergo the mission is getting rid of Qadhafi*. From the start of the military operation, NATO airplanes targeted strikes at Qadhafi's headquarters and bombed the regime's forces even when they were in retreat and far from any combatants.[57] NATO selectively enforced the arms embargo, focusing on arms being sent to regime forces while ignoring those delivered to the opposition, including by members of the U.S.-led coalition itself—particularly the United Arab Emirates and Qatar.[58] Nor did the United States or other NATO members press the Libyan opposition to test the seriousness of periodic regime cease-fire or negotiation proposals; instead, it called on regime forces to withdraw not just from Benghazi but from Misrata and other cities while supporting opposition offensives and refraining from pressing the rebels to negotiate.[59] In that sense, as Gates later candidly admitted, the notion that the U.S. mission was limited to protecting civilians was a "fiction," and in reality—even though he could not recall a specific decision that said, "Well, let's just take him out"—NATO operations were not going to cease until Qadhafi was gone.[60]

In an April 15 open letter discussing their mission, Obama, Cameron, and Sarkozy also essentially acknowledged the contradiction, writing that their "duty" and "mandate" under UN Security Council Resolution 1973 was to "protect civilians . . . not to remove Gaddafi by force," but also asserting that "it is impossible to imagine a future for Libya with Gaddafi in power." So long as he remained in power, they concluded, "NATO and its coalition partners must maintain their operations so that civilians remain protected and the pressure on the regime builds. Then a genuine transition from dictatorship to an inclusive constitutional process can really begin, led by a new generation of leaders. For that transition to succeed, Colonel Gaddafi must go, and go for good."[61] Among its other unintended consequences, this broad interpretation of using "all necessary measures" to protect civilians would persuade Moscow never again to allow ambiguous language in a Security Council resolution that could be used by the West to undertake regime change. Russian and Chinese leaders both saw NATO's military operation as a "bait and switch," one they would repeatedly seek to avoid in Syria by using their Security Council vetoes to protect Assad.

Because Qadhafi refused to cede power and his forces—understandably afraid of their fate in a post-Qadhafi Libya—fought hard, the war would take much longer than initially envisaged, but ultimately the Western-backed rebels would prevail. Tens of thousands of Libyans were killed or wounded in eight months of fighting, but on August 22 opposition forces stormed Qadhafi's compound in Tripoli, chased him from the capital, and declared victory over the regime.[62] It would take another two months for the rebels to consolidate their victory and find the former dictator. On October 20, forces representing the National Transitional Council captured the coastal city of Sirte, found the former dictator hiding in a steel culvert, and tortured and killed him without a trial.[63]

With Qadhafi's fall, the familiar temptation to declare victory kicked in among both pundits and officials. Already on

August 22, as the regime fell, Clinton's friend and sometime adviser Sidney Blumenthal emailed her, "Brava! You must go on camera. You must establish yourself in the historical record at this moment. The most important phrase is 'successful strategy.'" "You are vindicated."[64] Two days later, Anne-Marie Slaughter, the former State Department official, wrote that the intervention had proved skeptics "badly wrong," arguing that the outcome demonstrated how it was in the West's "strategic interest to help social revolutions fighting for the values we espouse and proclaim."[65] Visiting Tripoli just after its liberation, Nicholas Kristof—like so many early visitors to Baghdad in 2003—found "almost no looting . . . little apparent retaliation [against Qadhafi loyalists]," and "pro-Americanism that is now ubiquitous."[66] *The New York Times*'s Mark Landler wrote that the outcome offered "vindication" of Obama's approach—citing the analyst David Rothkopf's view that the intervention was "the kind of multilateral, affordable, effective endeavor that any foreign policy initiative aspires to"—and noted that even critics had to concede success.[67] That was true: the conservative writer and Obama critic Robert Kagan called the outcome in Libya a "great accomplishment for the Obama administration and for the president personally," while John McCain said that the Obama administration "deserves great credit" and "the world is a better place."[68] The prominent commentator Fareed Zakaria praised Obama's approach and concluded that it heralded a new era in U.S. foreign policy. "The question before Libya," Zakaria wrote, "was: Could such interventions be successful while keeping costs under control—both human and financial. Today's answer is: Yes."[69]

Leaders and officials also scrambled to take credit for the victory. On September 15, with Qadhafi still at large, Cameron and Sarkozy went to Tripoli, accompanied by Bernard-Henri Lévy.[70] Clinton herself followed not long afterward, announcing that she was "proud to stand here on the soil of a free Libya" while standing next to the beaming opposition leader, Mahmoud Jibril.[71] Only a few days later, when Clinton got word—in the middle of a televised interview from Kabul—that Qadhafi had been killed, she giddily exclaimed, "Wow! We came, we saw, he died!"[72] On September 29, the Republican senators McCain, Graham, Mark Kirk, and Marco Rubio also went to Tripoli, declaring it to be "surprisingly secure and orderly" and populated by Libyans who wanted "to build a secure, prosperous and democratic nation that rejects violent extremism, allies itself with America and our allies, and promotes the peaceful ideals of the Arab Spring."[73]

Even Obama, who always sought to avoid "spiking the football" and who had issued a cautious statement in August after Tripoli fell, could not help but celebrate the demise of a dictator whose overthrow he had done so much to bring about. "The dark shadow of tyranny has been lifted," Obama said in the Rose Garden on October 20, calling on Libyans to "build an inclusive and tolerant and democratic Libya that stands as the ultimate rebuke" to Qadhafi. "Without putting a single U.S. service member on the ground, we achieved our objectives, and our NATO mission will soon come to an end. We've demonstrated what collective action can achieve in the twenty-first century."[74] Two of Obama's top officials at NATO, the U.S. permanent representative, Ivo Daalder, and NATO's supreme allied commander, James Stavridis, agreed. "By any measure," they wrote in *Foreign Affairs,* "NATO succeeded in Libya. It saved tens of thousands of lives from almost certain destruction. It conducted an air campaign of unparalleled precision, which, although not perfect, greatly minimized collateral damage. It enabled the Libyan opposition to overthrow one of the world's longest-ruling dictators. And it accomplished all of this without a single allied casualty and at a cost—$1.1 billion for the U.S. and several billion dollars overall—that was a fraction of that spent on previous interventions in the Balkans, Afghanistan, and Iraq."[75]

U.S. and NATO leaders had a lot to be proud of, but declaration of victory in Libya—as in so many other cases of regime change that came before it—would prove to be premature. Indeed, far from putting the country on the path to democracy, the war would leave it even more unstable and produce a wide range of unintended, and undesirable, consequences.

The first problem, as always, was the inability to fill the inevitable security vacuum created by the regime's collapse—especially in a country where no real institutions existed, where the population was deeply divided by tribe, region, and politics, and where outside powers used proxies to vie for influence. An early, ominous sign came on August 23, when during the fall of Tripoli the Qatari-backed Islamist leader Abd al-Hakim Belhaj—former head of the al-Qaeda-affiliated Libyan Islamic Fighting Group—declared himself leader of the liberation forces, infuriating other groups of rebel forces including Misratans, Zintanis, and Nafusa fighters who had previously supported Belhaj and Western-oriented TNC opposition leaders like Jibril.[76] Reporting back to Washington from Benghazi that week, Assistant Secretary of State Jeffrey Feltman noted that Jibril was still commuting to Libya from his residence in Doha and that TNC officials seemed to be more like "observers and chroniclers rather than the authors of the unfolding developments to the west." Feltman wondered whether "the extensive plans that the TNC has made about the post-Qadhafi transitional structures have any relevance for Tripoli."[77] Revenge killings, reprisals, and assassinations began almost immediately, and before long the government—such as it was—began paying militias in an attempt to keep the peace, because it had no forces of its own. The Libyan army had essentially disintegrated, and the collapsed economy could not provide alternative jobs, so the militias essentially took over. As Frederic Wehrey, a former U.S. Air Force officer who traveled frequently to Libya, summed it up, the situation was a classic Catch-22: "The anemic and provisional government insisted that the state could not be built until the revolutionaries (real and self-professed) gave up their guns. And the revolutionaries insisted they would not do so until the state was formed and their interests were secure."[78]

The first Libyan elections, which took place on July 7, 2012, were relatively promising, with a turnout of more than 60 percent, and Jibril was appointed transitional prime minister.[79] Obama declared it to be "another milestone on the extraordinary transition to democracy," but major obstacles were also clear from the start.[80] The newly elected General National Congress (GNC) was dominated by Islamists, and Jibril had to distance himself from any notion of secularism and pledge to make sharia law a main source of legislation while also trying to establish independence from the Western and regional powers who were seen to have installed him.[81] Jibril—as a former representative of the Qadhafi regime—was viewed skeptically by much of the population and had little authority, because "the ragtag populist army that had actually done the fighting against Colonel Qaddafi was not taking orders from the men in suits who believed they were Libya's new leaders," as Scott Shane and Jo Becker put it in *The New York Times*.[82] He was soon replaced as transitional prime minister by Abdurrahim el-Keib, as part of a deal struck by the militias who were now running the show. In October, el-Keib would be replaced by Ali Zeidan, a former diplomat who had served in the TNC. Under heavy pressure from militias, in May 2013 the GNC passed a "political isolation law" that banned even lower-level former Qadhafi officials from taking positions in the new government. Like aggressive de-Baathification in Iraq in 2003, the measure alienated significant parts of the population, increased unemployment, put thousands of resentful former security officials out on the streets, and deprived the new government of badly needed technical expertise.[83]

With no functioning government to speak of, human rights conditions deteriorated rapidly. The rebels expelled thirty thousand mostly black residents from Tawergha, while Human Rights Watch reported "the worst kind of vigilantism" and abuses that "appear to be so widespread and systematic that they may amount to crimes against humanity."[84] It was not long before the Islamic State—competing for influence among extremists with Ansar al-Sharia, the group responsible for the killing of U.S. ambassador Chris Stevens and three other U.S. officials in the attacks in Benghazi in September 2012—began to fill the vacuum, especially in the coastal towns such as Derna and Sirte.[85] By 2016 there were an estimated five thousand to sixty-five hundred IS fighters in Libya—more than in any country other than Syria and Iraq.[86]

As security deteriorated and the Libyan economy collapsed—with oil production falling to some 30 percent of prewar levels—Libyans began to flee the country in record numbers (mostly to Tunisia and Egypt), and Libya became a crossroads for African and other migrants desperately seeking to get to Europe.[87] The refugee flows and instability also affected neighboring states such as Chad, Algeria, and especially Mali, where insurgent Tuaregs, some of whom had been serving in Qadhafi's security services, took over the northern part of the country, leading to a military coup in Bamako in response. Over time, the al-Qaeda-affiliated extremist group Ansar Dine (Defenders of the Faith) gained strength from incoming fighters and arms from Libya and defeated the Tuaregs, imposed sharia law in the northern region, and declared independence, fueling a civil war. In another unintended consequence, France—which was among the strongest proponents of intervention in Libya—found itself obliged to send forces to Mali to reinforce the government, with the United States providing assistance with military logistics.[88] In other words, far from helping to stabilize the wider region, as many proponents of intervention in Libya argued it would, the intervention in many ways did the opposite.

The repercussions of the conflict and the regime's collapse also included massive regional arms flows, both from Qadhafi's now unsecured arsenals and from the new supplies that had been provided to anti-regime insurgents.[89] According to Gates, an arsenal of an estimated twenty thousand shoulder-fired surface-to-air missiles, SA-7s, "basically just disappeared into the maw of the Middle East and North Africa," while other reports concluded that machine guns, automatic rifles, and ammunition ended up in Syria, Yemen, Tunisia, Mali, Niger, Algeria, Sudan, Egypt, and Gaza, often in the hands of terrorists, insurgents, and criminals.[90] The U.S. State Department initiated a $40 million program to find and destroy arms caches, but the program had little success, in part because militias took advantage to import or steal additional arms that they would sell on to the Americans for a profit.[91]

As was often the case during and after previous Middle Eastern interventions, outside powers with competing agendas complicated efforts to mediate among factions on the ground. From the start of the conflict in Libya, Qatar and Turkey lined up behind Libya's mostly Islamist-oriented militias in Misrata and other largely western Libyan cities, while the United Arab Emirates, Saudi Arabia, and Egypt backed their mostly eastern-based opponents. In February 2014, Khalifa Haftar, a Qadhafi-era general who had been living in exile in the United States prior to the 2011 revolution, launched

Operation Dignity, a military operation designed to oust the Islamists and unify the country under his rule with the backing of the UAE, Saudi Arabia, and Egypt—all of which supplied money and arms and even undertook bombing raids on behalf of Haftar's forces. Haftar showed no interest in compromise or democracy, insisting that the only place for Libyan Islamists was "in prison, under the ground, or out of the country," one consequence of which was to drive some of the disparate Islamist factions to join forces—and to turn to Qatar and Turkey for support.[92] Critics would later argue that the United States did not do enough to prevent regional powers from arming their preferred proxies, but with no troops on the ground and little visibility into what was happening in Libya—for security reasons, the U.S. embassy was evacuated to Malta in July 2014—that proved easier said than done. "They march to their own drummer," one former senior State Department official told *The New York Times,* referring to the U.S. allies in the Gulf.[93]

After elections in June 2014 (which were marred by violence and in which turnout fell from 1.7 million to 630,000), in which non-Islamist parties won a majority of seats in the new House of Representatives (HOR), Libya's Supreme Court annulled the elections under pressure from Islamist militias. Elected members of the HOR rejected the court's ruling and continued to operate, while the largely Islamist factions that filed the constitutional challenge maintained that the previous GNC remained the legitimate parliament.[94] By the end of the year, Libya had two competing governments, parliaments, and central bank heads, all backed by competing militias supported by a range of outside powers. Rather than a stable new government, let alone a functioning democracy, the country had entered a state of multisided civil war with no obvious way to resolve it.[95]

Finally, but perhaps most consequential of all, the intervention in Libya created a catastrophic degree of moral hazard. The willingness of the United States and NATO—the most powerful militaries in the world—to materially back an armed rebellion in Libya, just after having sided with revolutionary protesters in Egypt, inevitably encouraged similar rebellions elsewhere.[96] Indeed, with Western leaders explicitly expressing the hope that Libya might provide a model for Syria, within days of Qadhafi's death protesters in Homs were chanting, "Gaddafi is finished. It is your turn now Bashar!"[97] While many proponents of intervention argued that punishing and even overthrowing Qadhafi were necessary to deter other dictators from cracking down on their own rebellious opposition groups, instead it only encouraged those groups to escalate violence to a level that they had reason to believe would provoke outside intervention while making other dictators even more determined to do whatever necessary to crush the resistance.[98] In Syria, where the Assad regime and its backers in Moscow and Tehran resolved to prevent anything like Libya from ever happening, the destructive consequences of this dynamic would vastly eclipse those of Libya itself.

For many, including some top administration officials themselves, the lesson of failure in Libya was not that intervention was a mistake but that those who intervened failed to adequately follow up. For example, Susan Rice, ambassador to the United Nations at the time of the intervention, would write that we "failed to try hard enough and early enough to win the peace," while Bill Burns, at the time the undersecretary of state for political affairs, concluded that the problem was the "failure to plan for and sustain a realistic approach to security after Qadhafi fell."[99] France's then national security adviser, Jean-David Levitte, also insisted that "the mistake was not to intervene. It was not to stay. . . . We should have helped them create a proper police force."[100] Two prominent analysts at New America, Peter Bergen and Alyssa Sims, agreed that the "lack of planning for the day after the regime collapsed helped set the stage for a civil war," while the Brookings Institution's Shadi Hamid argued that the United States and its allies failed to "plan and act for the day after," with training missions, peacekeeping forces, advice on institutions, and efforts to restrain unhelpful allies from excessive meddling.[101] In April 2015, John McCain considered the situation in Libya a "disaster," complaining that the problem was that "we just basically left," unlike "at the end of World War II when we defeated the Germans."[102] AEI's Danielle Pletka agreed in 2016 that "had the Obama administration followed the ouster of Libyan tyrant Moammar Qaddafy with a plan to stabilize that nation . . . Libya would not now be a haven for ISIS and al Qaeda."[103]

Even Obama himself would end up articulating a version of this view, telling the United Nations in September 2015 that "our coalition could have and should have done more to fill a vacuum left behind."[104] In a spring 2016 interview with the editor of *The Atlantic,* Jeffrey Goldberg, Obama said, "When I go back and I ask myself what went wrong, there's room for criticism, because I had more faith in the Europeans, given Libya's proximity, being invested in the follow-up."[105] Around the same time, Obama told Chris Wallace of Fox News that the "worst mistake" of his presidency was "probably failing to plan for the day after, what I think was the right thing to do, in intervening in Libya."[106]

The "if only" reflex was understandable, but the idea that insecurity in postwar Libya could have been avoided with more "planning"—which critics often used as a euphemism for "ground troops"—misses the point. Indeed, the issue was not so much a failure to "plan" as that "voluminous plans dissolved on first contact with Libyan realities," as Frederic Wehrey observed.[107] To be sure, one constraint was Obama's own deep reluctance to put U.S. forces on the ground, having been elected president in part because of his strong opposition to regime change and occupation in Iraq. In the midst of a costly troop surge in Afghanistan, Obama was hardly eager to deploy even more troops in Libya, where U.S. interests were more limited. Especially after four Americans were killed in Benghazi in September 2012—a tragedy that Obama's opponents relentlessly and cynically used against the administration for political advantage—there was little appetite for taking on more risk.[108] Sizable majorities of Americans rejected the notion that the United States had a responsibility to act in Libya, and overwhelming majorities—82 percent in March 2011—opposed sending in ground troops.[109] In June 2011, the House of Representatives passed a bipartisan resolution urging Obama not to put troops on the ground in Libya by 268 to 145, and leading members of Congress from both parties repeatedly made clear their opposition to deploying U.S. forces.[110] Even strong proponents of U.S. military action such as John McCain and Joe Lieberman argued that U.S. ground forces would be "inappropriate" and "counterproductive," while Lindsey Graham insisted that Western forces would "undercut the opposition and . . . backfire."[111] Yet this would not prevent them, after Qadhafi's removal, from calling for a U.S. role in "safeguarding the immense stockpiles of weapons and dangerous materials that exist across the country . . . bringing Libya's many militias under the TNC's civilian authority . . . working toward their demobilization, disarmament and reintegration into Libyan society," and helping Libya "build a professional security force"—or from criticizing the subsequent failure to do all these things.[112]

In any case the issue of sending in peacekeepers was largely a moot point, because the Libyans themselves were strongly opposed to any outside military presence.[113] The TNC's founding statement made clear they wanted international support "without any direct military intervention on Libyan soil," a position they would maintain both during the conflict and in its aftermath.[114] As then NSC Libya expert Ben Fishman has pointed out, "they were adamant from the outset of the transition that they themselves should determine the country's future," which former State Department official Jeremy Shapiro described as a "sort of conspiracy. They were very keen to take responsibility for their country, and we were very keen to let them, for our own reasons."[115]

Then there was the enormous challenge of finding Libyan recruits who were competent, untainted by extremism, and willing to work together notwithstanding deep regional, tribal, and political divisions. With Congress unwilling to fund the training of Libyan forces, the administration tried to get the Libyan government to pay for training efforts, but despite repeated promises to do so, the checks never arrived. As Biden's national security adviser Antony Blinken later explained, "I know this sounds incredible, but for months and months and months on end we could not get anyone in authority in the government to just sign an agreement on anything, including our detailed offers of security assistance. . . . I think what we underestimated was how totally incoherent Libya was as a governing structure, especially in the absence of Qaddafi."[116] Ambassador Cretz agreed that "they just weren't in a position to absorb huge amounts of aid. . . . I think we could have done more to help construct a security force, but even on that score, you know, they were just not ready. I don't know how we would have overcome the strong—the obstinate positions of all the different militias that did not want to give a single inch of the authority that they had gotten from being, you know, the leaders of the revolution."[117] Deborah Jones, who took over as U.S. ambassador to Libya in June 2013, recalls personally listening to Prime Minister Ali Zeidan try to order his interior minister to accept a French offer to fund police training, only to see the proposal to do so continue to gather dust.[118]

Ultimately, unwilling or unable to provide training to Libyans in Libya because of the absence of security in country, the United States and some of its European partners attempted to set up a program to train a general-purpose force (GPF) at military bases in Bulgaria as well as at sites in the U.K. and Turkey, but the effort was a failure.[119] The mission in Turkey—already viewed skeptically by Turkey's geopolitical rivals in the coalition—suffered "astronomical attrition rates," while the training effort in the U.K. was plagued by defections, delinquency, and reports of crimes, including rape and robbery, among the recruits.[120] Many of the Libyans who did get trained and sent back to Libya quickly found themselves under attack from better-armed Libyan militias, and the government did not have the legitimacy or power to do anything about it.

Nobody was more exasperated by the lack of progress than Obama, who felt a responsibility for the results of the mission he had authorized and knew he would bear the political risk if it failed. He repeatedly tasked his top advisers to accelerate efforts to train Libyan security forces, including through NATO, and expressed frustration when the efforts showed such little progress. In October 2013, after making a call from the Oval Office to the Libyan prime minister, Ali Zeidan, who had been briefly abducted in a reported coup attempt, Obama angrily complained to me and my NSC colleague Prem Kumar about our and our allies' inability to keep the prime minister safe and made clear in no uncertain terms he wanted to see much faster progress on the standing up of Libya's general-purpose force.[121] We shared Obama's frustration and said we would do all we could, knowing, however, that Zeidan needed protection immediately and that the GPF, in the best of circumstances, would not be ready for many years.

Even if it had somehow been politically possible and practically feasible to send in a large number of U.S. and European "stabilization" forces, it is not clear that such a presence would have been effective or sustainable in the long run. To be sure, Western forces could have been sent in with a mission to seize and hold ports, airports, ministries; secure weapons stockpiles and other key infrastructure sites; confront militias; and counter crime and looting. But as the experiences in Afghanistan and Iraq had already demonstrated, such a deployment would require significant and enduring military commitments and would only raise questions like how the militias would be disarmed, how outside forces would respond if attacked by nationalist or extremist insurgents, and for how long Western publics and parliaments—all of whom had been promised before the intervention that ground troops had been ruled out—would support the deployments as costs and inevitable casualties escalated. It wasn't so much a lack of "planning" that doomed the effort as Libyan nationalism, Libyan dysfunction, intervention fatigue, U.S. domestic political opposition, the agendas of outside rivals, and an unwillingness among Western powers to bear the costs and risks of sending forces to the Middle East. Those obstacles could not just be wished away.

In an August 2014 interview with the *New York Times* columnist Thomas Friedman, Obama concluded that we had underestimated "the need to come in full force—if you were going to do this, then it's the day after Qaddafi's gone, and everybody's feeling good, and everybody's holding up posters saying, 'Thank you, America.' At that moment, there has to be a much more aggressive effort to rebuild societies that didn't have any civic traditions. You've had a despot there for 40 years in place—there are no traditions there to build on, unlike Tunisia, where there was a civil society and that's why they've been more successful in transitioning. So that's a lesson that I now apply every time I ask the question: Should we intervene militarily? Do we have an answer for the day after?"[122] In Libya, we didn't have an answer for the day after.

After Obama left office, the security situation in Libya deteriorated even further, and the Trump administration largely disengaged. A few months after taking office, Trump himself stated, "I do not see a role in Libya. I think the United States has right now enough roles."[123] Instead, Washington limited its efforts to counterterrorism actions against the Islamic State and largely left the diplomacy in the hands of the UN and the Europeans, who continued their efforts to mediate among the various warring Libyan factions. For the next several years, the UN special envoy for Libya, Ghassan Salamé, proposed measures to revive and amend a stalemated 2015 political agreement, but his efforts remained "stuck on nearly every count."[124] While almost all parties were committed to the UN-backed agreement in principle, in reality Egypt, the United Arab Emirates, and Saudi Arabia (along with Russia and France) continued to provide support for General Haftar's forces, while Qatar and Turkey backed the Misrata-based Islamist force, and Italy cut deals with western militias to counter the flow of migrants.[125]

In April 2019, Trump abruptly changed course and seemed to endorse Haftar, who had just launched a new military offensive on Tripoli, apparently hoping the general could fulfill his long-standing promise to unify the country under his own leadership through force of arms.[126] But aside from the issue of whether embracing a new Libyan strongman was the right approach, Haftar never demonstrated the ability to take over and stabilize the country, and as the civil war escalated and casualties mounted, the administration pivoted back again to focusing on trying to negotiate a cease-fire. The tragic reality was that Libya was broken, and—especially with Americans increasingly averse to intervention and regional powers lined up on opposite sides of the conflict—no one had a recipe or the means to put it back together.

It is impossible to know how Libya would have evolved had the United States not led a military intervention there in 2011. There was certainly a risk of a massacre in Benghazi, though as noted earlier, Qadhafi's bombastic threats were likely hyperbolic in an effort to deter protesters. His interest in avoiding Western military retaliation and history of cutting deals with armed groups—along with the fact that he refrained from widespread attacks on civilians in the numerous Libyan cities his forces retook from the opposition during the war—suggest that the risk of civilian massacres was lower than widely believed at the time.[127] Even if Libyan forces did march on Benghazi and elsewhere, the crackdown would likely have resulted in far fewer casualties—and ultimate instability—than did the civil war that took place after the United States and NATO intervened. To be sure, even if NATO hadn't intervened, other supporters of the Libyan opposition, such as Qatar and other Gulf states, might have armed and financed the rebels, but even that scenario would likely have been far less destructive than the conflict that broke out after Qadhafi's overthrow.

Obviously, an intervention that deposed Qadhafi and was followed by the deployment of effective peacekeeping forces that imposed stability, disarmed rival militias and extremists, contained refugee flows, and got Libya's oil industry and economy going again would have been preferable to leaving Qadhafi in place or allowing chaos to prevail. But no one has yet been able to explain where those forces would have come from, how a hostile U.S. Congress and skeptical public could have been persuaded to support them (especially given the overwhelming opposition to any presence in Libya at all after Benghazi), how the Libyans' staunch opposition to an outside military presence could have been overcome, or what those forces would have done in the face of likely armed resistance.

The alternatives to regime change in Libya—either not intervening at all or using military force to prevent regime attacks on Benghazi but stopping short of regime change (the ostensible original mission) would have been far from perfect. But either would have been preferable to an intervention that set off a vicious internal power struggle, drew in rival regional powers, alienated Russia and China, led to moral hazard in Syria and elsewhere, and—in so doing—ultimately undermined the very principle of humanitarian intervention itself.

CHAPTER 7

"Assad Must Go"

Syria, 2011 . . .

The carefully crafted written statement might not have been as dramatic as a speech from the Rose Garden or Oval Office, but it was the message that mattered: Bashar al-Assad's time was up. "We have consistently said that President Assad must lead a democratic transition or get out of the way," Obama declared in the statement released by the White House on August 18, 2011, just before leaving Washington for a ten-day summer vacation. "He has not led. For the sake of the Syrian people, the time has come for President Assad to step aside." Always averse to unilateral action and a fierce critic of the Bush administration's invasion and occupation of Iraq, Obama emphasized that "the United States cannot and will not impose this transition upon Syria. It is up to the Syrian people to choose their own leaders, and we have heard their strong desire that there not be foreign intervention in their movement." But he also made clear that the United States would now act to support "an effort to bring about a Syria that is democratic, just, and inclusive for all Syrians. We will support this outcome by pressuring President Assad to get out of the way of this transition, and standing up for the universal rights of the Syrian people along with others in the international community."[1] "As part of that effort," Obama added, the administration was announcing "unprecedented sanctions to deepen the financial isolation of the Assad regime and further disrupt its ability to finance a campaign of violence against the Syrian people." He froze Syrian government assets, banned U.S. investments in Syria, and prohibited Americans from dealing with the Syrian government or importing Syrian oil products, all in the name of pressuring Assad to step down. At the State Department later that afternoon, Secretary of State Hillary Clinton predicted that the sanctions would "strike at the heart of the regime." She called on U.S. allies to "get on the right side of history" and end their dealings with the Assad regime.[2]

Obama's statement marked the third time since the start of 2011—and the fifth since 2001—that the United States had officially come out in favor of removing a Middle Eastern regime and committed itself to working toward that goal. This time, the problem would be not what would happen in the aftermath of the regime's fall but rather the costs and the consequences of the failure to oust the regime in the first place. Notwithstanding increasing amounts of financial, political, diplomatic, and military support to opposition forces trying to force Assad from power during the following months and years, it would gradually become clear that the United States had adopted a policy goal it did not have the will to bring about at a cost—including a potentially indefinite military occupation—it was willing to bear. Far from falling quickly, as some U.S. officials hoped or expected, to remain in power, Assad proved himself willing to kill, torture, and displace millions of his own citizens, cynically manipulate sectarianism, and deepen his country's dependence on Iran and Russia. The result of U.S. efforts to unseat Assad was thus not the dictator's departure—let alone the "democratic, just, and inclusive" Syria that Obama called for—but rather one of the most destructive conflicts the world had seen since World War II, with unimaginable human, strategic, political, and economic costs and consequences.

Proponents of regime change at the time and later would argue that if only the United States had intervened earlier, more directly, or more forcefully—providing greater quantities and more advanced arms to the opposition, setting up a no-fly zone, or even undertaking air strikes against the regime—it could have succeeded in overthrowing the regime and preventing a slaughter, all without having to deploy troops. As one prominent columnist asserted in 2013, "The limited use of U.S. airpower and collaboration with forces on the ground could have quickly put an end to the Assad regime 18 months ago, preventing 60,000 deaths and rise of al-Qaeda."[3] Just as in previous efforts at regime change, however, such arguments underestimated the commitment that would have been necessary to get rid of Assad, the long-term consequences of making such a commitment, and the strong likelihood that the result would have been a political and security vacuum that—if not filled by the United States—would lead to an enduring civil war or the seizure of power by extremists. Arguments that the Syrian regime could have been changed with a modest increase in U.S. military support—almost no one, after all, advocated an Iraq War–like invasion or occupation—overlook the degree to which the United States *did* intervene in Syria, including militarily, and the evidence that escalation by Washington and its partners brought about only counter-escalation by the regime and its determined backers in Russia and Iran.

Looking back at the way the war in Syria unfolded, it is difficult to find some critical moment where the application of a limited degree of additional military force or some other U.S. step would have led to the toppling of the regime. Based on precedents elsewhere, and given Syria's unique makeup, it is even more difficult to imagine how such measures would have led to a stable situation on the ground in the absence of a large U.S. military force that might have to be deployed indefinitely. It is therefore hard to avoid the conclusion that if the United States was not prepared to accept the real costs and consequences of regime change—which are always greater than its proponents acknowledge—it would have been better not to pursue that goal in the first place. The tragic story of regime change in Syria would be one of ends that exceeded means, calls for the use of military force that overstated what it could accomplish, and well-intended efforts that ultimately did more to escalate and perpetuate the conflict than they did to help bring it to an end.

Obama did not exactly jump at the chance to pursue regime change in Syria, of course. Indeed, far from having come to office focused on getting rid of Assad (or anyone else), Obama initially set out to explore better relations with Damascus, a process that continued right until the start of the conflict. The new administration's top regional priority, alongside dealing with Iran, was Arab-Israeli peace, and Syria was positioned to play a critical role. Starting as early as June 2009, Clinton publicly articulated the case for getting beyond the U.S.-Syria disputes of the first decade of the twenty-first century, and top diplomats, including Special Envoy for Middle East Peace George Mitchell, traveled repeatedly to Damascus. In February 2010, Obama announced his intention to appoint a U.S. ambassador to Syria for the first time since 2005, when Bush had cut ties with Damascus over its support for extremist groups in Iraq and the murder of the Lebanese prime minister Rafik Hariri.[4] Another senior official Obama sent to meet with Assad was Undersecretary of State William Burns, who told the press after his February 2010 meeting that he was there "to convey President Obama's continuing interest in building better relations with Syria based upon mutual interest and mutual respect." Burns said he "had quite productive and extensive discussions with President Assad . . . about areas in which we disagree, but also . . . areas of common ground on which we can build."[5] Obama's choice for the new U.S. ambassador, Robert Ford, would arrive in Damascus in January 2011, around the same time another experienced Middle East hand, Frederic Hof, was secretly exploring prospects for a Syria-Israel peace agreement.[6] Far from trying to overthrow Assad, Obama and other top officials initially had high hopes of working with him.[7]

Even as Assad began to brutally crack down on initially nonviolent protesters in the spring of 2011, the administration sought to avoid confrontation and held out hope that a peaceful resolution could be found. In a March 27 television interview on CBS, Clinton said that "we deplore the violence in Syria" but suggested that political change and accommodation might still be possible. "There is a different leader in Syria now," she said. "Many of the members of Congress of both parties who have gone to Syria in recent months have said they believe he's a reformer."[8] She was referring in particular to the then chairman of the Senate Foreign Relations Committee, John Kerry, who met with Assad four times between 2009 and 2010. In March 2011, Kerry told an audience in Washington, D.C., "President Assad has been very generous with me in terms of the discussions we have had. . . . I asked President Assad to do certain things to build the relationship with the United States and sort of show the good faith that would help us to move the process forward. . . . So my judgment is that Syria will move;

Syria will change, as it embraces a legitimate relationship with the United States and the West and economic opportunity that comes with it and the participation that comes with it."[9]

As the Syrian rebellion escalated throughout the spring of 2011, critics began to press the administration to take tougher action. On April 28, Senators Lindsey Graham, John McCain, and Joe Lieberman put out a statement urging Obama "to state unequivocally—as he did in the case of Qaddafi and Mubarak—that it is time for Assad to go" and calling on him to "take tangible diplomatic and economic measures to isolate and pressure the Assad regime."[10] The same day, Senator Marco Rubio called on the administration to sever ties with Syria and recall the newly arrived U.S. ambassador.[11] On May 11, Senators Lieberman, McCain, Rubio, and Ben Cardin called on the administration to "sanction, condemn, and pressure the Syrian government" and joined twelve other senators in introducing a resolution asserting that Assad had "lost his legitimacy."[12] At this point, even hawks in Congress and the media were not (yet) calling for U.S. military involvement in Syria. John McCain called for doing "all that we can, short of military action," and Charles Krauthammer insisted that "nobody is asking for a Libya-style rescue."[13] But they were demanding that the United States punish the Syrian regime more severely, align itself with the protesters, and specifically call on Assad to go. The unspoken implication was that such measures would help dislodge the Syrian regime and lead to its replacement by something better, without the United States having to fire a shot.

Obama continued to resist such calls, however, in part because he believed explicit support from the unpopular United States could tarnish the protesters and give the regime a basis for accusing Washington of being behind them—the same reason he had refrained from closely associating himself with the

Iranians who took to the streets two years previously to protest a fraudulent election there. The administration wanted its role to be "behind what the voices in the region are saying," one administration official explained, while Assistant Secretary of State for Near Eastern Affairs Jeffrey Feltman told Congress that the United States wanted "to make sure that the story remains about the Syrian people and not about us."[14] Obama also worried about creating expectations of U.S. military action if he called specifically on Assad to go without a concrete plan to achieve that objective. The ongoing operation to unseat Qadhafi in Libya, after all, was proving far more difficult than many hoped or expected, and the last thing Obama wanted to do was commit to another open-ended military deployment in the Middle East. As former Clinton (and later Obama) administration official Martin Indyk explained to *The New York Times,* Libya was inevitably on everyone's mind: "If a Benghazi-style massacre is threatened, we would have to consider a humanitarian intervention under the same principle. Hard to imagine at this point when the death toll is 400. But if it rises to tens of thousands?"[15] It was not a question Obama wanted to answer.

After intense internal debate about how to handle the protests spreading across North Africa and the Middle East, on May 19—in a speech originally intended to focus on efforts to promote Arab-Israeli peace—Obama embraced democratic reform in the region. Speaking at the State Department, he stated that it would be the "policy of the United States to promote reform and transition to democracy. . . . Our support for these principles is not a secondary interest" but "a top priority that must be translated into concrete actions." Noting that transitions were already well advanced in Tunisia, Libya, and Egypt, Obama added that "support must also extend to nations where transitions have yet to take place"—a clear reference to Syria.

Still concerned about calling for regime change without the will to bring it about, Obama stopped short of an outright call for Assad's departure and maintained that "the future of Syria must be determined by its people." But, he added, "President Bashar al-Assad is standing in their way. His calls for dialogue and reform have rung hollow while he is imprisoning, torturing, and slaughtering his own people." Assad, Obama said, "can lead the transition or get out of the way."[16]

As Assad's crackdown grew ever more brutal over the summer of 2011, more voices within the administration started to make the case for going beyond vague statements that Assad had "lost legitimacy" or was "not indispensable" and explicitly calling on him to step down.[17] The regime's killing spree had reached the point where some administration officials came to conclude it was becoming unsustainable *not* to call for Assad's departure. Pressed by colleagues making that case, Deputy National Security Adviser Ben Rhodes, responsible for communications in the White House, concluded that "there was a moral stance to be taken, and a political message to be sent that Assad was irredeemable in the eyes of the free world." Rhodes and other senior officials knew that Assad "wasn't going to heed our command, but we had issued similar calls regarding Mubarak and Gaddafi, Clinton was on board, and the Treasury Department had a stronger package of sanctions ready to go."[18] Administration officials also knew that the United States still did not have a plan to force Assad from power, but they thought that problem might be mitigated by the fact that Assad's days seemed to be numbered in any case. Syria analysts and experts throughout the government consistently assessed that Assad could be toppled by the Syrian opposition within four to six months, and the "prevailing belief," as Fred Hof put it, "was that Assad would not last too long. If the Arab Spring had swept away Mubarak and others, and all these people were giants, who was Assad to resist this tidal force?"[19] Not long after I took over the Middle East portfolio at the White House in March 2013, one of the government's most experienced Syria hands assured me that Assad would be gone by Christmas.

Obama himself remained skeptical, but he said he would support the call for Assad to step down if key allies joined him in making it. He spoke to Chancellor Angela Merkel of Germany and President Nicolas Sarkozy of France on August 5, and to Prime Minister David Cameron of the U.K. on August 13, and they all agreed to issue their own joint call for Assad to step aside.[20] Turkey, a potentially important player that had invested heavily in diplomatic outreach to Assad, asked for a few more weeks to try to persuade the Syrian leader to reform, but U.S. patience had finally run out. The White House issued the statement, and regime change was again officially the policy of the United States.[21]

Given how things turned out, was Obama wrong to have called on Assad to step aside if he didn't have the will or the means to force him to do so? Obama himself rejects the notion, arguing that "denouncing a brutal regime's mistreatment of its people does not oblige the United States to invade the country and install a government you prefer."[22] That is certainly true, and it would have been irresponsible for the United States not to denounce Assad's horrifying treatment of his own citizens or to seek to impose costs on him for such behavior. But it is also true—even more in retrospect than at the time—that specifically calling for Assad to step aside raised expectations among the Syrian opposition and its supporters that the world's strongest power was going to take action to accomplish that goal, as it was doing at that very moment in Libya. After Obama avoided calling for Assad's departure for six months in part to avoid raising such expectations, doing so in a formal, prepared statement of U.S. government policy—a step that went well beyond "denouncing a brutal regime"—inevitably implied a shift in actions as well as goals. It was a signal to the U.S. government to start pursuing those goals and to Syrian protesters that it was going to do so. "With what Obama said," commented one Syrian opposition activist the day of Obama's statement, "it's going to become widespread now. I think we're going to see lots of people on the streets."[23] He was right about that, but not in the way he or others had in mind.

The U.S. embrace of the goal of Assad's departure raised the question of what the administration would do to try to bring it about. With Qadhafi still at large and the Libya war dragging on, Obama remained reluctant to get involved in another potential quagmire, a reluctance widely shared in the Pentagon, which of course hadn't been enthusiastic about the Libya intervention in the first place.[24] Robert Gates, who had sarcastically asked his colleagues if he could finish the two wars in Iraq and Afghanistan before starting another in Libya, had stepped down as secretary of defense in June 2011, but his successor, Leon Panetta, was no more eager to deploy U.S. forces to another war in the Middle East. Pentagon planners did not see viable military options for getting rid of Assad short of going to war, and the chairman of the Joint Chiefs of Staff, Martin Dempsey, warned that even a limited no-fly zone would have to deal with sophisticated Syrian air defenses and require as many as seventy thousand troops.[25] At State, Clinton came under increasing pressure from aides such as Robert Ford who warned that failing to support rebels perceived to be moderate and friendly to the United States would allow Islamist extremists to take over the opposition and would forge links with terrorists in Iraq. But Clinton was still dealing with the aftermath of military intervention in Libya and a rocky political transition in Egypt, limiting her enthusiasm for getting more involved militarily in Syria. According to her top foreign policy adviser, Jake Sullivan, "There was a divide within the administration, 'principals' versus those who worked the Syria file. Experts were more forward-leaning; principals more cautious." Administration Syria specialists like Ford, Hof, and the National Security Council's Syria team asked how the administration could justify acting against Qadhafi but not Assad, but as Sullivan recalled, "no one convinced Obama that attacking Assad would achieve a result better than the anarchy following NATO's bombardment of Libya."[26]

As an alternative to direct U.S. military intervention, in August 2012 the CIA director, David Petraeus—with support from Clinton, Panetta, and Dempsey—presented the president with a plan for arming and training the opposition.[27] The plan consisted of weapons deliveries and training for vetted, non-extremist opposition forces. To those—including Obama and the U.S. ambassador to the United Nations, Susan Rice—who doubted the plan's effectiveness and feared such arms could end up in the wrong hands, Clinton and Petraeus "argued that there was a big difference between Qatar and Saudi Arabia dumping weapons into the country and the United States responsibly training and equipping a non-extremist rebel force. And getting control of that mess was a big part of our plan's rationale." Clinton admitted that "the goal was not to build up a force strong enough to defeat the regime. Rather the idea was to give us a partner on the ground we could work with that could do enough to convince Assad and his backers that a military victory was impossible."[28] Panetta noted that he, Clinton, and Petraeus "believed that withholding weapons was impeding our ability to develop sway with those groups and subjecting them to withering fire from the regime."[29] Bill Burns, now the deputy secretary of state, also participated in the meeting and agreed that the case for doing more to bolster the opposition was "never about victory on the battlefield. It was about trying to demonstrate to Assad and his outside backers that he couldn't win militarily, and that his political options were going to narrow the longer the fighting continued. It was a way to manage the opposition, and to use our provision of training and equipment to help make them a more coherent and responsive force."[30]

Despite the almost unanimous support from his top advisers, Obama rejected the proposal. He worried about weapons falling into the wrong hands and was skeptical that hastily formed, inexperienced opposition forces could defeat a standing army backed by determined allies. As he later told Jeffrey Goldberg of *The Atlantic,* "When you have a professional army that is well armed and sponsored by two large states [Iran and Russia] who have huge stakes in this, and they are fighting against a farmer, a carpenter, an engineer who started out as protesters and suddenly now see themselves in the midst of a civil conflict . . . The notion that we could have—in a clean way that didn't commit U.S. military forces—changed the equation on the ground there was never true."[31] Obama also argued that the historical track record of U.S.-backed opposition forces was poor. "Very early in this process," he said later, "I actually asked the CIA to analyze examples of America financing and supplying arms to an insurgency in a country that actually worked out well. And they couldn't come up with much."[32] According to *The New York Times,* "The C.I.A. review . . . found that the agency's aid to insurgencies had generally failed in instances when no Americans worked on the ground with the foreign forces in the conflict zones, as is the administration's plan for training Syrian rebels."[33] One of the few places where U.S. armed support for insurgents had allegedly "worked" was Afghanistan, but the precedent of armed jihadis morphing into the Taliban and al-Qaeda did not exactly make Obama more comfortable with the proposal.[34]

The Petraeus plan would end up being the first of many "if only" moments in Syria, seen in retrospect as missed opportunities to act more decisively to get rid of the regime. Indeed, as Rhodes observed, "in the years that followed, this proposal would take on a mythical status as a road not taken that could have led to a different outcome."[35] Even Clinton herself would later say that "the failure to help build up a credible fighting force of the people who were the originators of the protests against Assad . . . left a big vacuum, which the jihadists have now filled."[36] But Rhodes also rightly points out that "the reality is that it was a small-scale recommendation to engage a portion of the opposition, providing them with a fraction of the support that Russia and Iran were providing the Assad regime."[37] It was telling that even proponents of the plan didn't think it would lead to Assad's departure, but instead focused on things like gaining "sway" with the opposition or preventing the opposition's defeat so that Assad would negotiate. As with all hypotheticals, we will never know for sure how the war might have evolved had Obama approved the plan, but the fact that later and far bigger efforts to arm and train the opposition—even when the regime had been weakened by years of war, attrition, and defections—never managed to force Assad to accept even a degree of power sharing, let alone drive him from power, suggests it is doubtful that a modest arm and train program in late 2012 would have made a decisive difference.[38]

The administration also tried diplomatic means to push Assad out, including by trying to persuade Russia to accept the need for him to go, much as it acquiesced in NATO's effort to overthrow Qadhafi. An apparent opportunity to do so arose when Russia surprisingly agreed to attend a UN-sponsored meeting in Geneva in late June 2012—with the participation of France, Germany, the U.K., Italy, the UAE, Saudi Arabia, Qatar, Turkey, Iraq, Kuwait, the EU, China, and the Arab League—to discuss a power-sharing plan drafted by former UN secretary-general Kofi Annan. Iran, the Assad regime's other main sponsor, was excluded from the meeting at U.S. insistence, partly because of other regional disputes but also because U.S. officials knew that Tehran would never agree to the U.S. objective of Assad's negotiated departure.

While not explicitly calling for Assad's departure, the plan called for the creation of a Syrian "government of national unity" that "could include members of the present government and the opposition and other groups" but would exclude "those whose continued presence and participation would undermine the credibility of the transition and jeopardize stability and reconciliation."[39] The latter was shorthand for members of the Assad regime with blood on their hands. In combative bilateral meetings with Secretary Clinton and in the wider discussions, the Russian foreign minister, Sergei Lavrov, stuck to Russia's hard-line position that it wasn't for outsiders to choose Syria's leaders and that any cease-fire would have to start with the "rebellious" opposition rather than the "legitimate" regime.[40] But after two days of vigorous back-and-forth, Russia agreed to the establishment of a "transitional governing body" that would "exercise full executive powers." The new body, the final Geneva communiqué said, "could include members of the present government and the opposition and other groups and shall be formed on the basis of mutual consent."[41]

For Clinton and other U.S. diplomats (as well as for the European and Arab participants), the principle of "mutual consent" was important because it meant that Assad had to go, as there was no way the opposition would accept his role in the transition.[42] I was personally surprised they had agreed to it, having heard Lavrov and other Russian officials insist repeatedly they would never call on Assad to leave. But it was quickly clear that Russia, in fact, had a very different interpretation of the text—an early indication of Moscow's deep opposition to regime change. Deflating U.S. and others' hopes, Lavrov told the press immediately after the meeting that the group's final communiqué included no demand for Assad to step down—for Russia, "mutual consent" meant Assad had to agree as well—and pointed out that the final text did not include Annan's proposed call to exclude anyone who would "undermine negotiations on a new government."[43] For years thereafter, including at subsequent—and ultimately futile—follow-on negotiations in Geneva, U.S. diplomats would insist that the Geneva communiqué meant that Assad could have no role in Syria's future government, while the Russians would deny any such thing. Far from Russia's joining U.S. efforts to oust Assad—a constant unfulfilled hope of U.S. diplomacy—Moscow would end up as the Syrian dictator's savior and protector.

The effort to work with Russia would prove to be another area where the United States underestimated the difficulty of regime change in Syria. Not only did Moscow under Vladimir Putin want to reestablish itself as a major player in the Middle East and to limit American influence there, but its opposition to the very principle of regime change—notwithstanding its abstention on Libya, which it came to regret—was profound. Putin, who had returned to the Kremlin in 2012, had hated seeing pro-Russian governments ousted in Serbia in 2000, Georgia in 2003, Ukraine in 2005, and Kyrgyzstan in 2010, and he was troubled by the way NATO got rid of Qadhafi in Libya in 2011. By 2012, Putin had seen enough, and he was determined to prevent regime change from happening in Syria (as he would be in Ukraine, in 2014). From Russia's point of view, the idea that local rebellions against dictators could lead the United States and its NATO allies to use military force to oust unpopular dictatorships was unfathomable—not least lest discontented Russians get similar ideas. U.S. support for protesters after flawed Duma elections in December 2011, after all, had stung Putin (and made him determined for revenge against Hillary Clinton, whom he falsely blamed for having incited the protesters).[44]

Russia also feared—not unreasonably, in this case—that if Assad did fall, he would be replaced not with a stable, pro-Western democracy (which would be "bad enough," from Putin's point of view) but with chaos and extremism as in places like Afghanistan and Somalia.[45] Thus whereas Russian officials always insisted that they had no love lost for Assad, in reality Russia was never really open to alternatives to him, and U.S. officials were mistaken ever to believe that it was. Hopeful American diplomats always welcomed the first part of Russia's discourse on Syria—"We are not wedded to Assad"—but failed to take adequate account of the rest: "But it's not for us to determine Syria's leader, and we won't help push him out (so that you can put your allies in his place)."

One reason why it proved harder to topple the Syrian regime than many expected was that officials and analysts underestimated Assad's resilience and misread the nature of his regime. It was not a new problem. A decade earlier, with neoconservative hubris at its peak, former George W. Bush speechwriter David Frum and former Reagan administration Defense Department official Richard Perle claimed, "If all our problems were as easy as Syria, the war on terror would have ended a year ago." Their "only question" about Syria—given its weak economy, energy dependence, and presumed fear of U.S. military power—was, "Why have we put up with it as long as we have?"[46] But the notion that Assad could so easily be forced from power, or even that a political compromise with him might be possible, turned out to be deeply misguided.

In contrast with his father, Hafez al-Assad, a career military officer who had famously killed up to thirty thousand people in the city of Hama in February 1982, Bashar was seen by some as not having the stomach to fight.[47] According to this assessment, the "easygoing," "gentleman-like" Bashar wanted to live the quiet life of an eye doctor in London (a branch of medicine he allegedly chose because he didn't like the sight of blood). And he found himself as Syria's president only because his brother Bassel, who had been groomed for the post, had been killed in a car accident in 1994.[48] This led to the misplaced hope that Bashar could somehow be pressured into either sharing power or giving it up entirely, perhaps persuaded to abandon Syria for a life of luxury in exile with his glamorous, British-born wife, Asma. But that proved to be a misreading of both Syria and Assad, who saw leaving or even sharing power as a certain death sentence. Instead, as journalist Sam Dagher noted, the younger Assad had internalized "the regime's most important maxim: To stay in power you must maintain people's fear of the state and its tools of repression, notwithstanding your promises of reform and the margins of freedom you permit."[49] If anything, Bashar had to take an even tougher line than his father to make up for the legitimacy he lacked.

Syria was not like Egypt or Tunisia, where dictators left power mostly peacefully, or even like Libya, where Qadhafi had no major sectarian cards to play or powerful outside allies to rely on. Instead—and more like Saddam Hussein's

Iraq—it was a dictatorship in which power was maintained by a minority (in this case Alawite) through the ruthless use of force, intimidation, and manipulation of sectarian divisions. Notwithstanding its criminality and corruption and miserable economic performance, the regime maintained significant support from minorities (not just Alawites, but Christians, Druze, and others) who feared that regime change would leave them vulnerable to the country's Sunni majority—a fear understandably fueled by the precedent in Iraq, where it was the Sunnis who lost power and position to a sectarian Shia majority. Many moderate Sunnis, including among the business community, also stuck with the regime, if only out of fear of the alternative. As former Netherlands Syria envoy Nikolaos van Dam has pointed out, "The power of the regime has been systematically underestimated by many Western politicians and others as well. This was partly a result of wishful thinking and partly a lack of knowledge of a regime that had been able to gather experience for over half a century on how to stay in power in the most unscrupulous manner. Appointing loyal supporters at sensitive key positions, eliminating (assassinating or imprisoning) those who were even only suspected of opposing the regime, has enhanced its power position for a long time."[50]

Proponents of using military force in Syria often described their objectives not as regime change or Assad's defeat but as a means to "compel [Assad] to the negotiating table," "initiate diplomacy," or provide "breathing space in which decent leaders can begin to consolidate power."[51] Officials in the Situation Room sometimes proposed measures that would "get Assad's attention" or serve the purpose of a "brushback pitch" in baseball, designed to warn a batter to step back to avoid potential harm. The flaw in such thinking was that for Assad "diplomacy" was an effort to remove him from power, and "political transition" was shorthand for regime change. The issue wasn't getting his attention or getting him to the negotiating table; it was taking away his power, his wealth, and possibly his life, which would have required more than economic pressure or a warning shot.

Bashar's determination to fight and confidence he could succeed were also bolstered by his ability to get backing not just from Russia but from Iran, which also differentiated Syria from other "Arab Spring" countries. For Tehran, Syria was a rare ally in the region and a critical air and land bridge to Hezbollah, Iran's powerful, Lebanon-based proxy force, and Assad knew how much Iran needed him. In the spring of 2013, with U.S. officials still optimistic about opposition military gains, Assad called in more than two thousand battle-hardened Hezbollah fighters in a campaign to take back opposition-held Qusair, a critical outpost along the regime supply lines between Damascus and Aleppo.[52] The defeat of the rebels at Qusair was a stark further sign that opposition escalation would be met not by capitulation or compromise but by counter-escalation by the regime and its backers in Tehran and Moscow. It tested whether the United States and other opposition supporters would themselves be prepared to counter-escalate, with all the consequences that doing so would entail.[53]

One advocate within the Obama administration for more robust efforts to oust Assad—even in the face of this resistance—was the new secretary of state, John Kerry. Kerry came in, he told me at the time, determined to "move the White House" on Syria, a reference to the perception—and in fact the reality—that officials at the State Department were more supportive of intervention in Syria than President Obama and his top NSC officials. This State-NSC gap resulted in part from bureaucratic politics—the fact that the diplomats at State were the ones constantly engaging with often sympathetic opposition figures and allies in the region appealing for help, while the White House was generally more attuned to domestic constraints, public and congressional opinion, the Pentagon's reluctance to take military action, and competing priorities.

When I joined Kerry on a March 2013 trip to Britain, France, Germany, Italy, Turkey, Egypt, Saudi Arabia, and the United Arab Emirates, I saw just as he did how desperate regional partners were for greater U.S. involvement, practically pleading with the United States to put "skin in the game." They said the opposition needed a "team captain"—an expression often used by King Abdullah of Jordan—and only the United States could play that role. Such pleas would have had an impact on any U.S. diplomat, and they bolstered Kerry's arguments for U.S. action and reinforced the sense that others would wage war on Syria even if the United States declined to get involved.

In the case of Syria, these bureaucratic factors were magnified by the differing personalities, temperaments, and worldviews of the president and the secretary of state. In contrast to Obama's more pessimistic, "realist" worldview and cautious approach to international military engagement, Kerry was an energetic, can-do optimist who rarely saw a problem he did not think he could solve. Perhaps ironic for someone who had originally become a public figure by concluding that military efforts in Vietnam had failed, when it came to Syria, Kerry was convinced that U.S. military power could be effectively deployed to bolster diplomacy.[54] In the U.S. policy debate, the next several years would be marked by Kerry—along with other top officials at State (including Deputy Secretary Burns and Undersecretary for Political Affairs Wendy Sherman)—pressing vigorously for greater U.S. engagement in Syria, and Obama—along with top officials at the White House (led by

Rice and Chief of Staff Denis McDonough)—resisting steps that they feared would lead the United States down a slippery slope toward war. Rice herself would later observe that when she was national security adviser from 2013 to 2017, "the Principals fought over Syria longer and harder than on any issue during my tenure. John Kerry, [CIA director] John Brennan, and Samantha Power argued for the U.S. to do more—provide more lethal weapons to the rebels, take targeted strikes against Assad or his air force, and, perhaps, establish safe zones for civilians. Others, including me and Denis McDonough, Secretary Ash Carter, and Chairman of the Joint Chiefs Martin Dempsey and later Joe Dunford, were equally tortured by the suffering in Syria but opposed deeper U.S. military involvement."[55] Obama himself, like everyone involved in Syria policy, agonized over the suffering of Syrian civilians, but he remained skeptical about America's ability to positively change the course of events without bearing costs and creating consequences that had little public or congressional support.

Obama's skepticism did not prevent him from tasking the administration with constantly considering, and in many cases ultimately approving, measures to increase pressure on Assad. In the spring of 2013, an NSC-led interagency process focused on consideration of what participants called "accelerants"—measures that might speed up Assad's departure, still seen by most to be both inevitable and necessary. Obama's critics (both inside and outside the government) insisted that "between nothing and invasion lie many intermediate measures."[56] Many such measures—from the direct use of U.S. military force to arming and training the opposition, possible covert actions, stepped-up sanctions, or diplomatic initiatives such as official recognition of the Syrian opposition—were considered exhaustively.

High on the list were proposals to impose no-fly zones.

Proponents of such measures—including members of Congress, pundits, and former military and civilian officials—argued that doing so could tip the military balance in the opposition's favor and save civilian lives.[57] But while the Pentagon dutifully prepared options and presented them for consideration, it remained skeptical about costs, effectiveness, and the potential for escalation, and so did Obama. In a July 19, 2013, letter to Senator Carl Levin of the Armed Services Committee, Chairman Dempsey wrote that a no-fly zone over Syria would require "hundreds of ground- and sea-based aircraft, intelligence and electronic warfare support, and enablers for refueling and communications."[58] He estimated the costs of such a deployment at "$500 million initially, averaging as much as a billion dollars per month over the course of a year." Dempsey also worried about what some strategists called "catastrophic success": "We must anticipate and be prepared for the unintended consequences of our action. Should the regime's institutions collapse in the absence of a viable opposition, we could inadvertently empower extremists or unleash the very chemical weapons we seek to control." General Philip Breedlove, NATO's supreme allied commander, U.S. European Command, also made the case that a no-fly zone was "quite frankly an act of war" that would "absolutely be harder than Libya."[59]

As an alternative to comprehensive no-fly zones, military planners also examined more limited options such as cratering runways, hitting planes on the ground, or using Patriot missile systems and/or standoff weapons based in Turkey or other neighboring countries to stop Syrian planes from flying. But all these options carried their own limits and complications. Cratered runways could quickly and easily be repaired. Syrian aircraft on the ground could be targeted, but even the successful destruction of airplanes would just lead Assad to conduct his air strikes with harder-to-target helicopters, missiles, and rockets. Trying to impose a no-fly zone using Patriots in Turkey would not only leave significant gaps in coverage but also make the United States dependent on Ankara—which by this point had turned decisively against Assad and wanted to pull the United States into the very direct military conflict Obama sought to avoid. And in any case, military officials assessed that around 90 percent of the civilians killed in Syria were victims not of air strikes but of direct fire from machine guns, artillery, and short-range rockets, so even eliminating the regime's air advantage would not significantly reduce the killing.[60] This was the same problem that in Libya led NATO to go well beyond a no-fly zone and instead target Qadhafi's ground forces and command posts. Indeed, Obama worried that if he approved the no-fly zones, it would not be long before critics demanded he take further steps, including direct strikes on the regime. "If you eliminate one capability of a potential adversary," Dempsey pointed out, you could soon be asked to "do more against the rest."[61]

The administration also considered options for creating "safe zones" for Syrian refugees and opposition forces. Advocates of such measures argued that they would not only provide refuge for displaced civilians but could be used as places where opposition forces could regroup.[62] To avoid the risk of escalation, or bolstering bad actors, some proponents of these measures proposed conditioning U.S. assistance on "pledges from groups to work together and respect democratic principles" or on using weapons only "defensively."[63]

But these proposals, too, raised serious questions to which the administration never had satisfying answers. Who would provide the forces to police the zones, given the strong public and congressional opposition to "boots on the ground" (especially after Benghazi), Europe's inability to find forces even for Libya, and the deep rivalries among regional powers? When

U.S.-backed forces within the zones inevitably committed human rights abuses, partnered with extremists, or launched offensive attacks—regardless of whatever commitments they might have made as preconditions for U.S. support—would we really cut them off? If Assad attacked the zones—rightly seeing them as places where opposition fighters would regroup before pursuing attacks on the regime—would U.S. forces strike the regime directly in response? If strikes against the regime led to extremist groups advancing on Damascus alongside our proxies, would we strike them too—resulting in air strikes against both sides at the same time? (This surreal scenario came up more than once in the Situation Room.) If action against the Assad regime led Iran-backed Shia militias to start attacking U.S. troops in Iraq, as they did during the Iraq War, would we respond militarily against them and their sponsors in Iran as well? Could the United States agree with the Turks on how to manage a potential zone along their border, given their hostility to the Kurdish fighters in that zone? And what if the regime and other actors just forced populations they didn't want into the safe zone, creating a humanitarian nightmare and making the United States complicit in "ethnic cleansing"? As Deputy National Security Adviser Antony Blinken—who himself supported more extensive U.S. intervention—pointed out, every time he and others advocated for deeper U.S. involvement, Obama would ask what the endgame was, and "no one could answer with confidence that we would not wind up on a slippery slope, getting in deeper and deeper than we intended."[64]

After resisting doing so all spring, on June 13, 2013, the administration did announce an increase in military assistance to Syrians fighting Assad. With opposition forces losing momentum, and following numerous cases of reported chemical weapons use by regime forces, the White House put out a statement by Rhodes announcing that "the President has augmented the provision of non-lethal assistance to the civilian opposition, and also authorized the expansion of our assistance to the Supreme Military Council (SMC), and we will be consulting with Congress on these matters in the coming weeks."[65] The official trigger for this step was the regime's reported use of chemical weapons, which Obama had said would "change his calculus" about intervening in Syria, but it also served the purpose of sending a message to the regime and showing Congress, the public, and allies in the region that the United States was "doing something." Asked in a conference call with reporters if the announcement meant arming the rebels, Rhodes explained that we would not "detail every single type of support that we are providing, but [suffice it] to say it's important to note that it is both the political and the military opposition that . . . is and will be receiving U.S. assistance."[66] The statement followed intensive debate among NSC lawyers about whether U.S. officials could publicly declare that they were providing military assistance to Syrians, because there was no clear legal basis for doing so. In the end, they agreed the statement could be made so long as no specifics were given. This opened the path to a vast expansion of support for Syrian military opposition forces—described later by the then national security adviser, Rice, as "arming and later training vetted Syrian rebels who were fighting Assad"—even if it was one that administration officials could not discuss in any detail at the time.[67] The eventual scope of U.S. military support to the Syrian opposition—later reported to be "one of the costliest covert action programs in the history of the C.I.A." and potentially responsible for tens of thousands of regime or allied casualties—belied the notion that the United States did not intervene in Syria. In fact, it demonstrated all too well that it would take more than military support to the opposition to overthrow the regime or even compel it to compromise.[68]

Another critical moment in the debate about possible military action came on August 21, when the Assad regime fired rockets carrying sarin gas at opposition forces in the Damascus suburb of Ghouta, killing more than fourteen hundred people, including many children. When word of the massacre's scale reached Obama, he said this was the type of attack he was referring to when he had said the previous August that the use of chemical weapons would be a "red line" for him, and he immediately tasked the Pentagon with preparing a military response. When intelligence analysts confirmed later that week with high confidence that it was a chemical weapons (CW) attack and that the regime was responsible—it was important to Obama not to risk a repeat of the reliance on faulty intelligence ahead of the Iraq War—he approved a Pentagon plan to undertake military strikes against Syrian CW production and delivery facilities, with the goal of degrading the CW program and deterring future use.

On August 29, following the British Parliament's refusal to support U.K. participation in the strikes, I joined Obama in the Oval Office for his calls to the British prime minister, Cameron, and the French president, François Hollande. Given the respective historical U.S. relationships with the two countries, both of which I had dealt with closely for years, it was striking for me to hear the French leader pledge unreservedly to join the United States in military action while the British leader sheepishly conveyed his regrets. Immediately after the calls, Obama pulsed a small group of advisers (the group included Vice President Biden, National Security Adviser Rice, Homeland Security Adviser Lisa Monaco, Ben Rhodes, me, and the NSC official responsible for Europe, Karen Donfried), and we all agreed that military strikes should proceed notwithstanding the British Parliament's decision. Obama himself said little but did not disagree. After chairing an NSC meeting the next day to make final preparations, he ordered the military to plan to conduct the strikes—dozens of Tomahawk cruise missiles fired from five *Arleigh Burke*–class destroyers in the Mediterranean—that weekend.[69]

At the last minute, however, Obama had second thoughts and decided to request congressional authorization to undertake military action.[70] He later gave a number of reasons for his change of heart: UN weapons inspectors were still on the ground and at risk; a missile strike would degrade but not eliminate the CW program; the risk that Assad might emerge stronger after surviving limited strikes (requiring the United States potentially to have to strike over and over again—the "slippery slope"); the British decision not to participate; and, importantly, the absence of clear domestic and international legal bases for the strikes.[71] As a presidential candidate, Obama had taken a firm position on the limits of presidential authority to use military force without congressional backing—a fact of which the White House counsel, Kathryn Ruemmler, reminded him during the NSC meeting, to his evident irritation—and he wanted legislators to share the responsibility for any military action. When it became clear in early September that congressional authorization was not forthcoming, Obama seized the opportunity of a Russian proposal to work with the Syrian government to voluntarily give up its chemical weapons, and plans for military action were again set aside.[72]

For years afterward, critics would look back at this—just as with the Petraeus train and equip plan—as another "if only" moment. "If we had bombed as was planned, things would be different today," said the French prime minister, Manuel Valls, in 2016.[73] The American analyst Robert Kagan agreed, asserting a year later that "the world would be a different place today if Obama had carried out his threat to attack Syria."[74] As president, Donald Trump would even go so far as to assert, "If

President Obama had crossed his stated Red Line in the Sand, the Syrian disaster would have ended long ago!" It was a garbled and hyperbolic claim that was inconsistent with his own earlier opposition to air strikes, but one that was not so far off from what a lot of more serious analysts also believed.[75] John Kerry later wrote that he "thought that these strikes could create a diplomatic opening and bring countries together around an endgame that could lead to a post-Assad Syria with the institutions of the State preserved. Assad's protectors in Iran and Russia would learn there were limits to Assad's freedom of action and ability to gain advantage on the ground." Kerry "believed that if Russia's calculation changed, they might encourage either a negotiated exit for Assad and the creation of a transition government (more acceptable regime elements alongside secular opposition representatives) or an election in which the people of Syria would select their future leader. Most of all, Assad might see that he couldn't gas his way out of a civil war."[76]

In fact, however, as with the Petraeus plan, there is little reason to believe that limited air strikes designed to deter and degrade chemical weapons use would have done much to advance the cause of regime change in Syria. In a similar operation in Iraq in 1998, after all, hundreds of cruise missile and air strikes on Iraqi military sites degraded Iraq's potential WMD capabilities but had little effect on Saddam Hussein's rule, which ended only when the United States invaded Iraq in 2003. Similarly, in Libya, the opening U.S. salvo of more than a hundred cruise missiles effectively eliminated the country's air defense system and served to send a message to Qadhafi, but he would nonetheless fight on for another eight months, and Libya was a much easier target for regime change than Syria. Destroying some valued regime assets or chemical weapons delivery systems as planned might well have deterred further use of sarin gas (I supported the strikes for that reason), but as Trump's own limited strikes in April 2017 and April 2018 would demonstrate, this would not have significantly altered the battlefield balance or in any way threatened Assad's hold on power.[77] The notion that air strikes alone could lead to the regime's demise—let alone lead to a stable replacement—was another case of advocates of regime change putting their faith in hope more than logic or experience (or, in some cases, advocating a policy designed to lead to military escalation).

The continued lack of success of efforts to strengthen the opposition versus Assad—and ongoing congressional and allied pressure for action—led President Obama in May 2014 to propose the new, $5 billion Counterterrorism Partnerships Fund to strengthen Syria's neighbors that included $500 million for a train and equip program under the Department of Defense. The idea was that the addition of Defense Department resources could significantly bolster the existing efforts to strengthen the opposition militarily and that an overt program would at least allow the administration to point to visible efforts to do so, thereby not just responding to public and congressional criticism but signaling to Assad that the United States was committed to the opposition. I and some others at the NSC argued internally that the program's international legal basis was highly questionable (it had no UN authorization and could not really be described as self-defense), that it might "cannibalize" resources from other efforts to arm and train the opposition, and that the United States would have responsibility for protecting the force if it came under attack, as it surely would, given its mission. Obama appeared to share such concerns but ultimately approved the program, under heavy political pressure to act more assertively and apparently convinced that if the United States didn't more visibly support the opposition, others would just do so anyway. Initially conceived for the purpose of putting military pressure on Assad, however, the force's mission was changed in the summer of 2014 to target the surging Islamic State, which solidified the legal basis but made it much harder to find recruits, most of whom were motivated to fight only Assad, not their fellow Sunnis who were themselves fighting the regime. The recruitment effort proved so challenging that CENTCOM's commander, General Lloyd Austin, had to admit at a September 2015 congressional hearing that even after months of recruiting, the force consisted of only "four or five" trained counter-IS fighters.[78] Even when a somewhat larger group was assembled shortly after arriving in Syria, it was reportedly ambushed by the al-Nusra Front, which stole its ammunition, trucks, and equipment.[79]

The effort was such a debacle that the White House ended up distancing itself from its own proposal, essentially admitting that Obama had never believed in it in the first place. "Many of our critics had proposed this specific option as essentially the cure-all for all of the policy challenges that we're facing in Syria right now," the press secretary, Josh Earnest, said. "That is not something that this administration ever believed, but it is something that our critics will have to answer for."[80] If the Assad regime was going to be ousted, it was going to take a lot more than a modest training program focused on the Islamic State to do it.

By mid-2014, it was becoming increasingly clear that U.S. policy was not working, and was not going to work. The United States and its allies had a political objective, Assad's departure, but were not prepared to devote anywhere near the necessary means to achieve that goal. And it was also becoming clear that the strategy behind that goal—increasing support to the Syrian opposition to force Assad to accept a "political transition"—was based on wishful thinking about the determination of the regime to fight to the bitter end, the capacity of the opposition to drive Assad from power, and the role that outside actors such as Russia and Iran could and would play in protecting the regime.

It had also become clear—as Obama had argued from the start—that creating an armed opposition capable of toppling a determined regime was a far greater, and riskier, task than proponents of regime change in Syria claimed. In theory, as an alternative to direct military intervention, it made eminent sense to "identify elements on the ground most effective, easily supplied, and amenable to help," or to "build a new Syrian opposition capable of defeating both Bashar al-Assad and the more militant Islamists," as various advocates of arming the opposition proposed.[81] In reality, however, the Syrian opposition was weak, deeply divided, and outgunned by Assad's Russia- and Iran-backed standing army and sectarian militias, and the idea of creating a powerful, unified, "moderate" military opposition to Assad was a fantasy. The opposition was made up of as many as fifteen hundred insurgent groups with conflicting goals and no central command, and while the United States made extensive efforts to bring them together, it could never overcome the determination of outside actors such as Saudi Arabia, the UAE, Qatar, and Turkey to pursue their own agendas and support their respective clients, many of whom were deeply opposed to one another.[82] As Swedish Syrian expert Aron Lund caustically noted, "Using a chaotic, hundred-headed Sunni guerrilla force to tweak the Syrian president's personal cost-benefit analysis of a political transition was like trying to perform heart surgery with a chainsaw, and blood soon spurted all over the map."[83] Kerry tried valiantly to coordinate all these diverse groups through regular meetings with the countries that were supporting the opposition. Although cooperation did get better over time, the deep differences among them were ultimately impossible to overcome, and they all rightly gambled that the United States was not going to cut strategic ties with them over this issue. Pledges by all participants to channel all their military support through the opposition's Supreme Military Council were consistently violated as each sponsoring power sought to empower its proxies while swearing to the United States and others that it was supporting only groups that were vetted and collectively approved. And while regional partners who wanted to intensify the fight against Assad always claimed to be able to call on large numbers of vetted and capable fighters in the "Free Syrian Army," such forces never seemed to materialize.

As lessons from Afghanistan some twenty-five years earlier might have suggested, arming jihadist rebels would inevitably have unintended consequences, and preventing extremists from dominating the opposition would prove to be an impossible task—perhaps not surprising under conditions of a savage civil war.[84] "All of the opposition worked with [the al-Qaeda affiliate] Nusra," according to Syria specialist Charles Lister, "because they were very good on the battlefield."[85] Regional actors—determined to overthrow Assad at all costs—proved willing to fund, arm, and otherwise support those extremists, including with some of the weapons that were flowing out of Libya. "We had partners," noted Assistant Secretary of Defense Derek Chollet, "who were just throwing all sorts of resources at the conflict. Many of those resources ended up in the wrong hands."[86] As *The New York Times* reported, "Most of the arms shipped at the behest of Saudi Arabia and Qatar to supply Syrian rebel groups fighting the government of Bashar al-Assad are going to hard-line Islamic jihadists, and not the more secular opposition groups that the West wants to bolster, according to American officials and Middle Eastern diplomats. . . . 'The opposition groups that are receiving the most of the lethal aid are exactly the ones we don't want to have it,' said one American official."[87] In an October 3, 2014, speech at Harvard University, Vice President Joe Biden was distinctly off message, but not far from the truth, when he said many of our allies in the region were "so determined to take down Assad and essentially have a proxy Sunni-Shia war . . . they poured hundreds of millions of dollars and tens of thousands of tons of weapons into anyone who would fight against Assad. Except that the people who were being supplied were al-Nusra and al Qaeda and the extremist elements of jihadis coming from other parts of the world."[88] The decision to try to overthrow Assad had unleashed forces that U.S. officials had not foreseen and did not have the power to control.

In September 2015, with opposition forces now dominated by extremists and armed with heavier weapons advancing toward Damascus, Russia responded by deploying hundreds of troops and heavy equipment (including T-90 battle tanks and armored personnel carriers), dozens of fixed-and rotary-wing aircraft (including Su-30s, Su-24s, and Su-25s), fourteen helicopters (Mi-24 Hind gunships and Mi-17 transport helicopters), and naval assets including guided-missile destroyers and supply ships armed with cruise missiles.[89] The deployment was the logical consequence of Moscow's strong determination to prevent Assad from falling and a demonstration that opposition escalation would be met by counter-escalation unless the United States and others were prepared to counter-escalate in turn, which they were not. Thus the prospect of ending the Assad regime diminished further, because from then on even limited military options such as setting up a no-fly zone would mean dealing with even more sophisticated Russian air defense systems and killing Russian military personnel—leading to a potentially serious military clash with a major military power.

Arguments for the use of force, and continued efforts to get rid of the regime, did not go away entirely. Kerry continued to advocate military strikes to "send a message" to Assad and enhance diplomatic leverage, but as one press report put it, Obama was "not moved, and not amused."[90] In June 2016, several dozen U.S. diplomats used the State Department "dissent channel" to argue for "a judicious use of stand-off and air weapons, which would undergird and drive a more focused and hard-nosed U.S.-led diplomatic process." They called for "the use of military force as an option to enforce [cease-fire arrangements] and compel the Syrian regime to abide by its terms as well as to negotiate a political solution in good faith." The diplomats' frustration was understandable, but by then the concept of Assad negotiating in good faith was implausible, and it was hard to see what realistic diplomatic compromise could conceivably result from a "judicious" use of force.[91]

When in the summer of 2016 the Assad regime, backed by Russian airpower, launched a relentless assault on the major northern city of Aleppo—the eastern half of which had been in opposition hands since the start of the war—the administration again debated all the previously considered options for using force to stop it, but once again refrained for all the same reasons as before.[92] Kerry, John Brennan, and Samantha Power continued to support air strikes and expanded efforts to arm the Syrian opposition, but Obama refused to approve military action.[93] As horrific as the killing in Aleppo was, he still could not envisage a scenario in which air strikes, shooting down Syrian or Russian planes, or giving more and more advanced arms to the opposition led to anything other than military escalation, a perpetuation of the war, and deeper U.S. involvement in what he believed to be an unwinnable conflict.

Instead, the Obama administration focused its final year

in office on the ongoing campaign against the Islamic State as well as on supporting Syrian refugees, providing humanitarian assistance, stabilizing Syria's neighbors, and attempting to work with Russia to de-escalate the conflict through the negotiation of national cease-fires. Recognizing reality, it had gradually lowered its political objective from "the Assad regime must be replaced" to "Assad and his cronies must go" to "Assad and his cronies must eventually go" to effectively putting off regime change entirely for the foreseeable future. Even Kerry, who had come in determined to intensify efforts to oust Assad and as late as 2016 was still trying to leverage anti-IS military efforts to put political pressure on Assad, admitted that the goal of regime change was now practically out of reach and that the use of military force was off the table. As he told a group of Syrian opposition activists in September 2016, "I think you're looking at three people, four people in the administration who have all argued for use of force, and I lost the argument."[94] The Obama administration had embraced the highly desirable political objective of regime change in Syria, but it never found the means to achieve that goal without bearing costs and risks that it was not prepared to accept. The painful result was that more than five years after Obama had called for Assad to step down, it was Obama who was stepping down, while the Syrian dictator remained in power.

By the time Trump took office in January 2017, regime change in Syria was effectively no longer U.S. policy. Before running for president, Trump tweeted in June 2013 that "we should stay the hell out of Syria, the 'rebels' are just as bad as the current regime," and he strongly urged Obama not to strike Assad over chemical weapons use in September that year before later criticizing him for failing to do so.[95] As a presidential candidate,

Trump blamed "mistakes in Iraq, Egypt and Libya" for helping to "throw the region in chaos" and said "it all began with a dangerous idea that we could make western democracies out of countries that had no experience or interests in becoming a western democracy."[96] Where Syria was concerned, he specifically argued that the Islamic State was a "far bigger problem than Assad," that it was "madness, and idiocy" to be fighting both of them at the same time, and that he would "talk to [Assad]" and "get along with him."[97] In an interview just after his election, Trump explained that his "attitude was you're fighting Syria, Syria is fighting ISIS, and you have to get rid of ISIS. . . . Now we're backing rebels against Syria, and we have no idea who these people are."[98]

Reflecting these views after Trump took office, on March 30, 2017, the U.S. ambassador to the United Nations, Nikki Haley, stated that the administration's "priority is no longer to . . . focus on getting Assad out," while Secretary of State Rex Tillerson explained that the "longer-term status of President Assad will be decided by the Syrian people."[99] When Trump did conduct air strikes against Syria for using chemical weapons in April 2017, he said his "attitude toward Syria and Assad [had] changed very much," but the limited scope of the strikes made clear that regime change was not the objective, a point underscored by senior administration officials.[100] The fact that the targeted CW strikes had little effect on Assad's grip on power and the broader political and military course of the war raised further doubts about any notion that limited bombing could have maximal political effects.

In July 2017, Trump announced on Twitter that he was "ending massive, dangerous and wasteful payments to Syrian rebels fighting Assad," removing any pretense that the United States was still in the business of toppling Assad militarily.[101] Over the next three years, Trump officials would occasionally assert they were still seeking to get rid of Assad—Tillerson, for example, maintained that objective in a major Syria speech in January 2018—but it was far from a priority, and the gap between action and rhetoric was huge.[102] Getting rid of Assad was certainly not anything Trump was going to expend blood or treasure—or risk confrontation with Russia—to achieve.

Further underscoring that regime change was no longer the goal, in December 2018, Trump suddenly announced his intention to withdraw all remaining U.S. troops from Syria and stated—contrary to what many of his top foreign policy officials had only recently been claiming—that their purpose did not even include putting political pressure on Assad. "We have defeated ISIS in Syria," he tweeted on December 19, "my only reason for being there during the Trump presidency."[103] In a video recording issued the same day, he said, "Our boys, our young women, our men—they're coming back, and they're coming back now."[104] The announcement took U.S. allies, partners on the ground, and even senior U.S. officials by surprise, and some—including Secretary of Defense James Mattis and the top administration official responsible for the fight against the Islamic State, Brett McGurk—were so dismayed by the policy shift and the chaotic nature of the decision making that they promptly resigned from the administration. While opposition from Congress, other officials, and the military led Trump to reverse the immediate withdrawal order, the signal of the president's intentions could not have been clearer.

With the United States—the chosen "team captain"—having clearly given up on regime change in Syria, its international partners—most of whom had already reconciled themselves to the reality of living with Assad—did so as well. Turkey—once perhaps the strongest proponent of overthrowing Assad militarily—increasingly prioritized its fight to deny autonomy to the Syrian Kurds and was now working with Russia and Iran on diplomatic solutions that would depend on cooperation with Assad. Saudi Arabia, whose main concern had always been its geopolitical competition with Iran, not repression in Syria, continued to explore the possibility of reconciliation with Assad if he distanced himself from Tehran.[105] In Europe, Britain became consumed with internal debates over Brexit, and after May 2017 a new French president, Emmanuel Macron, criticized France's promotion of regime change in Syria and said "nobody has shown me a legitimate successor to Assad."[106] Jordan and the United Arab Emirates, both concerned more with extremism than with Assad, ended their support for the anti-Assad opposition, and in early 2019—not surprisingly right after Trump had announced the sudden U.S. troop withdrawal—the UAE and Bahrain announced they were reopening their embassies in Damascus and reestablishing diplomatic relations with Syria. In September 2019, a delegation from the Assad regime was warmly greeted by the Arab League leadership at the UN General Assembly meetings in New York, and in October, Iraq joined Lebanon and Tunisia in formally calling for Syria to be readmitted to the Arab League, from which it had been expelled in November 2011.[107] Assad had not been rehabilitated, but for the countries that had put so much pressure on the United States to embrace the goal of regime change in 2011, the pursuit of that goal was effectively over.

And it was over for the United States as well. In October 2019, Trump announced that the United States would allow Turkey to conduct a military operation against its Kurdish enemies in northern Syria and to set up a "safe zone" there. "The endless and ridiculous wars are ENDING!" Trump tweeted before announcing the withdrawal of virtually all U.S. troops from Syria. Without the protection of U.S. forces and under attack by Turkey, the desperate Kurds and Arabs who had fought alongside Americans to defeat the Islamic State had little choice but to turn to Assad for protection and to allow regime forces back onto parts of the nearly one-third of Syrian territory they were controlling. Without firing a shot, Assad's forces promptly returned to parts of the country they had not occupied since the early stages of the war. Starting in December, Assad's air forces, backed by Russia, undertook a furious assault on remaining opposition forces in the northern province of Idlib, as the United States and most of its former partners in Syria looked passively on.[108] Further twists and turns in Syria policy were, no doubt, to be expected. But the goal of regime change, embraced with such hope more than eight years previously, had been set aside.

We can never know how the situation in Syria would have evolved had the United States intervened earlier, more forcefully, and more directly in an effort to oust Bashar al-Assad from power. Proponents of doing so, however, have tended to underestimate the degree of military intervention required to oust a regime like Assad's, the track record of dictators in the region fighting to the death rather than giving up power through a "political transition," the difficulty of limiting the role of extremists in an armed opposition, and the determination of Russia, Iran, and Hezbollah to prevent Assad from falling—even if that meant massacring large numbers of civilians. And the argument that *earlier* support for the opposition would have been effective overlooks the reality that earlier support would almost certainly have also led to *earlier* counter-escalation by Russia and Iran, and to deal with that, the United States and its allies would have had to be prepared to counter-escalate in turn, with all the consequences doing so would entail. The United States could, no doubt, have resolved to do whatever necessary to see regime change through, regardless of how the regime, Russia, Iran, and Hezbollah responded, and then, like in Afghanistan and Iraq, undertaken to try to stabilize a broken Syria in the aftermath of war and in the face of deep divisions and determined opposition. But it is far from clear that such an approach would have prevented mass killing, refugee flows, human rights abuses, and increased extremism, and virtually certain that it would have had other, unpredictable, costs and consequences—including the potential for Afghanistan- or Somalia-like anarchy or Iraq-like insurgency. Those outcomes, in turn, would have required Americans to undertake the costly and indefinite commitments that every relevant precedent suggests would have been required.

All the alternatives to making such commitments were also admittedly more than unappealing, and certainly the course of action chosen—calling for regime change but limiting the means to achieve it—proved catastrophic. What does seem clear is that if the United States was not prepared to escalate significantly in Syria and accept the consequences of doing so, it would have been better off refraining from pursuing regime change in the first place. A policy of sanctioning Assad and his supporters (as leverage for more limited political goals), providing more humanitarian and refugee assistance to Syrians, working to cut off financial flows and foreign fighters behind the extremist opposition (instead of abetting them), deterring chemical weapons use through the threat of force, and pressing the regime and its sponsors to accept at least a degree of de facto regional devolution would have had its own moral and humanitarian costs. But it would have been a vastly better course of action than was an eight-year effort to get rid of Assad that would culminate in grudging acceptance that he would remain in power and regain the territory he had lost. To paraphrase Winston Churchill, living with the Assad regime in the first place might have been the worst possible policy, except for all the others.

CONCLUSION

Why Regime Change in the Middle East Always Goes Wrong

There are a lot of differences among the stories of regime change discussed in this book, but there are some important similarities as well. In every case, the efforts to oust an existing regime and put a better one in its place proved far more costly than predicted, failed to bring about stability (sometimes actually leading to more instability), and produced a wide range of unintended, and undesirable, consequences. As different as each individual episode was, and as varied as were the methods used, the history of regime change in the post–World War II Middle East is a history of repeated patterns, in which policy makers underestimated the challenges of ousting a regime, overstated the threat faced by the United States, embraced the optimistic narratives of exiles or local actors with little power and vested interests, prematurely declared victory, failed to anticipate the chaos that would inevitably ensue after regime collapse, and ultimately found themselves bearing the costs—in some cases more than a trillion dollars and thousands of American lives—for many years or even decades to come. They were all hard cases, and in most there were also benefits to removing regimes that deserved no sympathy. But even so, considering every attempted U.S.-led regime change operation in the Middle East since 1953, there are no examples of clear success, several catastrophic failures, and a track record in which costs have always been higher, benefits fewer, and the results more unpredictable than policy makers and proponents had promised.

Why is regime change in the Middle East so hard? Why does it always prove more difficult—and produce worse outcomes—than expected? Why do American leaders and pundits keep thinking we can "get it right" and fall for the delusion that this time will be different? And are there any realistic alternatives to a policy that so regularly fails? There is no single answer to these questions, and it is important to acknowledge that in every case in question the policy alternatives were unappealing as well. But looking back over seventy years of U.S. attempts to change governments in the Middle East—and thinking about how best to approach the region in the future—some important lessons do emerge.

Removing a Regime Is the "Easy Part"

The clearest lesson from almost seven decades of experience with regime change is that it is far easier to remove a problematic regime than to put a better one in its place. In almost every case, when an existing regime is destroyed, a political and security vacuum is created, and a competition for power begins. In the absence of security, people feel no alternative but to organize and arm themselves and to turn to kin, tribes, and sects for safety, exacerbating sectarianism and internal rivalries and sometimes leading to demands for secession. These actions inevitably threaten other ethnic or political groups, creating the domestic equivalent of the "security dilemma" in international relations, which posits that measures taken by one party to improve its security can actually undermine it by making other parties feel less secure.[1] During the campaign to oust an existing regime, disparate groups may join forces to oppose their common enemy's hold on power, creating the illusion of unity, but their common interests dissipate almost immediately once the regime is gone. Whether the anticommunist warlords in Afghanistan, Saddam Hussein's opponents in Iraq, the coalition of strange bedfellows that led to the revolution in Egypt, or the various rebel militias in Libya, opposition groups with little in common quickly turn against each other in competition for power once the regime falls. All too often—unsurprisingly in the context of growing anarchy—the most extreme or violent groups prevail, "moderates" are sidelined, and those excluded from power work to undermine those who seized it. As former British official Emma Sky lamented after spending years trying to help stabilize post-Saddam Iraq, "Those the US-led Coalition excluded from power sought to undermine the new order that was introduced. And those we empowered sought to use the country's resources for their own interests, to subvert the nascent democratic institutions, and to use the security forces we trained and equipped to intimidate their rivals."[2]

The security vacuum after a regime change not only sets up a struggle for power within states but generates ruthless competition among regional rivals as well. As seen in Afghanistan, Iraq, Libya, and Egypt when governments fall (or even wobble, as in Syria), regional and even global powers rush in, hoping to put their own proxies in power and pull the country into their orbit. Iran, Saudi Arabia, Qatar, Turkey, and the United Arab Emirates, as well as more distant actors such as Russia, China, India, Pakistan, and the United States, all use their money, arms, relationships, and sometimes direct military force to compete for power, control, and influence—fueling violence, instability, and sectarianism in the process. All those actors intervened on opposite sides in the vacuums created by the Arab Spring, taking their geopolitical competition onto new terrain. In the process, they intensified and perpetuated regional and proxy conflicts that, tragically, have continued to rage.

Security Vacuums Can Be Even Worse Than Repressive Regimes

In the run-up to the 2003 Iraq War, the Reagan administration defense secretary Caspar Weinberger testified to Congress, "People say there will be chaos. I disagree, but I must confess frankly that even chaos would be better than Saddam."[3] Neither the prediction nor the assessment would hold up very well over time, because the chaos, violence, and rise in local and global extremism that followed Saddam Hussein's fall were even more deadly and costly—for both Iraqis and Americans—than what preceded them. In Afghanistan, too, the ouster of Najibullah's communist government led to a vicious civil war that killed more than 500,000 civilians and displaced more than half the country's population before the country was eventually overrun by the Taliban, which proceeded to provide safe haven for al-Qaeda as it undertook attacks against the United States. In Libya, NATO's intervention to remove Qadhafi was followed by an enduring civil war that has led to the deaths of many more Libyans than had died before the intervention and that spilled over into some neighboring countries and pulled regional powers into the conflict.[4] And in Syria, an unsuccessful attempt at regime change dramatically escalated a conflict that resulted in the brutal deaths of more than half a million Syrians and the displacement of more than thirteen million, a global refugee crisis, and the rise of the Islamic State. Secretary of

State Condoleezza Rice's repeated assertion around the time of the Iraq War that pursuing "stability at the expense of democracy" had produced neither was broadly true, but it turned out to have a corollary—that pursuing democracy at the expense of stability might also produce neither, but at much higher cost.[5] A saying attributed to the thirteenth-century Muslim theologian Ibn Taymiyyah—"better sixty years of tyranny than one night of anarchy"—goes too far, but it does underscore the point that getting rid of a regime that promotes insecurity makes little sense if the result is more insecurity than existed in the first place.[6]

Locals Don't Always Welcome "Liberators"

The former British prime minister Harold Macmillan once quipped that the French wartime leader Charles de Gaulle never forgave the British and the Americans for liberating his country. The same feelings of resentment toward putative "liberators" help explain why it is so hard for the United States and other external actors to impose order from the outside. In de Gaulle's case, this nationalist resentment led only to a stubborn foreign policy of emphasizing France's independence and occasional provocations such as expelling U.S. troops from French territory or vetoing British membership in the European Community. But in the case of regime change in the Middle East—where interveners have rarely been greeted as liberators for very long—it has frequently led to violent resistance.

Nationalism is a powerful force with deep historical and possibly even evolutionary roots. Because being part of a community—whether a family, tribe, city, or country—has been necessary for human safety since the beginning of time, people have evolved to be deeply mistrustful of outsiders, about whom they often make snap and even irrational judgments. "Our brains," the neuroscientist Robert Sapolsky has pointed out, "distinguish between in-group members and outsiders in a fraction of a second, and they encourage us to be kind to the former but hostile to the latter."[7] This doesn't mean that people can never welcome outside political assistance, but it does help explain both why it is so hard to create a stable state in the absence of common national myths and why local populations are so resistant to foreign interference.[8]

Examples abound of populations motivated by nationalism turning against outside interveners. In Iran after 1953, antipathy toward the United States for having empowered the repressive shah fueled bitter anti-Americanism—eventually including hostage taking and terrorism—that the Islamic regime was able to manipulate to its advantage for years to come. In Afghanistan, where deep suspicion of foreigners helped fuel the violent Afghan resistance against the Soviet occupation, Hamid Karzai could never escape the impression among Afghans that he was put in power and supported by foreigners, and the departure of U.S. troops has long been among the opposition Taliban's most central rallying cries. As Carter Malkasian, a former military adviser to U.S. commanders in Afghanistan, has put it, the Taliban's animating idea was "resistance to occupation." "The very presence of Americans in Afghanistan was an assault on what it meant to be Afghan. It inspired Afghans to defend their honor, their religion, and their homeland."[9]

In Iraq, there was also great resentment of "exiles who had ridden in on the back of American tanks," as the writer George Packer put it, and it was easy for Iraqis who had been excluded from power—especially Sunnis but plenty of Shia groups as well—to rally public opinion against occupying U.S. forces.[10] As the former Coalition Provisional Authority official Rory Stewart and the scholar Gerald Knaus later noted,

"The [Iraqi] population was not prepared to give us the benefit of the doubt. Many Iraqis assumed we had come to steal the oil, crush a potential rival, or stamp on Islam and Arabia. . . . Most of the population disliked the U.S.-led coalition simply because it was the U.S.-led coalition."[11] By 2008, the Iraqis were insisting that all American troops leave the country, even though a surge in those troops had just helped stifle a raging insurgency. In Syria, according to the scholar Joshua Landis, "as soon as [moderate rebels] began taking money and orders from America, they were tarred by radicals as CIA agents who were corrupt and traitors to the revolution. America was toxic, and everything it touched turned to sand in its hands."[12]

Indeed, while many Americans like to believe their interventions are generous, benign, and widely appreciated, that is rarely how they are perceived locally. The Iraq invasion in particular had a devastating impact on regional attitudes toward the United States, with large majorities in nearly all countries in the region holding unfavorable views of the United States every year since, and even larger majorities saying the United States is playing a "negative role" in Iraq.[13] Recent surveys show that nearly 80 percent of Arabs have a negative view of U.S. foreign policy, and 82 percent even see the United States as a threat to the region's stability.[14] "What seem to be universal values to us," the scholar Dominic Tierney has pointed out, "look like imperialism to others."[15] Such attitudes hardly facilitate Americans' efforts to play the role of liberators when toppling even unpopular governments in the region.

"Clients" Have Their Own Interests

Regime change might be worth the high costs if it consistently led to the installation of governments that acted according to

American wishes, or even worked effectively with the United States to pursue common goals. Unfortunately, it rarely does. Indeed, the very fact of appearing to have been put in power with outside assistance raises questions about the legitimacy of the new leaders, who often seek to bolster that legitimacy by standing up to those who helped them come to power. As political scientist Ely Ratner has pointed out, "Incumbents, who are vulnerable to accusations of American puppetry, respond [to criticism] by distancing themselves from their pro-American policies of the past, with hope to parry the political challenge. The result is that in the wake of U.S. support, democratic transitions rarely lead to positive foreign-policy realignment toward the United States."[16]

Blurring the lines between supposed servants and masters, Mohammad Reza Shah, Hamid Karzai, Nouri al-Maliki, Mohammad Morsi, Mahmoud Jibril, and others would all end up defying Washington on a range of domestic and international issues, knowing that their original sponsors had little choice but to continue to support them. Critics often complain that the United States fails to exercise effective leverage over its clients, but threats to abandon leaders the United States helped install are often hollow, and the clients know it. Actually replacing those leaders with new ones simply re-creates the problem.

Newly installed regimes also often defy their original sponsors because the new leaders reflect enduring national interests and goals of states more than they shape them. As political scientists Alexander Downes and Lindsey O'Rourke have put it, "State interests have deeper roots than the beliefs or policies of any one leader. Changing a state's leader, therefore, is not synonymous with changing its interests. . . . And once in power, the new leader is focused on ensuring his or her own political survival, a task that is often undermined by implementing the intervener's agenda."[17] When the shah of Iran supported the 1973–74 Arab oil embargo against the United States, then White House official Robert Hormats complained bitterly that the shah had "screwed us!" But in fact the shah was simply pursuing Iranian interests and knew Washington could do little about it.[18] The same principle applied when post-Saddam Iraq aligned itself geopolitically with Iran (to the point of putting pro-Iranian Shia militias on the government payroll and allowing Iranian overflights to deliver arms to the Assad regime); Afghanistan's Karzai refused to support U.S. military operations and publicly denounced U.S. leaders; Mubarak's successors in Egypt defied Washington by repressing dissent, altering the constitution, harassing U.S. nongovernmental organizations, and secretly trading with North Korea; and post-Qadhafi Libyan leaders rejected secularism and worked closely with foreign powers—Turkey and Qatar in some cases and the UAE, Saudi Arabia, Egypt, and Russia in others—to advance their internal goals in defiance of U.S. preferences.

None of this means that all regimes from any given country are alike or that a new government will not be more compatible with American interests than its predecessor, but it does mean an alignment with American policy or interests is far from guaranteed, even after a regime is replaced. The fact that Russia remains a strategic competitor and rival of the United States more than thirty years after the fall of the Soviet regime suggests that deeply rooted national threat perceptions, interests, and ambitions may endure long after any particular regime is removed.[19]

Regional Spoilers Thwart Success

It is frequently assumed in Washington that regional or international partners will help bear the burdens and assume the costs of regime change. As seen in previous chapters, many Iraq War proponents argued that the United States wouldn't have to contribute large numbers of peacekeepers because Iraq's neighbors would do so; in Afghanistan many believed NATO's involvement and a UN mandate would significantly reduce American burdens; and in Libya President Obama purposefully embraced a strategy of limiting U.S. involvement before later having to admit that he had expected too much from his European allies.[20] Unfortunately, not only are allied contributions typically far less than hoped or expected, but all too often regional spoilers intervene to complicate U.S. efforts to impose stability. Far from being helpful, many regional and global players have an interest in seeing the United States fail and have the leverage to bring that failure about.

In Afghanistan, of course, the United States assembled an impressive international coalition, backed by a UN Security Council mandate, and even U.S. rivals such as Iran and Russia initially played mostly helpful roles. But these and other regional powers had their own interests and agendas, including the empowerment of their preferred proxies and the weakening of the United States. As Barnett Rubin has observed, most of Afghanistan's neighbors see the U.S. military presence there "as a threat to them and not as a credible counterterrorism force."[21] Pakistan, in particular, has overwhelmingly prioritized its competition with India over democracy in Afghanistan, regional stability, or even its relationship with the United States, leading it to provide a safe haven for the Taliban and other extremist groups so long as they helped guarantee its "strategic depth" and counterbalanced Indian influence. Successive U.S. administrations—Bush, Obama, and Trump—all resolved to pressure Pakistan to be more supportive of the elected Afghan government, but none succeeded. Trump even cut hundreds of millions of dollars in U.S. military assistance to Pakistan while announcing that it had "much to lose by continuing to harbor terrorists," before essentially pivoting less than a year later to an approach that recognized Pakistan's central role and offered concessions to the Taliban.[22] The simple reality was that without Pakistan's willingness to deny the Taliban a sanctuary, which was not forthcoming, it was impossible for the Afghan government to survive without indefinite U.S. military support.

Regional spoilers also helped ensure the failure of regime change in Iraq. As the U.S. Army's own study of the Iraq War concluded, "The coalition's transition strategy never satisfactorily addressed the issue of destabilizing interventions by Iraq's neighbors in 2004–2006—especially the Syrian and Iranian regimes. The Syrian regime allowed its territory to become a base for Ba'athist militants and militant jihadists who infiltrated into Iraq and fueled a sectarian terror campaign there. . . . Meanwhile, on Iraq's eastern border, Iran funneled support to Shi'a militant proxies fighting U.S. and coalition forces and conducting large-scale sectarian cleansing in central Iraq."[23] These regional actors had nowhere near the same military capabilities as the United States, but they didn't need them; they only needed committed supporters, motivated proxies, geographical proximity, and a willingness to kill Americans and their allies with roadside bombs, rockets, and advanced improvised explosive devices.

In Syria, U.S. adversaries such as Russia and Iran were able to prevent successful regime change, responding to every U.S.-led escalation with even more ruthless escalation of their own—ruthlessness and escalation that Washington would have had to be willing to match to get rid of Assad. In Libya the competition between the Qatar-Turkey alliance on one side and the UAE-Saudi-Egypt alliance on the other thwarted international efforts to end the fighting. And in Egypt itself the

United States could not prevent the Emiratis and Saudis from fomenting and supporting a military coup against the Morsi regime. The bottom line is that in the wake of regime change close regional neighbors often have greater interests, knowledge, access on the ground, and staying power than the United States.

Unintended Consequences Are Inevitable

As senior U.S. officials debated intervention in Libya in 2011, Secretary of Defense Robert Gates—the most experienced member of Obama's cabinet—reminded his colleagues that "when you start a war you never know how it will go."[24] Gates's warning was an understatement: in every single case, however carefully prepared, regime change in the Middle East has had unanticipated and unwelcome consequences.

Perhaps the most powerful example was the first U.S. intervention in Afghanistan, which as Andrew Bacevich rightly observed "reflected the unwitting tendency, while intently focusing on solving one problem, to exacerbate another and plant the seeds of a third."[25] Support for the mujahideen in the 1980s helped to undermine the Soviet Union, but it also led to more than a decade of chaos, a civil war, brutal and backward Taliban rule, a global jihadist movement, and ultimately another indefinite U.S. military intervention. By helping the jihadists bring down one superpower—the Soviet Union—Americans inadvertently gave them confidence they could bring down another: the United States itself. Even Gates, who supported U.S. assistance to the mujahideen at the time as a senior CIA official, later asked, "Did [those who joined the anti-regime campaign] know they were going to give rise to the Taliban? Did *we* know we were going to help give rise to the

Taliban? You cannot ever pretend to know the future and to know the long-term consequences of your actions."[26]

Unintended consequences were the norm elsewhere as well. In Iran, Mosaddeq the prickly nationalist was ousted, but the shah's subsequent corruption and repression ultimately led to an Islamic revolution and decades of anti-Americanism, state-sponsored terrorism, and regional destabilization. In Iraq, the United States removed Saddam Hussein, but in doing so, it inadvertently empowered Iran, fueled jihadism, demonstrated to dictators around the world the potential value of possessing nuclear weapons (to deter regime change), increased doubts all over the world about the benevolence of U.S. power, and soured the American public on military intervention for decades to come. The U.S. Army's study of the Iraq War concluded that "Iran was the only winner"—not exactly the original plan.[27]

In Libya, Qadhafi's ouster contributed to arms proliferation across the region, instability in Chad and Mali (which prompted further Western military intervention), and Russia's resolve never again to allow the UN Security Council to pass such a resolution that would facilitate regime change—which came to haunt the opposition in Syria. Whereas many regime change advocates in Libya hoped that Qadhafi's overthrow would lead other dictators to "seek peaceful transitions," it ended up doing the opposite, with Assad cracking down all the more ruthlessly on his opponents.[28] And one of the unintended consequences of *that* development was support for efforts to overthrow Assad violently, which led to a surge in extremists who spilled over into neighboring Iraq and undermined the government there. To be sure, as I have pointed out, in all these cases, inaction would have had costs and consequences as well. But in every case action also turned out to have high—and unpredictable—costs.

In the immediate wake of the Iraq War, David Frum and Richard Perle wrote that "when it is in our power and our interest, we should toss dictators aside with no more compunction than a police sharpshooter feels when he downs a hostage-taker."[29] In fact, police sharpshooters tend to pull the trigger only after careful preparation and as a last resort, and so should governments, because once the shooting starts, you never know what will happen.

Regime Change Creates Moral Hazard

Just as the expectation of bank bailouts can lead to risky behavior by investors, or flood insurance can lead people to build houses where they shouldn't, military intervention to remove dictators can create perverse incentives in the target countries and beyond. Credibly threatening to remove a hostile regime (or actually doing so) can give hope to populations in other countries that they too can win their freedom, ostensibly a good thing. In practice, however, the threat or execution of regime change can also lead those populations to escalate violence, which often leads to counter-escalation by better armed regimes. This was certainly the case in Libya, where NATO's intervention to help the rebels overthrow the government suggested to members of the opposition in Syria that if they could only escalate violence to a high enough level, the world's most powerful militaries would intervene on their behalf as well. The result was not Assad's ouster or a diplomatic compromise but the greatest humanitarian catastrophe since World War II, a refugee crisis, the destabilization of Syria's neighbors, the growth of the Islamic State, and political spillover into Europe and beyond.

Proponents of regime change, of course, would argue that the solution to such problems is not to avoid inciting violent rebellions in the first place but to back them so that they succeed. But not only is that far easier said than done—for all the reasons just discussed—but even if "success" could somehow be achieved in one place by devoting enough resources to it, that success itself might produce the need for even greater efforts elsewhere. It is difficult, in other words, to intervene militarily on behalf of one deserving group facing oppression without inevitably inspiring others—in Syria, Iraq, Iran, Yemen, Kurdistan, or elsewhere—to expect the same kind of support if they provoke a degree of violence too great for the West to ignore.

Americans Don't Know Enough About the Middle East

Regime change and nation building in transparent countries where American officials have extensive presence and experience would be hard enough, but it turns out to be exceedingly difficult in complex countries where that expertise is in short supply. This was famously the situation in Iraq, where U.S. policy makers badly miscalculated the effects of a U.S. intervention on the Iraqi population, relying, in some cases, on their own, highly limited, personal interaction with selected Iraqis with hidden—or not so hidden—agendas. Giving mostly young, inexperienced officials without local language skills responsibilities for governance in a majority-Arab country of more than thirty million people turned out to be a more challenging task than proponents of the Iraq War apparently assumed.

But the lack of knowledge and experience was the case elsewhere as well. In Afghanistan in the 1980s, with almost no presence on the ground, the CIA outsourced efforts to support the mujahideen to Pakistan and Saudi Arabia, which naturally took advantage to prioritize their own interests and steer weapons to their preferred proxies. After 2003, busy policy makers, who were simultaneously trying to manage an all-consuming war in Iraq and deal with growing terrorist threats and more, struggled to navigate an Afghanistan-Pakistan relationship that was a puzzle even to locals and experts. As the journalist Steve Coll noted, "Hardly anyone among the secretaries or deputy secretaries managing policy had long, direct experience with Pakistan. They might have gotten to know their counterparts in the Pakistan Army or the Foreign Ministry and formed a few impressions from these relationships and from reading. Yet their responsibilities at State, the Pentagon, or the CIA spanned the world, and it was impossible for most of them to untangle complexities within complexities involving the Wazirs, the Mehsuds, or the structure of the Afghan Taliban's revival." The U.S. government did have some genuine experts on the region, such as the national intelligence officer for South Asia, Peter Lavoy, but there was only so much midlevel officials could do. "In the Situation Room," Coll noted, "Lavoy learned, the best that might be realistically hoped for from overwhelmed decision makers, up to and including the president, was a willingness to avoid cartoonish, stubborn, black-and-white judgments, and to accept 'It's complicated.'"[30] Bush and Obama's Afghanistan "czar," Douglas Lute, would later himself admit, "We were devoid of a fundamental understanding of Afghanistan—we didn't know what we were doing. . . . We didn't have the foggiest notion of what we were undertaking."[31]

In Libya, the United States had no embassy for twenty-six years after 1980 and then, after the 2012 Benghazi tragedy, found itself trying to help install a stable Libyan government with practically no presence on the ground. Under extreme political pressure to avoid casualties after Benghazi, the Obama administration had extended debates about whether to authorize the presence of a single civilian in country (ultimately it did so), but that individual and an embassy based in Malta for security reasons did not exactly give Washington a good window into emerging Libyan politics. U.S. ambassador to the United Nations Samantha Power later wrote that given our own inability to accurately predict *American* political behavior, we could "hardy expect to have a crystal ball when it came to accurately predicting outcomes where the culture was not our own."[32] This all-too-true statement might have suggested the need for caution elsewhere in the region as well. Indeed, I recall briefings in the White House Situation Room about even some of the hundreds of different rebel groups in Syria that the United States was supporting—however well "vetted"—where the briefers themselves admitted they had trouble keeping track of what those groups were doing because we lacked a diplomatic presence on the ground.[33] As international relations scholar Stephen Walt noted after reviewing the literature on intervention going back to Iraq and Afghanistan, "Personal accounts from participants in these efforts make it abundantly clear that the people responsible for these efforts did not know which local leaders to trust or support, did not understand the complex and subtle networks of allegiance and authority in which they were trying to work, and inevitably trampled on local customs and sensitivities."[34]

In the absence of detailed local knowledge, U.S. policy is susceptible to manipulation from parties, often exiles from the target countries, with their own vested interests. The most famous example is of course Ahmed Chalabi, the Iraqi exile who helped to convince top Bush administration officials that Saddam Hussein had weapons of mass destruction and that American forces would be greeted as liberators, before eventually being arrested for working to advance the interests of Iran and calling himself and his colleagues "heroes in error."[35]

Other Iraqi exiles—including those who helped mislead Western intelligence agencies with deliberately false information—also took advantage of limited U.S. expertise and the powerful tendency of decision makers to hear what they wanted to hear.[36] Similar dynamics would take place in Libya, Syria, and elsewhere, where even well-meaning exiles understandably determined to get rid of the dictators in their homeland told Americans and others what they wanted to hear in order to win the support of the most powerful countries of the world.

Some five hundred years ago, Machiavelli wrote, "It ought to be considered how vain are the faith and promises of those who find themselves deprived of their country. . . . Such is the extreme desire in them to return home, that they naturally believe many things that are false and add many others by art, so that between those they believe and those they say they believe, they fill you with hope, so that relying on them you will incur expenses in vain, or you undertake an enterprise in which you ruin yourself."[37] The Italian strategist was not writing about policy challenges in the modern Middle East, but he might as well have been.

U.S. Staying Power Is Limited

Regime change might be more effective if Americans were prepared to devote unlimited resources to governance, nation building, and security once a new regime was put in place, and to maintain its commitments as long as necessary regardless of costs and casualties. Unfortunately, American patience and staying power are finite, and once the immediate crisis passes and threat perceptions diminish, it is hard to sustain the high costs and heavy resource commitments—especially to places where vital U.S. interests are not necessarily at stake. After the

United States essentially abandoned Afghanistan in the 1990s after driving out the Soviets for geopolitical reasons, former CIA station chief Milt Bearden asked, "Did we really give a shit about the long-term future of Nangarhar? Maybe not. As it turned out, guess what? We didn't."[38]

The diminishing public willingness to support the costs of the wars in Iraq and Afghanistan is a good illustration of how support for regime change falls over time. In 2003, after the 9/11 attacks and administration warnings about mushroom clouds, 72 percent of Americans thought intervention in Iraq to overthrow Saddam Hussein was the right decision, and only 22 percent thought it was the wrong decision. By 2008, however, only 38 percent thought it was the right decision and 54 percent thought it was the wrong one.[39] By 2019, only 32 percent of Americans said invading Iraq was worth it, with 62 percent saying the war was a mistake.[40]

Public support for the war in Afghanistan lasted longer, gradually falling from an early 2002 peak, when only 6 percent of Americans thought sending troops there was a mistake, to 2004, when the "mistake" percentage reached 25 percent, to 2014, when, for the first time, a majority of those who answered thought sending troops was a mistake.[41] By 2019, 59 percent of Americans believed the Afghanistan war was not worth fighting compared with 40 percent who said it was.[42] Support for both wars among military veterans who served in Iraq and Afghanistan is similarly weak: in a 2019 poll, 64 percent of veterans said the Iraq War was "not worth fighting considering the costs versus benefits to the United States" versus 33 percent who thought it was worth fighting, with 58 percent of veterans saying Afghanistan was not worth fighting and 38 percent saying it was.[43]

In Libya and Syria there was little public support for intervention to begin with. Congressional opposition to the deployment of ground troops to Libya—among Republicans and Democrats alike—was so strong, especially after Benghazi, that the debate about stabilization forces was largely moot. In Syria, too, Obama's strong personal aversion to getting dragged into another Middle East war played a major role in limiting U.S. involvement, but in many ways he was merely reflecting public and congressional opinion. To be sure, Americans will never support foreign military intervention without strong leadership from the top, but there are limits to how far out in front of the public a president can afford to get before paying a political price.

The 2016 presidential elections only reinforced this point. After criticism of Obama's alleged lack of engagement and withdrawal from Iraq, and with a booming U.S. economy, one might have expected the foreign policy pendulum to swing back in the direction of internationalism as has often been the case in the past. Instead, even in that year's Republican primaries, the candidates representing assertive military engagement were crushed by a businessman with no foreign policy experience who claimed intervention in the Middle East was a waste of money and promised to bring the troops home. For all their criticism of Obama's alleged weakness or passivity, only one of the nineteen Republican candidates for president—Senator Lindsey Graham of South Carolina—was calling for even a modest deployment of additional troops to Iraq and Syria, and he got so little support he didn't even make it to the first primaries. In the general election, Trump campaigned against foreign intervention and defeated Hillary Clinton, a former secretary of state and member of the Senate Armed Services Committee who was more supportive of U.S. military deployments abroad. By 2019, with U.S. troops still in Iraq and Afghanistan, and Libya and Syria still highly unstable, only 27 percent of Americans believed that "intervening militarily in other countries to solve conflicts" makes the United States safer, while 46 percent believed it made us less safe.[44]

The problem of falling domestic support and staying power is of course not unique to the United States. In a study of twenty-six completed military occupations in the world since 1815, the scholar David Edelstein concluded that only seven succeeded (France in 1815, North Korea in 1945, and Germany, Japan, Austria, Italy, and Okinawa after World War II), in part because "both occupied populations and occupying powers grow weary of extended occupations, undermining their success."[45]

Democracy Is Elusive, Especially in the Middle East

In his 1991 book, *Exporting Democracy,* the political theorist Joshua Muravchik claimed that "democracy can indeed be spread by the sword" and that, while not easy, promoting democracy is something we had done before and would "become easier now" because the Cold War was over.[46] That it hasn't exactly worked out that way should not have come as a surprise. In the contemporary Middle East, the conditions for democratic development are poor, and the assumptions that getting rid of an autocratic regime will allow democracy to suddenly flourish are misguided.

While there are no clear recipes for democratic development, extensive scholarly research suggests that the main necessary ingredients include a degree of economic development; ethnic, political, and cultural homogeneity (or at least a shared national narrative); and the previous existence of democratic norms, practices, and institutions.[47] Unfortunately, the contemporary Middle East is lacking in all these attributes, making democracy promotion there even harder than elsewhere. Political scientists Alfred Stepan and Graeme Robertson have noted that democracy is more elusive in the Middle East because most of the states in the region are not nation-states. They have artificial borders drawn by colonial powers and populations that lack "a strong affective attachment to, and identity with, the specific institutions and symbols of the political community within the country's boundaries."[48] Because of this lack of internal unity, they have also been largely held together only by internal security forces—the *mukhabarat*—further impeding the potential for economic development.[49]

Even in places where democracy has eventually developed, it was often a process that took decades or centuries. As the scholar and former ambassador to the UN Jeane Kirkpatrick has pointed out, "In Britain, the road from the Magna Carta to the Act of Settlement, to the great Reform Bills of 1832, 1867, and 1885, took seven centuries to traverse. American history gives no better grounds for believing that democracy comes easily, quickly, or for the asking. A war of independence, an unsuccessful constitution, a civil war, a long process of gradual enfranchisement marked our progress toward constitutional democratic government. The French path was still more difficult. Terror, dictatorship, monarchy, instability, and incompetence followed on the revolution that was to usher in a millennium of brotherhood. Only in the 20th century did the democratic principle finally gain wide acceptance in France and not until after World War II were the principles of order and democracy, popular sovereignty and authority, finally reconciled in institutions strong enough to contain conflicting currents of public opinion."[50]

None of this means that democracy is impossible in the Middle East. But it does suggest—along with nearly seventy years of empirical evidence—that pursuing regime change in the Middle East on the basis that it will quickly lead to democratic development would be wishful thinking in the extreme. The United States should support democracy, human rights, and individual liberty wherever and however it can, for the sake of humanity and its own self-interest. But linking the case for regime change to the spread of democracy has proven to be misguided in every case.

Even Lots of Money and Troops Are Not Enough

In their comprehensive study of the U.S. role in nation building from 1945 to 2003, a group of analysts from the Rand Corporation concluded in 2003 that the most important ingredient for success was the "level of effort" by the United States, "measured in time, manpower, and money."[51] The authors looked at cases including Germany and Japan after World War II, Somalia, Haiti, Bosnia, and Kosovo after U.S.-led interventions, and Afghanistan since the Taliban were overthrown in 2001. They underscored the positive correlation between the number of U.S. troops deployed and per capita assistance, on the one hand, and the ultimate outcome in terms of political stability, prosperity, and democracy, on the other. The implication of the study—completed not long after the invasion of Iraq—was that the United States would have a far better chance to make regime change in Iraq a success if it devoted adequate resources to the task.

There can be little doubt that adequate resources are a necessary element in successful nation building; Afghanistan in the 1990s and Libya in the second decade of the twenty-first century are good examples of how limited effort can lead to limited results. But the two decades of U.S. experience since the invasion of Iraq also demonstrate that even a high level of effort is not sufficient when the conditions for success do not exist. As the Rand authors acknowledged, in addition to massive outside efforts, Germany and Japan had advantages that included "already highly developed, economically advanced societies," circumstances that simply did not apply in Afghanistan or Iraq.[52] In those two cases, the United States and others at various times deployed more than 100,000 troops and spent trillions of dollars, yet fell well short of creating stable, self-sustaining countries, let alone democracies. After almost twenty years of such investments, it's hard to argue that the problem was simply the "level of effort measured in time, manpower, and money." Instead, it seems necessary to conclude that even enormous amounts of resources are not enough to produce success if the right conditions are not in place.

Do these lessons mean regime change—in the Middle East or anywhere else—is never warranted and can never succeed? Should the United States, based on this depressing track record, resolve never to adopt regime change as policy? It is impossible to rule out that there could be cases where the risk of nuclear weapons proliferation or use, mass terrorism, genocide, or a direct attack on the United States would be such that the benefits of removing a threatening regime would exceed the costs of doing so. But if history is any guide, such cases will be rare to nonexistent, and even where they may exist, they demand far more caution, humility, and honesty about the likely costs and consequences than has been the case. Even in a case as seemingly compelling as Afghanistan in the 1980s, if Americans could have been told in advance what would follow the overthrow of the Soviet-backed government—a protracted civil war that killed a million civilians, the birth of the global jihadist movement, half a decade of dystopian Taliban rule, mass terrorist attacks on the United States, and the need for another regime change operation in Afghanistan that would cost more than two thousand American lives and expenditures of more than $50 billion a year for nearly two decades—it is far from clear they would have supported it in the first place. In Iran, Iraq, Egypt, Libya, and Syria, the case for intervening to get rid of a regime also initially seemed compelling, until the costs and results became known.

The usual response to this argument is that policy makers should have just followed up more effectively. It is hard to argue, however, that regime change in the Middle East is a good conceptual idea but that the Eisenhower, Carter, Reagan, Bush I, Clinton, Bush II, Obama, and Trump administrations happened to get implementation wrong—in every case over a nearly seventy-year period, sometimes by doing too much and sometimes by doing too little—and that the next president who tries it will get it right. The iron rule of regime change in the Middle East seems to be that its costs will be higher than expected, unintended consequences will emerge, and results will leave much to be desired.

Another frequent response to skepticism about regime change is the assertion that however costly it might be, there is sometimes simply no alternative to it. As Charles Krauthammer argued in 2004, defending the invasion of Iraq and efforts to "bring democracy" to the Middle East, "There is not a single, remotely plausible alternative strategy for attacking the monster behind 9/11."[53] Two years later, Secretary of State Condoleezza Rice was still arguing, "I frankly haven't heard an alternative posed for how we fight the war on terror except on the offense," while Robert Kagan suggested in 2006 that even critics of the Bush administration's policies of intervention and nation building were not offering "an alternative doctrine."[54] These and many other proponents of regime change both in years past and today argue that even if the costs are high and the results imperfect, the United States has no choice but to act because any alternative course of action is worse. As occasional Trump adviser Senator Tom Cotton put it in June 2017, making the case for regime change in Iran, "I don't see how anyone can say America can be safe as long as you have in power a theocratic despotism."[55]

It's true, as I've acknowledged throughout this book, that there were never *good* alternatives to regime change in the challenging cases we've looked at. But it's also true that even in these hard cases there were usually better options than intervening to oust and replace—by whatever method—the regime. In virtually every case, more modest aims and measures—from efforts to assist civilian populations, deterrence of external aggression, targeted sanctions, diplomatic pressure, humanitarian relief, or *in some cases even doing nothing*—would have worked out better for both the United States and the local populations than what often turned out to be hugely ambitious, expensive, unsuccessful, and counterproductive regime change operations. The Hippocratic oath to "do no harm" is not always an option in international diplomacy, where sometimes security threats or humanitarian crises require action that inevitably does harm. But as any physician would acknowledge, turning to aggressive, invasive treatment under the wrong circumstances can be worse than containing and managing problems, however real.

In most cases, in fact, the best alternative to regime change looks a lot like the containment strategy that won the Cold War—accepting that some problems must be managed rather than solved while using diplomacy, engagement, defense, development, alliances, assistance, and the force of our own example to buy time and promote peaceful, long-term change. When the costs and results of regime change are considered, what

George Kennan almost seventy-five years ago called "long-term, patient but firm and vigilant containment" turns out to be a better approach, even when facing dangerous, adversarial, and repressive regimes.

Proponents of regime change, of course, often argue the opposite: that the lesson of the Cold War—and particularly the way it was waged by the hawkish Ronald Reagan—was that the United States achieved regime change in Moscow through a "maximum pressure" campaign that forced the Soviet Union's collapse. In this version of history, Reagan "abandoned containment" in 1983 and brought about regime change in Moscow through a policy of massive defense spending, economic warfare, support for proxies, and an ideological offensive. The implication—sometimes made explicit in current debates about Iran, North Korea, Syria, or Venezuela—is that a similar approach is what is required to get rid of problematic regimes today.[56] It was not a coincidence that shortly after the U.S. withdrawal from the Iran nuclear deal Secretary of State Mike Pompeo chose the Ronald Reagan Library in Simi Valley, California, as the venue for a speech to the Iranian diaspora.[57]

In fact, while ideological confrontation, sanctions, and a military buildup obviously played a role in the ultimate decline of the Soviet Union, this version of history overlooks the reality that regime change was never the near-term goal of U.S. strategy toward Moscow, even though the Soviet regime threatened U.S. interests far more than any Middle East dictatorship ever has. There were, of course, early proponents of regime change—or even preventive war—in Russia, but those approaches were rejected even by Cold War hawks like Paul Nitze and John Foster Dulles, who focused instead on competing with the Soviets for influence in the third world and accepted the reality that political change in Moscow was not in America's power to achieve at acceptable cost.[58] As Richard

Haass has written, "Seeking regime change, or rollback, was deemed too risky, even reckless, given what could result if a desperate Soviet leadership lashed out with all the force at its disposal."[59]

In the late 1970s, a new generation of cold warriors—including members of the anti-Soviet Committee on the Present Danger—renewed the calls for "offensive" measures to weaken the Soviet Union internally, but they, too, failed to win over policy makers.[60] While Reagan criticized the "evil empire" and denounced accommodation of Moscow, his policies reflected the need to manage the problem for the foreseeable future, and his vision for destroying communism was only a "plan and hope for the long term," as he put it to the British Parliament in 1982.[61] Reagan himself later admitted that when he declared, "Mr. Gorbachev, tear down this wall!" during a speech in Berlin in June 1987, he "never dreamed that in less than three years the wall would come down."[62] Secretary of State George Shultz has said that Reagan did not have a strategy of "spending the Soviets into the ground" through an arms race, and U.S. ambassador to Moscow Jack Matlock added that there was no strategy for "bringing down" the Soviet Union.[63] As the Cold War historian John Lewis Gaddis put it, "At no point did . . . the Reagan administration give anything like serious attention to how they might actually overthrow the Soviet regime, or to what they would do in the unlikely event that such a thing should come about." While the United States took the lead in containing Moscow's influence in the postwar world, "it did not seek nor was it prepared for any effort to remove the Soviet government from its position of authority."[64]

Also relevant in today's context is that Reagan's approach to the Soviet Union—building on that of all his postwar predecessors—included extensive diplomatic engagement and the pursuit of arms control, even while the Soviet regime was mistreating its citizens at home and expanding its influence abroad. As Gaddis has also noted, Reagan began looking to improve relations with the Soviet Union from the moment he entered the White House and "began shifting American policy in that direction as early as the first months of 1983, almost two years before Mikhail Gorbachev came to power."[65] His approach did not change even after the Soviets shot down a South Korean civilian airliner in September 1983, killing 269 passengers, or when the hard-line apparatchik Konstantin Chernenko took over the Soviet leadership in February 1984. Indeed only a few days after Chernenko took office—in the first of a series of letters not unlike those Obama would write to Iran's supreme leader, Ali Khamenei, almost thirty years later—Reagan wrote the Soviet leader to say, "The U.S. firmly intends to defend our interests and those of our allies, but we do not seek to challenge the security of the Soviet Union and its people." "I want you to know," he emphasized in a private, handwritten note the following month, "that neither I nor the American people hold any offensive intentions toward you or the Soviet people. Our constant and urgent purpose must be . . . a lasting reduction of tensions between us. I pledge to you my profound commitment toward that end."[66] Reagan's message in his first meeting with the Soviet foreign minister, Andrei Gromyko, in September 1984 was also that "the Soviet Union had nothing to fear from us" and that the United States wanted "nothing less than a realistic, constructive, long-term relationship with the Soviet Union."[67] This was not the approach of someone bent on achieving regime change in Moscow anytime soon, or who thought that refusing to talk was the best way to achieve it. In his study of the neoconservative movement, historian Justin Vaïsse concluded that "over the years Reagan moved steadily away from the neoconservatives, in the end adopting policies in defiance of their wishes that probably contributed just as much to 'winning the Cold War' as anything they proposed."[68]

Containment, it should be noted, was not then and should not today imply inaction or indifference. The range of policy options for dealing with the tremendous challenges in the region includes measures such as no-fly zones to protect local populations; selective air strikes to degrade and deter potential WMD use or development; the maintenance of U.S. forces in the region to deter regional war and ensure the free flow of energy; direct military interventions such as the campaign pursued by both Obama and Trump against the Islamic State; sanctions to deny adversaries weapons and technologies; incentives for governments to respect human rights and develop democratic institutions and penalties when they do not; investment in economic development, education, and exchanges; and a better resourced and revitalized diplomatic corps. Such tools can be used judiciously to advance U.S. interests while acknowledging the limits of what can reasonably be accomplished.

Nor does containment require giving up hope for future progress or rule out working for eventual political change. As Kennan wrote in his 1947 "X" article, "The possibilities for American policy *are by no means limited to . . . hoping for the best.* . . . The United States has it in its power to increase enormously the strains under which Soviet policy must operate . . . and in this way to promote tendencies which must eventually find their outlet in either the break-up or the gradual mellowing of Soviet power."[69]

In the end, of course, the Soviet regime did disappear, but it is worth noting that change came about only after decades of containment and generational change, that the United States had no control over its timing, and that it was neither outside intervention nor bottom-up revolution but the regime itself—in the form of the Communist Party general secretary, Mikhail Gorbachev—that ultimately recognized the need to try to reform and salvage a crumbling system.[70]

There are obviously major differences between the Soviet Union of the Cold War and the countries of the Middle East where the United States has tried or contemplated regime change. But there are important similarities as well, in that the very existence of the Soviet Union was a threat to the United States and a disaster for its own people, yet U.S. leaders wisely refrained from efforts to pursue near-term regime change there, rightly calculating that the costs of doing so would exceed the benefits. The point is that U.S. interests were better served by containing and managing the problem through robust defensive measures, strong alliances, the preservation of an attractive, functioning democratic and capitalist system at home, patience, diplomatic engagement, and arms control than they would have been by efforts to overthrow the regime by coup, sanctions, or military intervention.

It is true that the prospects for political change in most of the countries in the Middle East where regime change might be contemplated today do not seem propitious. But then again they did not seem very propitious in Moscow either, and there are both empirical and theoretical reasons for believing that engagement, diplomacy, and economic development actually provide greater prospects for stability, peaceful relations, and long-term democratization than outside-imposed regime change. As political scientists Ronald Inglehart and Christian Welzel have argued, economic development and modernization help to create "a self-reinforcing process that transforms social life and political institutions, bringing rising mass participation in politics and—in the long run—making democratic political institutions increasingly likely."[71] As we have seen in countries as diverse as Chile, Indonesia, the Philippines, Serbia,

South Korea, Taiwan, and Vietnam, industrialization and economic growth—even in military autocracies—contributed to the expansion of the middle class, rising educational levels, demands for greater individual freedom, the rule of law, and increased international engagement.

There is obviously nothing automatic about this process—thirty years of development in China have not made it more cooperative or democratic—and the process is less likely if the country is ruled by an insecure ideological (or minority) regime that fears that democratization could threaten its very existence (and the privileges that come with its rule). But it is equally true that the prospects for positive change are even worse if the country in question is politically and economically isolated or facing a foreign-sponsored insurgency. The precedent of Iraq under Saddam Hussein, and the situations in North Korea, Iran, Cuba, and Venezuela today, hardly suggest that sanctions and isolation are the best ways to encourage democracy, human rights, and regional cooperation. In the case of North Korea such policies have also failed to prevent nuclear and ballistic missile proliferation. "By doing what we so often do," Fareed Zakaria has pointed out, "we cut these countries off from the most powerful agents of change in the modern world—commerce, contact, information."[72] Economic and political engagement with distasteful regimes obviously comes at a cost—more revenues for nefarious activities and the structures of repression—but the reality is that even when resources are scarce, the dictators and their cronies are the last to suffer. And the painful truth is that economic sanctions and isolation have a poor track record of producing revolutions and never induce leaders to give up power voluntarily. This is because—as former Treasury and CIA official David Cohen and scholar Zoe Weinberg have written—"the costs of relinquishing power will always exceed the benefit of sanctions relief."[73]

Proponents of regime change, especially since 9/11, also argue that the spread of weapons of mass destruction and terrorism makes containment obsolete. A core premise of the wars in Afghanistan and Iraq, after all, was that the United States could not afford to run even a small risk that terrorists would get their hands on weapons of mass destruction and that avoiding that risk was worth practically any cost. Almost twenty years later, however, the benefits of regime change as an insurance policy remain hypothetical—we might or might not have reduced proliferation risks—whereas the costs of implementing that policy are clear and enormous. All too often, regime change operations to prevent terrorism and mass atrocities have led to only more terrorism and mass atrocities, while regime change operations to prevent weapons of mass destruction have instead provided an incentive for the regime in question and others to pursue such weapons. By contrast, alternative arrangements for preventing weapons of mass destruction proliferation and terrorism—including intelligence cooperation, targeted sanctions, homeland security and defense efforts, arms control agreements, and deterrence—have proven far more cost-effective than ambitious efforts to remake societies after ousting hostile regimes. The 2015 Iran nuclear agreement, for example, was an imperfect arrangement that did little to solve the problems of Iranian support for terrorism, human rights violations, or interference in its neighbors' affairs. But it put in place mechanisms to reduce the nuclear proliferation risk, bought time for Iran to potentially evolve, avoided the costs and consequences of military intervention, and demonstrated the possibility of resolving even deep differences through international cooperation and diplomatic agreement. To assume that economic warfare, armed or unarmed support for opposition groups, a military coup, or military strikes linked to Iran's nuclear program would lead to the replacement of the current

Iranian regime with a more friendly, peaceful, democratic, and stable one would be to ignore the track record of similar efforts throughout the region over the past seventy years.

The regime change temptation will never go away. So long as there are states that threaten U.S. interests and mistreat their people—in other words, for the foreseeable future—U.S. leaders and pundits will periodically be pulled toward the idea that we can use our unparalleled military, diplomatic, and economic power to get rid of bad regimes and replace them with better ones. The bias of American political culture, resulting from the country's record of achievement and belief in its own exceptionalism, is to believe every problem has a solution, and the bias of the U.S. government is to act forcefully to try to solve those problems, no matter how difficult they might appear. The long, diverse, and tragic history of regime change in the Middle East, however, suggests that such temptations—like most other quick fixes that come along in life and politics—should be resisted. The next time U.S. leaders propose intervening in the Middle East to change a hostile regime, it can safely be assumed that such an enterprise will be more costly, less successful, and more replete with unintended consequences than proponents of such action realize or admit. So far at least, it has never been the other way around.

Acknowledgments

I am deeply grateful to the many friends, colleagues, former officials, family members, and anonymous reviewers who helped make this a better book.

I could not have asked for or imagined a better place to write it than at the Council on Foreign Relations (CFR) in Washington, D.C., surrounded by smart colleagues and supported by a first-rate team. CFR president Richard Haass not only urged me to write the book and gave me the time and space to do so, but—as a central participant himself in some of the developments it covers—took the time to give me invaluable comments on the manuscript. CFR director of studies Jim Lindsay did the same—he read every word more than once, asked probing questions, and provided incisive comments to ensure the final product met the Council's demanding standards of quality and fair-minded research. Jim also arranged to have the manuscript read by three anonymous expert reviewers—to whom I am grateful for their thorough comments and helpful suggestions. Mary and David Boies provided support for the endowed chair that has enabled me to research and write this book. I thank them sincerely for their generosity to the Council and support for its important work.

No one at the Council or elsewhere did more than my research associate Chris Brodsky, who spent most of the past eighteen months in his cubicle surrounded by tall stacks of (at last count 180) books about U.S. foreign policy in the Middle East. Beyond surviving this obvious workplace hazard, Chris was a tireless researcher, a superb sounding board, a knowledgeable and careful reader and critic, and an all-around great partner in every aspect of this project. I can't thank him enough.

Chris's predecessor, Alex Decina—a fluent Arabic speaker with extensive experience in the region—was instrumental in doing the early research that helped me get the project off the ground. Another CFR research associate, Zachary Shapiro, not only helped with research but provided smart and challenging comments on early drafts. Patricia Lee Dorff, Anya Schmemann, Jenny Mallamo, Susan Nelson, and the rest of the terrific CFR publications and communications teams were generous with their expertise and support. Several CFR interns—Emily Koenig, Katherine Nazemi, Ido Levy, and Shelby Butt—did a great job tracking down obscure details, checking facts, and providing ideas. Whatever flaws and errors the final result contains are of course my responsibility alone.

This book covers a lot of historical and regional ground, and I could not have written it without input from former colleagues in government and some top experts and practitioners. For sharing their recollections and making often detailed comments on all or part of the manuscript, I am grateful to: Peter Bergen, Alex Bick, Robert Blackwill, Jarrett Blanc, Bill Burns, Derek Chollet, Ruth Citrin, Ivo Daalder, Megan Doherty, Karen Donfried, Jon Finer, Ben Fishman, Robert Ford, Mark Gasiorowski, Avril Haines, Martin Indyk, Deborah Jones, Prem Kumar, Kelly Magsamen, Rob Malley, Mike McFaul, Brett McGurk, Andrew Miller, Robert Moore, Jim O'Brien, Anne Patterson, Samantha Power, Ben Rhodes, Bruce Riedel, Dennis Ross, Karim

Sadjadpour, Julia Santucci, Dan Shapiro, Jeremy Shapiro, Liz Sherwood-Randall, Emma Sky, Jake Sullivan, Omer Taspinar, Justin Vaïsse, Tamara Cofman Wittes, and Mona Yacoubian.

Thanks also to Anne Withers and Mike Smith at the National Security Council, and to Behar Godani and Anne Barbaro at the State Department, who on behalf of their respective agencies conducted the prepublication review thoroughly and expeditiously. The book covers issues I dealt with while a senior administration official, but all opinions and characterizations in this book are mine alone and do not necessarily represent those of the U.S. government.

My longtime agent, Andrew Wylie, started encouraging me to write about my time in government from the moment I left the administration, and I'm glad I took his advice. Andrew helped me find the ideal home for the book at St. Martin's Press, where my editor, Pronoy Sarkar, has been a total pro and a pleasure to work with. I thank Jennifer Fernandez for expertly guiding me through the production process.

I will always be grateful to President Barack Obama—and to Secretary of State Hillary Clinton and National Security Adviser Tom Donilon, who hired me at the State Department and National Security Council, respectively—for giving me the opportunity and privilege to serve in government and deal with these critical issues at a critical time. I also thank Susan Rice, who served with distinction as national security adviser—and my boss—starting in 2013, and who recruited me onto the Obama campaign in the first place, all the way back in 2007. As this book makes clear, there are no easy answers to the problems of the Middle East (or anywhere else), but I was deeply honored to work for President Obama and his entire team of talented, dedicated, decent patriots, who worked tirelessly to manage them.

Finally, biggest thanks of all to Rachel, Noah, Ben, and Dinah (aka "Temples"). Anyone who has served in government knows how demanding it is on families, but I have been lucky to have Rachel by my side ever since I first dipped my toes in these waters decades ago, and to have three kids who were toddlers when I first worked at the NSC and are now delightful, smart, funny, and engaging young adults. This book is dedicated to the four of them.

Notes

Introduction: The Regime Change Temptation

1 "Remarks by President Trump on Iran Strategy," White House, Oct. 13, 2017, www.whitehouse.gov/briefings-statements/remarks-president-trump-iran-strategy/.

2 See Mike Pompeo, "After the Deal: A New Iran Strategy," www.heritage.org/defense/event/after-the-deal-new-iran-strategy; Jason Rezaian, "Mike Pompeo Gives a Silly Speech on Iran," *Washington Post*, May 21, 2018, www.washingtonpost.com/news/global-opinions/wp/2018/05/21/mike-pompeo-gives-a-silly-speech-on-iran/. Pompeo later suggested the administration wanted Iran to "just be like Norway." "Iran Should Behave Like a Normal Nation: Pompeo," ABC News Videos, Jan. 13, 2020, news.yahoo.com/iran-behave-normal-nation-pompeo-222743151.html.

3 Donald J. Trump (@realDonaldTrump), Twitter, Jan. 1, 2018, 7:44 a.m., twitter.com/realdonaldtrump/status/947810806430826496?lang=en. Also see Mike Pence, "Unlike Obama, Trump Will Not Be Silent on Iran," *Washington Post*, Jan. 3, 2018, www.washingtonpost.com/opinions/this-time-we-will-not-be-silent-on-iran/2018/01/03/d1cfc34e-f0cc-11e7-97bf-bba379b809ab_story.html. On the Iran Action Group, see Krishnadev Calmur, "The U.S. Is Developing a New Way to Weaken Iran," *The Atlantic*, Aug. 17, 2018, www.theatlantic.com/international/archive/2018/08/us-iran/567751/.

4 Eliot A. Cohen, "A Reckoning for Obama's Foreign Policy Legacy," *The Atlantic*, May 15, 2018, www.theatlantic.com/ideas/archive/2018/05/lessons-obama-era-foreign-policy-officials-should-learn-from-trump/560387/.

5 "Transcript: Mike Pompeo Talks with Michael Morell on Intelligence Matters," CBS News, May 1, 2019, www.cbsnews.com/news/transcript-mike-pompeo-talks-with-michael-morell-on-intelligence-matters/.

6 Donald J. Trump (@realDonaldTrump), Twitter, May 19, 2019, 4:25

p.m., twitter.com/realdonaldtrump/status/1130207891049332737?lang=en; Seung Min Kim, "Threats Would Mean 'Official End of Iran,' Trump Warns in Tweet," *Washington Post*, May 19, 2019, www.washingtonpost.com/politics/threats-would-mean-official-end-of-iran-trump-warns-in-tweet/2019/05/19/ae347c82-7a81-11e9-a66c-d36e482aa873_story.html.

7 I described some of the parallels in Philip Gordon, "Trump's Iran Strategy Looks Awfully Familiar," *Politico*, Oct. 16, 2017, www.politico.com/magazine/story/2017/10/16/donald-trump-iran-nuclear-deal-215717. Also see David A. Graham, "It's 2003 All Over Again: It Doesn't Require Much Squinting to See the Ways the Iran Crisis Resembles the Lead-Up to the Iraq War," *The Atlantic*, Jan. 6, 2020, www.theatlantic.com/ideas/archive/2020/01/its-beginning-to-look-a-lot-like-2003/604477/; Michael Hirsh and Lara Seligman, "Echoes of Iraq in Trump's Confrontation with Iran," *Foreign Policy*, May 8, 2019, foreignpolicy.com/2019/05/08/echoes-of-iraq-war-in-trump-confrontation-with-iran/. On Trump exaggerating the intelligence, see David E. Sanger and Rick Gladstone, "Contradicting Trump, U.N. Monitor Says Iran Complies with Nuclear Deal," *New York Times*, Aug. 31, 2017, www.nytimes.com/2017/08/31/world/middleeast/un-nuclear-iran-trump.html; David E. Sanger and Julian E. Barnes, "On North Korea and Iran, Intelligence Chiefs Contradict Trump," *New York Times*, Jan. 29, 2019, www.nytimes.com/2019/01/29/us/politics/kim-jong-trump.html.

8 Philip Gordon, "The Middle East Is Falling Apart: America Isn't to Blame. There's No Easy Fix," *Politico*, June 4, 2015, www.politico.com/magazine/story/2015/06/america-not-to-blame-for-middle-east-falling-apart-118611.

9 David Remnick, "Negotiating the Whirlwind," *New Yorker*, Dec. 14, 2015, www.newyorker.com/magazine/2015/12/21/negotiating-the-whirlwind; Jeffrey Goldberg, "Obama's Former Middle East Adviser: 'We Should Have Bombed Assad,'" *The Atlantic*, April 20, 2016, www.theatlantic.com/international/archive/2016/04/philip-gordon-barack-obama-doctrine/479031/.

10 I have included Afghanistan in this study because of its geographical proximity to and similarities with the precedents in the Middle East as more traditionally defined. These factors make the lessons of the two U.S. interventions there far more relevant than other precedents in Europe, Latin America, or Asia. I have not included cases such as U.S. coup planning in Syria in the late 1950s, because while the plans existed they never really became the basis for sustained U.S. policy. The Syria cases are discussed in Douglas Little, "Cold War and Covert Action: The United States and Syria, 1945–1958," *Middle East Journal* 44, no. 1 (Winter 1990): 51–75, www.jstor.org/stable/pdf/4328056.pdf?refreqid=excelsior%3A7bb7efb0fc41716bb5cd591ceb22ff75.

11 Examples include Lindsey A. O'Rourke, *Covert Regime Change: America's*

Secret Cold War (Ithaca, N.Y.: Cornell University Press, 2018); Alexander B. Downes and Lindsey A. O'Rourke, "You Can't Always Get What You Want: Why Foreign-Imposed Regime Change Seldom Improves Interstate Relations," *International Security* 41, no. 2 (Fall 2016): 43–89; Alexander B. Downes and Jonathan Monten, "Forced to Be Free? Why Foreign-Imposed Regime Change Rarely Leads to Democratization," *International Security* 37, no. 4 (Spring 2013): 90–131; Bruce Bueno de Mesquita and George W. Downs, "Intervention and Democracy," *International Organization* 60, no. 3 (Summer 2006); Jeffrey Pickering and Mark Peceny, "Forcing Democracy at Gunpoint," *International Studies Quarterly* 50, no. 3 (Sept. 2006); Stephen Haggard and Lydia Tiede, "The Rule of Law in Post-conflict Settings: The Empirical Record," *International Studies Quarterly* 58, no. 3 (2014); Goran Peic and Dan Reiter, "Foreign-Imposed Regime Change State Power, and Civil War Onset, 1920–2004," *British Journal of Political Science* 41, no. 3 (July 2011): 453–75. Also see Stephen M. Walt, "Why Is the US So Bad at Promoting Democracy in Other Countries?," *Foreign Policy*, April 25, 2016, foreignpolicy.com/2016/04/25/why-is-america-so-bad-at-promoting-democracy-in-other-countries/.

12 Lawrence F. Kaplan and William Kristol, *The War over Iraq: Saddam's Tyranny and America's Mission* (San Francisco: Encounter Books, 2003), 99 (emphasis added).

13 William Kristol and Robert Kagan, "Introduction: National Interest and Global Responsibility," in *Present Dangers: Crisis and Opportunity in American Defense Policy*, ed. Robert Kagan and William Kristol (San Francisco: Encounter Books, 2000), 19.

14 Joshua Muravchik, *Exporting Democracy: Fulfilling America's Destiny* (Washington, D.C.: American Enterprise Institute, 1992), 81–82.

15 Danielle Pletka, "'Regime Change' Has Often Succeeded," *New York Times*, July 25, 2016, www.nytimes.com/roomfordebate/2016/02/28/pursuing-regime-change-in-the-middle-east/regime-change-has-often-succeeded.

16 At peak levels, the United States deployed 1.6 million combat and occupation forces in Germany, and 350,000 troops in Japan. James Dobbins et al., *America's Role in Nation-Building: From Germany to Iraq* (Washington, D.C.: Rand, 2003), xiii–xxii, 9–10, 30.

17 *Guatemala, Memory of Silence: Report on the Commission for Historical Clarification: Conclusions and Recommendations* (New York: United Nations, 1999).

18 Stephen Kinzer, *Overthrow: America's Century of Regime Change from Hawaii to Iraq* (New York: Times Books, 2006), 207.

19 "Paper Prepared by the 5412 Committee," *Foreign Relations of the United States (hereafter cited as FRUS), 1958–1960, Cuba*, vol. 6, doc. 481, history.state.gov/historicaldocuments/frus1958-60v06/d481.

20 Fox Butterfield, "Senior Official in CIA Is Linked to North's Effort on

Contra Arms," *New York Times*, Jan. 21, 1987; David Johnston, "The Iran-Contra Report: The Overview; Walsh Criticizes Reagan and Bush over Iran-Contra," *New York Times*, Jan. 19, 1994.

21 For an excellent assessment of U.S. policy toward Serbia under Milosevic, and how it differs from Syria, see Gregory L. Schulte, "Regime Change Without Military Force: Lessons from Overthrowing Milosevic," *Prism: A Journal of the Center for Complex Operations* 4, no. 2 (2013), cco.ndu.edu/Portals/96/Documents/prism/prism_4-2/prism45-56_Schulte.pdf.

22 Kinzer, *Overthrow*. Other examples include Ivan Eland, "The Empire Strikes Out: The 'New Imperialism' and Its Fatal Flaws," *Cato Institute Policy Analysis*, no. 459, Nov. 26, 2002; Sheila Carapico and Chris Toensing, "The Strategic Logic of the Iraq Blunder," *Middle East Research and Information Project* (Summer 2006); Nafeez Ahmed, "Iraq Invasion Was About Oil," *Guardian*, March 20, 2014; and Michael Klare, *Blood and Oil* (New York: Holt Books, 2004).

23 Michael Crowley, "'Keep the Oil': Trump Revives Charged Slogan for New Syria Troop Mission," *New York Times*, Oct. 26, 2019, www.nytimes.com/2019/10/26/us/politics/trump-syria-oil-fields.html; Dino Grandoni, "The Energy 202: Trump's Desire 'to Take' Syrian Oil Presents a Barrelful of Problems," *Washington Post*, Oct. 28, 2019, www.washingtonpost.com/news/powerpost/paloma/the-energy-202/2019/10/28/the-energy-202-trump-s-desire-to-take-syrian-oil-presents-a-barrelful-of-problems/5db5df8088e0fa5ad928dafb/; Robin Wright, "Trump's Baffling Plan to Pillage Syria's Oil," *New Yorker*, Oct. 30, 2019, www.newyorker.com/news/our-columnists/trumps-baffling-plan-to-pillage-syrias-oil.

24 In October 2019, Trump deployed U.S. forces in eastern Syria to "secure" and "protect" the oil fields there, but notwithstanding his repeated claims the United States did not actually take any of the oil for its own use. For some U.S. military leaders, allowing Trump to believe or claim the U.S. had taken the oil was simply the price to be paid for maintaining counterterrorism forces in Syria, "like feeding a baby its medicine in yogurt or applesauce," according to one U.S. official. Karen DeYoung, Dan Lamothe, Missy Ryan, and Michael Birnbaum, "Trump Decided to Leave Troops in Syria After Conversations About Oil, Officials Say," *Washington Post*, Oct. 25, 2019, https://www.washingtonpost.com/world/us-defense-secretary-mark-esper-says-us-will-leave-forces-in-syria-to-defend-oil-fields-from-islamic-state/2019/10/25/fd131f1a-f723-11e9-829d-87b12c2f85dd_story.html; Alex Ward, "Trump: We Should Keep Syria's Oil. The Pentagon: Nope," *Vox*, Nov. 7, 2019, www.vox.com/policy-and-politics/2019/11/7/20953612/trump-syria-oil-kurds-isis.

25 For an excellent study of Americans' tendency to overestimate their ability to remake the world in their image, see Peter Beinart, *The Icarus Syndrome: A History of American Hubris* (New York: HarperPerennial, 2010). And on their tendency to do so in the Middle East in particular, see Martin Indyk,

Innocent Abroad: An Intimate Account of American Peace Diplomacy in the Middle East (New York: Simon & Schuster, 2009).

Chapter 1: Original Sin

1 Kermit Roosevelt, *Countercoup* (New York: McGraw-Hill, 1979), 107.
2 Christopher de Bellaigue, *Muhammad Mossadegh and a Tragic Anglo-American Coup* (New York: HarperPerennial, 2013).
3 "1951 Man of the Year: Mohammed Mosaddegh," *Time*, Jan. 7, 1952, www.freeprotocols.org/content/republished/doc.public/politics/iran/mossadeq/1951TimesManOfTheYear/main.pdf.
4 Originally founded in 1909 as the Anglo-Persian Oil Company, AIOC was renamed Anglo-Iranian by Reza Shah in 1935.
5 Ervand Abrahamian, *The Coup: 1953, the CIA, and the Roots of Modern U.S.-Iranian Relations* (New York: New Press, 2013), 11–15.
6 See Kenneth M. Pollack, *The Persian Puzzle: The Conflict Between Iran and America* (New York: Random House, 2005), 56.
7 Mark J. Gasiorowski, "The 1953 Coup d'État Against Mosaddeq," in *Mohammad Mosaddeq and the 1953 Coup in Iran*, ed. Mark J. Gasiorowski and Malcolm Byrne (Syracuse, N.Y.: Syracuse University Press, 2004), 229.
8 Kinzer, *Overthrow*, 124, and Stephen Kinzer, *All the Shah's Men: An American Coup and the Roots of Middle East Terror* (Hoboken, N.J.: John Wiley and Sons, 2008), 98.
9 Grady, interview with *Wall Street Journal*, June 9, 1951, cited in Kinzer, *All the Shah's Men*, 93.
10 Barry Rubin, *Paved with Good Intentions: The American Experience and Iran* (New York: Penguin Books, 1980), 47.
11 Mark J. Gasiorowski, "U.S. Perceptions of the Communist Threat in Iran During the Mossadegh Era," *Journal of Cold War Studies* (Summer 2019): 185–221.
12 Nov. 26, 1951, Foreign Office cable, cited in Abrahamian, *Coup*, 174.
13 Woodhouse was accompanied by Sam Falle of the Foreign Office. Gasiorowski, "1953 Coup d'État Against Mosaddeq," 227.
14 C. M. Woodhouse, *Something Ventured* (London: Granada, 1982), 117, cited in Kinzer, *All the Shah's Men*, 3–4.
15 Kinzer, *Overthrow*, 122; "Memorandum of Discussion at the 135th Meeting of the National Security Council, Washington, March 4, 1953," *FRUS, 1952–1954, Iran, 1951–1954*, vol. 10.
16 Gasiorowski, "1953 Coup d'État Against Mosaddeq," 232.
17 James Risen, "Secrets of History: The C.I.A. in Iran," *New York Times, April 16*, 2000, archive.nytimes.com/www.nytimes.com/library/world/mideast/041600iran-cia-index.html; James Risen, "How a Plot Convulsed Iran in '53 (and '79)," *New York Times*, April 19, 2000, archive.nytimes.com/www.nytimes.com/learning/teachers/featured_articles/20000419wednesday.html.

18 Kinzer, *All the Shah's Men*, 156.

19 Gasiorowski, "U.S. Perceptions of the Communist Threat," 195–221; Gasiorowski, email correspondence with author, Aug. 22, 2019.

20 "The Secretary of State to the Embassy in Iran," *FRUS, 1952–1954, Iran, 1951–1954*, vol. 10.

21 "Telegram from the Embassy in Iran to the Department of State," *FRUS, 1952–1954, Iran, 1951–1954*, doc. 203.

22 Both quotations from Rubin, *Paved with Good Intentions*, 78, 80.

23 The NIE did warn, however, that "if present trends in Iran continued unchecked beyond the end of 1953, rising internal tensions . . . might lead to a breakdown of government authority and open the way for at least a gradual assumption of control by Tudeh." "National Intelligence Estimate," *FRUS, 1952–1954, Iran, 1951–1954*, doc. 143; Gasiorowski, "1953 Coup d'État Against Mosaddeq," 230–31.

24 Malcolm Byrne, introduction to Gasiorowski and Byrne, *Mohammad Mosaddeq and the 1953 Coup*, xviii. Also see Maziar Behrooz, "The 1953 Coup in Iran and the Legacy of the Tudeh," in ibid.; and Abrahamian, *Coup*, 174–76.

25 James A. Bill, *The Eagle and the Lion: The Tragedy of American-Iranian Relations* (New Haven, Conn.: Yale University Press, 1988), 91–95; Hugh Wilford, *America's Great Game: The CIA's Secret Arabists and the Shaping of the Modern Middle East* (New York: Basic Books, 2013), 163–64; Gasiorowski, "1953 Coup d'État Against Mosaddeq," 233.

26 The quotation is from CIA official Richard Cottam, who was involved in the agency's press and propaganda effort, cited in Kinzer, *All the Shah's Men*, 6.

27 The detailed coup plans are best summarized in Gasiorowski, "1953 Coup d'État Against Mosaddeq," 233–40.

28 Also influential in persuading the shah to support the coup was General Norman Schwarzkopf, a top U.S. military officer who had become close to the shah while commanding the Iranian gendarmerie from 1942 to 1948. Schwarzkopf was the father of the general of the same name who would command coalition forces in the 1991 invasion of Iraq. Gasiorowski, "1953 Coup d'État Against Mosaddeq," 247.

29 Eisenhower formally rejected Mosaddeq's aid request on June 30, 1953. "Telegram from the Department of State to the Embassy in Iran," *FRUS, 1952–1954, Iran, 1951–1954*, doc. 230.

30 "Telegram from the Central Intelligence Agency to the Station in Iran," *FRUS, 1952–1954, Iran, 1951–1954*, doc. 278.

31 Gasiorowski, "1953 Coup d'État Against Mosaddeq," 255, 259. Also Kinzer, *All the Shah's Men*, 168, 183.

32 Gasiorowski, "1953 Coup d'État Against Mosaddeq," 257; Kinzer, *All the Shah's Men*, 191; Risen, "How a Plot Convulsed Iran in '53 (and in '79)."

33 AIOC, renamed British Petroleum, also got 40 percent, while Royal

Dutch Shell got 14 percent, and Compagnie Française des Pétroles (later Total SA), got 6 percent.

34 Rubin, *Paved with Good Intentions*, 93.

35 Pollack, *Persian Puzzle*, 73; Abrahamian, *Coup*, 213.

36 Rubin points out that "the prime minister had always been the shah's appointee; now he became, in effect, the shah's executive assistant." Rubin, *Paved with Good Intentions*, 93.

37 Abrahamian, *Coup*, 214; Gasiorowski, "1953 Coup d'État Against Mosaddeq," in Gasiorowski and Byrne, *Mohammad Mosaddeq and the 1953 Coup*, 257–58.

38 National Security Archive, "New Findings on Clerical Involvement in the 1953 Coup in Iran," Washington, D.C., March 7, 2018, nsarchive.gwu.edu/briefing-book/iran/2018-03-07/new-findings-clerical-involvement-1953-coup-iran.

39 Pollack, *Persian Puzzle*, 118–19; Said Arjomand, *The Turban for the Crown: The Islamic Revolution in Iran* (New York: Oxford University Press, 1988), 91–94; Bill, *The Eagle and the Lion*, 218.

40 Byrne, introduction to Gasiorowski and Byrne, *Mohammad Mosaddeq and the 1953 Coup*, xv.

41 In a 1962 speech at the White House, Kennedy warned that "those who make peaceful revolution impossible will make violent revolution inevitable," a comment the shah took to be directed at Iran. Cited in Pollack, *Persian Puzzle*, 81.

42 Roham Alvandi, *Nixon, Kissinger, and the Shah: The United States and Iran in the Cold War* (Oxford: Oxford University Press, 2016), 49.

43 Tehran 1019 to State, March 19, 1970, *FRUS, 1969–1976*, vol. E-4, 55, history.state.gov/historicaldocuments/frus1969-76ve04/d55, cited in Alvandi, *Nixon, Kissinger, and the Shah*, 49.

44 Cited in Bernard Gwertzman, "Shah Cautions U.S. Against Arms Cut," *New York Times*, Aug. 7, 1976.

45 Woodhouse added, "At the time we were simply relieved that a threat to British interests had been removed." Woodhouse, *Something Ventured*, 131.

46 Eisenhower, Oct. 8, 1953, diary entry, https://www.eisenhowerlibrary.gov/sites/default/files/file/declass_fy10_1953_10_08.pdf.

47 Henry A. Kissinger, *White House Years* (Boston: Little, Brown, 1979), 1261.

48 Many of these measures are discussed in Pollack, *Persian Puzzle*, 105–6. Also see Mohammad Ataie, "Is Iran Abnormal?" *Lobelog*, Sept. 9, 2019, lobelog.com/is-iran-abnormal/.

49 In the summer of 1976, just before Carter's election, a report by the inspector general of the U.S. Foreign Service concluded that "the Government of Iran exerts the determining influence" in the relationship with the United States, because Iran contributed more financially to the United States than the other way around, and "he who pays the piper

calls the tune." Report cited in Gary Sick, *All Fall Down: America's Tragic Encounter with Iran* (New York: Random House, 1985), 20. Similarly, a 1978 study at Harvard by Robert L. Paarlberg came to the conclusion that in bilateral disputes with the United States, Iran prevailed far more frequently after the 1953 coup (when the shah was supposed to be America's puppet) than it did before. Robert L. Paarlberg, "The Advantageous Alliance: U.S. Relations with Iran, 1920–1975," in *Diplomatic Dispute: U.S. Conflict with Iran, Japan, and Mexico*, ed. Robert L. Paarlberg (Cambridge, Mass.: Harvard University Center for International Affairs, 1978), 17–53.

50 Rubin, *Paved with Good Intentions*, 55.

51 Byrne, introduction to Gasiorowski and Byrne, *Mohammad Mosaddeq and the 1953 Coup in Iran*, xv.

52 National Security Archive, "Iran 1953: US Envoy to Baghdad Suggested to Fleeing Shah He Not Acknowledge Foreign Role in Coup. Shah 'Agreed,' Declassified Cable Says," ed. Malcolm Byrne, posted July 2, 2014.

53 Eisenhower diary entry in "Editorial Note," *FRUS, 1952–1954, Iran, 1951–1954*, doc. 328.

54 Richard Harkness and Gladys Harkness, "The Mysterious Doings of CIA," *Saturday Evening Post*, Nov. 6, 1954.

55 Darioush Bayandor, *Iran and the CIA: The Fall of Mosaddeq Revisited* (London: Palgrave, 2010); Abbas Milani, *The Shah* (New York: St. Martin's Press, 2011); Ray Takeyh, "What Really Happened in Iran: The CIA, the Ouster of Mosaddeq, and the Restoration of the Shah," *Foreign Affairs*, June 16, 2014; Ray Takeyh, "The Myths of 1953," *Weekly Standard*, July 14, 2017.

56 Takeyh, "What Really Happened in Iran."

57 "Iran One Year Later: The Trump Administration's Policy, Looking Back and Looking Forward," Center for Strategic and International Studies, May 8, 2019, www.youtube.com/watch?v=7jEoSW9Sd68; Gregory Brew, "Misreading the 1953 Coup," *Lobelog*, May 20, 2019, lobelog.com/misreading-the-1953-coup/.

58 Mark J. Gasiorowski, "Why Did Mosaddeq Fall?" in Gasiorowski and Byrne, *Mohammad Mosaddeq and the 1953 Coup*, 276. Also see Mark J. Gasiorowski, "The Causes of Iran's 1953 Coup: A Critique of Darioush Bayandor's *Iran and the CIA*," *Iranian Studies*, July 13, 2012; Roham Alvandi and Mark J. Gasiorowski, "The United States Overthrew Iran's Last Democratic Leader," *Foreign Policy*, Oct. 30, 2019, foreignpolicy.com/2019/10/30/the-united-states-overthrew-irans-last-democratic-leader/. Mosaddeq's biographer Christopher de Bellaigue agrees it was "a military coup sponsored [and] organized by foreigners," while former CIA analyst Kenneth Pollack stresses that Iranian attempts to score points by blaming the United States for the coup do not negate the reality that "the United States *did* help to overthrow Mossadeq, and it *was* complicit in the establishment of Mohammad Reza Shah that succeeded him." See

Christopher de Bellaigue, "Iran 1953: 'A Casual Coup with a Few Dollars,'" discussion at the Asia Society, May 17, 2012, www.youtube.com/watch?v=BEjSuUYxvP4; Pollack, *Persian Puzzle*, 69.

59 See Dan Merica and Jason Hanna, "In Declassified Document, CIA Acknowledges Role in '53 Iran Coup," www.cnn.com/2013/08/19/politics/cia-iran-1953-coup/ (emphasis added).

60 George Washington University National Security Archive, CIA, History, *The Battle for Iran,* author's name excised, n.d. (ca. mid-1970s), 28, nsarchive2.gwu.edu/NSAEBB/NSAEBB435/docs/CIA%20-%20Battle%20for%20Iran%20-%202013%20release.PDF.

61 "CIA Confirms Role in 1953: Documents Provide New Details on Mossadeq Overthrow and Its Aftermath," ed. Malcolm Byrne, National Security Archive, nsarchive2.gwu.edu/NSAEBB/NSAEBB435/.

62 National Security Archive, "New Findings on Clerical Involvement in the 1953 Coup in Iran"; "1953 Iran Coup: New U.S. Documents Confirm British Approached U.S. in Late 1952 About Ousting Mosaddeq," ed. Malcolm Byrne and Mark Gasiorowski, National Security Archive, nsarchive.gwu.edu/briefing-book/iran/2017-08-08/1953-iran-coup-new-us-documents-confirm-british-approached-us-late.

63 On October 8, 1953, diary entry, see "Editorial Note," FRUS, *1952–1954, Iran, 1951–1954*, doc. 328.

64 Ibid.

65 Gwen Kinkead, "Kermit Roosevelt: Brief Life of a Harvard Conspirator, 1916–2000," *Harvard Magazine*, Jan.–Feb. 2011, harvardmagazine.com/2011/01/kermit-roosevelt.

Chapter 2: "We Won"

1 Steve Coll, *Ghost Wars: The Secret History of the CIA, Afghanistan, and Bin Laden, from the Soviet Invasion to September 10, 2001* (New York: Penguin Books, 2005), 50; Robert Gates, *From the Shadows: The Ultimate Insider's Story of Five Presidents and How They Won the Cold War* (New York: Simon & Schuster, 2006), 133.

2 Jimmy Carter, *White House Diary* (New York: Farrar, Straus and Giroux, 2010), 382.

3 Cited in Gates, *From the Shadows*, 144.

4 Ibid., 146; Coll, *Ghost Wars*, 46.

5 Gates, *From the Shadows*, 149.

6 "Reflections on Soviet Intervention in Afghanistan," Memorandum from the President's Assistant for National Security Affairs (Brzezinski) to President Carter, Dec. 26, 1979, Department of State, *FRUS, 1977–1980, vol. 12, Afghanistan,* history.state.gov/historicaldocuments/frus1977-80v12/d97, cited in Coll, *Ghost Wars*, 51. Also Kurt Lohbeck, *Holy War, Unholy Victory: Eyewitness to the CIA's Secret War in Afghanistan* (Washington, D.C.: Regnery Gateway, 1993), 43.

7 "Presidential Decisions on Pakistan, Afghanistan, and India," Memorandum

from the President's Assistant for National Security Affairs (Brzezinski) to Secretary of State Vance, Jan. 2, 1980, Department of State, *FRUS, 1977–1980, vol. 12, Afghanistan*, doc. 128, history.state.gov/historicaldocuments/frus1977-80v12/d128.

8 "Special Coordination Committee Meeting," Jan. 17, 1980, declassified document NLS-33-5-12-I-6, Brzezinski Collection, Carter Library, cited in Justin Vaïsse, *Zbigniew Brzezinski: America's Grand Strategist* (Cambridge, Mass.: Harvard University Press, 2018), 309. Also see Zbigniew Brzezinski, *Power and Principle: Memoirs of the National Security Adviser, 1977–1981* (New York: Farrar, Straus, Giroux, 1982), 430–37.

9 Steve Galster, "Afghanistan: The Making of U.S. Policy, 1973–1990," Sept. 11th Sourcebooks, National Security Archive, George Washington University, Oct. 9, 2001, 12, www2gwu.edu/~nsarchive/NSAEBB/NSAEBB57/essay.html.

10 Frank Anderson, "Cold War Interviews," National Security Archive, George Washington University, Aug. 1997, cited in Bruce Riedel, *What We Won: America's Secret War in Afghanistan, 1979–89* (Washington, D.C.: Brookings Institution Press, 2014), 113.

11 Robert Pear, "Arming Afghan Guerrillas: A Huge Effort Led by U.S.," *New York Times*, April 18, 1988, www.nytimes.com/1988/04/18/world/arming-afghan-guerrillas-a-huge-effort-led-by-us.html.

12 Bob Woodward and Charles R. Babcock, "U.S. Covert Aid to Afghans on the Rise," *Washington Post*, Jan. 13, 1985.

13 Hamilton Jordan, *Crisis: The Last Year of the Carter Presidency* (New York: Putnam, 1982), 101.

14 Coll, *Ghost Wars*, 65. See Gates, *From the Shadows*, 251; Peter L. Bergen, *Holy War Inc.: Inside the Secret World of Osama bin Laden* (New York: Free Press, 2001), 68.

15 Barnett R. Rubin, *The Fragmentation of Afghanistan: State Formation and Collapse in the International System* (New Haven, Conn.: Yale University Press, 1995), 197; Steve Coll, "CIA in Afghanistan: In CIA's Covert War, Where to Draw the Line Was Key," *Washington Post*, July 20, 1992.

16 Woodward and Babcock, "U.S. Covert Aid to Afghans on the Rise."

17 "S.Con.Res.74. A Concurrent Resolution to Encourage and Support the People of Afghanistan in Their Struggle to Be Free from Foreign Domination: 98th Congress (1983–1984)," www.congress.gov/bill/98th-congress/senate-concurrent-resolution/74/actions?r=7.

18 Pear, "Arming Afghan Guerrillas."

19 Woodward and Babcock, "U.S. Covert Aid to Afghans on the Rise."

20 Ronald Reagan, "Proclamation 4908—Afghanistan Day," March 10, 1982.

21 "Space Shuttle's Flight Dedicated to Afghans," *New York Times*, March 11, 1982, www.nytimes.com/1982/03/11/world/space-shuttle-s-flight-dedicated-to-afghans.html.

22 A YouTube video of Reagan meeting the rebels can be found at "Reagan reçoit les moujahidines Afghans à la Maison Blanche," www.youtube.com/watch?v=PAvF0N772io.

23 Pear, "Arming Afghan Guerrillas"; "Ronald Reagan, 40th President of the United States, 1981–1989: Address Before a Joint Session of Congress on the State of the Union," *American Presidency Project*, Feb. 4, 1986.

24 Gerald M. Boyd, "Reagan Terms Nicaraguan Rebels 'Moral Equivalent of Founding Fathers,'" *New York Times,* March 2, 1985.

25 Riedel, *What We Won,* 42–55. Also see Barnett R. Rubin, *Afghanistan from the Cold War Through the War on Terror* (Oxford: Oxford University Press, 2013); Olivier Roy, *Afghanistan: From Holy War to Civil War* (Princeton, N.J.: Darwin Press, 1995).

26 White House, National Security Decision Directive 166, "U.S. Policy, Programs, and Strategy in Afghanistan," fas.org/irp/offdocs/nsdd/nsdd-166.pdf.

27 Gates, *From the Shadows,* 349.

28 Coll, *Ghost Wars,* 125–27; Philip Zelikow, Ernest May, and Kirsten Lundberg, "Politics of a Covert Action: The US, the Mujahideen, and the Stinger Missile," John F. Kennedy School of Government, Nov. 9, 1999, case.hks.harvard.edu/politics-of-a-covert-action-the-u-s-the-mujahideen-and-the-stinger-missile/.

29 Milt Bearden and James Risen, *The Main Enemy: The Inside Story of the CIA's Final Showdown with the KGB* (New York: Random House, 2003), 240; Bergen, *Holy War Inc.,* 79; Mark Urban, *War in Afghanistan* (London: Macmillan, 1988), 244. According to George Crile, the funding represented 50 percent of the CIA operations budget in 1985 and would rise to 70 percent the following year. George Crile, *Charlie Wilson's War: The Extraordinary Story of How the Wildest Man in Congress and a Rogue CIA Agent Changed the History of Our Times* (New York: Grove Press, 2007), 339.

30 Crile, *Charlie Wilson's War,* 419.

31 Bergen, *Holy War Inc.,* 74.

32 Pear, "Arming Afghan Guerrillas."

33 Anatoly Dobrynin, *In Confidence: Moscow's Ambassador to America's Six Cold War Presidents (1962–1986)* (New York: Times Books, 1995), 435; Seth G. Jones, *Graveyard of Empires: America's War in Afghanistan* (New York: Norton, 2009), 18.

34 Rodric Braithwaite, *Afgantsy: The Russians in Afghanistan, 1979–1989* (Oxford: Oxford University Press, 2011), 272–73.

35 David B. Ottoway, "Agreement on Afghanistan Signed in Geneva," *Washington Post,* April 15, 1988, www.washingtonpost.com/archive/politics/1988/04/15/agreement-on-afghanistan-signed-in-geneva/c7288c64-6764-4e73-9bc5-7eeb48f7827d/?utm_term=.d5f5da9da98e.

36 Zalmay Khalilzad, "How the Good Guys Won in Afghanistan," *Washington Post,* Feb. 12, 1989.

37 Richard Mackenzie, "When Policy Tolls in a Fool's Paradise," *Insight*, Sept. 11, 1989.
38 Cited in Crile, *Charlie Wilson's War,* 504; Riedel, *What We Won,* 127; Coll, *Ghost Wars,* 185.
39 Khalilzad, "How the Good Guys Won in Afghanistan."
40 Director of Central Intelligence, "USSR: Withdrawal from Afghanistan," Special National Intelligence Estimate, March 1988, www.cia.gov/library/readingroom/docs/CIA-RDP09T00367R000200120001-3.pdf.
41 Ibid.; Riedel, *What We Won,* 129; Jones, *Graveyard of Empires,* 42.
42 For Zia, see Selig S. Harrison, "Who Will Win the Bloody Battle for Kabul?" *Washington Post*, Jan. 29, 1989, www.washingtonpost.com/archive/opinions/1989/01/29/who-will-win-the-bloody-battle-for-kabul/6ba0fd58-1e5f-4d91-874d-99e9d4e1ec0a/?noredirect=on&utm_term=.7deef4d0e7ef. For Bhutto, see Bruce Riedel, *Avoiding Armageddon: America, India, and Pakistan to the Brink and Back* (Washington, D.C.: Brookings Institution Press, 2013), 108; and Benazir Bhutto, *Daughter of the East: An Autobiography* (London: Hamish Hamilton, 1988), 400.
43 Reagan's comment came in the context of talks with the Soviets in Geneva on provisions for Afghanistan following a Soviet departure. Dennis Kux, *The United States and Pakistan, 1947–2000: Disenchanted Allies* (Baltimore: Johns Hopkins University Press, 2001), 289.
44 Richard Mackenzie, "Resistance Forces Seem Unable to Resist Infighting," with Glenn Simpson, *Insight*, Sept. 11, 1989.
45 Riedel, email correspondence with author, Aug. 26, 2019.
46 Coll, *Ghost Wars,* 208.
47 Ibid., 217.
48 Bergen, *Holy War Inc.,* 70.
49 Ibid., 68–70; Henry S. Bradsher, *Afghan Communism and Soviet Intervention* (Karachi, Pakistan: Oxford University Press, 1999), 220; Coll, "CIA in Afghanistan."
50 Coll, *Ghost Wars,* 174.
51 Harrison, "Who Will Win the Bloody Battle for Kabul?"
52 Michael T. Kaufman, "U.S. Said to Weigh Extensive Arms Sales to Pakistan," *New York Times*, March 5, 1981.
53 "Your Meeting with Pakistan President . . ." and "Visit of Zia-ul-Haq," in Christian F. Ostermann and Mircea Munteanu, "Towards an International History of the War in Afghanistan, 1979–1989," *Cold War International History Project,* Wilson Center, July 12, 2011, www.wilsoncenter.org/publication/towards-international-history-the-war-afghanistan-1979-1989.
54 "Classified Congressional Briefing on Pakistani Clandestine Nuclear-Related Procurement," July 26, 1987, nsarchive2.gwu.edu/nukevault/ebb446/docs/12.pdf; "Memorandum for the Undersecretary of State for

Political Affairs," Nov. 4, 1987, nsarchive2.gwu.edu/nukevault/ebb446/docs/20.pdf.

55 Coll, *Ghost Wars*, 165; Bergen, *Holy War Inc.*, 55.

56 Bergen, *Holy War Inc.*, 55.

57 Riedel, *What We Won*, 88; Bergen, *Holy War Inc.*, 55; Thomas Hegghammer, "The Rise of Muslim Foreign Fighters: Islam and the Globalization of Jihad," *International Security* 35, no. 3 (Winter 2010–11): 9, www.belfercenter.org/sites/default/files/files/publication/The_Rise_of_Muslim_Foreign_Fighters.pdf.

58 Jones, *Graveyard of Empires*; Lawrence Wright, *The Looming Tower: Al Qaeda and the Road to 9/11* (New York: Vintage, 2007), 110; Gilles Kepel, *Jihad: The Trail of Political Islam* (Cambridge, Mass.: Harvard University Press, 2002), 147.

59 Bhutto, *Daughter of the East*, 402.

60 Coll, *Ghost Wars*, 182.

61 Bergen, *Holy War Inc.*, 70.

62 Ibid., 73.

63 Ibid.

64 Thomas W. Lippman, "Aid to Afghan Rebels Returns to Haunt U.S.," *Washington Post*, July 26, 1993 (emphases added).

65 Gates, interview with Coll, in *Ghost Wars*, 168; Gates, *From the Shadows*, 424–25.

66 Andrew Bacevich, *America's War for the Greater Middle East: A Military History* (New York: Random House, 2017), 53.

67 Lippman, "Aid to Afghan Rebels Returns to Haunt U.S."

68 Gates, *From the Shadows*, 349.

69 Brzezinski, interview with *Le Nouvel Observateur*, "Brzezinski: Oui, la CIA est entrée en Afghanistan avant les Russes," *Le Nouvel Observateur*, Jan. 15, 1998, www.voltairenet.org/article165889.html.

70 Imtiyaz Gul Khan, "Afghanistan: Human Cost of Armed Conflict Since the Soviet Invasion," *Perceptions* (Winter 2012): 212–14; Jones, *Graveyard of Empires*, 25.

71 Tomsen cited in Coll, *Ghost Wars*, 239; Peter Tomsen, *The Wars of Afghanistan: Messianic Terrorism, Tribal Conflicts, and the Failures of Great Powers* (New York: PublicAffairs, 2013).

72 Zalmay Khalilzad, "Afghanistan: Time to Reengage," *Washington Post*, Oct. 7, 1996.

73 Riedel, *What We Won*, 132.

74 Bush's April 18, 2002, speech at the Virginia Military Institute cited in James Dao, "A Nation Challenged: The President; Bush Sets Role in Afghanistan Rebuilding," *New York Times*, April 18, 2002, www.nytimes.com/2002/04/18/world/a-nation-challenged-the-president-bush-sets-role-for-us-in-afghan-rebuilding.html.

75 "Joint Press Conference with Secretary Gates and Afghanistan President Karzai in Kabul, Afghanistan," news transcript, Department of

Defense, June 4, 2011, archive.defense.gov/Transcripts/Transcript.aspx?TranscriptID=4832.

76 Bergen, email exchange with author, Oct. 23, 2019.

Chapter 3: "We Have Turned a Corner"

1 Transcript of President Bush's speech to Congress, Sept. 20, 2001, www.npr.org/news/specials/americatransformed/reaction/010920.bushspeech.html.

2 Public Law 107-40, Sept. 18, 2001, www.congress.gov/107/plaws/publ40/PLAW-107publ40.pdf.

3 Barbara Lee, "Why I Opposed the Resolution to Authorize Force," Sept. 14, 2001, *Meridians* 2, no. 2 (2002), www.jstor.org/stable/40338529?seq=1#page_scan_tab_contents. Almost eighteen years later, the House of Representatives voted to repeal the 2001 AUMF. Tara Golshein, "House Democrats Vote to Repeal 9/11-Era Law Used to Authorize Perpetual War," *Vox*, June 19, 2019, www.vox.com/policy-and-politics/2019/6/19/18691936/house-democrats-vote-repeal-9-11-aumf-war-iran.

4 Rice, interview with Tony Snow, Fox News, Sept. 23, 2001, at www.washingtonpost.com/wp-srv/nation/specials/attacked/transcripts/foxtext092301.html.

5 Cheney cited in Bob Woodward, *Bush at War* (New York: Simon & Schuster, 2002), 127, 192.

6 Powell, interview, *This Week on Sunday*, ABC, Sept. 23, 2001, 2001–2009.state.gov/secretary/former/powell/remarks/2001/5011.htm.

7 Cited in Woodward, *Bush at War*, 130.

8 See Steve Coll, *Directorate S: The C.I.A. and America's Secret Wars in Afghanistan and Pakistan* (New York: Penguin, 2018), 80; Jones, *Graveyard of Empires*, 90.

9 "U.S. Strategy in Afghanistan," memo from Donald Rumsfeld to Doug Feith, Oct. 30, 2001, cited in "New Documents Detail America's Strategic Response to 9/11," National Security Archive, Sept. 11, 2011, nsarchive2.gwu.edu/NSAEBB/NSAEBB358a/doc18.pdf.

10 George W. Bush, "Prime Time News Conference," Washington, D.C., Oct. 11, 2001, cited in Ivo H. Daalder and James M. Lindsay, *America Unbound: The Bush Revolution in Foreign Policy* (Washington, D.C.: Brookings Institution Press, 2003), 106.

11 "A Nation Challenged: No Isolation from Evil, Bush Declares," *New York Times*, Nov. 11, 2001, www.nytimes.com/2001/11/11/world/a-nation-challenged-no-isolation-from-evil-bush-declares.html.

12 For Powell, see John Kifner with Eric Schmitt, "A Nation Challenged: The Military; Al Qaeda Routed from Afghanistan, U.S. Officials Say," *New York Times*, Dec. 17, 2001, www.nytimes.com/2001/12/17/world/nation-challenged-military-al-qaeda-routed-afghanistan-us-officials-say.html. For Bush, see Office of the Press Secretary, White House, "President

Delivers State of the Union Address," Jan. 29, 2002, georgewbush-whitehouse.archives.gov/news/releases/2002/01/20020129-11.html.

13 Rice's speech to the Johns Hopkins School of Advanced International Studies, April 29, 2002, georgewbush-whitehouse.archives.gov/news/releases/2002/04/20020429-9.html.

14 Tommy Franks, *American Soldier* (New York: Regan Books, 2004), 314, 325.

15 For an example of Rumsfeld's caution, see Matthew Engel, "Rumsfeld and Powell Fight over the Meaning of Victory," *Guardian*, Dec. 17, 2001, www.theguardian.com/world/2001/dec/18/afghanistan.matthewengel. For Wolfowitz, see "Deputy Secretary Wolfowitz Interview with CNN *Late Edition*," Dec. 9, 2001, Department of Defense News Transcript, https://archive.defense.gov/Transcripts/Transcript.aspx?TranscriptID=2620.

16 Donald Rumsfeld, *Known and Unknown: A Memoir* (New York: Sentinel, 2011), 405; Bacevich, *America's War for the Greater Middle East,* 231; Franks, *American Soldier*, 262.

17 Bacevich, *America's War for the Greater Middle East,* 232.

18 Charles Krauthammer, "Where Power Talks," *Washington Post,* Jan. 4, 2002, www.washingtonpost.com/archive/opinions/2002/01/04/where-power-talks/704fcb2f-f299-456e-908d-ba081e60877d/.

19 Max Boot, "The Case for American Empire," *Weekly Standard,* Oct. 15, 2001, www.weeklystandard.com/max-boot/the-case-for-american-empire. Boot would later distance himself from "unapologetic imperialism" while continuing to support "nation-building" in Afghanistan. See Max Boot, *The Corrosion of Conservativism: Why I Left the Right* (New York: Liveright, 2018), 50, 54; Max Boot, "Back to Nation-Building in Afghanistan? Good," *New York Times*, Aug. 22, 2017, www.nytimes.com/2017/08/22/opinion/president-trump-nation-building-afghanistan.html.

20 Milton Bearden, "Afghanistan: Graveyard of Empires," *Foreign Affairs,* Nov./Dec. 2001, www.foreignaffairs.com/articles/afghanistan/2001-11-01/afghanistan-graveyard-empires.

21 "U.S. Strategy in Afghanistan," Rumsfeld memo to Feith, Oct. 30, 2001; Bearden, "Afghanistan: Graveyard of Empires."

22 Rubin, *Afghanistan from the Cold War Through the War on Terror,* 17.

23 Woodward, *Bush at War*, 192.

24 David Rohde and David E. Sanger, "How a 'Good War' in Afghanistan Went Bad," *New York Times*, Aug. 12, 2007, www.nytimes.com/2007/08/12/world/asia/12afghan.html.

25 Ibid.

26 Jones, *Graveyard of Empires*, 110.

27 Ibid., 115, 126.

28 Rice cited in Daalder and Lindsay, *America Unbound,* 112.

29 For Franks's force recommendations, see Franks, *American Soldier*, 324,

334. On the numbers of weapons in Afghanistan at least as of 1992 after a decade of imports from both the Soviet Union and the United States, see Coll, *Ghost Wars*, 238.

30 In Bosnia there were 18.6 peacekeepers per thousand people and in Kosovo 20 per thousand, whereas in Afghanistan from 2003 to 2007 there were on average fewer than 2 peacekeepers per thousand Afghans. Dobbins et al., *America's Role in Nation-Building,* 136.

31 The initiative is discussed in Carter Malkasian, "How the Good War Turned Bad: America's Slow-Motion Failure in Afghanistan," *Foreign Affairs*, March/April 2020, https://www.foreignaffairs.com/articles/afghanistan/2020-02-10/how-good-war-went-bad.

32 Brian Knowlton, *International Herald Tribune*, "Rumsfeld Rejects Plan to Allow Mullah Omar 'to Live in Dignity': Taliban Fighters Agree to Surrender Kandahar," *New York Times,* Dec. 7, 2001, www.nytimes.com/2001/12/07/news/rumsfeld-rejects-planto-allow-mullah-omar-to-live-in-dignity-taliban.html.

33 Coll, *Directorate S*, 144.

34 Sean Naylor, *Not a Good Day to Die: The Untold Story of Operation Anaconda* (New York: Berkley Books, 2005).

35 Sean Naylor, "The Lessons of Anaconda," *New York Times*, March 2, 2003, www.nytimes.com/2003/03/02/opinion/the-lessons-of-anaconda.html.

36 Franks, *American Soldier*, 379.

37 Vernon Loeb, "Rumsfeld Announces End of Afghan Combat," *Washington Post*, May 2, 2003, www.washingtonpost.com/archive/politics/2003/05/02/rumsfeld-announces-end-of-afghan-combat/9507f2f8-a7e8-497c-be9d-5eae475f1b47/.

38 Jones, *Graveyard of Empires*, 148.

39 Robert Gates, *Duty: Memoirs of a Secretary at War* (New York: Vintage Books, 2015), 199.

40 James Dobbins, "Ending Afghanistan's Civil War," testimony presented before the House Armed Services Committee on Jan. 30, 2007 (Washington, D.C.: Rand CT-271); Gates, *Duty*, 199; Jason H. Campbell and Jeremy Shapiro, *Afghanistan Index,* Brookings Institution, Feb. 24, 2009, www.brookings.edu/wp-content/uploads/2016/07/index20090224.pdf.

41 Rohde and Sanger, "How a 'Good War' in Afghanistan Went Bad."

42 Philip H. Gordon, "Back Up NATO's Afghanistan Force," *International Herald Tribune*, Jan. 8, 2006; Philip H. Gordon, "Winter in Afghanistan," Brookings Institution, March 1, 2006, www.brookings.edu/opinions/winter-in-afghanistan/, originally published as "American Pie," *E!Sharp*, March/April 2006.

43 Coll, *Directorate S*, 298, 302–3.

44 NATO, "Joint Press Conference with General Dan McNeill, Commander of the NATO-Led International Security and Assistance Force (ISAF) in Afghanistan and Ambassador Daan Everts, NATO Senior

Civilian Representative," Sept. 13, 2007, www.nato.int/docu/speech/2007/s070912a.html.

45 From 2002 to 2008, U.S. military expenditure for Iraq came to $578 billion with financial assistance (development aid and foreign military financing) at $28 billion, while for Afghanistan the respective figures were $165 billion and $7.6 billion. Amy Belasco, "The Cost of Iraq, Afghanistan, and Other Global War on Terror Operations Since 9/11," Washington, D.C., Congressional Research Service, Dec. 8, 2014, 15 and 19.

46 Dov Zakheim, *A Vulcan's Tale: How the Bush Administration Mismanaged the Reconstruction of* Afghanistan (Washington, D.C.: Brookings Institution, 2011); Ronald Neumann, *The Other War: Winning and Losing in Afghanistan* (Washington, D.C.: Potomac Books, 2009); Jones, *Graveyard of Empires*, 124–29.

47 Rice cited in Coll, *Directorate S*, 306.

48 That was the first sentence in the administration's final Afghanistan report in December 2008, drafted primarily by the White House's coordinator for Afghanistan policy, General Douglas Lute, cited in ibid., 337.

49 Philip H. Gordon, *Winning the Right War: The Path to Security for America and the World* (New York: Henry Holt, 2007), 133.

50 Belasco, "Cost of Iraq, Afghanistan, and Other Global War on Terror Operations," 10–13. Also Ian S. Livingston and Michael E. O'Hanlon, *Afghanistan Index*, Brookings Institution, Sept. 29, 2017, 4–5, www.brookings.edu/wp-content/uploads/2016/07/21csi_20171002_afghanistan_index.pdf.

51 Todd Pitman, "Marines in Marjah Face Full-Blown Insurgency," *Boston Globe*, Oct. 8, 2010; Dexter Filkins, "Afghan Offensive Is New War Model," *New York Times*, Feb. 12, 2010; Bacevich, *America's War for the Greater Middle East*, 311.

52 Coll, *Directorate S*, 570.

53 Ibid., 392.

54 Ibid., 570.

55 Gerry J. Gilmore, "McChrystal: Surge Marks Turning Point in Conflict," *DOD News*, Dec. 2, 2009, archive.defense.gov/news/newsarticle.aspx?id=56919; "Top General Optimistic About Afghanistan," ABC News, Jan. 11, 2010, www.youtube.com/watch?v=ABdm3bdUeDE; Thomas Harding, "Operation Moshtarak: Gen. Stanley McChrystal Visits Subdued Former Taliban Capital," *Daily Telegraph*, Feb. 15, 2010, www.telegraph.co.uk/news/worldnews/asia/afghanistan/7243964/Operation-Moshtarak-Gen-Stanley-McChrystal-visits-subdued-former-Taliban-capital.html; Thom Shanker, "Top U.S. Commander Sees Progress in Afghanistan," *New York Times*, Feb. 4, 2010, www.nytimes.com/2010/02/05/world/asia/05gates.html.

56 "Obama Remarks on the Strategy in Afghanistan," *New York Times*, Dec. 16, 2010, www.nytimes.com/2010/12/17/world/asia/17afghan-text.html.

57 David Petraeus, Testimony before the Senate Armed Services Committee, March 15, 2011, www.isaf.nato.int/images/stories/File/Transcript/Petraeus%2003-15-11.pdf; Department of Defense News Transcript, Joint Press Conference with Secretary Gates and President Karzai from Kabul, Afghanistan, June 4, 2011, archive.defense.gov/Transcripts/Transcript.aspx?TranscriptID=4832.

58 White House Office of the Press Secretary, "Remarks of the President to Soldiers of the 10th Mountain Division at Fort Drum, New York," June 23, 2011, obamawhitehouse.archives.gov/the-press-office/2011/06/23/remarks-president-soldiers-10th-mountain-division-fort-drum-new-york.

59 Mark Urban, "Petraeus: Afghan War Has Turned a Corner," BBC, July 22, 2011, www.bbc.com/news/world-us-canada-14257679; Josh Rogin, "Petraeus's Optimism About Afghanistan Not Shared at CIA," *Foreign Policy*, April 27, 2011, foreignpolicy.com/2011/04/27/petraeuss-optimism-about-afghanistan-not-shared-at-cia/.

60 Post Staff Report, "US Surge Troops out of Afghanistan, Panetta Says," *New York Post*, Sept. 21, 2012.

61 Craig Whitlock, "At War with the Truth," *Washington Post*, Dec. 9, 2019, www.washingtonpost.com/graphics/2019/investigations/afghanistan-papers/afghanistan-war-confidential-documents/.

62 *Five-Year Afghanistan Report*, Department of Defense Archives, Oct. 2006, archive.defense.gov/home/dodupdate/For-the-record/documents/20062006d.html.

63 Bush's April 18, 2002, speech to the Virginia Military Institute, cited in Dao, "Nation Challenged: The President: Bush Sets Role for U.S. in Afghan Rebuilding."

64 Michael Hirsh and Jamie Tabarai, "Washington Losing Patience in Counterinsurgency in Afghanistan," *The Atlantic*, June 28, 2011, www.theatlantic.com/international/archive/2011/06/washington-losing-patience-with-counterinsurgency-in-afghanistan/240982/.

65 Cowper-Coles cited in Coll, *Directorate S*, 395.

66 Testimony of Rory Stewart, Senate Foreign Relations Committee Hearing, Sept. 16, 2009, "The Future in Afghanistan," www.foreign.senate.gov/imo/media/doc/StewartTestimony090916p1.pdf.

67 Coll, *Directorate S*, 393.

68 U.S. Department of Defense, Defense Casualty Analysis System, "U.S. Military Casualties—Operation Enduring Freedom (OEF) Casualty Summary by Month," dcas.dmdc.osd.mil/dcas/pages/report_oef_month.xhtml; Livingston and O'Hanlon, *Afghanistan Index*, 10.

69 Eric Schmitt, "U.S. Envoy's Cables Show Worries on Afghan Plan," *New York Times*, Jan. 25, 2010, archive.nytimes.com/www.nytimes.com/2010/01/26/world/asia/26strategy.html; Greg Jaffe, Scott Wilson, and Karen DeYoung, "U.S. Envoy Resists Troop Increase, Cites Karzai as Problem,"

Washington Post, Nov. 12, 2009, www.washingtonpost.com/wp-dyn/content/article/2009/11/11/AR2009111118432.html.

70 Zalmay Khalilzad, *The Envoy: From Kabul to the White House, My Journey Through a Turbulent World* (New York: St. Martin's Press, 2016), 127, 147; Jones, *Graveyard of Empires*, 94. The language on the government is from the December 2001 Bonn Declaration, "Agreement on Provisional Arrangements in Afghanistan Pending the Reestablishment of Permanent Government Institutions," https://www.refworld.org/docid/3f48f4754.html.

71 Bacevich, *America's War for the Greater Middle East*, 229–30.

72 Coll, *Directorate S*, 307.

73 Jaffe, Wilson, and DeYoung, "U.S. Envoy Resists Troop Increase, Cites Karzai as Problem."

74 Matthew Rosenberg, "Karzai Says He Was Assured CIA Would Continue Delivering Bags of Cash," *New York Times*, May 4, 2013, www.nytimes.com/2013/05/05/world/asia/karzai-said-he-was-assured-of-cash-deliveries-by-cia.html.

75 Alissa J. Rubin, "Karzai Bets on Vilifying U.S. to Shed His Image as a Lackey," *New York Times*, March 12, 2013, www.nytimes.com/2013/03/13/world/asia/karzais-bet-vilifying-us.html.

76 Coll, *Directorate S*, 378–79.

77 Adam Taylor, "Karzai Joins a Long List of Leaders Ungrateful for U.S. Support," *Washington Post*, Sept. 25, 2014.

78 Kevin Sieff, "Interview: Karzai Says 12-Year Afghanistan War Has Left Him Angry at U.S. Government," *Washington Post*, March 2, 2014.

79 Michael Hart, "Why We Couldn't Change Afghanistan," *The Atlantic*, Feb. 29, 2012.

80 George W. Bush, *Decision Points* (New York: Crown, 2010), 220.

81 Donald J. Trump (@realDonaldTrump), Twitter, Oct. 7, 2011, 3:43 p.m., twitter.com/realdonaldtrump/status/122396588336349184?lang=en; Donald J. Trump (@realDonaldTrump), Twitter, Feb. 27, 2012, 2:34 p.m., twitter.com/realdonaldtrump/status/174215838814044160?lang=en.

82 Bob Woodward, *Fear: Trump in the White House* (New York: Simon & Schuster, 2018), 123 and 315.

83 "Department of Defense Afghanistan Force Management Level Accounting and Reporting Practices Briefing by Pentagon Chief Spokesperson White and Joint Staff Director Lieutenant General McKenzie," Department of Defense, Aug. 30, 2017, www.defense.gov/Newsroom/Transcripts/Transcript/Article/1295700/department-of-defense-afghanistan-force-management-level-accounting-and-reporti/.

84 "Remarks by President Trump on the Strategy in Afghanistan and South Asia," Aug. 21, 2017, www.whitehouse.gov/briefings-statements/remarks-president-trump-strategy-afghanistan-south-asia/.

85 Tim Haines, "Tillerson on Afghanistan: We Will Not Seek Arbitrary

Deadlines; Decisions Will Be Informed by Progress," *Real Clear Politics*, Aug. 27, 2017, www.realclearpolitics.com/video/2017/08/27/tillerson_on_afghanistan_we_will_not_set_arbitrary_deadlines_decisions_will_be_informed_by_progress.html.

86 Associated Press, "Nikki Haley Calls Trump's Afghanistan Policy 'Strong' and 'an Entirely New Approach,'" *Post and Courier*, Aug. 22, 2017, www.postandcourier.com/news/nikki-haley-calls-president-trump-s-afghanistan-policy-strong-and/article_c0e8ce84-872e-11e7-ac26-af7322d5f82a.html.

87 "Soldier Excited to Take over Father's Old Afghanistan Patrol Route," *Onion*, Aug. 22, 2017, local.theonion.com/soldier-excited-to-take-over-father-s-old-afghanistan-p-1819580201.

88 Ellen Mitchell, "Top General in Afghanistan Says Taliban Fight Has 'Turned the Corner,'" *The Hill*, Nov. 28, 2017; Paul McLeary, "U.S. Has 'Turned the Corner' in Afghanistan, Top General Says," *Foreign Policy*, Nov. 28, 2017, foreignpolicy.com/2017/11/28/u-s-has-turned-the-corner-in-afghanistan-top-general-says/amp/.

89 Cited in Jeff Stein, "Donald Trump's Desire to 'Get the Hell out of Afghanistan' amid Taliban Gains Could Lead to Catastrophe," *Newsweek*, Sept. 21, 2018, www.newsweek.com/2018/10/26/donald-trump-get-hell-out-afghanistan-amid-taliban-gains-catastrophe-1132203.html.

90 Cost estimates range from around $841 billion to $1.07 trillion, depending on whether Veterans Affairs costs are included. Neta C. Crawford, "United States Budgetary Costs and Obligations of Post-9/11 Wars Through FY2020: $6.4 Trillion," Watson Institute, Brown University, Nov. 13, 2019, watson.brown.edu/costsofwar/files/cow/imce/papers/2019/US%20Budgetary%20Costs%20of%20Wars%20November%202019.pdf?utm_source=Daily%20on%20Defense%20(2019%20TEMPLATE)_11/15/2019&utm_medium=email&utm_campaign=WEX_Daily%20on%20Defense&rid=84648. Also Stein, "Donald Trump's Desire to 'Get the Hell out of Afghanistan' amid Taliban Gains Could Lead to Catastrophe."

91 Pamela Constable, "U.S. Watchdog's Report Details Serious Afghan Reversals," *Washington Post*, Nov. 1, 2018; Ashley Jackson, "The Taliban's Fight for Hearts and Minds," *Foreign Policy*, Sept. 12, 2018, foreignpolicy.com/2018/09/12/the-talibans-fight-for-hearts-and-minds-aghanistan/; Idrees Ali, "Watchdog Finds Little Progress in Afghanistan, Despite Military Optimism," Reuters, May 21, 2018, www.reuters.com/article/us-usa-afghanistan-military/watchdog-finds-little-progress-in-afghanistan-despite-u-s-military-optimism-idUSKCN1IM29M; Thomas H. Johnson, *Taliban Narratives: The Use and Power of Stories in the Afghanistan Conflict* (New York: Oxford University Press, 2017). For "wrong direction" figures, see Livingston and O'Hanlon, *Afghanistan Index*, 22.

92 According to Pew, the number of Americans who say the war in Afghanistan was the "right decision" was down from 69 percent in 2006 to 51 percent in 2014 to just 45 percent in 2018 (still a plurality, though, because 39 percent said it was the wrong decision, with others not answering). Baxter Oliphant, "After 17 Years of War in Afghanistan, More Say U.S. Has Failed Than Succeeded in Achieving Goals," Pew Research Center, Oct. 5, 2018, www.pewresearch.org/fact-tank/2018/10/05/after-17-years-of-war-in-afghanistan-more-say-u-s-has-failed-than-succeeded-in-achieving-its-goals/; Frank Newport, "More Americans Now View Afghan War as a Mistake," Gallup, Feb. 19, 2014, news.gallup.com/poll/167471/americans-view-afghanistan-war-mistake.aspx.

93 "Pentagon Says War in Afghanistan Costs Taxpayers $45 Billion per Year," *PBS NewsHour*, Feb. 6, 2018.

94 U.S. Central Command News Briefing, "Department of Defense Press Briefing by General Joseph Votel via Teleconference from Tampa, Florida, on Operations in the Central Command Area of Responsibility," Oct. 4, 2018, www.centcom.mil/MEDIA/Transcripts/Article/1655552/department-of-defense-press-briefing-by-general-joseph-votel-via-teleconference/.

95 David Petraeus and Vance Serchuk, "The U.S. Abandoned Iraq. Don't Repeat History in Afghanistan," *Wall Street Journal*, Aug. 9, 2019, www.wsj.com/articles/the-u-s-abandoned-iraq-dont-repeat-history-in-afghanistan-11565385301; Ryan Crocker, "I Was Ambassador to Afghanistan: This Deal Is a Surrender," *Washington Post*, Jan. 29, 2019; Michael Morell and Michael Vickers, "This Is Not the Moment to Retreat from Afghanistan," *Washington Post*, March 15, 2019, www.washingtonpost.com/opinions/2019/03/15/this-is-not-moment-retreat-afghanistan/?utm_term=.f2befa81cbb1; James Dobbins et al., *Consequences of a Precipitous U.S. Withdrawal from Afghanistan*, Rand Perspectives, Jan. 2019, www.rand.org/pubs/perspectives/PE326.html.

96 Sarah Dadouch, Susannah George, and Dan Lamothe, "U.S. Signs Peace Deal with Taliban Agreeing to Full Withdrawal of Troops from Afghanistan," *Washington Post*, Feb. 29, 2000, https://www.washingtonpost.com/world/asia_pacific/afghanistan-us-taliban-peace-deal-signing/2020/02/29/b952fb04-5a67-11ea-8efd-0f904bdd8057_story.html. The full text of the agreement can be found in David Welna and Colin Dwyer, "U.S. Signs Peace Deal with Taliban After Nearly Two Decades of War in Afghanistan," National Public Radio, https://www.npr.org/2020/02/29/810537586/u-s-signs-peace-deal-with-taliban-after-nearly-2-decades-of-war-in-afghanistan.

97 As of late 2019, only 19 percent of Americans polled believed that U.S. military involvement in Afghanistan had been successful in obtaining American strategic objectives. Shibley Telhami, director, "Critical Issues Poll: American Attitudes Toward the Middle East," poll conducted in

September 2019, available at https://criticalissues.umd.edu/sites/criticalissues.umd.edu/files/UMCIP%20Middle%20East%20Questionnaire.pdf. On the steady lowering of U.S. objectives in Afghanistan, see Kathy Gilsinan, "The U.S. Once Wanted Peace in Afghanistan," *The Atlantic*, Feb. 29, 2020, https://www.theatlantic.com/politics/archive/2020/02/united-states-taliban-afghanistan-peace-deal/607234/.

Chapter 4: "Mission Accomplished"

1 Ken Adelman, "'Cakewalk' Revisited," *Washington Post*, April 10, 2003, www.washingtonpost.com/archive/opinions/2003/04/10/cakewalk-revisited/9fc29e36-9230-4ccb-8f2f-7602f1df560f/?utm_term=.e7cc081fea35.

2 Ken Adelman, "Cakewalk in Iraq," *Washington Post*, Feb. 13, 2003, www.washingtonpost.com/archive/opinions/2002/02/13/cakewalk-in-iraq/cf09301c-c6c4-4f2e-8268-7c93017f5e93/?utm_term=.a4afbec815be.

3 David Brooks, "The Phony Debate," *Weekly Standard*, March 31, 2003, www.weeklystandard.com/david-brooks/the-phony-debate; David Brooks, "Optimism Rediscovered," *Weekly Standard*, April 6, 2003, www.weeklystandard.com/david-brooks/optimism-rediscovered.

4 David Brooks, "The Collapse of the Dream Palaces," *Weekly Standard*, April 28, 2003.

5 William Kristol, "September 11, 2001–April 9, 2003," *Weekly Standard*, April 28, 2003.

6 "U.S. Foreign Policy and the Future of Iraq," C-SPAN, April 22, 2003, www.c-span.org/video/?176282-1/us-foreign-policy-future-iraq&start=640.

7 Thomas Ricks, *Fiasco: The American Military Adventure in Iraq* (New York: Penguin Press, 2006), 145. Also see Jarrett Murphy, "Mission Accomplished 'Whodunit,'" CBS News, Oct. 29, 2003, www.cbsnews.com/news/mission-accomplished-whodunit/.

8 For estimates of the total costs of the war in Iraq, which range from around $850 billion to more than $2 trillion depending on what costs are included, see Belasco, "Cost of Iraq, Afghanistan, and Other Global War on Terror Operations Since 9/11"; Crawford, "United States Budgetary Costs and Obligations of Post-9/11 Wars Through FY2020: $6.4 Trillion." On U.S. casualties, the 5,500 number includes nonhostile fatalities, of which around 4,500 were killed in action. See Michael E. O'Hanlon, *Iraq Index: Tracking Variables of Reconstruction and Security in Post-Saddam Iraq*, Brookings Institution, Jan. 31, 2011, www.brookings.edu/wp-content/uploads/2016/07/index20120131.pdf; "Casualty Status," U.S. Department of Defense, March 19, 2019, dod.defense.gov/News/Casualty-Status/.

9 George Bush and Brent Scowcroft, *A World Transformed* (New York: Vintage, 1999), 433.

10 Ricks, *Fiasco*, 6, 25; "The Gulf War," *Frontline*, Jan. 9, 1996, www.pbs.org/wgbh/pages/frontline/gulf/; "Interview with Dick Cheney," C-SPAN, April 15, 1994, www.youtube.com/watch?v=w75ctsv2oPU; "*Meet the Press*: Interview with Dick Cheney," Aug. 27, 2000.

11 James A. Baker, "Why the U.S. Didn't March to Baghdad," *Los Angeles Times*, Sept. 8, 1996, articles.latimes.com/1996-09-08/opinion/op-41778_1_middle-east-peace.

12 Colin Powell, *My American Journey* (New York: Random House, 1995), 527; Norman Schwarzkopf, *It Doesn't Take a Hero: The Autobiography of General H. Norman Schwarzkopf* (New York: Bantam, 1992), 98.

13 Paul Wolfowitz, "Victory Came Too Easily; Review of Rick Atkinson, *Crusade: The Untold Story of the Gulf War*," *National Interest*, March 1, 1994, nationalinterest.org/bookreview/victory-came-too-easily-review-of-rick-atkinson-crusade-the-untold-story-of-the-1011.

14 For Bush's statement, see Reuters, "WAR IN THE GULF: Bush Statement; Excerpt from 2 Statements by Bush on Iraq's Proposal for Ending the Conflict," *New York Times*, Feb. 16, 1991, www.nytimes.com/1991/02/16/world/war-gulf-bush-statement-excerpts-2-statements-bush-iraq-s-proposal-for-ending.html. Also see Thomas L. Friedman, "AFTER THE WAR; Decision Not to Help Iraqi Rebels Puts U.S. in an Awkward Position," *New York Times*, April 4, 1991, www.nytimes.com/1991/04/04/world/after-the-war-decision-not-to-help-iraqi-rebels-puts-us-in-an-awkward-position.html; and Lev Grossman, "Did the U.S. Betray the Kurds in 1991?" CNN, April 7, 2003, www.cnn.com/2003/ALLPOLITICS/04/07/timep.betray.tm/.

15 E. J. Dionne Jr., "Kicking the 'Vietnam Syndrome,'" *Washington Post*, March 4, 1991, https://www.washingtonpost.com/archive/politics/1991/03/04/kicking-the-vietnam-syndrome/b6180288-4b9e-4d5f-b303-befa2275524d/.

16 Signatories of the letter included future Bush administration officials Elliott Abrams, Richard Armitage, John Bolton, Paula Dobriansky, Zalmay Khalilzad, Donald Rumsfeld, and Paul Wolfowitz. Project for a New American Century, Letter to President Clinton on Iraq, Jan. 26, 1998, web.archive.org/web/20131021171040/http:/www.newamericancentury.org/iraqclintonletter.htm.

17 Project for a New American Century, Letter to Gingrich and Lott on Iraq, May 29, 1998, www.economicsvoodoo.com/wp-content/uploads/PNAC-Letter-to-Gingrich-and-Lott-on-Iraq-May29-1988.pdf.

18 The Iraq Liberation Act passed by a vote of 360–38 in the House and was approved by unanimous consent in the Senate. Martin Indyk, *Innocent Abroad*, 192; and Ricks, *Fiasco*, 24–25.

19 For the criticisms of Desert Fox as well as the 2003 Iraq Survey Group's conclusion that they were "surprisingly effective" (Thomas Ricks's words), see Ricks, *Fiasco,* 16. Also see ISG leader David Kay's statement to a group of congressional committees, "Text of David Kay's Unclassified

Statement," Oct. 2, 2003, www.cnn.com/2003/ALLPOLITICS/10/02/kay.report/; and the "key findings" of the ISG at www.cia.gov/library/reports/general-reports-1/iraq_wmd_2004/chap4.html.

20 Richard Perle, "Iraq: Saddam Unbound," in Kagan and Kristol, *Present Dangers*, 99–100.

21 Paul Wolfowitz, "Statesmanship in the New Century," in ibid., 320.

22 Governor George W. Bush, "A Distinctly American Internationalism," Ronald Reagan Library, Simi Valley, Calif., Nov. 19, 1999, www.mtholyoke.edu/acad/intrel/bush/wspeech.htm. Bush also questioned the idea that it was the role of the United States to "go around the world and say this is the way it's got to be." "October 11, 2000, Presidential Debate," Oct. 11, 2000, transcript, Commission on Presidential Debates, www.debates.org/index.php?page=october-11-20000-debate-transcript.

23 Condoleezza Rice, "Promoting the National Interest," *Foreign Affairs*, Jan./Feb. 2000.

24 For Cheney, see Glenn Kessler, "U.S. Decision on Iraq Has Puzzling Past," *Washington Post*, Jan. 12, 2003. For Powell, see "Secretary of State Confirmation," C-SPAN, Jan. 17, 2001, www.c-span.org/video/?161898-1/secretary-state-nomination-hearing.

25 Colin Powell, "Press Briefing en Route to Cairo, Egypt," Feb. 23, 2001, 2001-2009.state.gov/secretary/former/powell/remarks/2001/931.htm; "Context of 'February 12, 2001: Rumsfeld Says Iraq Probably Not Nuclear Threat,'" *History Commons*, historycommons.org/context.jsp?item=complete_timeline_of_the_2003_invasion_of_iraq_1110#complete_timeline_of_the_2003_invasion_of_iraq_1110.

26 Khalilzad, *Envoy*, 99; Daalder and Lindsay, *America Unbound*, 130.

27 Daalder and Lindsay, *America Unbound*, 130.

28 For Bush, see Bush, *Decision Points*, 229; and Bob Woodward, *Plan of Attack* (New York: Simon & Schuster, 2004), 12, 27. For Cheney, see Kessler, "U.S. Decision on Iraq Has Puzzling Past." Also see the discussion in F. Gregory Gause, *The International Relations of the Persian Gulf* (New York: Cambridge University Press, 2010), 192.

29 Ron Suskind, *The One Percent Doctrine: Deep Inside America's Pursuit of Its Enemies Since 9/11* (New York: Simon & Schuster, 2006), 62, cited in George Tenet, *At the Center of the Storm: My Years at the CIA* (New York: HarperCollins, 2007), 264. Also Douglas Feith, *War and Decision: Inside the Pentagon at the Dawn of the War on Terrorism* (New York: HarperCollins, 2008), 227–28.

30 Bush quoted by Christopher Meyer, British ambassador to the United States, in a background interview for "Blair's War," *Frontline*, PBS, March 18, 2002. Also Woodward, *Bush at War*, 58–59.

31 George W. Bush, "Remarks in Welcoming Aid Workers Rescued from Afghanistan," Washington, D.C., Nov. 26, 2001, www.whitehouse.gov/news/releases/2001/11/20011126-1.html.

32 Joel D. Rayburn and Frank K. Sobchak, *The U.S. Army in the Iraq War, vol. 1, Invasion, Insurgency, Civil War, 2003–2006* (Carlisle, Pa.: Strategic Studies Institute, 2019), 32, publications.armywarcollege.edu/pubs/3667.pdf; Franks, *American Soldier*, 315, 345; David Frum, *The Right Man* (New York: Random House, 2003), 224.

33 Dick Cheney on Fox News, Dec. 11, 2001, www.foxnews.com/story/cheney-on-taliban-theyre-history.

34 "President Delivers State of the Union Address," White House Archives, Jan. 29, 2002, georgewbush-whitehouse.archives.gov/news/releases/2002/01/20020129-11.html; Secretary of State Colin Powell, Statement on President Bush's Budget Request for the State Department for 2003, Feb. 12, 2002, 2001-2009.state.gov/secretary/former/powell/remarks/2002/7957.htm; Colin Powell, "Interview on NBC's 'Meet the Press,'" Feb. 17, 2002, 2001-2009.state.gov/secretary/former/powell/remarks/2002/8071.htm; "Powell, Rice, Defend Bush 'Axis of Evil' Speech," CNN, Feb. 18, 2002, www.cnn.com/2002/US/02/17/bush.axis/.

35 Bush was first quoted in Michael Elliott and James Carney, "First Stop, Iraq," *Time*, March 24, 2003, 173. According to a source with firsthand knowledge, the participants in the meeting were McCain, Lieberman, and Graham, who were there to brief Rice on their meetings at the Munich Security Conference a few weeks beforehand.

36 Richard N. Haass, *War of Necessity, War of Choice: A Memoir of Two Iraq Wars* (New York: Simon & Schuster, 2009), 213.

37 Powell's dinner with Bush described in Woodward, *Bush at War*, 331–34; and Haass, *War of Necessity*, 214–15.

38 For a good survey of the various explanations for the war, which emphasizes this latter point, see Ahsan I. Butt, "Why Did the United States Invade Iraq in 2003?" *Security Studies*, Jan. 4, 2019, doi.org/10.1080/09635412.2019.1551567. Also see Michael J. Mazarr, *Leap of Faith: Hubris, Negligence, and America's Greatest Foreign Policy Tragedy* (New York: PublicAffairs, 2019), 7, 38–39, and 178–80; Lawrence Freedman, *A Choice of Enemies: America Confronts the Middle East* (New York: PublicAffairs, 2008), 397–99; National Security Archive, "The Iraq War Part II: Was There Even a Decision?" Electronic Briefing Book No. 328, ed. John Prados and Christopher Ames, nsarchive2.gwu.edu/NSAEBB/NSAEBB328/.

39 "Deputy Secretary Wolfowitz Interview with Sam Tannenhaus," *Vanity Fair*, May 9, 2003, archive.defense.gov/Transcripts/Transcript.aspx?TranscriptID=2594.

40 Robert Kagan and William Kristol, "What to Do About Iraq," *Weekly Standard*, Jan. 21, 2002, www.weeklystandard.com/robert-kagan-and-william-kristol/what-to-do-about-iraq-2064.

41 For Pletka, see "Overthrow Saddam?" *Middle East Quarterly* 6, no. 2 (June 1999), www.meforum.org/articles/other/overthrow-saddam; Richard Perle,

"Next Stop, Iraq?" speech to the Foreign Policy Research Institute, Philadelphia, Nov. 14, 2001, www.fpri.org/article/2001/11/next-stop-iraq/.

42 For Pollack's earlier skepticism, see Daniel Byman, Kenneth Pollack, and Gideon Rose, "The Rollback Fantasy," *Foreign Affairs,* Jan./Feb. 1999, www.foreignaffairs.com/articles/iraq/1999-01-01/rollback-fantasy. The quotation advocating invasion is from Kenneth M. Pollack, "Next Stop Baghdad?" *Foreign Affairs,* March/April 2002, www.foreignaffairs.com/articles/iraq/2002-03-01/next-stop-baghdad.

43 Kenneth M. Pollack, *The Threatening Storm: The Case for Invading Iraq* (New York: Random House, 2002).

44 David Brooks, "The 'Groundhog Day' War," *Weekly Standard,* Sept. 6, 2002, www.weeklystandard.com/david-brooks/the-groundhog-day-war (emphasis added).

45 "The Secret Downing Street Memo," July 23, 2002, published in *Sunday Times,* May 1, 2005.

46 "President Bush Delivers Graduation Speech at West Point," White House Archives, June 1, 2002, georgewbush-whitehouse.archives.gov/news/releases/2002/06/20020601-3.html.

47 "President Bush Outlines Iraqi Threat," White House Archives, Oct. 7, 2002, georgewbush-whitehouse.archives.gov/news/releases/2002/10/20021007-8.html.

48 "Interview with Condoleezza Rice; Pataki Talks About 9-11; Graham, Shelby Discuss War on Terrorism," CNN Transcripts, Sept. 8, 2002, transcripts.cnn.com/TRANSCRIPTS/0209/08/le.00.html. See also Ricks, *Fiasco*, 58, and George Packer, The *Assassins' Gate: America in Iraq* (New York: Farrar, Straus and Giroux, 2005), 62. Rice's comment, "history is littered with cases of inaction . . ." cited in Kaplan and Kristol, *War over Iraq*, 89. Also see "'Moral Case' for Deposing Saddam," BBC News, Aug. 15, 2002, news.bbc.co.uk/2/hi/americas/2193426.stm. Bush also frequently made the "mushroom cloud" point. See "Bush: Don't Wait for Mushroom Cloud," CNN, Oct. 8, 2002, edition.cnn.com/2002/ALLPOLITICS/10/07/bush.transcript/.

49 Dick Cheney, "Remarks to the Veterans of Foreign Wars 103rd National Convention," Nashville, Aug. 26, 2002. For full text, www.theguardian.com/world/2002/aug/27/usa.iraq. Also see discussion in Gause, *International Relations of the Persian Gulf,* 208; and Haass, *War of Necessity*, 218.

50 Rumsfeld at Department of Defense briefing, Sept. 26, 2002, www.c-span.org/video/?c4546748/debate.

51 "Meet the Press: Interview with Vice-President Dick Cheney," *Meet the Press*, Sept. 8, 2002, transcript at www.leadingtowar.com/PDFsources_claims_aluminum/2002_09_08_NBC.pdf.

52 "The Vice President Appears on NBC's *Meet the Press,"* Dec. 9, 2001, georgewbush-whitehouse.archives.gov/vicepresident/news-speeches/speeches/print/vp20011209.html.

53 Department of Defense, "Rumsfeld Calls Link Between Iraq, al Qaeda

'Not Debatable,'" archive.defense.gov/news/newsarticle.aspx?id=43413. For more, see Tenet, *Center of the Storm,* 302.

54 Michael Morell, *The Great War of Our Time: The CIA's Fight Against Terrorism—from al Qa'ida to ISIS* (New York: Twelve, 2015), 88.

55 National Intelligence Estimate, "Iraq's Continuing Programs for Weapons of Mass Destruction," Oct. 2002, fas.org/irp/cia/product/iraq-wmd-nie.pdf.

56 Tenet, *Center of the Storm*, 327–28; Morell, *Great War of Our Time*, 80–91; Daniel Schorn, "A Spy Speaks Out: Former Top CIA Official on 'Faulty' Intelligence Claims," *60 Minutes*, April 21, 2006, www.cbsnews.com/news/a-spy-speaks-out-21-04-2006/.

57 Packer, *Assassins' Gate*, 105–8.

58 Paul R. Pillar, *Intelligence and US Foreign Policy: Iraq, 9/11, and Misguided Reform* (New York: Columbia University Press, 2011), 155; Morell, *Great War of Our Time,* 85; Julian Borger, "The Spies Who Pushed for War," *Guardian*, July 17, 2003, www.theguardian.com/world/2003/jul/17/iraq.usa.

59 Tenet, *Center of the Storm*, 302.

60 Morell, *Great War of Our Time,* 87.

61 Cheney, interview with Tim Russert, *Meet the Press*, Sept. 8, 2002; "Interview with Vice President Dick Cheney," *PBS NewsHour*, Sept. 9, 2002, www.pbs.org/newshour/show/vice-president-dick-cheney.

62 "Text of President Bush's 2003 State of the Union Address," *Washington Post*, Jan. 28, 2003, www.washingtonpost.com/wp-srv/onpolitics/transcripts/bushtext_012803.html.

63 Chaim Kaufmann, "Threat Inflation and the Failure of the Marketplace of Ideas," *International Security* (Summer 2004); Butt, "Why Did the United States Invade Iraq in 2003?"; Mazarr, *Leap of Faith*, 314–16.

64 "Full Text of Colin Powell's Speech," *Guardian*, Feb. 5, 2003, www.theguardian.com/world/2003/feb/05/iraq.usa. Also Kaufmann, "Threat Inflation," 39.

65 Powell presentation to the UN Security Council, Feb. 5, 2003, news.un.org/en/story/2003/02/58372-powell-presents-us-case-security-council-iraqs-failure-disarm.

66 Steven R. Weisman, "Powell Calls His U.N. Speech a Lasting Blot on His Record," *New York Times*, Sept. 9, 2005, www.nytimes.com/2005/09/09/politics/powell-calls-his-un-speech-a-lasting-blot-on-his-record.html.

67 Kaplan and Kristol, *War over Iraq*, 98.

68 Ibid., 97.

69 "Full Text: George Bush's Speech to the American Enterprise Institute," *Guardian*, Feb. 27, 2003, www.theguardian.com/world/2003/feb/27/usa.iraq2.

70 Condoleezza Rice, "The Promise of Democratic Peace," *Washington Post*, Dec. 11, 2005, www.washingtonpost.com/wp-dyn/content/article/2005/12/09/AR2005120901711.html.

71 John B. Judis, "Imperial Amnesia," *Foreign Policy*, Oct. 27, 2009.
72 "Interview of the Vice President by Tim Russert, NBC News," March 16, 2003, cited in Packer, *Assassins' Gate*, 97–98 (emphasis added).
73 DOD Press Release, "Wolfowitz Talks to Arab-Americans About Ousting Hussein, Rebuilding Homeland," archive.defense.gov/news/newsarticle.aspx?id=29396. Transcript of interview with *Detroit News* available at "Wolfowitz IV with Nolan Finley of the Detroit News," www.scoop.co.nz/stories/WO0303/S00066.htm; Ricks, *Fiasco*, 96.
74 "Wolfowitz: Iraqis Will Greet Us as Liberators," testimony to House Budget Committee, Feb. 27, 2003, C-SPAN, www.c-span.org/video/?c4501109/wolfowitz-iraqis-greet-liberators.
75 Wolfowitz, interview with Jeffrey Goldberg, *New Yorker* Festival, Aug. 2003, see "Policy Toward Iraq," www.c-span.org/video/?178290-1/policy-iraq&start=4425 (emphasis added); Jeffrey Goldberg, "How Did I Get Iraq Wrong?" *Slate*, March 19, 2008, slate.com/news-and-politics/2008/03/i-didn-t-realize-how-incompetent-the-bush-administration-could-be.html.
76 Perle in Kagan and Kristol, *Present Dangers*, 102.
77 Sewell Chan, "Ahmad Chalabi, Iraqi Politician Who Pushed for U.S. Invasion, Dies at 71," *New York Times*, Nov. 3, 2015, www.nytimes.com/2015/11/04/world/middleeast/ahmad-chalabi-iraq-dead.html. Also see Walt Vanderbush, "Exiles and the Marketing of U.S. Policy Toward Cuba and Iraq," *Foreign Policy Analysis* 5, no. 3 (July 2009): 287–306, www.jstor.org/stable/pdf/24909780.pdf?ab_segments=0%252Fbasic_expensive%252Fcontrol&refreqid=excelsior%3A8be0008d98d2d08183589d0ee486230b; Dexter Filkins, "Where Plan A Left Ahmad Chalabi," *New York Times*, Nov. 5, 2006, www.nytimes.com/2006/11/05/magazine/05CHALABI.html; Jane Mayer, "The Manipulator," *New Yorker*, May 30, 2004, www.newyorker.com/magazine/2004/06/07/the-manipulator.
78 Jim Hoagland, "Now an Iraq War in Washington," *Washington Post*, April 9, 2001, www.globalpolicy.org/component/content/article/170/42306.html; Richard Perle, interview, "Truth, War, and Consequences," *Frontline*, July 10, 2003, www.pbs.org/wgbh/pages/frontline/shows/truth/interviews/perle.html.
79 Ricks, *Fiasco*, 123; Dexter Filkins and Kirk Semple, "Out-of-Favor Iraqi Exile Says U.S.-Led Force Raided Home," *New York Times*, May 20, 2004, www.nytimes.com/2004/05/20/international/middleeast/outoffavor-iraqi-exile-says-usled-force-raided-home.html.
80 On Rumsfeld's opposition to sending more troops, see Michael R. Gordon and Bernard E. Trainor, *Cobra II: The Inside Story of the Invasion and Occupation of Iraq* (New York: Random House, 2006), 32–34.
81 Packer, *Assassins' Gate*, 110.
82 James Dao, "Experts Warn of High Risk for American Invasion of Iraq,"

New York Times, Aug. 1, 2002, www.nytimes.com/2002/08/01/world/experts-warn-of-high-risk-for-american-invasion-of-iraq.html; Tim Weiner, "Crisis with Iraq: Baghdad's Foes; Opponents Find That Ousting Hussein Is Easier Said Than Done," *New York Times*, Nov. 16, 1998, www.nytimes.com/1998/11/16/world/crisis-with-iraq-baghdad-s-foes-opponents-find-that-ousting-hussein-easier-said.html; Ricks, *Fiasco, 22.*

83 James A. Baker III, "The Right Way to Change a Regime," *New York Times*, Aug. 25, 2002; Henry A. Kissinger, "Our Intervention in Iraq," *Washington Post*, Aug. 12, 2002, www.washingtonpost.com/archive/opinions/2002/08/12/our-intervention-in-iraq/cf84cd55-684f-4243-9234-d7d85ec7e6d5/; "Interview with Lawrence Eagleburger," *Fox Business News Sunday*, Aug. 18, 2002. For Hagel, see his testimony to the Senate Foreign Relations Committee in "Hearings to Examine Threats, Responses, and Regional Considerations Surrounding Iraq," Government Printing Office, July 31–Aug. 1, 2002, www.govinfo.gov/content/pkg/CHRG-107shrg81697/html/CHRG-107shrg81697.htm.

84 Brent Scowcroft, "Don't Attack Saddam," *Wall Street Journal*, Aug. 15, 2002, www.wsj.com/articles/SB102937177322806919.

85 The National Defense University, Army War College, and Council on Foreign Relations studies are discussed in Gause, *International Relations of the Persian Gulf*, 220–21; Packer, *Assassins' Gate*, 113; and Thomas E. Ricks, "Cheney Stands by His 'Last Throes' Remark," *Washington Post*, June 20, 2006, www.washingtonpost.com/wp-dyn/content/article/2006/06/19/AR2006061900699.html.

86 James Fallows, "The Fifty-First State?" *The Atlantic*, Nov. 2002, www.theatlantic.com/magazine/archive/2002/11/the-fifty-first-state/302612/; the professors' letter, organized by Harvard professor Stephen Walt, "War with Iraq Is *Not* in America's National Interest," *New York Times*, Sept. 26, 2002, sadat.umd.edu/sites/sadat.umd.edu/files/iraq_war_ad_2002_2.pdf.

87 John J. Mearsheimer and Stephen M. Walt, "Keeping Saddam Hussein in a Box," *New York Times*, Feb. 2, 2003, www.nytimes.com/2003/02/02/opinion/keeping-saddam-hussein-in-a-box.html.

88 Transcript: Obama's Speech Against the Iraq War, Oct. 2, 2002, posted on Jan. 20, 2009, at www.npr.org/templates/story/story.php?storyId=99591469.

89 The NIC assessments can be found at *Regional Consequences of Regime Change in Iraq,* www.cia.gov/library/readingroom/docs/DOC_0005299385.pdf; and *Principal Challenges in Post-Saddam Iraq,* www.cia.gov/library/readingroom/docs/DOC_0005674817.pdf.

90 Haass, *War of Necessity,* 181.

91 Warren Strobel, "Long-Classified Memo Surfaces Warning of 'Perfect Storm' from Invading Iraq," *Wall Street Journal*, March 13, 2019, www

.wsj.com/articles/long-classified-memo-surfaces-warning-of-perfect-storm-from-invading-iraq-11552486945. The memo, declassified and published in William J. Burns, *The Back Channel: A Memoir of U.S. Diplomacy and the Case for Its Renewal* (New York: Random House, 2019), can be found at www.wsj.com/public/resources/documents/2002MemotoPowell.pdf?mod=article_inline.

92 On the Future of Iraq Project and failure to prepare for postwar challenges, see Eric Schmitt and Joel Brinkley, "The Struggle for Iraq: Planning; State Dept. Study Foresaw Trouble Now Plaguing Iraq," *New York Times*, Oct. 19, 2003; Eric Schmitt and Joel Brinkley, "The Struggle for Iraq: Prewar Planning; Iraqi Leaders Say U.S. Was Warned of Disorder After Hussein, but Little Was Done," *New York Times*, Nov. 30, 2003: www.nytimes.com/2003/11/30/world/struggle-for-iraq-prewar-planning-iraqi-leaders-say-us-was-warned-disorder-after.html. For the study of historical lessons by the Policy Planning Staff, see the declassified September 26, 2002, memo from Haass to Powell, "Reconstruction in Iraq—Lessons of the Past," reprinted in Haass, *War of Necessity*, 279 (and the discussion on 255). Also see Gause, *International Relations of the Persian Gulf*, 219.

93 Boot, "Case for American Empire."

94 Kaplan and Kristol, *War over Iraq*, 98.

95 Pollack, "Next Stop Baghdad?"

96 Philip H. Gordon and Michael E. O'Hanlon, "Dealing with Iraq," *Financial Times*, Nov. 30, 2001. Also see Michael E. O'Hanlon and Philip H. Gordon, "Is Fighting Iraq Worth the Risks?" *New York Times*, July 25, 2002, www.nytimes.com/2002/07/25/opinion/is-fighting-iraq-worth-the-risks.html.

97 Martin Indyk, Michael E. O'Hanlon, and Philip H. Gordon, "The Iraq Ultimatum," *Slate*, Sept. 9, 2002, slate.com/news-and-politics/2002/09/what-bush-must-to-do-before-going-to-war.html; Philip H. Gordon, Martin Indyk, and Michael E. O'Hanlon, "Getting Serious About Iraq," *Survival* (Autumn 2002), www.brookings.edu/wp-content/uploads/2016/06/20020901.pdf; and Philip H. Gordon, "Iraq: The Transatlantic Debate" (Paris: EU Institute for Security Studies, Occasional Papers, No. 39, Nov. 2002), www.brookings.edu/wp-content/uploads/2016/06/gordon20021101.pdf.

98 Philip H. Gordon and Michael E. O'Hanlon, "A Tougher Target: The Afghanistan Model of Warfare Might Not Apply Very Well to Iraq," *Washington Post*, Dec. 26, 2001, www.washingtonpost.com/archive/opinions/2001/12/26/a-tougher-target/c41ec6ae-5266-43be-af6e-23de078b957e/?utm_term=.8076b9bb5bd2.

99 Adelman, "Cakewalk in Iraq."

100 Patrick Clawson, "Why Saddam Hussein Is Ripe for a Fall," *Washington Post*, Jan. 1, 2002, www.washingtonpost.com/archive/opinions/2002/01

/01/why-saddam-hussein-is-ripe-for-a-fall/60b7976b-8c55-4051-9e22-953a5c049c8f/?utm_term=.a4c4800a4557.

101 Eric Shinseki in a Senate Armed Services Committee hearing, Feb. 25, 2003, www.c-span.org/video/?175226-1/fiscal-year-2004-defense-budget&start=NaN&start=8014.

102 Paul Wolfowitz, "Statement on Defense Priorities," *Department of Defense Budget Priorities for Fiscal Year 2004*, Hearing before the House Committee on the Budget, 108th Cong., 1st sess. (Washington, D.C.: Government Printing Office, 2003), 8–10, www.govinfo.gov/content/pkg/CHRG-108hhrg85421/html/CHRG-108hhrg85421.htm.

103 Bob Davis, "Bush Economic Aide Says the Cost of the Iraq War May Top $100 Billion," *Wall Street Journal*, Sept. 16, 2002, www.wsj.com/articles/SB1032128134218066355.

104 "Rumsfeld Briefs Press," Jan. 19, 2003, transcripts.cnn.com/TRANSCRIPTS/0301/19/se.01.html.

105 William Nordhaus, "The Economic Consequences of a War with Iraq," in *War with Iraq: Costs, Consequences, and Alternatives*, ed. Carl Kaysen et al. (Cambridge, Mass.: American Academy of Arts and Sciences, 2002), 51–80, www.econ.yale.edu/~nordhaus/homepage/homepage/AAAS_War_Iraq_2.pdf; Wolfowitz, interview, *Good Morning America*, March 3, 2003, www.scoop.co.nz/stories/WO0303/S00011/wolfowitz-interview-with-good-morning-america.htm.

106 Testimony by Paul D. Wolfowitz, "Hearings Before a Subcommittee of the Committee on Appropriations House of Representatives," March 27, 2003, babel.hathitrust.org/cgi/pt?id=mdp.39015090415632;view=1up;seq=5; Gause, *International Relations of the Persian Gulf*, 218.

107 For Perle, see "Saddam's Ultimate Solution," *Wide Angle*, PBS, July 11, 2002, www.pbs.org/wnet/wideangle/interactives-extras/interviews/saddams-ultimate-solution-interview-richard-perle/1864/; for Pollack, "Next Stop Baghdad?"

108 Packer, *Assassins' Gate*, 116. USAID administrator Andrew Natsios on *Nightline* said $1.7 billion, cited in Ricks, *Fiasco*, 109; Dana Milbank and Robin Wright, "Off the Mark on Cost of War, Reception by Iraqis," *Washington Post*, March 19, 2004. Also see Amy Belasco and Larry Nowels, Congressional Research Service Report for Congress, *Supplemental Appropriations 2003: Iraq, Afghanistan, Global War on Terrorism, and Homeland Security*, updated April 18, 2003, fas.org/asmp/resources/govern/crs-rl31829.pdf.

109 "Netanyahu 2002: I Guarantee You," C-SPAN, Sept. 12, 2002, www.c-span.org/video/?c4529433/netanyahu-2002-guarantee.

110 Kaplan and Kristol, *War over Iraq*, 99.

111 Richard Perle, "Why the West Must Strike First Against Saddam Hussein," *Daily Telegraph*, Aug. 9, 2002.

112 Boot, "Case for American Empire."

113 Kagan and Kristol, "What to Do About Iraq."
114 Cited in Fallows, "Fifty-First State?"
115 Cited in ibid.
116 "President George W. Bush Speaks at AEI's Annual Dinner," Feb. 28, 2003, www.aei.org/publication/president-george-w-bush-speaks-at-aeis-annual-dinner/; "Remarks by President George W. Bush at the 20th Anniversary of the National Endowment for Democracy," www.ned.org/remarks-by-president-george-w-bush-at-the-20th-anniversary/.
117 Packer, *Assassins' Gate*, 194–95; Michael R. Gordon and Bernard E. Trainor, *The Endgame: The Inside Story of the Struggle for Iraq, from George W. Bush to Barack Obama* (New York: Vintage Books, 2012), 14.
118 L. Paul Bremer III, "How I Didn't Dismantle Iraq's Army," *New York Times*, Sept. 6, 2007.
119 Bush, *Decision Points*, 259; and the discussions in Ricks, *Fiasco*, 158–59; Haass, *War of Necessity*, 226; and Gordon and Trainor, *Cobra II*, 563.
120 Donald Rumsfeld, "Defense Department News Briefing," Pentagon, April 11, 2003.
121 Secretary of Defense Donald Rumsfeld, Department of Defense official transcript of June 18, 2003, press conference; Rumsfeld, interview with Wolf Blitzer, CNN, March 23, 2003, www.cnn.com/2003/US/03/23/cnna.irq.rumsfeld/index.html; Ricks, *Fiasco*, 249.
122 "Ladies and Gentlemen, We Got Him!!," www.youtube.com/watch?v=S02BHmWPZNs.
123 Max Boot, "Reconstructing Iraq," *Weekly Standard*, Sept. 15, 2003, www.weeklystandard.com/max-boot/reconstructing-iraq.
124 Danielle Pletka, "Troops in Iraq: More Isn't Better," *New York Times*, Sept. 23, 2003, www.nytimes.com/2003/09/23/opinion/troops-in-iraq-more-isn-t-better.html.
125 Fred Barnes, "The Bumpy Road to Democracy in Iraq," *Weekly Standard*, April 5, 2004, www.weeklystandard.com/fred-barnes/the-bumpy-road-to-democracy-in-iraq (emphasis added). For an excellent critique of the tendency of visitors to Iraq to draw unfounded conclusions from short visits—and to "[ascribe] their epiphanies to what are largely ceremonial visits"—see Jonathan Finer, "Green Zone Blinders," *Washington Post*, Aug. 18, 2007, www.washingtonpost.com/wp-dyn/content/article/2007/08/17/AR2007081701578_pf.html.
126 "'Iraq Insurgency in Last Throes,' Cheney Says," cnn.com, June 20, 2005; Packer, *Assassins' Gate*, 446. For the casualty figures, see O'Hanlon, *Iraq Index*.
127 Rice, "Promise of a Democratic Peace."
128 "Vice President's Remarks at the Gerald R. Ford Journalism Prize Luncheon Followed by Q&A," White House Archives, June 19, 2006, georgewbush-whitehouse.archives.gov/news/releases/2006/06/20060619-10.html; Cheney on *Meet the Press*, Sept. 10, 2006, www.nbcnews.com/id/14720480/ns/meet_the_press/t/transcript-sept/#.XHVS_qJKi70.

129 O'Hanlon, *Iraq Index*.
130 Rajiv Chandrasekaran, *Imperial Life in the Emerald City: Inside Iraq's Green Zone* (New York: Vintage, 2006), 146.
131 "Transcript of President Bush's Address to Nation on U.S. Policy in Iraq," *New York Times*, Jan. 11, 2007, www.nytimes.com/2007/01/11/us/11ptext.html; Gordon and Trainor, *Endgame*, 304, 378.
132 For a detailed description of surge operations, see Joel D. Rayburn et al., *The U.S. Army in the Iraq War, vol. 2, Surge and Withdrawal, 2007–2011* (Carlisle, Pa.: Strategic Studies Institute, 2019), 195–250, ssi.armywarcollege.edu/pubs/display.cfm?pubID=1376.
133 By February 2008, only 38 percent of Americans thought that going to war in Iraq was the right decision, compared with 54 percent who said the decision was wrong. Tom Rosentiel, "Public Attitudes Toward the War in Iraq: 2003–2008," Pew Research Center, March 19, 2008, www.pewresearch.org/2008/03/19/public-attitudes-toward-the-war-in-iraq-20032008/. Americans also strongly opposed the surge initially, by a margin of 61 percent to 35 percent in January 2007, though by the following summer 48 percent would say the surge was working. Frank Newport, "Public Opposes Troop Surge by 61% to 36% Margin," Gallup, Jan. 9, 2007, news.gallup.com/poll/26080/public-opposes-troop-surge-61-36-margin.aspx; Lydia Saad, "Nearly Half of U.S. Adults Now Applaud the Iraq Surge," Gallup, July 31, 2008, news.gallup.com/poll/109165/nearly-half-us-adults-now-applaud-iraq-surge.aspx. For more on the surge, see Carter Malkasian, *Illusions of Victory: The Anbar Awakening and the Rise of the Islamic State* (Oxford: Oxford University Press, 2017).
134 Gordon and Trainor, *Endgame*, 305, 430–31.
135 Ali Khedery, "Why We Stuck with Maliki," *Washington Post*, July 3, 2014; Ned Parker, "The Iraq We Left Behind: Welcome to the World's Next Failed State," *Foreign Affairs*, March 2, 2012.
136 John Kreiser, "Bush: No 'Graceful Exit' from Iraq," CBS News, Nov. 30, 2006, www.cbsnews.com/news/bush-no-graceful-exit-from-iraq/. Also see Emma Sky, *The Unraveling: High Hopes and Missed Opportunities in Iraq* (New York: PublicAffairs, 2015), 139.
137 Rayburn et al., *U.S. Army in the Iraq War, vol. 2, Surge and Withdrawal, 2007–2011*, 4.
138 John Hannah, "Iran-Backed Militia Are in Iraq to Stay," *Foreign Policy*, July 31, 2019.
139 See Obama's speech at Camp Lejeune, Feb. 27, 2009, obamawhitehouse.archives.gov/the-press-office/remarks-president-barack-obama-ndash-responsibly-ending-war-iraq. Also see Peter Baker, "With Pledges to Troops and Iraqis, Obama Details Pullout," *New York Times*, Feb. 27, 2009, www.nytimes.com/2009/02/28/washington/28troops.html; Gordon and Trainor, *Endgame*, 563.
140 Gordon and Trainor, *Endgame*, 632.

141 James Franklin Jeffrey, "Behind the U.S. Withdrawal from Iraq," *Wall Street Journal*, Nov. 2, 2014, www.wsj.com/articles/james-franklin-jeffrey-behind-the-u-s-withdrawal-from-iraq-1414972705; Gordon and Trainor, *Endgame*, 673.

142 "Remarks by the President on Ending the War in Iraq," White House Archives, Oct. 21, 2011, obamawhitehouse.archives.gov/the-press-office/2011/10/21/remarks-president-ending-war-iraq.

143 "Remarks by President Obama and Prime Minister al-Maliki of Iraq in a Joint Press Conference," White House Archives, Dec. 12, 2011, obamawhitehouse.archives.gov/the-press-office/2011/12/12/remarks-president-obama-and-prime-minister-al-maliki-iraq-joint-press-co.

144 The first quotation is from the then deputy national security adviser, Denis McDonough, cited in Josh Rogin, "How the Obama Administration Bungled the Iraq Withdrawal Negotiations," *Foreign Policy*, Oct. 21, 2011. The second is from the national security adviser to the vice president, Tony Blinken, in Antony J. Blinken, "Is Iraq on Track? Democracy and Disorder in Baghdad," *Foreign Affairs*, July/Aug. 2012.

145 Gordon and Trainor, *Endgame*, 547.

146 Parker, "Iraq We Left Behind."

147 Seth G. Jones et al., *Rolling Back the Islamic State* (Santa Monica, Calif.: Rand, 2017), 20, www.rand.org/pubs/research_reports/RR1912.html; George Packer, "The Common Enemy," *New Yorker*, Aug. 25, 2014, www.newyorker.com/magazine/2014/08/25/the-common-enemy.

148 Susan Rice, *Tough Love: My Story of the Things Worth Fighting For* (New York: Simon & Schuster, 2019), 421–22.

149 See, for example, Marc Thiessen, "Obama's Iraq Disaster," *Washington Post*, June 16, 2014, www.washingtonpost.com/opinions/marc-thiessen-obamas-iraq-disaster/2014/06/16/7151391e-f55b-11e3-a3a5-42be35962a52_story.html; William Kristol, "We Were Right to Fight in Iraq," *USA Today*, May 20, 2015, www.usatoday.com/story/opinion/2015/05/20/iraq-saddam-hussein-obama-bush-william-kristol-editorials-debates/27681429/; and the positions of the politicians Marco Rubio, John McCain, and Jeb Bush discussed in Stephen M. Walt, *The Hell of Good Intentions: America's Foreign Policy Elite and the Decline of U.S. Primacy* (New York: Farrar, Straus and Giroux, 2018), 333n9.

150 Jeffrey, "Behind the U.S. Withdrawal from Iraq."

151 In 2014, the United States would send forces back to Iraq on the basis of an exchange of letters with Prime Minister Maliki that did not receive parliamentary approval. The context, however—with ISIS marching toward Baghdad—was very different from that in 2011.

152 International Crisis Group, "Iraq's Paramilitary Groups: The Challenge of Rebuilding a Functioning State," Report No. 188, July 30, 2018, www.crisisgroup.org/middle-east-north-africa/gulf-and-arabian-peninsula/iraq/188-iraqs-paramilitary-groups-challenge-rebuilding-functioning-state.

153 Tamer El-Ghobashy and Mustafa Salim, "As Iraq's Shiite Militias Expand

Their Reach, Concerns About an ISIS Revival Grow," *Washington Post*, Jan. 9, 2019, www.washingtonpost.com/world/as-iraqs-shiite-militias-expand-their-reach-concerns-about-an-isis-revival-grow/2019/01/09/52da575e-eda9-11e8-8b47-bd0975fd6199_story.html?utm_term=.105b9cb233ac.

154 Loveday Morris, "How the Kurdish Independence Referendum Failed Spectacularly," *Washington Post*, Oct. 20, 2017, www.washingtonpost.com/world/how-the-kurdish-independence-referendum-backfired-/2017/10/20/3010c820-b371-11e7-9b93-b97043e57a22_story.html?utm_term=.1fcf7368deaa.

155 "A Positive Sign from the Middle East: Iraq's Democratic Election," *Washington Post*, May 14, 2018, www.washingtonpost.com/opinions/global-opinions/a-positive-sign-from-the-middle-east-iraqs-democratic-election/2018/05/14/fc72f494-579d-11e8-858f-12becb4d6067_story.html?utm_term=.ff14814f7a19.

156 John Hannah, "Iraq Needs Regime Change Again," *Foreign Policy*, Feb. 20, 2020, https://foreignpolicy.com/2020/02/20/iraq-needs-regime-change-again-allawi-protests-iran/.

Chapter 5: "The Transition Must Begin Now"

1 McFaul, phone conversation with author, May 9, 2019. The NSC party is also discussed in Michael Crowley, "We Caved: What Happened When Barack Obama's Idealistic Rhetoric Collided with the Cold Realities of War and Dictatorship in the Middle East and Beyond," *Politico*, Jan./Feb. 2016, www.politico.eu/article/we-caved-barack-obama-america-military-cairo/.

2 Fred Kaplan, "The Realist," *Politico*, March/April 2014, www.politico.com/magazine/story/2014/02/barack-obama-realist-foreign-policy-103861; David Brooks, "Obama Admires Bush," *New York Times*, May 16, 2008, www.nytimes.com/2008/05/16/opinion/16brooks.html.

3 George W. Bush, Second Inaugural Address, Jan. 20, 2005, www.npr.org/templates/story/story.php?storyId=4460172. On Bush and democracy promotion, see Elliott Abrams, *Realism and Democracy: American Foreign Policy After the Arab Spring* (New York: Cambridge University Press, 2017), 171–72.

4 Shapiro, discussion with author, Jan. 2018.

5 "Senator Barack Obama Speech on the Way Forward in Iraq," Chicago Council on Global Affairs, Nov. 20, 2006, obamaspeeches.com/094-A-Way-Forward-in-Iraq-Obama-Speech.htm.

6 "Text: Obama's Speech in Cairo," *New York Times*, June 4, 2009, www.nytimes.com/2009/06/04/us/politics/04obama.text.html.

7 White House, Office of the Vice President, "Remarks by Vice President Biden at the 45th Munich Conference on Security Policy," Feb. 7, 2009, obamawhitehouse.archives.gov/the-press-office/remarks-vice-president-biden-45th-munich-conference-security-policy.

8 The presidential directive remains classified, but it is discussed in some detail in Mark Landler, "Secret Report Ordered by Obama Identified Potential Uprisings," *New York Times*, Feb. 11, 2016, www.nytimes.com/2011/02/17/world/middleeast/17diplomacy.html; Ryan Lizza, "The Consequentialist: How the Arab Spring Remade Obama's Foreign Policy," *New Yorker*, April 25, 2011, www.newyorker.com/magazine/2011/05/02/the-consequentialist; David Ignatius, "Obama's Low-Key Strategy for the Middle East," *Washington Post*, March 6, 2011.

9 Crowley, "We Caved."

10 Samantha Power, *The Education of an Idealist* (New York: HarperCollins, 2019), 286.

11 Joel Brinkley, "How 'Democracy' Got to Be a Dirty Word," *SFGate*, April 5, 2009, www.sfgate.com/opinion/article/How-democracy-got-to-be-a-dirty-word-3165842.php.

12 Thomas Carothers, "Why Is the United States Shortchanging Its Commitment to Democracy?" *Washington Post*, Dec. 22, 2014, carnegieendowment.org/2014/12/22/why-is-united-states-shortchanging-its-commitment-to-democracy-pub-57593; Abrams, *Realism and Democracy*, 174; James Traub, *The Freedom Agenda: Why America Must Spread Democracy (Just Not the Way George Bush Did)* (New York: Picador, 2009), 247.

13 See Obama, interview with Justin Webb, BBC, June 2, 2009, "Obama: Mubarak Is 'Stalwart Ally' . . . 'Force for Stability and Good,'" www.youtube.com/watch?v=tmLX37f4ZgQ. Also see Fawas A. Gerges, *Obama and the Middle East: The End of America's Moment?* (New York: Palgrave Macmillan, 2012), 103–4, 158.

14 Remarks by Secretary of State Hillary Clinton, Forum for the Future: Partnership Dialogue Panel Session, U.S. Department of State transcript, Jan. 13, 2011, 2009-2017.state.gov/secretary/20092013clinton/rm/2011/01/154595.htm.

15 Hillary Rodham Clinton, *Hard Choices* (New York: Simon & Schuster, 2014), 285.

16 Peter Beaumont and Jack Shenker, "Egypt's Day of Fury: Cairo in Flames as Cities Become Battlegrounds," *Guardian*, Jan. 28, 2011, www.theguardian.com/world/2011/jan/28/egypt-cairo-protesters-defy-curfew-elbaradei-mubarak.

17 Secretary of State Hillary Clinton, Remarks with Spanish Foreign Minister Trinidad Jimenez After Meeting, Department of State Transcript, Jan. 25, 2011, 2009-2017.state.gov/secretary/20092013clinton/rm/2011/01/155280.htm, cited in Lizza, "Consequentialist."

18 Remarks by the President in State of the Union Address, White House Archives, Jan. 25, 2011, obamawhitehouse.archives.gov/the-press-office/2011/01/25/remarks-president-state-union-address.

19 Rhodes cited in David D. Kirkpatrick, *Into the Hands of the Soldiers:*

Freedom and Chaos in Egypt and the Middle East (New York: Random House, 2018), 35.

20 Official Transcript of President Obama's Remarks on Situation in Egypt, obamawhitehouse.archives.gov/the-press-office/2011/01/28/remarks-president-situation-egypt; "Obama: I Told Mubarak He Must Deliver on His Promises," CNN, Jan. 28, 2011, www.cnn.com/2011/WORLD/africa/01/28/egypt.protests.u.s.response/index.html.

21 Kirkpatrick, *Into the Hands of the Soldiers*, 43.

22 "Hosni Mubarak's Speech: Full Text," *Guardian*, Feb. 1, 2011, www.theguardian.com/world/2011/feb/02/president-hosni-mubarak-egypt-speech.

23 Ross, conversation with author, April 18, 2019.

24 Gates, *Duty*, 506.

25 Burns, *Back Channel*, 301; Abrams, *Realism and Democracy*, 35.

26 Magsamen, conversation with author, May 15, 2019.

27 Ben Rhodes, *The World as It Is: A Memoir of the Obama White House* (New York: Random House, 2018), 101.

28 Rhodes, conversation with author, Oct. 29, 2019.

29 Gates, *Duty*, 57; Crowley, "We Caved."

30 Clinton, *Hard Choices*, 287.

31 Ibid.; Gates, *Duty*, 505. For more on Obama's thinking and the Mubarak call, see David E. Sanger, *Confront and Conceal: Obama's Secret Wars and Surprising Use of American Power* (New York: Crown, 2012), 296–97.

32 Kirkpatrick, *Into the Hands of the Soldiers*, 44.

33 Remarks by the President on the Situation in Egypt, White House Archives, Feb. 1, 2011, obamawhitehouse.archives.gov/the-press-office/2011/02/01/remarks-president-situation-egypt.

34 Rhodes, *World as It Is*, 108.

35 White House, Office of the Press Secretary, Press Briefing by Press Secretary Robert Gibbs, Feb. 2, 2011, obamawhitehouse.archives.gov/the-press-office/2011/02/02/press-briefing-press-secretary-robert-gibbs-222011.

36 CNN Staff, "Egypt Takes Center Stage at Munich Security Conference," CNN, Feb. 5, 2011, www.cnn.com/2011/WORLD/europe/02/05/germany.security.conference/index.html.

37 Clinton, *Hard Choices*, 289; Burns, *Back Channel*, 302.

38 David Ignatius, "Hillary Clinton Was Right on Egypt," *Washington Post*, Jan. 28, 2016, www.washingtonpost.com/opinions/hillary-clinton-was-right-on-egypt/2016/01/28/fe7fe922-c609-11e5-8965-0607e0e265ce_story.html?noredirect=on&utm_term=.7a99ca7472ec.

39 U.S. Department of State, Briefing for the Traveling Press, Hillary Rodham Clinton, Feb. 6, 2011, 2009-2017.state.gov/secretary/20092013clinton/rm/2011/02/156051.htm.

40 Press Briefing by Press Secretary Robert Gibbs, Feb. 8, 2011, obamawhitehouse.archives.gov/the-press-office/2011/02/08/press-briefing-press

-secretary-robert-gibbs-282011; Lucy Madison, "Obama on Egypt: 'We Are Witnessing History Unfold,'" CBS News, Feb. 10, 2011, www.cbsnews.com/news/obama-on-egypt-we-are-witnessing-history-unfold/.

41 CNN Staff, "Egypt's Mubarak Resigns After 30-Year Rule," CNN, Feb. 11, 2011, www.cnn.com/2011/WORLD/africa/02/11/egypt.revolution/index.html.

42 "Obama's Remarks on the Resignation of Mubarak," *New York Times*, Feb. 11, 2011, www.nytimes.com/2011/02/12/world/middleeast/12diplo-text.html.

43 Rhodes, *World as It Is*, 108.

44 Marwa Awad and Dina Zayed, "Military Rulers Dissolve Egypt's Parliament," Reuters, Feb. 12, 2011; Steven Cook, *The Struggle for Egypt: From Nasser to Tahrir Square* (New York: Oxford University Press, 2012), 297.

45 David D. Kirkpatrick, "Egypt's Military Expands Power, Raising Alarms," *New York Times*, Oct. 14, 2011, www.nytimes.com/2011/10/15/world/middleeast/egypts-military-expands-power-raising-alarms.html; Leila Fadel, "Egyptians Seek to 'Reclaim' Revolution from Military Leaders," *Washington Post*, Sept. 30, 2011.

46 David D. Kirkpatrick, "Islamists Win 70% of Seats in the Egyptian Parliament," *New York Times*, Jan. 21, 2012, www.nytimes.com/2012/01/22/world/middleeast/muslim-brotherhood-wins-47-of-egypt-assembly-seats.html.

47 David D. Kirkpatrick, "Named Egypt's Winner, Islamist Makes History," *New York Times*, June 24, 2012, www.nytimes.com/2012/06/25/world/middleeast/mohamed-morsi-of-muslim-brotherhood-declared-as-egypts-president.html; Charles Levinson, Matt Bradley, and Tamer El-Ghobashy, "Islamist Wins Egyptian Vote," *Wall Street Journal*, June 25, 2012, www.wsj.com/articles/SB10001424052702304458604577486420858304122.

48 Clinton, *Hard Choices*, 289; Ignatius, "Hillary Clinton Was Right on Egypt."

49 See Kirkpatrick, *Into the Hands of the Soldiers*, 148.

50 Patterson, email communication with author, Jan. 6, 2020.

51 Statement by Press Secretary on Egypt, June 24, 2012, obamawhitehouse.archives.gov/the-press-office/2012/06/24/statement-press-secretary-egypt.

52 Joel Greenberg, "Anxious Israel Sends Guarded Response to Egypt," *Washington Post,* June 25, 2012, www.washingtonpost.com/world/middle_east/anxious-israel-sends-guarded-response-to-egypt/2012/06/24/gJQAZXNH1V_story.html?utm_term=.4fbecb31de45; Angus McDowall, "Mubarak's Departure Deals Blow to Saudis," *Wall Street Journal*, Feb. 12, 2011, www.wsj.com/articles/SB10001424052748703786804576138321598498188.

53 Kirkpatrick, "Named Egypt's Winner, Islamist Makes History."

54 Steven Lee Myers, "U.S. Move to Give Egypt $450 Million in Aid Meets Resistance," *New York Times*, Sept. 28, 2012, www.nytimes.com/2012/09/29/world/middleeast/white-house-move-to-give-egypt-450-million-in-aid-meets-resistance.html.

55 Derek Chollet, *The Long Game: How Obama Defied Washington and Redefined America's Role in the World* (New York: PublicAffairs, 2016), 118.

56 Eric Trager, *Arab Fall: How the Muslim Brotherhood Won and Lost Egypt in 891 Days* (Washington, D.C.: Georgetown University Press, 2013), 168; Kirkpatrick, *Into the Hands of the Soldiers,* 156.

57 Dennis Ross, "Egypt's New Leaders Must Accept Reality," *Washington Post,* Aug. 19, 2012, www.washingtonpost.com/opinions/dennis-ross-egypts-new-leaders-must-accept-reality/2012/08/19/46e60810-e8ad-11e1-936a-b801f1abab19_story.html?utm_term=.9325122afd77.

58 Michael Birnbaum, "Egypt's President Morsi Takes Sweeping New Powers," *Washington Post,* Nov. 22, 2012; Trager, *Arab Fall,* 175–77; Kirkpatrick, *Into the Hands of the Soldiers,* 178.

59 Kirkpatrick, *Into the Hands of the Soldiers,* 178.

60 Marwa Awad, "Clashes in Cairo After Mursi Seizes New Powers," Reuters, Nov. 23, 2012.

61 Michael Birnbaum, "Egypt's Morsi Appears to Accept Some Limits on His Power," *Washington Post,* Nov. 26, 2012; Stephanie McCrummen, "Egypt's Morsi Annuls Most of Contested Decree, Stays Firm on Dec 15. Referendum," *Washington Post,* Dec. 8, 2012, www.washingtonpost.com/world/middle_east/egyptian-president-poised-to-grant-military-broader-police-powers/2012/12/08/071a80f8-4131-11e2-ae43-cf491b837f7b_story.html?utm_term=.b999ebdd6913.

62 Kirkpatrick, *Into the Hands of the Soldiers,* 178.

63 Bruce Riedel, "Saudi Arabia Cheers the Coup in Egypt," Brookings Institution, July 7, 2013, www.brookings.edu/opinions/saudi-arabia-cheers-the-coup-in-egypt/.

64 On Saudi and Emirati support for Morsi's overthrow, see David Kirkpatrick, "Recordings Suggest Emirates and Egyptian Military Pushed Ousting of Morsi," *New York Times,* March 1, 2015, www.nytimes.com/2015/03/02/world/middleeast/recordings-suggest-emirates-and-egyptian-military-pushed-ousting-of-morsi.html; David Kirkpatrick, "Leaks Gain Credibility and Potential to Embarrass Egypt's Leaders," *New York Times,* May 12, 2015, www.nytimes.com/2015/05/13/world/middleeast/leaks-gain-credibility-and-potential-to-embarrass-egypts-leaders.html. On Saudi and Emirati subsidies, see "Saudi Arabia Pledges $5 Billion in Aid to Egypt," CBS News, July 9, 2013, www.cbsnews.com/news/saudi-arabia-pledges-5-billion-in-aid-to-egypt/; Rod Nordland, "Saudi Arabia Promises to Aid Egypt's Regime," *New York Times,* Aug. 19, 2013, www.nytimes.com/2013/08/20/world/middleeast/saudi-arabia-vows-to-back-egypts-rulers.html; Andrew

Critchlow, "Saudi and UAE Ready $20Bn Boost for Egypt's El-Sisi," *Telegraph*, June 1, 2014, www.telegraph.co.uk/finance/newsbysector/banksandfinance/10868522/Saudi-and-UAE-ready-20bn-boost-for-Egypts-El-Sisi.html; Trager, *Arab Fall*, 232.

65 Kirkpatrick, *Into the Hands of the Soldiers*, 212.

66 David D. Kirkpatrick, "Army Ousts Egypt's President; Morsi Is Taken into Military Custody," *New York Times*, July 3, 2013, www.nytimes.com/2013/07/04/world/middleeast/egypt.html.

67 John Hudson, "Obama Administration Won't Call Egypt's Coup a Coup," *Foreign Policy*, July 8, 2013, foreignpolicy.com/2013/07/08/obama-administration-wont-call-egypts-coup-a-coup/.

68 CNN Staff, "U.S. Opts Not to Define Egypt Ouster as a Coup; Tensions Rise Ahead of Planned Protests," CNN, July 25, 2013, www.cnn.com/2013/07/25/politics/obama-egypt/index.html?no-st=1555700537.

69 Dana Hughes, "Reporters Grill State Dept. on Egypt Coup Decision Punt," ABC News, July 26, 2013, abcnews.go.com/blogs/politics/2013/07/reporters-grill-state-dept-on-egypt-coup-decision-punt/.

70 Greg Botelho, Josh Levs, and Ian Lee, "Egypt on Edge After at Least 278 Killed in Bloodiest Day Since Revolution," CNN, Aug. 15, 2013, www.cnn.com/2013/08/14/world/meast/egypt-protests/index.html; "All According to Plan," Human Rights Watch, Aug. 12, 2014, www.hrw.org/report/2014/08/12/all-according-plan/raba-massacre-and-mass-killings-protesters-egypt; Kirkpatrick, "Army Ousts Egypt's President; Morsi Is Taken into Military Custody"; Mohamed Ezz, "Egypt Court Sentences 75 to Death over Deadly 2013 Protests," *New York Times*, Sept. 8, 2018, www.nytimes.com/2018/09/08/world/middleeast/egypt-protest-sentences.html.

71 Michael R. Gordon and Mark Landler, "In Crackdown Response, U.S. Temporarily Freezes Some Military Aid to Egypt," *New York Times*, Oct. 9, 2013, www.nytimes.com/2013/10/10/world/middleeast/obama-military-aid-to-egypt.html.

72 Jen Psaki, Press Statement on U.S. Assistance to Egypt, Oct. 9, 2013, 2009-2017.state.gov/r/pa/prs/ps/2013/10/215258.htm.

73 Secretary of State John Kerry, State Department Transcript of Interview with Hamid Mir of Geo TV, Aug. 1, 2013, 2009-2017.state.gov/secretary/remarks/2013/08/212626.htm; Matt Bradley and Saeed Shah, "Kerry Lauds Egypt Military for 'Restoring Democracy,'" *Wall Street Journal*, Aug. 1, 2013.

74 Secretary of State John Kerry, Department of State official transcript of June 22, 2014, press conference in Cairo, 2009-2017.state.gov/secretary/remarks/2014/06/228234.htm.

75 According to former Pentagon official Derek Chollet, Hagel spent more than thirty hours on the phone with Sisi during this period. Chollet, *Long Game*, 121. Chollet also told me that Hagel faithfully delivered the points in his calls but that Sisi made clear his intention to ignore them,

a point that further underscored the limits of U.S. influence. Chollet, conversation with author, Sept. 20, 2019.

76 White House, Office of the Press Secretary, "Remarks by President Obama in Address to the UN General Assembly," United Nations, New York, Sept. 24, 2013, obamawhitehouse.archives.gov/the-press-office/2013/09/24/remarks-president-obama-address-united-nations-general-assembly.

77 Kirkpatrick, *Into the Hands of the Soldiers*, 322; Chollet, *Long Game*, 122.

78 Geoff Dyer, "US Restores $1.3Bn Military Aid to Egypt," *Financial Times*, March 31, 2015, www.ft.com/content/f08ed734-d7f2-11e4-80de-00144feab7de; Derek Chollet, "The Part of Obama's Arms-to-Egypt Decision That Matters," *Defense One*, April 2, 2015, www.defenseone.com/ideas/2015/04/part-obamas-arms-egypt-deal-matters/109213/.

79 Andrew Miller, "Egypt: Security, Human Rights, and Reform," House Foreign Affairs Committee Middle East and North Africa Subcommittee Hearing, July 24, 2018, docs.house.gov/meetings/FA/FA13/20180724/108598/HHRG-115-FA13-Wstate-MillerA-20180724.pdf. Also "Egypt: Torture Epidemic May Be Crime Against Humanity," Human Rights Watch, Sept. 6, 2017, www.hrw.org/new/2017/09/06/egypt-torture-epidemic-may-be-crime-against-humanity.

80 Kirkpatrick, *Into the Hands of the Soldiers*, 331; Mark Landler, "Egypt's President, Hoping to Be Allowed to Stay in Office Until 2034, Basks in Trump's Embrace," *New York Times*, April 9, 2019, www.nytimes.com/2019/04/09/us/politics/trump-abdel-fattah-el-sisi.html.

81 Nancy A. Youssef, Vivian Salama, and Michael C. Bender, "Trump, Awaiting Egyptian Counterpart at Summit, Called Out for 'My Favorite Dictator,'" *Wall Street Journal*, Sept. 13, 2019, https://www.wsj.com/articles/trump-awaiting-egyptian-counterpart-at-summit-called-out-for-my-favorite-dictator-11568403645.

82 Sullivan, conversation with author, Oct. 28, 2019.

83 Ignatius, "Hillary Clinton Was Right on Egypt."

Chapter 6: "We Came, We Saw, He Died"

1 Jo Becker and Scott Shane, "Hillary Clinton, 'Smart Power,' and a Dictator's Fall," *New York Times*, Feb. 27, 2016, www.nytimes.com/2016/02/28/us/politics/hillary-clinton-libya.html?searchResultPosition=2.

2 "Libyan Ambassadors Defect En Masse," Al Jazeera, Feb. 22, 2011, www.aljazeera.com/news/africa/2011/02/201122275739377867.html; Colin Moynihan, "Libya's U.N. Diplomats Break with Qadhafi," *New York Times*, Feb. 21, 2011, www.nytimes.com/2011/02/22/world/africa/22nations.html.

3 David Kirkpatrick and Mona El-Naggar, "Qaddafi's Son Warns of Civil War as Libyan Protests Widen," *New York Times*, Feb. 20, 2011, www.nytimes.com/2011/02/21/world/africa/21libya.html.

4 BBC Staff, "Libya Protests: Gaddafi's Son Warns of Civil War," BBC,

Feb. 21, 2011, www.bbc.com/news/world-middle-east-12520586; CNN Staff, "Libya, World Reacts to Saif Gadhafi's Address," CNN, Feb. 21, 2011, www.cnn.com/2011/WORLD/africa/02/21/libya.gadhafi.speech.reax/index.html.

5 David Kirkpatrick and Kareem Fahim, "Qaddafi Warns of Assault on Benghazi as U.N. Vote Nears," *New York Times*, March 17, 2011, www.nytimes.com/2011/03/18/world/africa/18libya.html; Frederic Wehrey, *The Burning Shores: Inside the Battle for the New Libya* (New York: Farrar, Straus and Giroux, 2018), 39.

6 Ian Black, "Gaddafi Urges Violent Showdown and Tells Libya, 'I'll Die a Martyr,'" *Guardian*, Feb. 22, 2011, www.theguardian.com/world/2011/feb/22/muammar-gaddafi-urges-violent-showdown.

7 Alan J. Kuperman, "A Model Humanitarian Intervention? Reassessing NATO's Libya Campaign," *International Security* (Summer 2013): 105–36, www.jstor.org/stable/pdf/24480571.pdf?refreqid=excelsior%3Aa4b478659ff03f3e57ec6046c2df3127; Alan J. Kuperman, "Obama's Libya Debacle: How a Well-Meaning Intervention Ended in Failure," *Foreign Affairs* (March–April 2015), www.foreignaffairs.com/articles/libya/2019-02-18/obamas-libya-debacle; Hugh Roberts, "Who Said Gaddafi Had to Go?" *London Review of Books,* Nov. 17, 2011, www.lrb.co.uk/v33/n22/hugh-roberts/who-said-gaddafi-had-to-go; Richard N. Haass, "Hearing on the Perspective on the Crisis in Libya," Senate Committee on Foreign Relations, April 6, 2011, cfrd8-files.cfr.org/sites/default/files/pdf/2011/04/Haass.Testimony.4.6.11.pdf. On the 1996 Abu Salim prison massacre, see "Libya: June 1996 Killings at Abu Salim Prison," Human Rights Watch, June 27, 2006, www.hrw.org/news/2006/06/27/libya-june-1996-killings-abu-salim-prison; and Kareem Fahim, "Rebels Yank Open Gates of Infamous Libyan Prison, Seeking Clues to a Massacre," *New York Times*, Sept. 1, 2011, www.nytimes.com/2011/09/02/world/africa/02abusalim.html.

8 Joffé cited in House of Commons Foreign Affairs Committee, *Libya: Examination of Intervention and Collapse and the UK's Future Policy Options*, Third Report of Session 2016–17 (London: House of Commons), Sept. 14, 2016, 14. Alison Pargeter, a Libya expert based at the Royal United Services Institute, gave similar testimony to the committee, also cited in the House of Commons report, 13–14.

9 Readout of President Obama's Call with Chancellor Angela Merkel of Germany, White House Press Statement, Feb. 26, 2011, obamawhitehouse.archives.gov/the-press-office/2011/02/26/readout-president-obamas-call-chancellor-angela-merkel-germany.

10 "Holding the Qadhafi Government Accountable," Press Statement by Secretary of State Hillary Clinton, Feb. 26, 2011, 2009-2017.state.gov/secretary/20092013clinton/rm/2011/02/157187.htm.

11 Mark Landler, "Obama Tells Qaddafi to Quit and Authorizes Refugee

Airlifts," *New York Times*, March 3, 2011, www.nytimes.com/2011/03/04/world/africa/04president.html?mtrref=www.google.com&gwh=D47FD18CD5B7ACAE607576EC8B888EF6&gwt=pay.

12 "European Council Declaration," Press Statement by the European Commission, March 11, 2011, europa.eu/rapid/press-release_DOC-11-2_en.htm.

13 Chairman of the Senate Foreign Relations Committee John Kerry Statement During Hearing, March 2, 2011, www.foreign.senate.gov/press/chair/release/chairman-kerry-repeats-call-for-qadhafi-to-leave-and-urges-consideration-of-a-no-fly-zone-over-libya.

14 Bryon Jones, "What Can Be Done to End the Crisis in Libya?" CNN, March 4, 2011, www.cnn.com/2011/WORLD/africa/03/03/libya.crisis.what.next/index.html; John T. Bennet, "Sen. McCain Calls for Immediate No-Fly Zone over Libya's Skies," *The Hill*, March 14, 2011, thehill.com/blogs/floor-action/senate/149429-mccain-calls-for-immediate-no-fly-zone-over-libya.

15 Anne-Marie Slaughter, "Fiddling While Libya Burns," *New York Times*, March 13, 2011, www.nytimes.com/2011/03/14/opinion/14slaughter.html?mtrref=undefined; Nicholas Kristof, "Here's What We Can Do to Tackle Libya," *New York Times*, March 2, 2011, www.nytimes.com/2011/03/03/opinion/03kristof.html?mtrref=www.google.com; James Traub, "Stepping In," *Foreign Policy*, March 11, 2011, foreignpolicy.com/2011/03/11/stepping-in/.

16 Daniel Halper, "Experts Urge Obama to Act on Libya," *Washington Examiner*, March 25, 2011, www.washingtonexaminer.com/weekly-standard/experts-urge-obama-to-act-on-libya.

17 "Newt Gingrich: Libya No-Fly Zone Should Happen 'This Evening,'" *Huffington Post*, March 8, 2011, www.huffpost.com/entry/newt-gingrich-libya-no-fly-zone_n_832967.

18 Cited in Michael Zenko, "Think Again: Libya," *Foreign Policy*, April 28, 2011, foreignpolicy.com/2011/04/28/think-again-libya/. Also Elliott Abrams, "A Formula for Libya Unworthy of Our Country," *Weekly Standard*, April 25, 2011, www.weeklystandard.com/elliott-abrams/a-formula-for-libya-unworthy-of-our-country.

19 Nicholas Kristof, "The Case for a No-Fly Zone over Libya," *New York Times*, March 9, 2011, www.nytimes.com/2011/03/10/opinion/10kristof.html.

20 Comments of Abdel Hafeez Goga, the deputy head of the Benghazi-based provisional rebel government, cited in Matt Bradley and Charles Levinson, "Arab League Urges Libya 'No-Fly' Zone," *Wall Street Journal*, March 14, 2011, www.wsj.com/articles/SB10001424052748704838804576196681609529882; Levy, interview with Spiegel, *Spiegel Online*, March 30, 2011, www.spiegel.de/international/world/spiegel-interview-with-bernard-henri-levy-we-lost-a-great-deal-of-time-in-libya-because-of-the-germans-a-753797.html. Also see Micah Zenko, "Libya: 'Justifi-

cations' for Intervention," Council on Foreign Relations, June 24, 2011, www.cfr.org/blog/libya-justifications-intervention.

21 Slaughter, "Fiddling While Libya Burns."

22 "Donald Trump Supporting Libya Intervention in 2011," www.youtube.com/watch?v=OTqoz0RYvVM.

23 Maggie Haberman, "Donald Trump Questioned on Previous Positions on Libya and Iraq," *New York Times*, June 6, 2016, www.nytimes.com/2016/06/07/us/politics/donald-trump-questioned-about-previous-positions-on-libya-and-iraq.html.

24 Cited in Becker and Shane, "Hillary Clinton, 'Smart Power,' and a Dictator's Fall."

25 Rhodes, conversation with author, Oct. 29, 2019.

26 Becker and Shane, "Hillary Clinton, 'Smart Power,' and a Dictator's Fall."

27 Gates was paraphrasing General Douglas MacArthur. Secretary of Defense Robert Gates Speech at West Point, Feb. 25, 2011, archive.defense.gov/Speeches/Speech.aspx?SpeechID=1539.

28 Gates, *Duty*, 512.

29 Becker and Shane, "Hillary Clinton, 'Smart Power,' and a Dictator's Fall."

30 Secretary of Defense Robert Gates Testimony to Congress, Defense Department Fiscal Year 2012 Budget Request, March 2, 2011, www.c-span.org/video/?298247-1/defense-department-fiscal-year-2012-budget-request&start=4937.

31 Chairman, Joint Chiefs of Staff Admiral Mike Mullen, "DOD News Briefing," Pentagon, March 1, 2011, U.S. Department of Defense, archive.defense.gov/transcripts/transcript.aspx?transcriptid=4777.

32 William Daley, *Meet the Press*, March 6, 2011, www.nbcnews.com/id/41906285/ns/meet_the_press-transcripts/t/meet-press-transcript-march/#.XPmHfRZKi70.

33 Clinton, *Hard Choices*, 302.

34 Secretary of State Hillary Clinton Testimony to Congress, State Department 2012 Budget Request, March 10, 2011, www.c-span.org/video/?298424-1/state-department-2012-budget-request&start=4539.

35 Arab League Resolution 7360, March 12, 2011, responsibilitytoprotect.org/Arab%20League%20Ministerial%20level%20statement%2012%20march%202011%20-%20english(1).pdf.

36 The issue was complicated by the fact that at this very time Saudi Arabia was intervening militarily to support the Sunni monarchy in Bahrain, making clear that Gulf support for regime change in the region was highly selective.

37 Becker and Shane, "Hillary Clinton, 'Smart Power,' and a Dictator's Fall."

38 McCain cited in Zenko, "Libya: 'Justifications' for Intervention"; Hague cited in House of Commons Foreign Affairs Committee, *Libya: Examination of Intervention and Collapse and the UK's Future Policy Options*, 10.

39 House of Commons Foreign Affairs Committee, *Libya: Examination of*

Intervention and Collapse and the UK's Future Policy Options, Sept. 6, 2016, 13.

40 Miller, discussion with author, July 23, 2019. Miller notes that documents such as the TNC's March 29, 2011, "Vision of a Democratic Libya," committing the group to "dialogue, tolerance, cooperation . . . democracy . . . freedom of expression . . . political pluralism and the right of all Libyans to vote in free and fair elections," were drafted with significant U.S. input and then later touted by American officials as validations of the TNC's democratic nature. See Interim National Council, "A Vision of a Democratic Libya," March 29, 2011, www.aljazeera.com/mritems/Documents/2011/3/29/2011329113923943811The%20Interim%20Transitional%20National%20Council%20Statement.pdf.

41 Gates, *Duty*, 518; Helene Cooper and Steven Lee Myers, "Obama Takes Hard Line with Libya After Shift by Clinton," *New York Times*, March 18, 2011, www.nytimes.com/2011/03/19/world/africa/19policy.html; Paul Richter and Christi Parsons, "U.S. Intervention in Libya Now Seen as Cautionary Tale," *Los Angeles Times*, June 27, 2014, www.latimes.com/world/middleeast/la-fg-us-libya-20140627-story.html.

42 Rhodes, *World as It Is*, 113.

43 Gates, *Duty*, 518; Rhodes, *World as It Is*, 114; Chollet, *Long Game*, 98.

44 Chollet, *Long Game*, 98.

45 Gates, *Duty*, 519; Becker and Shane, "Hillary Clinton, 'Smart Power,' and a Dictator's Fall"; Cooper and Myers, "Obama Takes Hard Line with Libya After Shift by Clinton."

46 UN press release of UNSCR 1973, March 17, 2011, www.un.org/press/en/2011/sc10200.doc.htm.

47 Tom Donilon, "The Continuing Need for a Strong NATO," *Washington Post*, Oct. 27, 2011, www.washingtonpost.com/opinions/the-continuing-need-for-a-strong-nato/2011/10/26/gIQA3nYNNM_story.html. For background and details on the NATO operation, see Christopher S. Chivvis, *Toppling Qaddafi: Libya and the Limits of Liberal Intervention* (New York: Cambridge University Press, 2014).

48 Rhodes, *World as It Is*, 115; Cooper and Myers, "Obama Takes Hard Line with Libya After Shift by Clinton."

49 Chollet, *Long Game*, 106.

50 Chollet, conversation with author, Sept. 20, 2019.

51 Derek Chollet and Ben Fishman, "Who Lost Libya? Obama's Intervention in Retrospect," *Foreign Affairs*, April 20, 2015, www.foreignaffairs.com/articles/libya/2015-04-20/who-lost-libya.

52 Cretz quoted in Becker and Shane, "Hillary Clinton, 'Smart Power,' and a Dictator's Fall"; Chollet, *Long Game*, 107.

53 Remarks by the President on the Situation in Libya, March 18, 2011, obamawhitehouse.archives.gov/the-press-office/2011/03/18/remarks-president-situation-libya.

54 Press Gaggle by Press Secretary Jay Carney, White House Transcripts,

March 24, 2011, obamawhitehouse.archives.gov/the-press-office/2011/03/24/press-gaggle-press-secretary-jay-carney-3242011; Secretary of State Hillary Clinton, interview with Diane Sawyer, ABC News, March 22, 2011, Department of State Archives, 2009-2017.state.gov/secretary/20092013clinton/rm/2011/03/158841.htm.

55 "Remarks by President in Address to the Nation on Libya," White House Office of the Press Secretary, March 28, 2011, obamawhitehouse.archives.gov/the-press-office/2011/03/28/remarks-president-address-nation-libya.

56 Gordon, "Interview with Evan Davies of BBC Radio 4's Today Program," State Department Transcript, March 30, 2011, 2009-2017.state.gov/p/eur/rls/rm/2011/159379.htm; Deputy Secretary of State James Steinberg Statement Before the House Foreign Affairs Committee, March 31, 2011, 2009-2017.state.gov/s/d/former/steinberg/remarks/2011/169301.htm.

57 Kareem Fahim and David D. Kirkpatrick, "Airstrikes Clear Way for Libyan Rebels' First Major Advance," *New York Times*, March 26, 2011, www.nytimes.com/2011/03/27/world/africa/27libya.html.

58 Kuperman, "Model Humanitarian Intervention?" 114; Mark Mazzetti and Eric Schmitt, "C.I.A. Agents in Libya Aid Airstrikes and Meet Rebels," *New York Times*, March 30, 2011, www.nytimes.com/2011/03/31/world/africa/31intel.html; Mark Hosenball, "Exclusive: Obama Authorizes Secret Help for Libyan Rebels," Reuters, March 30, 2011, www.reuters.com/article/us-libya-usa-order/exclusive-obama-authorizes-secret-help-for-libya-rebels-idUSTRE72T6H220110330; House of Commons Foreign Affairs Committee, *Libya: Examination of Intervention and Collapse and the UK's Future Policy Options*, 16; Micah Zenko, "The Big Lie About the Libyan War," *Foreign Policy*, March 22, 2016, foreignpolicy.com/2016/03/22/libya-and-the-myth-of-humanitarian-intervention/.

59 For two of the proposals, see "Gaddafi Accepts Chavez Talks Offer," Al Jazeera, March 3, 2011, www.aljazeera.com/news/africa/2011/03/20113365739369754.html; and Peter Kenyon, "Libyan Rebels Reject AU Cease-Fire Plan," National Public Radio, April 11, 2011, www.npr.org/2011/04/11/135324882/libyan-rebels-reject-au-ceasefire-plan. Also see discussion in Roberts, "Who Said Gaddafi Had to Go?"

60 Gates cited in Becker and Shane, "Hillary Clinton, 'Smart Power,' and a Dictator's Fall." Gates's successor, Leon Panetta, would also later write, "Everyone in Washington knew but we couldn't officially acknowledge that our goal in Libya was regime change." Leon Panetta, *Worthy Fights: A Memoir of Leadership in War and Peace* (New York: Penguin Books, 2015), 354.

61 "Libya Letter by Obama, Cameron, and Sarkozy: Full Text," BBC News, April 15, 2011, www.bbc.com/news/world-africa-13090646.

62 Estimates of casualties during the Libya conflict vary widely. The journalist Seumas Milne suggests that 1,000–2,000 Libyans were killed before the intervention and from 10,000 to 50,000 afterward. Seumas Milne,

"If the Libyan War Was About Saving Lives, It Was a Catastrophic Failure," *Guardian*, Oct. 26, 2011, www.theguardian.com/commentisfree/2011/oct/26/libya-war-saving-lives-catastrophic-failure. The University of Sweden's conflict tracker cites 11,500 deaths as a result of political conflict from 2011 to 2018 in the Uppsala Conflict Data Program, Department of Peace and Conflict Research, Uppsala University, ucdp.uu.se/#country/620. A University of Tripoli study found that in total the Libyan war in the first year resulted in 21,490 killed, 19,700 injured, and 435,000 displaced. Mohamed A. Daw, Abdallah El-Bouzedi, and Aghnaya A. Dau, "Libyan Armed Conflict 2011: Mortality, Injury, and Population Displacement," *African Journal of Emergency Medicine* 5, no. 3 (2015): 101–7, www.sciencedirect.com/science/article/pii/S2211419X15000348. Also see Kuperman, "Obama's Libya Debacle."

63 Kareem Fahim, Anthony Shadid, and Rick Gladstone, "Violent End to an Era as Qaddafi Dies in Libya," *New York Times*, Oct. 20, 2011, www.nytimes.com/2011/10/21/world/africa/qaddafi-is-killed-as-libyan-forces-take-surt.html.

64 Blumenthal, email to Clinton, Aug. 22, 2011, foia.state.gov/searchapp/DOCUMENTS/HRCEmail_OctWeb/225/DOC_0C05786884/C05786884.pdf.

65 Anne-Marie Slaughter, "Why Libya Sceptics Were Proven Badly Wrong," *Financial Times*, Aug. 24, 2011, www.ft.com/content/18cb7f14-ce3c-11e0-99ec-00144feabdc0.

66 Nicholas Kristof, "Thank You, America!" *New York Times*, Aug. 31, 2011, www.nytimes.com/2011/09/01/opinion/kristof-from-libyans-thank-you-america.html.

67 Mark Landler, "For Obama, Some Vindication of Approach to War," *New York Times*, Oct. 20, 2011, www.nytimes.com/2011/10/21/world/africa/qaddafis-death-is-latest-victory-for-new-us-approach-to-war.html?_r=0&pagewanted=print.

68 Robert Kagan, "An Imperfect Triumph in Libya," *Washington Post*, Aug. 26, 2011, www.washingtonpost.com/opinions/an-imperfect-triumph-in-libya/2011/08/26/gIQA5gC9gJ_story.html?utm_term=.adefdd258525; John McCain, interview with Wolf Blitzer, *The Situation Room*, Oct. 20, 2011, www.realclearpolitics.com/articles/2011/10/20/interview_with_senator_john_mccain_111774.html.

69 Fareed Zakaria, "A New Era in U.S. Foreign Policy," CNN, Aug. 23, 2011, globalpublicsquare.blogs.cnn.com/2011/08/23/a-new-era-in-u-s-foreign-policy/.

70 Patrick Wintour, "Sarkozy and Cameron Arrive in Libya to Meet National Transitional Council," *Guardian*, Sept. 15, 2012, www.theguardian.com/politics/2011/sep/15/cameron-sarkozy-libya-visit-ntc.

71 Secretary of State Hillary Clinton, Remarks with Libyan Prime Minister Mahmoud Jibril, Oct. 18, 2011, 2009-2017.state.gov/secretary/20092013clinton/rm/2011/10/175782.htm.

72 Corbett Daly, "Clinton on Qaddafi, 'We Came, We Saw, He Died,'" CBS News, Oct. 20, 2011, www.cbsnews.com/news/clinton-on-qaddafi-we-came-we-saw-he-died/.

73 John McCain et al., "The Promise of a Pro-American Libya," *Wall Street Journal,* Oct. 7, 2011, www.wsj.com/articles/SB10001424052970203388804576613293623346516.

74 "Remarks on the Death of Former Leader Muammar Abu Minyar al Qadhafi of Libya," Oct. 20, 2011, www.govinfo.gov/content/pkg/DCPD-201100773/pdf/DCPD-201100773.pdf.

75 Ivo H. Daalder and James G. Stavridis, "NATO's Victory in Libya: The Right Way to Run an Intervention," *Foreign Affairs,* March/April 2012, www.foreignaffairs.com/articles/libya/2012-02-02/natos-victory-libya; Ivo H. Daalder and James G. Stavridis, "NATO's Success in Libya," *New York Times,* Oct. 30, 2011, www.nytimes.com/2011/10/31/opinion/31iht-eddaalder31.html.

76 Wehrey, *Burning Shores,* 62; Roberts, "Who Said Gaddafi Had to Go?"

77 Feltman email to Huma Abedin for Hillary Clinton, declassified email available at foia.state.gov/searchapp/DOCUMENTS/HRCEmail_SeptemberWeb/O-2015-08633-184/DOC_0C05781926/C05781926.pdf.

78 Wehrey, *Burning Shores,* 88.

79 David D. Kirkpatrick, "Braving Areas of Violence, Voters Try to Reshape Libya," *New York Times,* July 7, 2012, www.nytimes.com/2012/07/08/world/africa/libyans-vote-in-first-election-in-more-than-40-years.html.

80 Statement by the President on Libya, White House Archives, July 7, 2012, obamawhitehouse.archives.gov/the-press-office/2012/07/07/statement-president-libya.

81 David Kirkpatrick, "Election Results in Libya Break an Islamist Wave," *New York Times,* July 8, 2012, www.nytimes.com/2012/07/09/world/africa/libya-election-latest-results.html; Flavia Krause-Jackson and Caroline Alexander, "Jibril Turns Against Foreign Powers That Aided Qaddafi Overthrow," *World News Blog,* Nov. 23, 2011, efstaworldnews.wordpress.com/2011/11/23/jibril-turns-against-foreign-powers-that-aided-qaddafi-overthrow.

82 Scott Shane and Jo Becker, "A New Libya, with 'Very Little Time Left,'" *New York Times,* Feb. 27, 2016, www.nytimes.com/2016/02/28/us/politics/libya-isis-hillary-clinton.html.

83 Ghaith Shennib and Jessica Donati, "Libyan Parliament Bans Ex–Gaddafi Officials from Office," Reuters, May 5, 2013, www.reuters.com/article/us-libya-politics/libyan-parliament-bans-ex-gaddafi-officials-from-office-idUSBRE94405320130505; Roman David and Houda Mzioudet, "Personnel Change or Personal Change? Rethinking Libya's Political Isolation Law," Brookings Institution, March 2014, www.brookings.edu/wp-content/uploads/2016/06/Lustration-in-Libya-English.pdf; Steven A. Cook, *False Dawn: Protest, Democracy, and Violence in the New Middle East* (Oxford: Oxford University Press, 2017), 128.

84 "Libya: Wake-Up Call to Misrata's Leaders," Human Rights Watch, April 8, 2012, www.hrw.org/news/2012/04/08/libya-wake-call-misratas-leaders; Shane and Becker, "New Libya"; Kuperman, "Obama's Libya Debacle."

85 Wehrey, *Burning Shores*, 236; Tamer El-Ghobashy and Hassan Morajea, "Islamic State Tightens Grip on Libyan Stronghold of Sirte," *Wall Street Journal*, Nov. 29, 2015, www.wsj.com/articles/islamic-state-entrenches-in-sirte-libya-1448798153m; Suliman Ali Zway and David D. Kirkpatrick, "Western Officials Alarmed as ISIS Expands Territory in Libya," *New York Times*, May 31, 2015, www.nytimes.com/2015/06/01/world/africa/western-officials-alarmed-as-islamic-state-expands-territory-in-libya.html; David D. Kirkpatrick, "ISIS Finds New Frontier in Chaotic Libya," *New York Times*, March 10, 2015, www.nytimes.com/2015/03/11/world/africa/isis-seizes-opportunity-in-libyas-turmoil.html; David Lee Anderson, "ISIS Rises in Libya," *New Yorker*, Aug. 4, 2015, www.newyorker.com/news/news-desk/isis-rises-in-libya.

86 Department of Defense Briefing by General David M. Rodriguez, April 7, 2016, dod.defense.gov/News/Transcripts/Transcript-View/Article/715846/department-of-defense-briefing-by-gen-david-m-rodriguez/.

87 "Libya Crude Oil: Production, *CEIC*, 2002–2019," www.ceicdata.com/en/indicator/libya/crude-oil-production; Operational Portal: Refugee Situations Mediterranean Interactive, UN High Commissioner for Refugees, accessed July 23, 2019, data2.unhcr.org/en/situations/mediterranean.

88 Ernesto Londoño, "U.S. Expands Aid to French Mission in Mali," *Washington Post*, Jan. 26, 2013, www.washingtonpost.com/world/national-security/us-expands-aid-to-french-mission-in-mali/2013/01/26/3d56bb5c-6821-11e2-83c7-38d5fac94235_story.html?noredirect=on&utm_term=.f2d67e481f49; Eric Schmitt, "U.S. Military Offers Support, but Not Troops, to Aid France in Africa," *New York Times*, May 12, 2017, www.nytimes.com/2017/05/12/world/africa/africa-us-military-aid-france.html.

89 James Risen, Mark Mazzetti, and Michael S. Schmidt, "U.S.-Approved Arms for Libya Rebels Fell into Jihadis' Hands," *New York Times*, Dec. 5, 2012, www.nytimes.com/2012/12/06/world/africa/weapons-sent-to-libyan-rebels-with-us-approval-fell-into-islamist-hands.html.

90 See report by the U.K. Foreign and Commonwealth Office on the spread of weapons from Libya into the Sahel: "Investigating Cross-Border Weapon Transfers in the Sahel," Nov. 2016, www.conflictarm.com/reports/investigating-cross-border-weapon-transfers-in-the-sahel/; Risen, Mazzetti, and Schmidt, "U.S.-Approved Arms for Libya Rebels Fell into Jihadis' Hands."

91 Sharyl Attkisson, "Thousands of Libyan Missiles from Qaddafi Era Missing in Action," CBS News, March 25, 2013, www.cbsnews.com/news/thousands-of-libyan-missiles-from-qaddafi-era-missing-in-action/; C. J. Chivers, "How to Control Libya Missiles? Buy Them Up," *New York*

Times, Dec. 22, 2011, www.nytimes.com/2011/12/23/world/africa/us-seeks-program-to-buy-up-missiles-loose-in-libya.html; David Ignatius, "Libyan Missiles on the Loose," *Washington Post*, May 8, 2012, www.washingtonpost.com/opinions/libyan-missiles-on-the-loose/2012/05/08/gIQA1FCUBU_story.html; Remarks by Andrew J. Shapiro, Addressing the Challenge of MANPADS Proliferation, U.S. State Department Transcript, Feb. 2, 2012, 2009-2017.state.gov/t/pm/rls/rm/183097.htm.

92 Haftar quoted on Islamists in Wehrey, *Burning Shores*, 182.

93 Risen, Mazzetti, and Schmidt, "U.S.-Approved Arms for Libya Rebels Fell into Jihadis' Hands."

94 Kuperman, "Obama's Libya Debacle"; Wehrey, *Burning Shores*, 166.

95 David D. Kirkpatrick, "Strife in Libya Could Presage Long Civil War," *New York Times*, Aug. 24, 2014, www.nytimes.com/2014/08/25/world/africa/libyan-unrest.html?module=inline; Frederic Wehrey, "Can Libya Survive a Civil War That's Only Getting Worse," *Defense One*, Feb. 9, 2015, www.defenseone.com/threats/2015/02/can-libya-survive-civil-war-s-only-getting-worse/104886/.

96 Kuperman, "Model Humanitarian Intervention?" 129–31.

97 Khaled Yacoub Oweis, "Qadhafi's Killing Fuels Syria's Friday Protests," Reuters, Oct. 21, 2011, www.reuters.com/article/us-syria-protests/gaddafis-killing-fuels-syrias-friday-protests-idUSTRE79K22P20111021. For Sarkozy's and Cameron's hope that the Libyan revolution would be a model for Syrians, see "Cameron and Sarkozy Meet Libya's New Leaders in Tripoli," *Guardian*, Sept. 15, 2011, www.theguardian.com/world/2011/sep/15/cameron-sarkozy-libya-leader-tripoli.

98 According to former Syrian general Manaf Tlass, a close friend of Bashar al-Assad's who later defected, "The determination of Bashar and his family to survive and crush the challenge to their rule increased further after Hafez's longtime ally Gaddafi was brutally lynched by a mob." See Sam Dagher, *Assad or We Burn the Country: How One Family's Lust for Power Destroyed Syria* (New York: Little, Brown, 2019), 280.

99 Rice, *Tough Love*, 294; Burns, *Back Channel*, 335.

100 Jo Becker and Scott Shane, "In Their Own Words: The Libya Tragedy," *New York Times*, Feb. 27, 2016, www.nytimes.com/interactive/2016/02/28/us/politics/libya-quotes.html.

101 Peter Bergen and Alyssa Sims, "Seven Years After Obama's 'Worst Mistake,' Libya Killing Is Rampant," CNN, June 20, 2018, www.cnn.com/2018/06/20/opinions/libya-chaos-civilian-deaths-bergen-sims/index.html; Shadi Hamid, "Everyone Says the Libya Intervention Was a Failure. They're Wrong," Brookings Institution, April 12, 2016, www.brookings.edu/blog/markaz/2016/04/12/everyone-says-the-libya-intervention-was-a-failure-theyre-wrong/.

102 McCain, interview with Wolf Blitzer, *The Situation Room*, April 20, 2015, votesmart.org/public-statement/1111924/cnn-the-situation-room

-transcript-yemen-libya-isis-and-ramadi-nomination-of-loretta-lynch-hillary-clintons-presidential-bid#.XTc5ZetKi70.

103 Pletka, "'Regime Change' Has Often Succeeded."

104 Remarks by President Obama to the United Nations General Assembly, Sept. 28, 2015, obamawhitehouse.archives.gov/the-press-office/2015/09/28/remarks-president-obama-united-nations-general-assembly.

105 Jeffrey Goldberg, "The Obama Doctrine," *The Atlantic,* April 2016, www.theatlantic.com/magazine/archive/2016/04/the-obama-doctrine/471525/.

106 President Barack Obama, interview with Chris Wallace, Fox News, April 10, 2016, video.foxnews.com/v/4839779084001/#sp=show-clips.

107 Wehrey, *Burning Shores*, 67. Also see Brendan R. Gallagher, *The Day After: Why America Wins the War but Loses the Peace* (Ithaca, N.Y.: Cornell University Press, 2019), 162.

108 Chollet, *Long Game*, 147.

109 Pew Research Center, "Public Wary of Military Intervention in Libya; Broad Concern That U.S. Military Is Overcommitted," March 23, 2011, www.pewresearch.org/fact-tank/2011/03/23/public-wary-of-u-s-military-intervention-in-libya/.

110 Alan Silverleib, "House Rips Obama Libya Policy," CNN, June 3, 2011, www.cnn.com/2011/POLITICS/06/03/house.libya/index.html; Jennifer Steinhauer, "House Rebukes Obama for Continuing Libyan Mission Without Its Consent," *New York Times*, June 3, 2011, www.nytimes.com/2011/06/04/world/africa/04policy.html.

111 Joe Lieberman and John McCain, "In Libya, Regime Change Should Be the Goal," *Wall Street Journal,* April 1, 2011, www.wsj.com/articles/SB10001424052748703806304576233112828325424; Transcript of John McCain's interview with Christiane Amanpour, *This Week*, ABC News, March 6, 2011, votesmart.org/public-statement/591879/abc-this-week-with-christiane-amanpour-transcript#.XS4U4OtKi70; Graham, interview with Wolf Blitzer, CNN Transcripts, March 30, 2011, cnn-pressroom.blogs.cnn.com/2011/03/30/sen-graham-on-cia-in-libya/.

112 McCain et al., "Promise of a Pro-American Libya."

113 Wehrey, *Burning Shores,* 158.

114 Founding Statement of the Interim Transitional National Council, March 5, 2011, www.webcitation.org/5x0wuZ8r2.

115 Shane and Becker, "New Libya."

116 Ibid.; Becker and Shane, "In Their Own Words."

117 Cretz cited in Becker and Shane, "In Their Own Words."

118 Jones, email to author, Jan. 5, 2020.

119 Benjamin Nickels, "Pitfalls for Libya's General Purpose Force," Carnegie Endowment for International Peace, Oct. 10, 2013, carnegieendowment.org/sada/53273; "U.S. Military Working on Plan to Train Thousands of Libyans," Reuters, Nov. 17, 2013, www.reuters.com/article/us-usa

-libya-training/u-s-military-working-on-plan-to-train-thousands-of-libyans-idUSBRE9AG0F620131117?feedType=RSS&feedName=topNews&utm_source=dlvr.it&utm_medium=twitter&dlvrit=992637.

120 Frederic Wehrey, "The Foreign Policy Essay: Mosul on the Mediterranean? The Islamic State in Libya and U.S. Counterterrorism Dilemmas," *Lawfare*, Dec. 17, 2014, www.lawfareblog.com/foreign-policy-essay-mosul-mediterranean-islamic-state-libya-and-us-counterterrorism-dilemmas; Missy Ryan, "Libya's War on Isis: How the West Had a Hand in the Country's Descent from Euphoria to Chaos," *Independent*, Aug. 7, 2015, www.independent.co.uk/news/world/africa/libyas-war-on-isis-how-the-west-had-a-hand-in-the-countrys-descent-from-euphoria-into-chaos-10446040.html; Wehrey, *Burning Shores*, 158.

121 On the kidnapping, see Chris Stephen, "Libyan PM Ali Zeidan Says Kidnapping Was Coup Attempt," *Guardian*, Oct. 11, 2013, www.theguardian.com/world/2013/oct/11/libyan-pm-ali-zeidan-kidnap-coup-attempt.

122 Thomas L. Friedman, "Obama on the World," *New York Times*, Aug. 8, 2014, www.nytimes.com/2014/08/09/opinion/president-obama-thomas-l-friedman-iraq-and-world-affairs.html.

123 "President Trump: 'I Do Not See a Role in Libya,'" C-SPAN, April 20, 2017, www.c-span.org/video/?c4666751/president-trump-i-role-libya; Glenn Thrush, "No U.S. Military Role in Libya, Trump Says, Rejecting Italy's Pleas," *New York Times*, April 20, 2017, www.nytimes.com/2017/04/20/us/politics/trump-italy-prime-minister-paolo-gentiloni.html.

124 Frederic Wehrey and Wolfram Lacher, "The Wrong Way to Fix Libya: Early Elections Would Be a Disaster," *Foreign Affairs*, June 19, 2018. On the 2015 Libyan Political Agreement, see Aziz El Yaakoubi, "Libyan Factions Sign U.N. Deal to Form Unity Government," Reuters, Dec. 17, 2015, www.reuters.com/article/us-libya-security-idUSKBN0U00WP20151217.

125 Wehrey and Lacher, "Wrong Way to Fix Libya."

126 Frederic Wehrey, "In Tripoli," *London Review of Books*, July 19, 2019, carnegieendowment.org/2019/07/16/in-tripoli-pub-79516; David D. Kirkpatrick, "Trump Endorses an Aspiring Libyan Strongman, Reversing Policy," *New York Times*, April 19, 2019, www.nytimes.com/2019/04/19/world/middleeast/trump-libya-khalifa-hifter.html; Philip H. Gordon and Andrew Miller, "Trump's Support for Haftar Won't Help Libya," *Foreign Policy*, April 24, 2019, foreignpolicy.com/2019/04/24/trumps-support-for-haftar-wont-help-libya/.

127 Kuperman, "Model Humanitarian Intervention?" 112.

Chapter 7: "Assad Must Go"

1 White House, "President Obama: 'The Future of Syria Must Be Determined by Its People, but President Bashar al-Assad Is Standing in Their Way,'" Aug. 18, 2011, obamawhitehouse.archives.gov/blog/2011

/08/18/president-obama-future-syria-must-be-determined-its-people -president-bashar-al-assad; Jason Ukman and Liz Sly, "Obama: Syrian President Assad Must Step Down," *Washington Post*, Aug. 19, 2011, www .washingtonpost.com/blogs/checkpoint-washington/post/obama-syrian -president-assad-must-step-down/2011/08/18/gIQAM75UNJ_blog .html.

2 Scott Wilson and Joby Warrick, "Assad Must Go, Obama Says," *Washington Post*, Aug. 18, 2011, www.washingtonpost.com/politics/assad-must -go-obama-says/2011/08/18/gIQAelheOJ_story.html.

3 Jackson Diehl, "What the Iraq War Taught Me About Syria," *Washington Post*, March 31, 2013, www.washingtonpost.com/opinions/jackson-diehl -what-the-iraq-war-taught-me-about-syria/2013/03/31/5ef2e6d0-97b2 -11e2-814b-063623d80a60_story.html.

4 Mark Landler, "Obama Will Send Envoy to Syria, Officials Say," *New York Times*, June 24, 2009, www.nytimes.com/2009/06/24/world /middleeast/24syria.html; "A Conversation with U.S. Secretary of State Hillary Rodham Clinton," Council on Foreign Relations, July 15, 2009, www.cfr.org/event/conversation-us-secretary-state-hillary-rodham -clinton-1.

5 "Remarks by Under Secretary of State for Political Affairs William J. Burns Following Meeting with Syrian President Dr. Bashar al-Assad," State Department Archives, Feb. 17, 2010, 2009-2017.state.gov/p/us/rm /2010/136717.htm. Burns was less optimistic in private, reporting to Secretary Clinton that based on their past behavior, "it made little sense to get our hopes up about the Syrians." Burns, *Back Channel*, 323.

6 Isabel Kershner, "Secret Israel-Syria Peace Talks Involved Golan Heights Exit," *New York Times*, Oct. 12, 2012, www.nytimes.com/2012/10/13 /world/middleeast/secret-israel-syria-peace-talks-involved-golan-heights -exit.html.

7 Frederic Hof, "I Got Syria So Wrong," *Politico*, Oct. 14, 2015, www .politico.com/magazine/story/2015/10/syria-civil-war-213242.

8 Clinton, interview with Bob Schieffer, *Face the Nation*, CBS, March 27, 2011, State Department Archives, 2009-2017.state.gov/secretary /20092013clinton/rm/2011/03/159210.htm.

9 "Senator John Kerry on U.S. Policy Toward the Middle East," Carnegie Endowment for International Peace, Washington, D.C., March 16, 2011, carnegieendowment.org/files/0317carnegie-johnkerry.pdf; James Traub, "How John Kerry Tries to Put Out Diplomatic Fires," *New York Times,* July 14, 2011, www.nytimes.com/2011/07/17/magazine/john -kerry-our-man-in-kabul.html; Farah Stockman, "Kerry's Softer Stance on Syria Scrutinized," *Boston Globe,* April 28, 2011, archive.boston.com /news/nation/washington/articles/2011/04/28/kerrys_softer_stance_on _syria_scrutinized/?page=1; Sarah Birke, "John Kerry Meets Syria's Assad," *Wall Street Journal*, April 1, 2010, www.wsj.com/articles/SB10001 424052702303395904575157713877756160. Kerry had also met with

Assad twice in 2005 and 2006, and in June 2008 had authored an op-ed with Senator Chuck Hagel, Obama's future defense secretary, advocating engagement with Syria. "It's Time to Talk to Syria," *Wall Street Journal*, June 5, 2008, www.wsj.com/articles/SB121262346490946859.

10 "Graham, McCain, and Lieberman Statement on Syria," April 28, 2011, www.lgraham.senate.gov/public/index.cfm/2011/4/post-9cc074e6-802a-23ad-4884-8893ce0e7083.

11 Marco Rubio, "How America Must Respond to the Massacre in Syria," *Foreign Policy*, April 28, 2011, foreignpolicy.com/2011/04/28/how-america-must-respond-to-the-massacre-in-syria/.

12 Josh Rogin, "16 Senators: Syria's Assad Has Lost His Legitimacy," *Foreign Policy*, May 11, 2011, foreignpolicy.com/2011/05/11/16-senators-syrias-assad-has-lost-his-legitimacy/. The bill is available at www.govtrack.us/congress/bills/112/sres180/text.

13 "Remarks by Senator John McCain at the Dean Acheson Lecture at U.S. Institute of Peace," May 19, 2011, web.archive.org/web/20130317220851/www.mccain.senate.gov/public/index.cfm?FuseAction=PressOffice.Speeches&ContentRecord_id=0A52E626-9BBF-8C1B-AF06-9AC2360D7C8C; Charles Krauthammer, "Syria's 'Reformer,'" *Washington Post*, March 31, 2011, www.washingtonpost.com/opinions/syrias-reformer/2011/03/31/AFy4JFCC_story.html.

14 For the administration official, see Scott Wilson, "Syrian Tanks, Soldiers, Lay Siege to Southern Towns," *Washington Post*, April 26, 2011, www.washingtonpost.com/world/syrian-tanks-soldiers-lay-siege-to-southern-towns/2011/04/25/AFUscBlE_story.html. Feltman cited in Mary Beth Sheridan and Colum Lynch, "As Syrian Crackdown Continues, Obama Administration to Call for Assad's Resignation," *Washington Post*, Aug. 10, 2011, www.washingtonpost.com/world/national-security/as-syrian-crackdown-continues-obama-administration-to-call-for-assads-resignation/2011/08/10/gIQAQjRN7I_story.html.

15 Mark Landler, "U.S. Moves Cautiously Against Syrian Leaders," *New York Times*, April 29, 2011, www.nytimes.com/2011/04/30/world/middleeast/30policy.html.

16 "President Barack Obama Speech at the U.S. Department of State," White House Archives transcript, May 19, 2011, obamawhitehouse.archives.gov/the-press-office/2011/05/19/remarks-president-middle-east-and-north-africa.

17 Sheridan and Lynch, "As Syrian Crackdown Continues, Obama Administration to Call for Assad's Resignation." Clinton said Assad was "not indispensable" on July 11, 2011, in "Secretary of State Hillary Clinton Remarks with European Union High Representative for Foreign Affairs and Security Policy Catherine Ashton After Their Meeting," Department of State Archives, July 11, 2011, 2009-2017.state.gov/secretary/20092013clinton/rm/2011/07/168027.htm.

18 Rhodes, *World as It Is*, 157–58.

19 On U.S. intelligence assessments, see Steven Mufson, "'Assad Must Go': These 3 Little Words Are Huge Obstacle for Obama on Syria," *Washington Post,* Oct. 19, 2015, www.washingtonpost.com/business/economy/assad-must-go-these-three-little-words-present-a-huge-obstacle-for-obama-on-syria/2015/10/19/6a76baba-71ec-11e5-9cbb-790369643cf9_story.html; and Mark Mazzetti, Robert F. Worth, and Michael R. Gordon, "Obama's Uncertain Path amid Syria Bloodshed," *New York Times,* Oct. 22, 2013, www.nytimes.com/2013/10/23/world/middleeast/obamas-uncertain-path-amid-syria-bloodshed.html. Hof himself would testify to Congress in December 2011 that the administration's view was that "this regime is the equivalent of a dead man walking." Matthew Lee, "U.S.: Assad's Syria 'a Dead Man Walking,'" *Christian Science Monitor*, Dec. 14, 2011, www.csmonitor.com/World/Latest-News-Wires/2011/1214/US-Assad-s-Syria-a-dead-man-walking.

20 Joint U.K., French, and German statement on Syria, Aug. 18, 2011, www.gov.uk/government/news/joint-uk-french-and-german-statement-on-syria.

21 Kirit Radia, "Obama Calls on Syria's Assad to Step Down, Freezes Assets," ABC News, Aug. 18, 2011, abcnews.go.com/International/obama-calls-syrias-assad-step-freezes-assets/story?id=14330428.

22 Goldberg, "Obama Doctrine."

23 Wilson and Warrick, "Assad Must Go, Obama Says."

24 Mazzetti, Worth, and Gordon, "Obama's Uncertain Path amid Syria Bloodshed"; Adam Entous, "Inside Obama's Syria Debate," *Wall Street Journal,* March 29, 2013, www.wsj.com/articles/SB10001424127887323639604578368930961739030.

25 Mazzetti, Worth, and Gordon, "Obama's Uncertain Path amid Syria Bloodshed."

26 Charles Glass, "Tell Me How This Ends," *Harper's Magazine*, Feb. 2019.

27 Mazzetti, Worth, and Gordon, "Obama's Uncertain Path amid Syria Bloodshed." Also see Clinton, *Hard Choices*, 391–92; and Panetta, *Worthy Fights*, 449.

28 Clinton, *Hard Choices*, 391–92.

29 Panetta, *Worthy Fights*, 449.

30 Burns, *Back Channel*, 327.

31 Goldberg, "Obama Doctrine."

32 David Remnick, "Going the Distance: On and off the Road with Barack Obama," *New Yorker,* Jan. 19, 2014, www.newyorker.com/magazine/2014/01/27/going-the-distance-david-remnick.

33 Mark Mazzetti, "C.I.A. Study of Covert Aid Fueled Skepticism About Helping Syrian Rebels," *New York Times*, Oct. 14, 2014, www.nytimes.com/2014/10/15/us/politics/cia-study-says-arming-rebels-seldom-works.html.

34 Burns, *Back Channel*, 328,
35 Rhodes, *World as It Is*, 197.
36 Clinton in Goldberg, "Obama Doctrine."
37 Rhodes, *World as It Is*, 197.
38 For a good assessment of counterfactuals in Syria, and rebuttal of the notion that implementation of the Petraeus plan would have toppled Assad or ended the conflict, see Mona Yacoubian, "Critical Junctures in United States Policy Toward Syria: An Assessment of the Counterfactuals," United States Holocaust Memorial Museum, Aug. 2017, www.ushmm.org/m/pdfs/Yacoubian-Critical-Junctures-US-Policy-Syria.pdf.
39 Kofi A. Annan, "Forging a Peace Plan for Syria," *Washington Post*, June 28, 2012, www.washingtonpost.com/opinions/kofi-annan-forging-a-peace-plan-for-syria/2012/06/28/gJQAEtU19V_story.html.
40 Andrew Quinn, "Clinton in Russia to Face Off on Annan Syria Plan," Reuters, June 28, 2012, www.reuters.com/article/us-syria-crisis-clinton-idUSBRE85R1JP20120628.
41 Final Communiqué of the Action Group for Syria (Geneva Communiqué), June 30, 2012, peacemaker.un.org/sites/peacemaker.un.org/files/SY_120630_Final%20Communique%20of%20the%20Action%20Group%20for%20Syria.pdf.
42 Hillary Rodham Clinton, "Press Availability Following the Meeting of the Action Group on Syria," June 30, 2012, Geneva, 2009-2017.state.gov/secretary/20092013clinton/rm/2012/06/194328.htm.
43 Karen DeYoung, "Syria Conference Fails to Specify Plan for Assad," *Washington Post*, June 30, 2012, www.washingtonpost.com/world/national-security/syria-conference-fails-to-specify-plan-for-assad/2012/06/30/gJQAsPfeEW_story.html. Also see the discussion in Michael McFaul, *From the Cold War to Hot Peace: An American Ambassador in Putin's Russia* (New York: Houghton Mifflin Harcourt, 2018), 14.
44 David M. Herszenhorn and Ellen Barry, "Putin Contends Clinton Incited Unrest over Vote," *New York Times*, Dec. 8, 2011, www.nytimes.com/2011/12/09/world/europe/putin-accuses-clinton-of-instigating-russian-protests.html; Michael Crowley, "Why Putin Hates Hillary," *Politico*, Aug. 25, 2016, www.politico.com/story/2016/07/clinton-putin-226153.
45 On Putin's concerns about regime change and fears that chaos in Syria would threaten Russian interests, see Alina Polyakova, "Russia Is a Great Power Once Again," *The Atlantic*, Feb. 26, 2018, www.theatlantic.com/international/archive/2018/02/russia-syria-putin-assad-trump-isis-ghouta/554270/; Sarah A. Topol, "What Does Putin Really Want?" *New York Times Magazine*, June 25, 2019, www.nytimes.com/2019/06/25/magazine/russia-united-states-world-politics.html; and Robert Burns, "Kremlin Convinced U.S. Intent on Regime Change in Russia," Associated Press, June 28, 2017, www.chicagotribune.com/nation-world/ct-russia-united-states-tensions-20170628-story.html.

46 David Frum and Richard Perle, *An End to Evil: How to Win the War on Terror* (New York: Random House, 2003), 114.

47 On Hama killings, see Thomas L. Friedman, *From Beirut to Jerusalem* (New York: Farrar, Straus and Giroux, 1989), 76–105.

48 See Dagher, *Assad or We Burn the Country*, 75–82; Annia Ciezadlo, "Bashar Al Assad: An Intimate Profile of a Mass Murderer," *New Republic*, Dec. 19, 2013, newrepublic.com/article/115993/bashar-al-assad-profile-syrias-mass-murderer; Majid Rafizadeh, "How Bashar al-Assad Became So Hated," *The Atlantic*, April 17, 2013, www.theatlantic.com/international/archive/2013/04/how-bashar-al-assad-became-so-hated/275058/.

49 Dagher, *Assad or We Burn the Country*, 90.

50 Nikolaos van Dam, *Destroying a Nation: The Civil War in Syria* (London: I. B. Tauris, 2017), 174–75. For other good insights into the structures and working of the Assad regime, see Dagher, *Assad or We Burn the Country;* Rania Abouzeid, *No Turning Back: Life, Loss, and Hope in Wartime Syria* (New York: W. W. Norton, 2018); Robert Worth, *A Rage for Order: The Middle East in Turmoil, from Tahrir Square to ISIS* (New York: Farrar, Straus and Giroux, 2016); Michel Duclos, *La longue nuit syrienne: Dix années de diplomatie impuissante* (Paris: L'Observatoire, 2019); David Lesch, *Syria: The Fall of the House of Assad* (New Haven, Conn.: Yale University Press, 2013); and Fabrice Balanche, "Sectarianism in Syria's Civil War: A Geopolitical Study," Washington Institute for Near East Policy, Jan. 2018, www.washingtoninstitute.org/uploads/Documents/pubs/SyriaAtlasCOMPLETE-3.pdf.

51 Examples cited from Anne-Marie Slaughter, "Don't Fight in Iraq and Ignore Syria," *New York Times*, June 17, 2014, www.nytimes.com/2014/06/18/opinion/dont-fight-in-iraq-and-ignore-syria.html; and John Kerry, *Every Day Is Extra* (New York: Simon & Schuster, 2018), 527.

52 Martin Chulov, "Hezbollah's Role in Syrian Conflict Ushers New Reality for Its Supporters," *Guardian*, May 24, 2013, www.theguardian.com/world/2013/may/24/hezbollah-syria-new-reality-supporters; Anne Barnard, "Hezbollah Commits to an All-Out Fight to Save Assad," *New York Times*, May 25, 2013, www.nytimes.com/2013/05/26/world/middleeast/syrian-army-and-hezbollah-step-up-raids-on-rebels.html; Loveday Morris, "In Syria, Hezbollah Forces Mass Around Aleppo to Aid Assad," *Washington Post*, June 2, 2013, www.washingtonpost.com/world/middle_east/hezbollah-boosting-assads-forces-in-northern-syria/2013/06/02/3bb59c7e-cb9e-11e2-8f6b-67f40e176f03_story.html.

53 Christopher Phillips, *The Battle for Syria: International Rivalry in the New Middle East* (New Haven, Conn.: Yale University Press, 2016), 157–58.

54 Remnick, "Negotiating the Whirlwind."

55 Rice, *Tough Love*, 367.

56 Charles Krauthammer, "Message from the Ruins of Qusair," *Washington Post*, June 6, 2013, www.washingtonpost.com/opinions/charles

-krauthammer-message-from-the-ruins-of-qusair/2013/06/06/32b64cc0-ced9-11e2-8f6b-67f40e176f03_story.html.

57 For some of the many calls for a no-fly zone, see Fox News Staff, "Lieberman Suggests No-Fly Zone an Option in Syria if Violence Escalates," Fox News, March 27, 2011, www.foxnews.com/politics/lieberman-suggests-no-fly-zone-an-option-in-syria-if-violence-escalates; John McCain, interview, CNN, June 13, 2013, edition.cnn.com/TRANSCRIPTS/1306/13/sitroom.01.html; "Levin, McCain Urge President to Take 'More Active Steps' in Syria," March 21, 2013, web.archive.org/web/20140321171405/www.levin.senate.gov/newsroom/press/release/levin-mccain-urge-president-to-take-more-active-steps-in-syria/?section=alltypes; Burgess Everett, "McCain, Graham Call for No-Fly Zone," *Politico*, June 13, 2013, www.politico.com/story/2013/06/syria-no-fly-zone-092766; Jack Keane and Danielle Pletka, "Jack Keane and Danielle Pletka: How to Stop Assad's Slaughter," *Wall Street Journal*, May 22, 2013, www.wsj.com/articles/SB100014241278873237446045784772035 21015598; Lindsey Graham, Comments on the Senate floor on June 13, 2013.

58 Jeremy Herb, "Gen. Dempsey: Syria No-Fly Zone Could Cost US $1B per Month," *The Hill*, July 22, 2013, thehill.com/policy/defense/312675-gen-dempsey-syria-no-fly-zone-could-cost-1b-per-month. The Dempsey letter can be found at https://abcnews.go.com/blogs/politics/2013/07/gen-martin-dempsey-lays-out-us-military-options-for-syria.

59 John Vandiver, "Breedlove: No-Fly Zone over Syria Would Constitute 'Act of War,'" *Stars and Stripes*, May 31, 2013, www.stripes.com/news/breedlove-no-fly-zone-over-syria-would-constitute-act-of-war-1.223788.

60 The 90 percent figure is cited by Dempsey in Anna Mulrine, "A No-Fly Zone over Syria? Harder to Do Than in Libya, Warns Top US General," *Christian Science Monitor*, April 30, 2013, www.csmonitor.com/USA/Politics/monitor_breakfast/2013/0430/A-no-fly-zone-over-Syria-Harder-to-do-than-in-Libya-warns-top-US-general. Also see Micah Zenko, "Responsibility to Protect? Why None of the Plans for Intervening in Syria Actually Tries to Save Civilians," *Foreign Policy*, Sept. 17, 2013, foreignpolicy.com/2013/09/17/responsibility-to-protect/; and Karen Yourish, K. K. Rebecca Lai, and Derek Watkins, "Deaths in Syria," *New York Times*, Sept. 14, 2015, www.nytimes.com/interactive/2015/09/14/world/middleeast/syria-war-deaths.html.

61 Dempsey cited in Mulrine, "No-Fly Zone over Syria?"

62 For some of the many proposals, see Josh Rogin, "McCain Resolution Calls for Safe Zones and Arming the Syrian Opposition," *Foreign Policy*, March 28, 2012, foreignpolicy.com/2012/03/28/mccain-resolution-calls-for-safe-zones-and-arming-the-syrian-opposition/; Anne-Marie Slaughter, "Syrian Intervention Is Justifiable, and Just," *Washington Post*, June 8, 2012, www.washingtonpost.com/opinions/syrian-intervention-is-justifiable-and-just

/2012/06/08/gJQARHGjOV_story.html; and Mark Palmer and Paul Wolfowitz, "The Case for Arming the Syrian Opposition," *Wall Street Journal*, March 6, 2012, www.wsj.com/articles/SB10001424052970203986604577257201200177274.

63 For the first quotation, see Max Boot, interview with the Council on Foreign Relations, Dec. 11, 2012, www.cfr.org/expert-roundup/what-should-us-policy-be-syria. The case for only "defensive" weapons is made in Palmer and Wolfowitz, "Case for Arming the Syrian Opposition"; and Anne-Marie Slaughter, "How to Halt the Butchery in Syria," *New York Times*, Feb. 23, 2012, www.nytimes.com/2012/02/24/opinion/how-to-halt-the-butchery-in-syria.html.

64 Cited in Glass, "Tell Me How This Ends."

65 "Statement by Deputy National Security Advisor for Strategic Communications Ben Rhodes on Syrian Chemical Weapons Use," White House Archives, June 13, 2013, obamawhitehouse.archives.gov/the-press-office/2013/06/13/statement-deputy-national-security-advisor-strategic-communications-ben-; Mark Mazzetti, Michael R. Gordon, and Mark Landler, "U.S. Is Said to Plan to Send Weapons to Syrian Rebels," *New York Times*, June 13, 2013, www.nytimes.com/2013/06/14/world/middleeast/syria-chemical-weapons.html.

66 "On-the-Record Conference Call by Deputy National Security Advisor for Strategic Communications Ben Rhodes on Syria," White House Archives, June 13, 2013, obamawhitehouse.archives.gov/the-press-office/2013/06/13/record-conference-call-deputy-national-security-advisor-strategic-commun.

67 Rice, *Tough Love*, 367–68. Also Ernesto Londoño and Greg Miller, "CIA Begins Weapons Delivery to Syrian Rebels," *Washington Post*, Sept. 11, 2013, www.washingtonpost.com/world/national-security/cia-begins-weapons-delivery-to-syrian-rebels/2013/09/11/9fcf2ed8-1b0c-11e3-a628-7e6dde8f889d_story.html.

68 Mark Mazzetti, Adam Goldman, and Michael S. Schmidt, "Behind the Sudden Death of a $1 Billion Secret C.I.A. War in Syria," *New York Times*, Aug. 2, 2017, www.nytimes.com/2017/08/02/world/middleeast/cia-syria-rebel-arm-train-trump.html; Aron Lund, "How Assad's Enemies Gave Up on the Syrian Opposition," Century Foundation, Oct. 17, 2017; Jeremy Shapiro, "Obama's Syria Policy Is a Perfect Case Study on How Bad Foreign Policy Is Made," *Vox*, March 16, 2016, www.vox.com/2016/3/16/11244980/obama-syria-policy. The source for the Syrian regime and allied casualty estimate is an official cited in David Ignatius, "What the Demise of the CIA's Anti-Assad Program Means," *Washington Post*, July 20, 2017, www.washingtonpost.com/opinions/what-the-demise-of-the-cias-anti-assad-program-means/2017/07/20/f6467240-6d87-11e7-b9e2-2056e768a7e5_story.html. For a game theory–based assessment of how arming the rebels may have increased casualties and prolonged the war, see Andrew H. Kidd, "Subsidizing Rebels, Taxing

Atrocities: Saving Lives in Civil Wars," Simon-Skjodt Center for the Prevention of Genocide, United States Holocaust Memorial Museum, Series of Occasional Papers, No. 4/August 2017, www.ushmm.org/m/pdfs/Kydd-Game-Theory.pdf.

69 Mark Landler, David E. Sanger, and Thom Shanker, "Obama Set for Limited Strike on Syria as British Vote No," *New York Times,* Aug. 29, 2013, www.nytimes.com/2013/08/30/us/politics/obama-syria.html.

70 Ben Rhodes, "Inside the White House During the Syrian 'Red Line' Crisis," *The Atlantic*, June 3, 2018, www.theatlantic.com/international/archive/2018/06/inside-the-white-house-during-the-syrian-red-line-crisis/561887/; Rice, *Tough Love*, 362–65; Rhodes, *World as It Is*, 235–36; Mark Landler, *Alter Egos: Hillary Clinton, Barack Obama, and the Twilight Struggle over American Power* (New York: Random House, 2016), 204–7.

71 Goldberg, "Obama Doctrine."

72 Rice, *Tough Love*, 364–65; Rhodes, *World as It Is*, 240; Power, *Education of an Idealist*, 382–86; Kerry, *Every Day Is Extra*, 537; Chollet, *Long Game*, 132.

73 Valls cited in Goldberg, "Obama Doctrine."

74 Robert Kagan, "It'll Take More Than a Missile Strike to Clean Up Obama's Mess in Syria," *Washington Post*, April 7, 2017, www.washingtonpost.com/opinions/itll-take-more-than-a-missile-strike-to-clean-up-obamas-mess-in-syria/2017/04/07/c3e1b384-1bb9-11e7-bcc2-7d1a0973e7b2_story.html.

75 Donald J. Trump (@realDonaldTrump), Twitter, April 8, 2018, 9:12 a.m., twitter.com/realdonaldtrump/status/982969547283161090?lang=en.

76 Kerry, *Every Day Is Extra*, 526–27.

77 I discuss my support for the targeted CW strikes in Goldberg, "Obama's Middle East Adviser: 'We Should Have Bombed Assad.'"

78 "U.S. Strategy Against ISIS," C-SPAN, Sept. 16, 2015, www.c-span.org/video/?328129-1/hearing-military-operations-islamic-state; Spencer Ackerman, "US Has Trained Only 'Four or Five' Syrian Fighters Against Isis, Top General Testifies," *Guardian*, Sept. 16, 2015, www.theguardian.com/us-news/2015/sep/16/us-military-syrian-isis-fighters.

79 Nabih Bulos, "US-Trained Division 30 Rebels 'Betray US and Hand Weapons Over to al-Qaeda's Affiliate in Syria,'" *Telegraph*, Sept. 22, 2015, www.telegraph.co.uk/news/worldnews/middleeast/syria/11882195/US-trained-Division-30-rebels-betrayed-US-and-hand-weapons-over-to-al-Qaedas-affiliate-in-Syria.html.

80 White House, Office of the Press Secretary, "Press Briefing by the Press Secretary Josh Earnest, 9/16/2015," obamawhitehouse.archives.gov/the-press-office/2015/09/17/press-briefing-press-secretary-josh-earnest-9162015; and Peter Baker, "Finger-Pointing, but few Answers, After a Syria Solution Fails," *New York Times*, Sept. 15, 2015, www.nytimes

.com/2015/09/18/world/finger-pointing-but-few-answers-after-a-syria-solution-fails.html.

81 Max Boot and Michael Doran, "5 Reasons to Intervene in Syria Now," *New York Times*, Sept. 26, 2012, www.nytimes.com/2012/09/27/opinion/5-reasons-to-intervene-in-syria-now.html; Kenneth M. Pollack, "An Army to Defeat Assad: How to Turn Syria's Opposition into a Real Fighting Force," *Foreign Affairs*, Sept./Oct. 2014, www.foreignaffairs.com/articles/middle-east/2014-08-18/army-defeat-assad.

82 Glass, "Tell Me How This Ends." Also David R. Shedd, deputy director of the DIA, who estimated twelve hundred opposition groups in Syria in July 2013: Remarks by Deputy Director of the Defense Intelligence Agency David R. Shedd, Aspen Institute, July 2013, www.youtube.com/watch?v=V26Ibp6dg8Q.

83 Lund, "How Assad's Enemies Gave Up on the Syrian Opposition."

84 See the prescient warning about both of these risks by the CIA veteran Bruce Riedel, "Will Arming Syrian Rebels Lead to Disaster?" *Daily Beast*, June 15, 2013, www.thedailybeast.com/will-arming-syrian-rebels-lead-to-disaster.

85 Lister cited in Glass, "Tell Me How This Ends." Also see Charles Lister, "Al Qaeda Is Starting to Swallow the Syrian Opposition," *Foreign Policy*, March 15 2017, foreignpolicy.com/2017/03/15/al-qaeda-is-swallowing-the-syrian-opposition/; Nour Malas, "As Syrian Islamists Gain, It's Rebel Against Rebel," *Wall Street Journal*, May 29, 2013, www.wsj.com/articles/SB10001424127887323975004578499100684326558; Marc Lynch, "Shopping Option C for Syria," *Foreign Policy*, Feb. 14, 2013, foreignpolicy.com/2013/02/14/shopping-option-c-for-syria/; Sam Heller, "A Deadly Delusion: Were Syria's Rebels Ever Going to Defeat the Jihadists?" *War on the Rocks*, Aug. 10, 2017, warontherocks.com/2017/08/a-deadly-delusion-were-syrias-rebels-ever-going-to-defeat-the-jihadists/; Rania Abouzeid, "Syrian Opposition Groups Stop Pretending," *New Yorker*, Sept. 26, 2013, www.newyorker.com/news/news-desk/syrian-opposition-groups-stop-pretending.

86 Lund, "How Assad's Enemies Gave Up on the Syrian Opposition." Also see Yacoubian, "Critical Junctures in United States Policy Toward Syria."

87 David E. Sanger, "Rebel Arms Flow Is Said to Benefit Jihadists in Syria," *New York Times*, Oct. 14, 2012, www.nytimes.com/2012/10/15/world/middleeast/jihadists-receiving-most-arms-sent-to-syrian-rebels.html; C. J. Chivers, Eric Schmitt, and Mark Mazzetti, "In Turnabout, Syria Rebels Get Libyan Weapons," *New York Times*, June 21, 2013, www.nytimes.com/2013/06/22/world/africa/in-a-turnabout-syria-rebels-get-libyan-weapons.html; "Final Report of the Panel of Experts Established Pursuant to Resolution 1973 (2011) Concerning Libya," United Nations Security Council, March 9, 2013, www.securitycouncilreport.org/atf/cf/%7B65BFCF9B-6D27-4E9C-8CD3-CF6E4FF96FF9%7D/s_2013_99.pdf.

88 "Joe Biden Apologizes to UAE After Militants Remarks," NBC News, Oct. 3, 2014, www.nbcnews.com/politics/politics-news/joe-biden-apologizes-uae-after-militants-remarks-n218956.

89 Eric Schmitt and Michael R. Gordon, "Russian Moves in Syria Widen Role in Mideast," *New York Times*, Sept. 14, 2015, www.nytimes.com/2015/09/15/world/middleeast/russian-moves-in-syria-widen-role-in-mideast.html; Steven Lee Myers and Eric Schmitt, "Russian Military Uses Syria as Proving Ground, and West Takes Notice," *New York Times*, Oct. 14, 2015, www.nytimes.com/2015/10/15/world/middleeast/russian-military-uses-syria-as-proving-ground-and-west-takes-notice.html; Thomas Gibbons-Neff, "This Is the Airpower Russia Has in Syria," *Washington Post*, Sept. 30, 2015, www.washingtonpost.com/news/checkpoint/wp/2015/09/21/these-are-the-28-jets-russia-now-has-in-syria/.

90 Nick Gass, "Obama Ruled Out New Calls for Missile Strikes in Syria," *Politico*, March 10, 2016, www.politico.com/story/2016/03/obama-kerry-syria-220526.

91 "State Department Draft Dissent Memo on Syria," *New York Times*, June 17, 2016, www.nytimes.com/interactive/2016/06/17/world/middleeast/document-state-dept-syria.html?_r=0&module=inline. Also see Jeremy Shapiro, "Speaking Nonsense to Power: Misadventures in Dissent over Syria," *War on the Rocks*, June 24, 2016, warontherocks.com/2016/06/speaking-nonsense-to-power-misadventures-in-dissent-over-syria/.

92 "Exclusive: Obama, Aides Expected to Weigh Syria Military Options on Friday," Reuters, Oct. 13, 2016, www.reuters.com/article/us-mideast-crisis-syria-options-exclusiv-idUSKCN12D2B2.

93 Greg Miller and Adam Entous, "Plans to Send Heavier Weapons to CIA-Backed Rebels in Syria Stall amid White House Skepticism," *Washington Post*, Oct. 23, 2016, www.washingtonpost.com/world/national-security/plans-to-send-heavier-weapons-to-cia-backed-rebels-in-syria-stall-amid-white-house-skepticism/2016/10/23/f166ddac-96ee-11e6-bb29-bf2701dbe0a3_story.html.

94 Anne Barnard, "Audio Reveals What John Kerry Told Syrians Behind Closed Doors," *New York Times*, Sept. 30, 2016, www.nytimes.com/interactive/2016/09/30/world/middleeast/john-kerry-syria-audio.html.

95 Donald J. Trump (@realDonaldTrump), Twitter, June 15, 2013, 8:33 p.m., twitter.com/realDonaldTrump/status/346063000056254464; Donald J. Trump (@realDonaldTrump), Twitter, Sept. 5, 2013, 7:13 a.m., twitter.com/realdonaldtrump/status/375577511473983488?lang=en.

96 "Transcript: Donald Trump's Foreign Policy Speech," April 27, 2016, *New York Times*, www.nytimes.com/2016/04/28/us/politics/transcript-trump-foreign-policy.html; Washington Post Staff, "Wednesday's GOP Debate Transcript, Annotated," *Washington Post*, Sept. 16, 2015, www.washingtonpost.com/news/the-fix/wp/2015/09/16/annotated-transcript-september-16-gop-debate/.

97 "Transcript: Donald Trump Expounds on His Foreign Policy Views," *New York Times*, March 26, 2016, www.nytimes.com/2016/03/27/us/politics/donald-trump-transcript.html.

98 Monica Langley and Gerard Baker, "Donald Trump, in Exclusive Interview, Tells WSJ He Is Willing to Keep Parts of Obama Health Law," *Wall Street Journal*, Nov. 11, 2016, www.wsj.com/articles/donald-trump-willing-to-keep-parts-of-health-law-1478895339.

99 Michelle Nichols, "U.S. Priority on Syria No Longer Focused on 'Getting Assad Out': Haley," Reuters, March 31, 2017, www.reuters.com/article/us-mideast-crisis-syria-usa-haley/u-s-priority-on-syria-no-longer-focused-on-getting-assad-out-haley-idUSKBN1712QL. For Tillerson, see Elise Labott, Nicole Gaouette, and Richard Roth, "US Signals Openness to Assad Staying Put," CNN, March 30, 2017, www.cnn.com/2017/03/30/politics/tillerson-haley-syria-assad-turkey/index.html.

100 Donald Trump, "Remarks by President Trump and His Majesty King Abdullah II of Jordan in Joint Press Conference," White House, April 5, 2017, www.whitehouse.gov/briefings-statements/remarks-president-trump-majesty-king-abdullah-ii-jordan-joint-press-conference/; Nikki Haley, "Amb Haley at an Emergency UN Security Council Meeting on Chemical Weapons in Syria," U.S. Embassy in Syria, April 5, 2017, sy.usembassy.gov/amb-haley-emergency-un-security-council-meeting-chemical-weapons-syria/; Tim Hains, "Tillerson on Syria: Military Posture Towards Assad Has Not Changed; Trump Not Seeking Regime Change," RealClearPolitics, April 9, 2017, www.realclearpolitics.com/video/2017/04/09/tillerson_military_posture_towards_syria_has_not_changed_not_seeking_regime_change.html; "Press Conference by Secretary Mattis and Gen. Votel in the Pentagon Briefing Room," Department of Defense Transcripts, April 11, 2017, www.defense.gov/Newsroom/Transcripts/Transcript/Article/1148604/press-conference-by-secretary-mattis-and-gen-votel-in-the-pentagon-briefing-room/.

101 Donald J. Trump (@realDonaldTrump), Twitter, July 24, 2017, 10:23 p.m., twitter.com/realdonaldtrump/status/889672374458646528?lang=en. On the program's cancellation, see Greg Jaffe and Adam Entous, "Trump Ends Covert CIA Program to Arm Anti-Assad Rebels in Syria, a Move Sought by Moscow," *Washington Post*, July 19, 2017, www.washingtonpost.com/world/national-security/trump-ends-covert-cia-program-to-arm-anti-assad-rebels-in-syria-a-move-sought-by-moscow/2017/07/19/b6821a62-6beb-11e7-96ab-5f38140b38cc_story.html.

102 "Remarks on the Way Forward for the United States Regarding Syria: Secretary of State Rex Tillerson at the Hoover Institution," Jan. 25, 2018, www.hoover.org/news/rex-tillerson-hoover-institution.

103 Donald J. Trump (@realDonaldTrump), Twitter, Dec. 19, 2018, 9:29 a.m., twitter.com/realdonaldtrump/status/1075397797929775105.

104 Donald J. Trump (@realDonaldTrump), Twitter, Dec. 19, 2018, 6:10 p.m., twitter.com/realDonaldTrump/status/1075528854402256896.

105 Jack Stubbs and Ellen Francis, "Assad Claims Saudi Arabia Offered to Help Him if He Cuts Ties with Iran," *Independent*, Oct. 14, 2016, www.independent.co.uk/news/world/middle-east/saudi-arabia-assad-syria-cut-ties-with-iran-a7360786.html.

106 "France's Macron Says Sees No Legitimate Successor to Syria's Assad," Reuters, June 21, 2017, www.reuters.com/article/us-mideast-crisis-syria-france/frances-macron-says-sees-no-legitimate-successor-to-syrias-assad-idUSKBN19C2E7.

107 "Despite Suspension, Syria FM Greets Arab League Chief at UN," Agence France-Presse, Sept. 28, 2019, www.france24.com/en/20190927-despite-suspension-syria-fm-greets-arab-league-chief-at-un; Joyce Karam (@Joyce_Karam), "Secretary General of Arab League warmly welcomes #Syria regime delegation at UN in New York," Twitter, Sept. 27, 2019, 3:38 p.m., twitter.com/joyce_karam/status/1177668922545512449; "Iraq to Officially Call for Syria to Return to Arab League," *Middle East Monitor*, Oct. 14, 2019, www.middleeastmonitor.com/20191014-iraq-to-officially-call-for-syria-return-to-arab-league/. Lebanon and Tunisia had begun calling for Syria to be readmitted to the Arab League in January 2019. Bassem Mroue, "Lebanon Calls for Readmitting Syria to Arab League," Associated Press, Jan. 18, 2019, www.apnews.com/fdeb759e998048dd972bb3a095628be9; "Tunisia Calls for Arab League to Readmit Syria," Al Jazeera, Jan. 26, 2019, www.aljazeera.com/news/2019/01/tunisia-calls-arab-league-readmit-syria-190126112356574.html.

108 Vivian Yee and Hwaida Saad, "Syrian Offensive Sends Tens of Thousands Fleeing," *New York Times*, Dec. 23, 2019, https://www.nytimes.com/2019/12/23/world/middleeast/syria-idlib-russia-aid-refugees.html.

Conclusion: Why Regime Change in the Middle East Always Goes Wrong

1 Barry R. Posen, "The Security Dilemma and Ethnic Conflict," *Survival* (Spring 1993): 27–47, www.rochelleterman.com/ir/sites/default/files/posen-1993.pdf; Chaim Kaufmann, "Possible and Impossible Solutions to Ethnic Civil Wars," *International Security* 20, no. 4 (1996): 147, www.jstor.org/stable/pdf/2539045.pdf?refreqid=excelsior%3Adeb12c13aa0742afd36111849f1297f7; Daniel Byman, "Regime Change in the Middle East," *Political Science Quarterly* 127, no. 1 (2012): 33; Downes and Monten, "Forced to Be Free?" 104–5.

2 Sky, *Unraveling,* xi.

3 Caspar Weinberger, "Hearings to Examine Threats, Responses, and Regional Considerations Surrounding Iraq," U.S. Senate, Committee on Foreign Relations, July 31–Aug. 1, 2002, www.govinfo.gov/content/pkg/CHRG-107shrg81697/pdf/CHRG-107shrg81697.pdf.

4 On wartime casualties, see Daw, El-Bouzedi, and Dau, "Libyan Armed Conflict 2011"; and Kuperman, "Model Humanitarian Intervention?" Precise figures are not available for deaths following Qadhafi's fall, but most estimates put fatalities in the range of twenty thousand to twenty-five thousand or more. Clionadh Raleigh et al., "Introducing ACLED-Armed Conflict Location and Event Data," *Journal of Peace Research* 47, no. 5 (2010): 651–60 (updated data set originally posted in 2010), www.acleddata.com/data/; Hana Salama, "Counting Casualties: Operationalizing SDG Indicator 16.1.2 in Libya," Small Arms Survey, Geneva, Feb. 2018, www.smallarmssurvey.org/fileadmin/docs/T-Briefing-Papers/SAS-SANA-BP-Counting-Casualties-Libya.pdf; "World Digest: July 9, 2019," *Washington Post*, July 9, 2019, www.washingtonpost.com/national/world-digest-july-9-2019/2019/07/09/870bfa46-a253-11e9-bd56-eac6bb02d01d_story.html.

5 Secretary Condoleezza Rice, Remarks at the University of Cairo, June 20, 2005, 2001-2009.state.gov/secretary/rm/2005/48328.htm.

6 Noah Feldman, "Luncheon Speech: Better Sixty Years of Tyranny Than One Night of Anarchy," *International and Comparative Law Review* 31, no. 1 (2009), digitalcommons.lmu.edu/ilr/vol31/iss1/6.

7 Robert Sapolsky, "This Is Your Brain on Nationalism," *Foreign Affairs*, March/April 2019, www.foreignaffairs.com/articles/2019-02-12/your-brain-nationalism.

8 Stephen M. Walt, "You Can't Defeat Nationalism, So Stop Trying," *Foreign Policy*, June 4, 2019, foreignpolicy.com/2019/06/04/you-cant-defeat-nationalism-so-stop-trying/; Amy Chua, *Political Tribes: Group Instinct and the Fate of Nations* (New York: Penguin Press, 2018), esp. 95–97.

9 Malkasian, "How the Good War Turned Bad: America's Slow-Motion Failure in Afghanistan," *Foreign Affairs*, March/April 2020).

10 Packer, *Assassins' Gate*, 177.

11 Rory Stewart and Gerald Knaus, *Can Intervention Work?* (New York: W. W. Norton, 2011), xxii.

12 Landis cited in John Judis, "America's Failure—and Russia and Iran's Success—in Syria's Cataclysmic Civil War," *TPM*, Jan. 10, 2017, talkingpointsmemo.com/cafe/americas-failure-russia-success-in-syrias-war.

13 In 2018, for example, favorable/unfavorable views of U.S. foreign policy in ten regional countries were as follows: Egypt: 8/92; Lebanon: 48/52; Jordan: 37/63; Saudi Arabia: 86/14; UAE: 78/22; Iraq: 8/92; Turkey: 15/85; Iran: 32/68, cited in James Zogby, *Middle East Public Opinion 2018*, Prepared for the Bani Yas Forum, 2018, static1.squarespace.com/static/52750dd3e4b08c252c723404/t/5c0fcb2e758d461f72dc37ca/1544538926539/2018+SBY+FINAL+WEB.pdf. In the immediate wake of the Iraq invasion, favorable views of the United States in most regional countries were in the single digits. Shibley Telhami, "A View from the Arab World: A Survey in Five Arab Countries," Brookings Institution, March 13, 2003, www.brookings.edu/wp-content/uploads/2016

/06/survey20030313.pdf; Pew Research Experts, "Views of a Changing World 2003: War with Iraq Further Divides Global Publics," Pew Global Attitudes Survey, June 2003, www.pewresearch.org/global/2003/06/03/views-of-a-changing-world-2003/.

14 Arab Center for Research and Policy Studies, 2017–18 Arab Opinion Index, May 9, 2018, www.dohainstitute.org/en/News/Pages/ACRPS-Releases-Arab-Index-2017-2018.aspx; Devon Haynie, "Poll: Arabs See U.S. as a Threat," *U.S. News & World Report*, April 11, 2017, www.usnews.com/news/best-countries/articles/2017-04-11/poll-arabs-believe-israel-us-are-biggest-threat-to-the-region.

15 Dominic Tierney, *How We Fight: Crusades, Quagmires, and the American Way of War* (New York: Hachette, 2010), 50.

16 Ely Ratner, "Reaping What You Sow: Democratic Transitions and Foreign Policy Realignment," *Journal of Conflict Resolution* 53, no. 3 (June 2009): 390–418, www.jstor.org/stable/pdf/20684592.pdf?ab_segments=0%252Fdefault-2%252Fcontrol&refreqid=excelsior%3A9cc7e02815d54d514039bf5e1b5eea09.

17 Downes and O'Rourke, "You Can't Always Get What You Want."

18 Cited in Pollack, *Persian Puzzle*, 107.

19 Robert D. Blackwill and Philip H. Gordon, "Containing Russia: Responding to Moscow's Intervention in U.S. Democracy and Growing Geopolitical Challenge," Council on Foreign Relations Special Report, Jan. 2018, www.cfr.org/report/containing-russia.

20 Goldberg, "Obama Doctrine."

21 Rubin cited in Yaroslav Trofimov, "Pakistan's Fear of India Fuels Afghan War," *Wall Street Journal*, April 24, 2017, www.wsj.com/articles/pakistans-fear-of-india-fuels-afghan-war-1503567005.

22 Gordon Lubold, Eli Stockols, and Peter Nicholas, "Trump Takes New Tack in Afghanistan Fight," *Wall Street Journal*, Aug. 21, 2017, www.wsj.com/articles/trump-ups-the-ante-in-afghanistan-fight-1503360382?mod=article_inline; Mark Landler and Gardiner Harris, "Trump, Citing Pakistan as 'Safe Haven' for Terrorists, Freezes Aid," *New York Times*, Jan. 4, 2018, www.nytimes.com/2018/01/04/us/politics/trump-pakistan-aid.html; Remarks by President Trump on the Strategy in Afghanistan and South Asia, White House, Aug. 21, 2017, www.whitehouse.gov/briefings-statements/remarks-president-trump-strategy-afghanistan-south-asia/.

23 Rayburn and Sobchak, *U.S. Army in the Iraq War, vol. 1, Invasion, Insurgency, Civil War, 2003–2006*, 657.

24 Gates, *Duty*, 511.

25 Bacevich, *America's War for the Greater Middle East*, 22.

26 Dan Zak, "Robert Gates: A Man Still at War," *Washington Post*, Jan. 12, 2014, www.washingtonpost.com/lifestyle/style/robert-gates-says-hes-at-peace-but-in-his-new-memoir-his-duty-seems-to-weigh-heavily/2014/01/12/54f1a8b0-7943-11e3-b1c5-739e63e9c9a7_story.html.

27 Rayburn et al., *U.S. Army in the Iraq War, vol. 2, Surge and Withdrawal, 2007–2011,* 639.
28 Kagan, "Imperfect Triumph in Libya." Also see Nicholas Kristof, "Hugs from Libyans," *New York Times,* March 23, 2011, www.nytimes.com/2011/03/24/opinion/24kristof.html.
29 Frum and Perle, *End to Evil,* 110, 114, 141.
30 Coll, *Directorate S,* 290.
31 Douglas Lute, Lessons Learned Interview, *Washington Post,* Feb. 20, 2015, www.washingtonpost.com/graphics/2019/investigations/afghanistan-papers/documents-database/?document=lute_doug_ll_01_d5_02202015.
32 Power, *Education of an Idealist,* 306.
33 Eric Schmitt and Mark Mazzetti, "U.S. Intelligence Official Says Syrian War Could Last for Years," *New York Times,* July 20, 2013, www.nytimes.com/2013/07/21/world/middleeast/us-intelligence-official-says-syrian-war-could-last-for-years.html; Mark Hosenball and Phil Stewart, "Kerry Portrait of Syria Rebels at Odds with Intelligence Reports," Reuters, Sept. 5, 2013, www.reuters.com/article/us-syria-crisis-usa-rebels/kerry-portrait-of-syria-rebels-at-odds-with-intelligence-reports-idUSBRE98405L20130905.
34 Walt, *Hell of Good Intentions,* 81. On the failure to understand the societies where the United States intervened, Walt cites Peter W. Galbraith, *The End of Iraq: How American Incompetence Created a War Without End* (New York: Simon & Schuster, 2007); Peter Van Buren, *We Meant Well: How I Helped Lose the Battle for the Hearts and Minds of the Iraqi People* (New York: Metropolitan Books, 2012); Rajiv Chandrasekaran, *Little America: The War Within the War for Afghanistan* (New York: Alfred A. Knopf, 2012); Sky, *Unraveling*; Daniel Bolger, *Why We Lost: A General's Inside Account of the Iraq and Afghanistan Wars* (Boston: Houghton Mifflin Harcourt, 2014); Carter Malkasian, *War Comes to Garmser: Thirty Years of Conflict on the Afghan Frontier* (New York: Oxford University Press, 2013); and Anand Gopal, *No Good Men Among the Living: America, the Taliban, and the War Through Afghan Eyes* (New York: Metropolitan Books, 2014). Other such works include Malkasian, *Illusions of Victory*; and Bacevich, *America's War for the Greater Middle East.*
35 Cited in Jack Fairweather and Anton LaGuardia, "Chalabi Stands By Faulty Intelligence That Toppled Saddam's Regime," *Daily Telegraph,* Feb. 19, 2004.
36 Douglas Jehl, "C.I.A. Chief Orders 'Curveball' Review," *New York Times,* April 8, 2005, www.nytimes.com/2005/04/08/politics/cia-chief-orders-curveball-review.html.
37 Niccolò Machiavelli, *Discourses on Livy,* trans. Harvey C. Mansfield and Nathan Tarcov (Chicago: University of Chicago Press, 1998), chap. 31. Thanks to Brett McGurk for making me aware of this quotation.
38 Bearden, interview with Coll, in *Ghost Wars,* 173.

39 Rosentiel, "Public Attitudes Toward the War in Iraq: 2003–2008."
40 Ruth Igielnik and Kim Parker, "Majorities of U.S. Veterans, Public Say the Wars in Iraq and Afghanistan Were Not Worth Fighting," Pew Research Center, July 10, 2019, www.pewresearch.org/fact-tank/2019/07/10/majorities-of-u-s-veterans-public-say-the-wars-in-iraq-and-afghanistan-were-not-worth-fighting/.
41 Newport, "Most Americans Now View Afghanistan War as a Mistake."
42 Igielnik and Parker, "Majorities of U.S. Veterans, Public Say the Wars in Iraq and Afghanistan Were Not Worth Fighting."
43 Ibid.
44 Dina Smeltz et al., *Rejecting Retreat: Americans Support U.S. Engagement in Global Affairs*, Chicago Council on Global Affairs, Sept. 6, 2019, 16, www.thechicagocouncil.org/sites/default/files/report_ccs19_rejecting-retreat_20190909.pdf.
45 See David M. Edelstein, *Occupational Hazards: Success and Failure in Military Occupation* (Ithaca, N.Y.: Cornell University Press, 2008), 1.
46 Muravchik, *Exporting Democracy*, 117, 222.
47 See Downes and Monten, "Forced to Be Free?" 104–5; Larry Diamond, *The Spirit of Democracy: The Struggle to Build Free Societies Throughout the World* (New York: Times Books, 2008), 95–96; Ronald Inglehart and Christian Welzel, "How Development Leads to Democracy: What We Know About Modernization Today," *Foreign Affairs* 88, no. 2 (2009): 33–48; Jan Teorell, *Determinants of Democratization: Explaining Regime Change in the World, 1972–2006* (Cambridge: Cambridge University Press, 2010); Donald Horowitz, *Ethnic Groups in Conflict* (Berkeley: University of California Press, 1985), 291–332; Bruce E. Moon, "Long Time Coming: Prospects for Democracy in Iraq," *International Security* 33, no. 4 (Spring 2009): 115–48; Jason Brownlee, "Can America Nation-Build?" *World Politics* 59, no. 2 (Jan. 2007): 314–40.
48 Alfred Stepan and Graeme Robertson, "An 'Arab' More Than 'Muslim' Electoral Gap," *Journal of Democracy* 14, no. 3 (2003), muse.jhu.edu/article/44541. Also Sanford Lakoff, "The Reality of Muslim Exceptionalism," *Journal of Democracy* 15, no. 4 (2004), www.journalofdemocracy.org/article/reality-muslim-exceptionalism.
49 Abrams, *Realism and Democracy*, 115–16; Etel Solingen, "Transcending Disciplinary Divides: A Comparative Framework on the International Relations of the Middle East," Project on Middle East Political Science, Aug. 31, 2015, http://pomeps.org/wp-content/uploads/2015/09/POMEPS_Studies_16_IR_Web1.pdf, 52–62. Also see Adam Garfinkle, "The Impossible Imperative? Conjuring Arab Democracy," *National Interest* (Fall 2002).
50 Jeane J. Kirkpatrick, "Dictatorships and Double Standards," *Commentary*, Nov. 1, 1979.
51 Dobbins et al., *America's Role in Nation-Building*, xxv.
52 Ibid., xix.

53 Charles Krauthammer, "Democratic Realism," Irving Kristol Lecture/AEI Annual Dinner, Feb. 10, 2004, www.aei.org/publication/democratic-realism/.

54 Glenn Kessler, "Rice Bucks Tradition with Pre-election Appearance," *Washington Post*, Nov. 4, 2006; Robert Kagan, "Staying the Course, Win or Lose," *Washington Post*, Nov. 2, 2006.

55 Cited in Michael Crowley, "Trump Allies Push White House to Consider Regime Change in Tehran," *Politico*, June 25, 2017.

56 Mark Dubowitz, "Confront Iran the Reagan Way," *Wall Street Journal*, July 4, 2017, www.wsj.com/articles/confront-iran-the-reagan-way-1499197879; Ray Takeyh and Reuel Marc Gerecht, "Don't Fear Regime Change in Iran," *Wall Street Journal*, June 11, 2018, www.wsj.com/articles/dont-fear-regime-change-in-iran-1528756928; Marc Thiessen, "Trump's Sanctions Are Working. But It Will Take More to Topple the Regime," *Washington Post*, May 21, 2019, www.washingtonpost.com/opinions/2019/05/21/trumps-iran-sanctions-are-working-itll-take-more-topple-regime/; Jake Novak, "How Ronald Reagan Would Have Handled North Korea," CNBC News, Aug. 10, 2017, www.cnbc.com/2017/08/10/how-ronald-reagan-would-have-handled-north-korea-commentary.html; Joseph Bosco, "Reagan and the Case for Tactical Nukes in South Korea," *The Diplomat*, Nov. 2, 2017, thediplomat.com/2017/11/reagan-and-the-case-for-tactical-nukes-in-south-korea/; Lindsey Graham, "Match Words with Actions in Venezuela, Mr. President," *Wall Street Journal*, March 22, 2019, www.wsj.com/articles/match-words-with-actions-in-venezuela-mr-president-11558565556.

57 Sarah Parvini and Melissa Etehad, "Blasting Iran's Regime as 'Not Normal,' Pompeo Calls On Iranian Americans for Support in California Visit," *Los Angeles Times*, July 22, 2019, www.latimes.com/politics/la-na-pompeo-iran-talk-20180722-story.html.

58 See John Lewis Gaddis, *Strategies of Containment: A Critical Appraisal of American National Security Policy During the Cold War*, rev. ed. (New York: Oxford University Press, 2005), 153–54; Marc Trachtenberg, "A 'Wasting Asset': American Strategy and the Shifting Nuclear Balance, 1949–1954," *International Security* (Winter 1988–89): 5; Russell D. Buhite and William Christopher Hamel, "War for Peace: The Question of an American Preventive War Against the Soviet Union, 1945–55," *Diplomatic History* 14 (Summer 1990): 367–84; John Lewis Gaddis, *The United States and the End of the Cold War: Implications, Reconsiderations, Provocations* (Oxford: Oxford University Press, 1992), 20–46.

59 Richard N. Haass, "Regime Change and Its Limits," *Foreign Affairs*, July 1, 2005, www.foreignaffairs.com/articles/north-korea/2005-07-01/regime-change-and-its-limits.

60 Aaron Wildavsky, "Containment Plus Pluralization," in *Beyond Containment: Alternative Policies Toward the Soviet Union* (San Francisco: Institute for Contemporary Studies, 1983), 129–30.

61 Reagan's address to members of the British Parliament, London, June 8, 1982, *Public Papers of the Presidents: 1982* (Washington, D.C.: General Services Administration, National Archives and Records Service, Office of the Federal Register, 1983), 744–47.

62 Ronald Reagan, *An American Life* (New York: Simon & Schuster, 1990), 683.

63 Melvin Leffler, "Ronald Reagan and the Cold War: What Mattered Most," *Texas National Security Review*, May 2018, 75–77, 91.

64 Gaddis, *United States and the End of the Cold War*, 26.

65 Ibid., 130.

66 Correspondence from Ronald Reagan to Konstantin U. Chernenko, March 1984, April 1984, correspondence with Soviet leaders file, Ronald Reagan Library, Simi Valley, Calif., cited in Victor Sebestyen, *Revolution 1989: The Fall of the Soviet Empire* (New York: Pantheon Books, 2009), 93.

67 Francis X. Clines, "Reagan, Meeting Gromyko, Asks for Closer Ties," *New York Times*, Sept. 24, 1984, www.nytimes.com/1984/09/24/world/reagan-meeting-gromyko-asks-for-closer-ties.html; Reagan, *American Life*, 604–5.

68 Justin Vaïsse, *Neoconservatism: The Biography of a Movement* (Cambridge, Mass.: Harvard University Press, 2010), 189. Also see Beinart, *Icarus Syndrome*, 237.

69 X [George F. Kennan], "The Sources of Soviet Conduct," *Foreign Affairs*, July 1947, www.foreignaffairs.com/articles/russian-federation/1947-07-01/sources-soviet-conduct (emphasis added).

70 Gaddis, *United States and the End of the Cold War*, 131.

71 Inglehart and Welzel, "How Development Leads to Democracy."

72 Fareed Zakaria, "How to Change Ugly Regimes," *Newsweek*, June 26, 2005, https://www.newsweek.com/fareed-zakaria-how-change-ugly-regimes-120417.

73 David S. Cohen and Zoe A. Y. Weinberg, "Sanctions Can't Spark Regime Change: The Trouble with Trump's Approach to Venezuela and Iran," *Foreign Affairs*, April 29, 2019; Raul Gallegos, "What America Doesn't Get About Dictatorships," *New York Times*, June 20, 2019. Some of this section draws on Philip Gordon, "Will the Nuclear Deal Transform Iran?" *American Interest*, May 3, 2016.

Index